Survey Research Methods

Survey
Research
Methods

A Reader

Edited by
Eleanor Singer and
Stanley Presser

The University of Chicago Press

Chicago and London

The University of Chicago Press, Chicago 60637
The University of Chicago Press, Ltd., London
© 1989 by The University of Chicago
All rights reserved. Published 1989
Printed in the United States of America
94 93 92 91 90 89 5 4 3 2 1

Library of Congress Cataloging-in-Publication Data
Survey research methods : a reader / edited by Eleanor Singer and Stanley Presser.
     p.   cm.
    Includes bibliographical references and index.
    ISBN 0-226-76108-8 : $34.00. ISBN 0-226-76109-6 (pbk.) : $16.95
    1. Social surveys.   I. Singer, Eleanor.   II. Presser, Stanley,
1950–
HN29.S733 1989
301'.0723—dc19   88-29520
                                                                CIP

The paper used in this publication meets the minimum requirements of the American National Standard for Information Sciences—Permanence of Paper for Printed Library Materials, ANSI Z39.48-1984. ∞™

CONTENTS

Mode of Administration

The Interviewer

Validation

EDITORS' INTRODUCTION

More social research is done today by means of surveys than by any other method. Research on people's characteristics, attitudes, and behaviors in fields as diverse as health, politics, and esthetics is carried out by administering standardized questionnaires to respondents selected from a defined population by probability methods. And the results of such research appear in daily newspapers and magazines as well as in scholarly books and journals.

Along with increasing use of the method itself has come increasing attention to its reliability and validity (see esp. Turner and Martin, 1984). The past fifteen years in particular—beginning roughly with the publication of Sudman and Bradburn's *Response Effects in Surveys* in 1974—have seen an enormous expansion of research on survey methodology, especially on the relation between survey methods and survey responses. Much of this research has appeared in the pages of *Public Opinion Quarterly,* from which the selections in this reader are drawn.

Sources of Survey Variability

Researchers have long recognized that estimates obtained by means of sample surveys vary because measurements are carried out on only some, not all, of the elements of a population. Even if all the elements of a sample could be enumerated with complete accuracy, the characteristics of that sample would still differ from those of other samples and from the parent population simply because they were derived from some, rather than all, population members. That variability is known as "sampling error."

But survey estimates will differ for a variety of reasons in addition to those having to do with sampling. These reasons can be grouped under the headings of coverage and cooperation, questionnaire, interviewer, and mode of administration.

Each of these components of the survey process, in turn, gives rise to several sources of variation. For example, coverage and cooperation errors give rise to variations in response attributable to failure to include all population elements in the sampling frame, failure to make contact with all members of the sample, and failure to complete an interview with every eligible member. Or, to take another example, interviewers may differ in the responses they get because they differ in training or experience, because they have different expectations about a study, or because their demographic characteristics influence the answers they get to certain kinds of questions.

In the past fifty years sampling theory has developed to the point where variations in survey estimates arising from this source can be calculated quite precisely, even for surveys involving very complex sampling designs. But for most other sources of variation, knowledge is much more rudimentary, and estimates of the magnitude of variation introduced by each source—and, perforce, of the total variation attributable to survey methods—do not yet exist. The readings that follow are all concerned, in one way or another, with measuring or reducing such unwanted variation in survey estimates.

Survey Variability and Survey Error

Because the earliest investigations of survey variability had to do with those resulting from sampling, we are accustomed to equating survey variability with survey error. But when we move from discussions of variability introduced by sampling to that introduced by other elements of the survey process, the equation of variability with error becomes less clear-cut.

For some such elements, the concept of nonsampling "error" may indeed be applicable. For example, if a large number of interviewers is working on a survey, one can estimate the variability in responses introduced by interviewers (treated as a "sample" from the "population" of all interviewers), and one might think of this "interviewer error" as analogous to sampling error. In principle, it is also possible to conceptualize a "universe" of questions that would tap a particular attitude. A random sample of questions from such a universe would then yield an estimate of the attitude, and variations between the results from several samples of questions could also be thought of as analogous to sampling error. But ordinarily, one does not have a large number of wordings for the same question, because changing the wording of a question may—and often does—change its meaning for respondents. Accordingly, differently worded questions may lead to different responses because they are, in effect, different questions. In that case, it makes sense to think about variability of response, but the analogy to sampling error—which involves a population mean and sample deviations from the mean—breaks down.[1]

Because the field is still in flux, writers concerned with sources of

1. For a discussion of the possibility of extending the concept of "sampling" to other elements of the survey process, see Cook, 1988.

variation in survey responses often use different terms for the same or similar concepts. Sudman and Bradburn, in their early treatment of the topic, used the term "response effects"—a term neutral with respect to the presence or size of error. Some subsequent writers have followed their lead, but others have tended to talk about "response errors" or "nonsampling errors," a practice that leads, by extension, to the notion of "total survey error," consisting of both sampling and nonsampling errors (cf. Andersen et al., 1979). This variation in terminology is reflected in the selections that follow.

Organization of the Book

For the past fifty years, *Public Opinion Quarterly* has published articles analyzing survey methods and has reported on research designed to improve them. A selection of the best of these recent articles has been included in this book.

The readings that follow offer a comprehensive introduction to what is currently known about how survey methods affect survey responses, quite apart from sampling error. They have been grouped into five main sections. Four of them correspond to the major sources of response variation identified above: sample, questionnaire, mode of administration, and interviewer. The fifth, on validation, is concerned with how well surveys measure what they purport to measure.

In part because of space limitations and in part because few, if any, articles on the topic have appeared in the journal, two areas relevant to survey methods research are not covered at all in this reader. One is the area of ethics, especially issues of confidentiality and informed consent (cf. National Research Council, 1979; Singer, 1978; Singer and Frankel, 1983; and Singer, 1984). The other, which is touched on by Traugott, Groves, and Lepkowski, is the issue of survey costs, in particular, the relationship between survey cost and survey error (cf. Groves, 1989; Sudman, 1967).

Each of the five sections is preceded by an introduction that places its articles in context. The introductions relate the articles to one another as well as to work published elsewhere, and they try to identify promising lines of research as well as existing gaps in knowledge. Where it is warranted, they also point out limitations of the articles that have been included.

In its intent, the book is similar to a review article on survey methods. But the emphasis is less on critical commentary than it is on providing actual instances of the best current research on various sources of response effects. Thus, it enables readers to evaluate the evidence for such effects and to learn by example how to conduct similar methods research.[2]

Severe space constraints have created difficult problems of selection. In order to reduce these somewhat, an arbitrary decision was made to limit the content to articles published since 1970, though earlier articles are sometimes referred to in the section introductions. Even so, more good articles were available than could be accommodated in one book, and the final selection was often simply arbitrary: an equally good article had, for reasons of space, to be left out. Where possible, the section introductions try to call attention to such articles, as well as to relevant books and articles appearing in other journals; these can profitably be used by students and teachers to supplement the readings included here. The references listed at the end of each article constitute an additional source of such supplementary readings.

We would like to thank Herbert Abelson, Leo Bogart, Gladys Lang, Bud Roper, Howard Schuman, and David Sills—members of POQ's Advisory Committee in 1987—for encouraging us to proceed with this project, and Sandra Whisler, Bob Shirrell, and Nell Dillon-Ermers at the University of Chicago Press, who did likewise. We also want to express our particular appreciation to Howard Schuman and Seymour Sudman for their helpful comments on some of the introductions. We are indebted to the authors of the articles reprinted here, as well as to holders of the original copyrights—Columbia University Press, the Trustees of Columbia University, and AAPOR—for permission to reproduce their works. We hope that readers will find as much intellectual stimulation in using the volume as we did in putting it together.

References

Andersen, Ronald, Judith Kasper, and Martin R. Frankel (1979)
    Total Survey Error. San Francisco: Jossey-Bass.
Converse, Jean M. (1987)
    Survey Research in the United States: Roots and Emergence, 1890–1960. Berkeley
    and Los Angeles: University of California Press.
Cook, Tom D. (1988)
    "The generalization of causal connections in research theory and practice." In L.
    Sechrest, J. Bunker, and E. Perrin (eds.), Improving Methods in Nonexperimental
    Research. Beverly Hills, CA: Sage.
Groves, Robert M. (1989)
    Survey Errors and Survey Costs. New York: Wiley.

2. For a general introduction to survey methods, see Lansing and Morgan, 1971; Moser and Kalton, 1979; or Rossi, Wright, and Anderson, 1983. For a fascinating history of the early days of survey research, including some of its enduring methodological controversies, see Converse, 1987.

Lansing, John B., and James N. Morgan (1971)
  Economic Survey Methods. Ann Arbor, MI: Institute for Social Research.
Moser, Claus, and Graham Kalton (1979)
  Survey Methods in Social Investigations. 2d ed. London: Heinemann.
National Research Council (1979)
  Privacy and Confidentiality as Factors in Survey Response. Washington: National
  Academy of Sciences.
Rossi, Peter H., James Wright, and Andy Anderson (1983)
  Handbook of Survey Research. New York: Academic Press.
Singer, Eleanor (1978)
  "Informed consent: Effect on response rate and response quality in social
  surveys." American Sociological Review 43:144–162.
Singer, Eleanor (1984)
  "Public reactions to some ethical issues of social research: Attitudes and
  behavior." Journal of Consumer Research 11:501–509.
Singer, Eleanor, and Martin R. Frankel (1983)
  "Informed consent procedures in telephone interviews." American Sociological
  Review 47:416–426.
Sudman, Seymour (1967)
  Reducing the Cost of Surveys. Chicago: Aldine.
Sudman, Seymour, and Norman M. Bradburn (1974)
  Response Effects in Surveys. Chicago: Aldine.
Turner, Charles F., and Elizabeth Martin, eds. (1984)
  Surveying Subjective Phenomena. New York: Russell Sage Foundation.

THE SAMPLE: Coverage and Cooperation

Survey estimates vary in predictable ways when they derive from a sample rather than the population as a whole; this source of variability, which depends on sample size and the complexity of the sampling plan, is known as sampling error. But, in addition, two other classes of factors related to sampling also affect the estimates obtained. Both of these involve the adequacy with which a sample represents an underlying population. One has to do with the completeness of the sampling frame—the list of elements from which the sample is drawn. The other has to do with contact and cooperation—the correspondence between the sample elements selected and those actually measured.

The readings in this section all speak to problems of coverage and completion, not basic sampling variability. (For a good introduction to probability sampling, see Kalton, 1983.) Those by Tull and Albaum and by Rothbart, Fine, and Sudman are concerned with problems related to sampling frames. Tull and Albaum consider biases that arise when surveys are done by telephone and access to a telephone varies throughout the population in a nonrandom way.[1] Although these biases have been reduced as telephone coverage of the population has increased (see, e.g., Thornberry and Massey, 1988), they have not been eliminated. Of course, problems related to sampling frames are not limited to telephone surveys.

The article by Rothbart, Fine, and Sudman deals with a different sort of frame issue. These researchers wanted to study a relatively rare population: Vietnam War veterans, for whom no frame was available. They describe a technique known as "multiplicity sampling" for locating the members of such a population, and they discuss some of the errors associated with it.[2]

The remaining articles in this section deal with variations in the ability to make contact with respondents and persuade them to be interviewed. Steeh provides careful documentation of an impression held by many survey researchers—that response rates have declined over time. Such an analysis is possible in this case because the necessary data have been kept by the Survey Research Center at the Univer-

1. As Kviz (1978) pointed out in a subsequent article, the differences between telephone households and the general population are generally smaller than those between telephone households and households without telephones, which are the comparisons tested by Tull and Albaum.
2. For other approaches to the problem of sampling relatively "rare" populations, see Tourangeau and Smith, 1985. Reed (1975) describes a strategy for locating such groups in existing surveys, for purposes of secondary analysis.

sity of Michigan for many years, and definition of the elements making up the response rate has remained reasonably constant. These two requirements for longitudinal research on response rates—standardized definitions and careful record keeping—are unfortunately rare, making comparisons between organizations and over time difficult.

In recent years nonresponse to one important recurring cross-sectional study, the General Social Survey, has run about 25%. In the article reprinted here, Smith attempts to estimate the bias due to this "hidden 25%" by experimenting with different ways of measuring the characteristics of nonresponders, both noncontacts and refusals.

The final two articles describe efforts to reduce nonresponse. Because one sizable source of nonresponse is failure to contact sample members, it is important to schedule interview attempts when people are likely to be home. Vigderhous reports on an investigation of the most fruitful times—seasons, days, hours—to find respondents at home for a telephone survey. (For related studies, see Weeks et al., 1980; Weeks, Kulka, and Pierson, 1987.)

Another way of reducing nonresponse is to increase the number of interview attempts or, in the case of mail surveys, the number of follow-ups. In what have come to be known as "mixed-mode" designs, researchers use more than one method to try to contact and/or persuade respondents; for example, nonrespondents to a mail survey may be contacted by telephone, or respondents who are to be interviewed by phone may first be sent a letter describing the survey. The article by Traugott, Groves, and Lepkowski describes a recent application of this idea, which in this case involves combining directory-based and random-digit-dialed samples and sending advance letters to those households for which an address as well as a telephone number is available.

Aside from noncontact, the major source of nonresponse is refusal to participate in the interview. Persuading respondents to cooperate is a matter of offering them some incentive: an appeal to self-interest or to altruism, for example (cf. Dillman, 1978). One obvious choice is money, and researchers have experimented (mainly in mail surveys) with monetary incentives ranging from small token payments or gifts to substantial rewards (see, e.g., Armstrong, 1975; Berry and Kanouse, 1987; Gunn and Rhodes, 1981; Mizes, Fleece, and Roos, 1984; Schewe and Cournoyer, 1976). Although the findings from these studies have not all been consistent, the weight of evidence suggests that monetary incentives increase response rates, probably by stimulating returns with fewer follow-ups. Response quality appears not to be compromised by such incentives, nor does the representativeness of the resulting sample. Some, however, regard the use of monetary incentives as inappropriate in most situations and as setting an unfortunate precedent (e.g., Sheatsley and Loft, 1981).

Some think that the proliferation of surveys, together with growing concerns about confidentiality, is increasing the public's reluctance to participate in interviews. Such evidence as exists provides no support for these claims, but since it is based on people who cooperate rather than on those who refuse, this evidence is by no means definitive.

References

Armstrong, J. Scott (1975)
"Monetary incentives in mail surveys." Public Opinion Quarterly 39:111–116.
Berry, Sandra H., and David E. Kanouse (1987)
"Physician response to a mailed survey: An experiment in timing of payment."
Public Opinion Quarterly 51:102–114.
Dillman, Don A. (1978)
Mail and Telephone Surveys: The Total Design Method. New York: Wiley.
Gunn, Walter J., and Isabelle N. Rhodes (1981)
"Physician response rates to a telephone survey: Effects of monetary incentive level." Public Opinion Quarterly 45:109–115.
Kalton, Graham (1983)
Introduction to Survey Sampling. Beverly Hills, CA: Sage.
Kviz, Frederick J. (1978)
"Random digit dialing and sample bias." Public Opinion Quarterly 42:544–546.
Mizes, J. Scott, E. Louis Fleece, and Cindy L. Roos (1984)
"Incentives for increasing return rates: Magnitude levels, response bias, and format." Public Opinion Quarterly 48:794–800.
Reed, John S. (1975)
"Needles in haystacks: Studying 'rare' populations by secondary analysis of sample surveys." Public Opinion Quarterly 39:514–522.
Schewe, Charles D., and Cournoyer, Norman G. (1976)
"Prepaid vs. promised monctary incentives to questionnaire response: Further evidence." Public Opinion Quarterly 40:105–107.
Sheatsley, Paul B., and Loft, John D. (1981)
"Comment." Public Opinion Quarterly 45:571–572.
Thornberry, Owen T., Jr., and James T. Massey (1988)
"Trends in U.S. telephone coverage across time and subgroups." In Robert M. Groves et al. (eds.) Telephone Survey Methodology. New York: Wiley.
Tourangeau, Roger, and A. Wade Smith (1985)
"Finding subgroups for surveys." Public Opinion Quarterly 49:351–365.
Weeks, Michael F., B. L. Jones, R. E. Folsom, Jr., and C. H. Benrud (1980)
"Optimal times to contact sample households." Public Opinion Quarterly 44:101–114.
Weeks, Michael F., Richard A. Kulka, and Stephanie A. Pierson (1987)
"Optimal call scheduling for a telephone survey." Public Opinion Quarterly 51:540–549.

Bias in
Random Digit Dialed Surveys

DONALD S. TULL AND GERALD S. ALBAUM

THE SURVEY DESIGNER who is considering using the telephone directory as a frame for a sample survey of households has to make an assessment of the effects of excluding unlisted subscribers and nonsubscribers from the sample. Both are sources of potential bias that, depending upon the designer's judgments, may be dealt with by means ranging from ignoring them to employing special procedures up to abandoning the telephone directory in favor of some alternative sampling frame.

An alternative sampling frame that has received a considerable amount of attention is the one generated by the random digit dialing (RDD) procedure, either by itself,[1] or together with the telephone directory.[2] This method of dealing with the problem of unlisted subscribers has been used directly in telephone surveys and as a means of obtaining addresses of unlisted subscribers for mail and personal interview surveys.[3]

A number of studies have been made and reported on the effects of excluding unlisted telephone subscribers from surveys.[4] These studies are of considerable assistance in assessing this potential source of bias and thus are of help to the designer in deciding whether or not to use the RDD procedure as the sampling frame in lieu of the telephone directory. For instance, Sudman (1976:65) suggests that random digit dialing is most appropriate for the central cities and some of the suburbs of large SMSAs, where "as many as 40 percent of all phones may be unlisted." In areas outside the SMSAs, where the fraction of unlisted numbers is gen-

---

[1] For a description of the procedures involved in using randomly selected telephone numbers as a sampling frame, see Cooper (1964) or Glasser and Metzger (1972).

[2] A description of RDD procedures when used to supplement the telephone directory is given in Sudman (1973).

[3] For examples of surveys in which RDD was used to generate the sample, see Cooper (1964), Glasser and Metzger (1972, 1975), and Hauck and Cox (1974).

[4] For other estimates of the biasing effects of excluding unlisted telephone subscribers from samples, see Brunner and Brunner (1971), Leuthold and Scheele (1971), Roslow and Roslow (1972), and Glasser and Metzger (1972, 1975).

Donald S. Tull and Gerald S. Albaum are Professors in the College of Business Administration, University of Oregon.

© 1977 by the American Association for Public Opinion Research. This essay originally appeared in *Public Opinion Quarterly*, volume 41, number 3.

erally less than 5 percent, he feels that the added value of random digit dialing is "probably not worth the small reduction in bias, remembéring that households without phones are still excluded."

It is the potential bias resulting from the exclusion of nonsubscribers that is the concern of the present study. In 1970, over 13 percent of all households were without telephone service. What are the biases, if any, that result from the exclusion of these households in RDD surveys?

To answer this question, values for selected demographic and housing characteristics and for the ownership of a number of durable products are estimated from a simulated RDD survey using Census of Population data. Similar estimates are shown for households with no telephone available. Chi-square values are calculated for the two estimates for each of the demographic housing and ownership characteristics considered.

The Data Base for the Estimates

The Public Use Samples of the 1970 Census of Population and Census of Housing (U.S. Bureau of the Census, 1972) contain selected data for each of a sample of households. Among the data provided for each household are whether or not a telephone was available, data on a number of demographic and housing unit characteristics, and whether or not each of a number of consumer durable products was owned. Data from both the 15 percent, 1 in 10,000 and the 5 percent, 1 in 10,000 Public Use Samples were used. The sample sizes were 6,333 and 6,346, respectively.

The information obtained about telephone service was whether or not a telephone was "available" rather than whether the household actually was a telephone subscriber. Those households reporting having a telephone "available" included ones using neighbor's telephones (or a telephone in the hall) to make and receive calls as well as the households subscribing to telephone service. The resulting data therefore provide a somewhat inflated estimate of telephone subscription and correspondingly reduced estimates of the biases resulting from excluding nonsubscribers from the sample. Such biases are small, however,[5] and are unlikely to affect the conclusions drawn from the data.

Comparison of Simulated RDD Survey and Households with No Telephone Available

By cross-tabulating values for selected demographic variable, housing unit characteristics, and ownership of durable products for those house-

---

[5] In a study done in 1965 involving telephone availability, the Bureau of Census reports that "in most cases the telephone was located within the unit occupied by the household. In a *small proportion of cases, however* [emphasis added], the telephone was located outside the living quarters but in a place readily accessible to the household, such as in a common hall of an apartment building" (U.S. Bureau of the Census, 1965:2).

Table 1. Comparison of Results of Simulated RDD Survey with Estimated Population Values

	Value from Simulated RDD Survey[a]		Households with No Telephone Available[b]		Estimated Population Values		χ² Values
	N	%	N	%	N	%	
Demographic Characteristics							
Sex of Head of Household							
Male	4,379	79.75	612	72.68	4,991	78.81	χ² = 21.8
Female	1,112	20.25	230	27.32	1,342	21.19	p < .001
							due to sampling
Total	5,491	100.0	842	100.0	6,333	100.0	variation
Race of Head of Household							
White	4,992	90.9	626	74.3	5,618	88.7	χ² = 202.2
Black	450	8.2	200	23.8	650	10.3	p < .001
Other	49	0.9	16	1.9	65	1.0	due to sampling
							variation
Total	5,491	100.0	842	100.0	6,333	100.0	
Age of Head of Household							
Under 20 years	19	0.3	15	1.8	34	0.5	χ² = 84.9
20–39	1,768	32.2	372	44.2	2,140	33.8	p < .001
40–59	2,176	39.6	236	28.0	2,412	38.1	due to sampling
60 and over	1,528	27.8	219	26.0	1,747	27.6	variation
Total	5,491	100.0	842	100.0	6,333	100.0	
Marital Status of Head of Household							
Spouse present	3,911	71.2	442	52.5	4,353	68.7	χ² = 179.7
Spouse absent	73	1.3	20	2.3	93	1.7	p < .001
Widowed	737	13.4	132	15.6	869	13.7	due to sampling
Divorced	267	4.9	57	6.8	324	5.1	variation
Separated	119	2.2	53	6.3	172	2.7	
Never married	384	7.0	138	16.4	522	8.2	
Total	5,491	100.0	842	100.0	6,333	100.0	
Income							
Loss or no income	119	2.2	42	5.0	161	2.5	χ² = 210.8
$1–9,999	3,823	69.6	753	89.4	4,576	72.3	p < .001
$10,000–19,999	1,292	23.5	42	5.0	1,334	21.1	due to sampling
$20,000–29,999	168	3.1	3	.3	171	2.7	variation
$30,000 and over	89	1.6	2	.2	91	1.4	
Total	5,491	100.0	842	100.0	6,333	100.0	
Education of Head of Household							
Less than grade 7	456	8.3	187	22.2	643	10.2	χ² = 271.1
Grades 7–8	869	15.8	183	21.7	1,052	16.6	p < .001
Some high school	997	18.2	190	22.6	1,187	18.7	due to sampling
							variation

Table 1 (Continued)

	Value from Simulated RDD Survey[a]		Households with no Telephone Available[b]		Estimated Population Values		χ^2 Values
	N	%	N	%	N	%	
High school graduate	1,607	29.3	188	22.3	1,795	28.3	
Some college	739	13.5	66	7.8	805	12.7	
College graduate	434	7.9	18	2.1	452	7.1	
Graduate School	389	7.1	10	1.2	399	6.3	
Total	5,491	100.0	842	100.0	6,333	100.0	
Employer of Head of Household							
Private concern	3,356	61.1	559	66.4	3,915	61.8	$\chi^2 = 58.7$
Federal government	357	6.5	27	3.2	384	6.1	$p < .001$ due to sampling variation
State government	166	3.0	21	2.5	187	3.0	
Local government	320	5.8	28	3.3	348	5.5	
Self-employed	692	12.6	67	8.0	759	12.0	
Not applicable[c]	600	10.9	140	16.6	740	11.7	
Total	5,491	100.0	842	100.0	6,333	100.0	
Location							
City, suburb	4,479	81.6	595	70.7	5,074	80.1	$\chi^2 = 54.5$
Rural	1,012	18.4	247	29.3	1,259	19.9	$p < .001$ due to sampling
Total	5,491	100.0	842	100.0	6,333	100.0	variation
Housing Unit Characteristics							
Type							
1 family detached	3,790	69.0	422	50.1	4,212	66.5	$\chi^2 = 174.7$
1 family attached	167	3.0	23	2.7	190	3.0	$p < .001$
2 family bldg.	447	8.1	88	10.5	535	8.4	due to sampling
3–4 family bldg.	251	4.6	66	7.8	317	5.0	variation
5–9 family bldg.	187	3.4	62	7.4	249	3.9	
10–19 family bldg.	162	3.0	47	5.6	209	3.3	
20–49 family bldg.	154	2.8	38	4.5	192	3.1	
50 and over family bldg.	201	3.7	32	3.8	233	3.7	
Mobile home or trailer	132	2.4	64	7.6	196	3.1	
Total	5,491	100.0	842	100.0	6,333	100.0	
Age of Unit							
1 year or less	140	2.5	30	3.6	170	2.7	$\chi^2 = 80.4$
2–5 years	598	10.9	64	7.6	662	10.5	$p < .001$
6–10 years	680	12.4	62	7.4	742	11.7	due to sampling
11–20 years	1,259	22.9	125	14.8	1,384	21.9	variation
21–30 years	710	12.9	141	16.7	851	13.4	
More than 30 years	2,104	38.3	420	49.9	2,524	39.9	
Total	5,491	100.0	842	100.0	6,333	100.0	

Table 1 (Continued)

	Value from Simulated RDD Survey[a]		Households with no Telephone Available[b]		Estimated Population Values		χ^2 Values
	N	%	N	%	N	%	
Tenure							
Owned or being bought	3,655	66.6	286	34.0	3,941	62.2	$\chi^2 = 341.4^d$
Cooperative or condominium	43	0.8	3	0.4	46	0.7	$p < .001$
Rented	1,793	32.7	553	65.6	2,346	37.0	due to sampling variation
Total	5,491	100.0	842	100.0	6,333	100.0	
Ownership of Selected Durables							
Air conditioning							
None	3,295	60.0	706	83.8	4,001	63.2	$\chi^2 = 184.8$
1 room unit	1,061	19.3	88	10.5	1,149	18.1	$p < .001$
2 or more individual room units	429	7.8	19	2.3	448	7.1	due to sampling variation
Central system	706	12.9	29	3.4	735	11.6	
Total	5,491	100.0	842	100.0	6,333	100.0	
Automobiles[e]							
None	756	13.8	316	37.5	1,072	16.9	$\chi^2 = 388.9$
1	2,573	46.9	418	49.6	2,991	47.2	$p < .001$
2	1,807	32.9	95	11.3	1,902	30.0	due to sampling variation
3 or more	355	6.5	13	1.5	368	5.8	
Total	5,491	100.0	842	100.0	6,333	100.0	
Clothes Dryer							
Electric heated	1,821	32.6	54	7.1	1,875	29.5	$\chi^2 = 364.5$
Gas heated	792	14.2	23	3.0	815	12.8	$p < .001$
None	2,977	53.3	679	89.8	3,656	57.6	due to sampling variation
Total	5,590	100.0	756	100.0	6,346	100.0	
Clothes Washing Machine							
Automatic	3,579	64.0	197	26.1	3,776	59.5	$\chi^2 = 412.2$
Wringer	590	10.6	129	17.1	719	11.3	$p < .001$
None	1,421	25.4	430	56.9	1,851	29.2	due to sampling variation
Total	5,590	100.0	756	100.0	6,346	100.0	
Dishwasher (built-in or portable)							
Yes	1,140	20.4	17	2.2	1,157	18.2	$\chi^2 = 145.9$
No	4,450	79.6	739	97.8	5,189	81.8	$p < .001$
Total	5,590	100.0	756	100.0	6,346	100.0	due to sampling variation

Table 1 (Continued)

	Value from Simulated RDD Survey[a]		Households with no Telephone Available[b]		Estimated Population Values		χ² Values
	N	%	N	%	N	%	
Home Food Freezer (separate from refrigerator)							
Yes	1,663	29.7	93	12.3	1,756	27.7	χ² = 100.4
No	3,927	70.3	663	87.7	4,590	72.3	p < .001
							due to sampling
Total	5,590	100.0	756	100.0	6,346	100.0	variation
Television Set							
1	3,648	65.3	590	78.0	4,238	66.8	χ² = 320.2
2 or more	1,760	31.5	59	7.8	1,819	28.7	p < .001
None	182	3.3	107	14.2	289	4.6	due to sampling
							variation
Total	5,590	100.0	756	100.0	6,346	100.0	

[a] Values for demographic characteristics, housing unit characteristics, and for ownership of air conditioning units and automobiles are those for households in the 15 percent, 1 in 10,000 Public Use Sample who reported having a telephone available. Data for ownership of clothes dryers, clothes washing machine, dishwashers, home food freezer, and television sets, are those for households in the 5 percent, 1 in 10,000 Public Use Sample who reported having a telephone available.

[b] Data sources as in ff. 1 above but values are for households reporting not having a telephone available.

[c] Primarily unemployed, disabled, and those not seeking work.

[d] Calculated with "cooperative or condominium" grouped with "owned or being bought" buyers because of small cell size in former.

[e] Owned or regularly driven by members of the household (includes company cars).

holds having a telephone available, it was possible to simulate an RDD survey. The same cross-tabulations were also made for households not having a telephone available. The results are shown in Table 1.

The differences between the simulated RDD survey values and the values for the households with no telephone available were significant in all cases at the .001 level. This level of significance resulted despite the reduction in the biases that stemmed from the use of availability rather than subscription as a measure of whether or not telephone service was being received.

The biases were generally in the direction one would expect. Households with a telephone available were more likely to have white, male heads of a higher average age, income, and education level, and to have the spouse present than those households with no telephone available. Telephone-available household heads were also more likely to be self-employed or to work for a governmental agency than the heads of households with no telephone service.

A higher proportion of telephone-available households tended to live in single-family detached housing units that they were buying, that were newer on the average, and were located in cities or suburbs. They also were more likely to own at least one automobile, have air conditioning, washing machines and dryers, dishwashers, home food freezers, and more than one television set than were the no-telephone-available households.

It should be remembered that the estimates of the biases present in RDD surveys were (probably) artificially reduced by the use of the "telephone available" definition. However, these estimates were made from data collected in 1970 and, since a higher proportion of households subscribe to telephone service now than then, the *actual* biases present in random digit dialed surveys due to exclusion of nonsubscribers should be less now than they were then.

After having observed the nature and direction of the biases, the survey designer would be well advised to note that, at most, the differences between the values estimated from the simulated RDD survey and the estimated population values amount to only a few percentage points. This may be well within the accuracy requirements of the next survey to be designed.

References

Brunner, James A., and G. Allen Brunner
  1971 "Are voluntarily unlisted telephone subscribers really different?" Journal of Marketing Research 8:121-124.
Cooper, Sanford L.
  1964 "Random sampling by telephone: a new and improved method." Journal of Marketing Research 1:45–48.
Glasser, Gerald J., and Gale D. Metzger
  1972 "Random digit dialing as a method of telephone sampling." Journal of Marketing Research 9:59–64.
  1975 "National estimates of nonlisted telephone households and their characteristics." Journal of Marketing Research 12:359-361.
Hauck, Mathew, and Michael Cox
  1974 "Locating a sample by random digit dialing." Public Opinion Quarterly 38:253-260.
Leuthold, David A., and Raymond Scheele
  1971 "Patterns of bias in samples based on telephone directories." Public Opinion Quarterly 35:249-257.
Sudman, Seymour
  1973 "The uses of telephone directories for survey sampling." Journal of Marketing Research 10:204-207.
  1976 Applied Sampling. New York: Academic Press.
U.S. Bureau fo the Census
  1965 Characteristics of Households with Telephones, March 1965. Series P-20, No. 146. Wahington, DC.: Government Printing Office.
  1972 Public Use of Samples of Basic Records from the 1970 Census: Description and Technical Documentation. Washington, D.C.: Government Printing Office.

On Finding and Interviewing
the Needles in the Haystack:
The Use of Multiplicity Sampling

GEORGE S. ROTHBART, MICHELLE FINE, AND
SEYMOUR SUDMAN

THE Vietnam Era Project of the Center for Policy Research has for the last several years been studying the male Vietnam veteran and his nonveteran peers. We collected comprehensive life history data for the purpose of assessing current functioning and the impact of the Vietnam War upon occupational and educational careers, upon interpersonal relations, and upon psychological mood and symptomatology. The veterans in this group constitute a rare and relatively difficult to access population when contrasted with a typical survey population. To draw a representative sample of sufficient size and

---

Abstract A multiplicity sample of a relatively rare population—Vietnam era veterans—provides insight into the following field issues: yield, location problems, coverage bias, and the effect of inclusion rule, i.e., eligible kin nominators. Here, the latter included parents, siblings, aunts and uncles. The resultant yield was double that of a conventional sample but was much higher for black and Mexican-American veterans than for whites. Location problems (on which there was little prior knowledge) were less serious than anticipated, requiring persistence but not extravagant expenditures to solve. Undercoverage bias was reduced by "nonselective" screening; this raised location cost, however. Relative yield, an indicator of selection bias, varied by kin category. Parents showed a higher relative yield than did siblings, while aunts and uncles were strikingly low in nominations relative to their numbers.

George S. Rothbart is Senior Research Associate, Center for Policy Research. Michelle Fine is Assistant Professor of Psychology and Education, University of Pennsylvania. Seymour Sudman is Professor of Business Adminsstration and Research Professor, Survey Research Laboratory, University of Illinois, Urbana. The research for this study was supported by a grant from the National Institute for Mental Health, IOROMH 26832-SP, and a contract from the Veterans Administration, V101 (134) P610. The interpretations here are the sole responsibility of the authors and do not necessarily reflect the view of the National Institute of Mental Health or the Veterans Administration. The authors wish to acknowledge the professional contribution of Kane, Parsons and Associates of New York, who did the novel and demanding field work for this research.

affordable cost, it was necessary to depart from conventional probability methods for sampling this category of respondent and its even rarer subcategories. In this departure respondents to a screening questionaire that was designed to find eligible persons within called households were asked an additional question: whether or not they could nominate relatives who met the screening criteria and who lived outside the household. Such a procedure falls under the heading of multiplicity sampling from kinship networks as discussed by Monroe Sirken (1970, 1974, and 1979). While the *theory* of network sampling has been well developed so that it is possible to make unbiased estimates of sample statistics and to compute sampling variances, much still remains to be learned about actual field experiences with this method. In this paper we report on our experience with and developmental application of multiplicity sampling when used in conducting a conventional sample survey.

The problems involved in sampling rare populations, and therefore the methods for their solution, are becoming increasingly important in survey research. This is so for at least two reasons. First, social researchers are increasingly being asked to conduct studies of persons with special characteristics—such as laid-off workers or people with certain categories of illness—so as to provide policy-relevant data. As research becomes more pointed, more informed by what has gone before, and more oriented toward practical implications, general population surveys often prove inadequate. Second, field-drawn samples have become increasingly essential to successful surveys. While it is possible to study some rare populations by utilizing institutional lists, lists are, unfortunately, often biased. But even where lists are good ones, the increased emphasis on privacy and informed consent frequently results in denial of access. The sampling methods described here, by radically increasing the yield of screening interviews, allow surveys to be conducted without recourse to lists and have the capacity to produce a sample of superior quality.

Beginning in late 1978, we conducted a study in seven sites in the Midwest, South, and West Coast (in Los Angeles) with a total sample size of 1,000 males. This sample was stratified by race and veteran status. Of the respondents, 550 are veterans; half of the veterans are Vietnam veterans. The sample is 25 percent black for all sites, and 25 percent Mexican-American (Chicano) for the Los Angeles sample. We decided to use network sampling to select *all* veterans, white and black, with service in Vietnam and service elsewhere. This decision enabled us to keep screening costs to a minimum, while allowing us to include a substantial proportion of minority veterans across sites with quite varied racial composition.

The Design Phase

Before we launched into a full-blown application of multiplicity, a pilot study was conducted to (1) provide answers to sampling questions, and (2) identify any problems we might encounter with the multiplicity procedure. We had four basic questions that needed to be answered.

1. How would multiplicity influence the overall yield for the sample?

2. How extensive should the kin counting rule be? For example, should nephews be included, as well as sons and brothers or would the inclusion of nephews introduce additional location problems and difficulty in estimating the probability of nomination?

3. What location problems could we anticipate in finding the nominated respondents? Would metropolitan sites, with greater possibilities for isolation, produce high loss rates?

4. What problems would we confront in trying to extract sufficient information from the nominator?

The pilot study provided sufficient information to answer, at least partially, these questions. It is our belief, in retrospect, that any attempt to employ a multiplicity sampling procedure should be preceded by a pilot study so that problems particular to the population being investigated can be considered in the design of the sampling procedure. Most important, no way of estimating multiplicity yield in advance is presently available except the use of a pilot study.

The pilot study involved 705 total calls, with 293 contacts completed, to test the multiplicity procedure. It was done only with potential nominators; no nominees were contacted. The result was that with the inclusion of nephews, the overall yield with multiplicity was 1.91 times the yield of household sampling. Although the pilot did not produce as much information as desired about potential location problems, it did seem to indicate the value of including nephews in the counting rule, and it minimized our worries about nominator reticence. Nominators appeared quite willing and able to provide information to the extent that they had such information available.

In the actual survey, a standard screening questionnaire was administered to each household asking about age-eligible males in the home. Regardless of whether or not a male was part of the household, each respondent to a screening call was given a brief explanation of the reason for our interest in kin, and then was asked if he or she had a son who was a veteran in the age group and, if yes, "does he live in the study area?" These questions were repeated for "brother" and "nephew." If a multiplicity nomination was offered—son, brother, or nephew—location information on the nominee was solicited, as well as supplementary information on the nominator. The latter included information on how to recontact the nominator, since a surprising number of such phone contacts are difficult to locate when recalled. This part of the screening interview needed particular care.

Multiplicity sampling requires the collection of three kinds of special information: first, information on location of the nominator; second, the location and characteristics of a potential respondent, provided by a nominator; and third, information needed to weight the final data. In the case of enumerative multiplicity studies, this latter information was provided by the nominator and is calculated by determining the number of households within the screening area eligible to report the respondent. As the inclusion rule becomes wider, going from sons to siblings to nephews, gathering these data requires increasingly elaborate information on kinship network from the nominator, some of it about kin of the nominee to whom the nominator is unrelated. In what we shall call survey multiplicity—i.e., our own case, in which the nominee is actually interviewed—this information is gathered directly from the nominee, who can provide it more easily and perhaps more accurately than can the nominator. This means the addition of a brief kinship questionnaire, which elicits information about the number of persons in various eligible kin positions and whether they live in separate households.

Let us first discuss some of the potential difficulties of the method. One problem that may occur in all forms of network sampling is overcoverage bias. Sometimes a person named as being in a certain category would turn out not to be in that category, e.g., someone cited as a Vietnam veteran would have served in Germany (and even, occasionally, had not been in the armed forces at all). In survey multiplicity, these individuals can be eliminated after the initial contact and thus do not have a substantive effect oh bias.[1] But overcoverage may be a source of error in calculating the characteristics and size of the nonlocatable group. The answer, though not neces-

---

[1] We followed a "nonselective" principle in designing our screening procedure. The nominator was not asked to supply any information beyond "approximate" membership in the category, nor was screening done for place of service (e.g., Vietnam). Veterans who had served during the wrong period, or were currently too old, or had served in the wrong place were eliminated only after direct contact, so as to avoid undercoverage resulting from nominator error. This principle is an especially good one to follow as the sampled category becomes rarer and the knowledge necessary for correct identification is abstruse, as in the case of physically or mentally ill persons (in the latter instance, considerations of stigma would also militate against a specific question). To improve the yield of sampling, it is only necessary to *increase the likelihood* that the nominee is actually in the desired category. The tradeoff is that the identified person must be contacted, thus increasing location cost.

sarily always practical, is to keep the nonlocatable group as small as possible.

Locating nominees turns out only to be a problem of persistence and modest investment of resources. This was surprising, since in our earlier experience in gathering network data, we had learned that individuals often had difficulty supplying the addresses of friends and more than occasionally even had difficulty supplying their full names. Thus, we started out with a bit of worry.

The answer to our early fears is easy, if one has the benefit of hindsight. We might have asked ourselves how members of networks locate one another in instances where they only possess minimal location data. The answer is that they *search* for the information. They call an intermediary, for example. Maybe the veteran is a nephew—a sister's son. They can call the sister, whose number they do know. Obviously we could do the same. Almost all of this locating can ordinarily be done on the telephone. We learned an important fact in the process of this telephoning. Some of the nominees were not members of the household at which they could be located—or, occasionally, of *any* household. It was easy enough to find them, however, once we were fortified with a name and list of possible locations. Without such prior knowledge, as in the usual household sample, it is likely that they would have been missed altogether.

Results

The essence of sampling is pecuniary, i.e., the estimation of the characteristics of a large population with a minimum amount of costly data gathering. Therefore, let us begin our discussion of the data on multiplicity sampling with a discussion of screening yield and cost-effectiveness and follow with a discussion of the characteristics of the sample, various inclusion rules, and issues regarding bias.

The data reported here are drawn from information on eligible veterans generated in screening interviews. In order to fulfill the design calling for 550 veterans in particular sample cells, 8,698 completed screening interviews had to be conducted. These interviews produced 535 veterans of the Vietnam era who met sample eligibility requirements and who lived within contacted households. We shall refer to these veterans as "direct hits." The incidence, therefore was, 535/8,698 = 6.2 percent—a distinctly rare population. An additional 476 veteran kin were obtained by multiplicity nomination from the same 8,698 households, for a total of 1,011 veterans produced in screening. The need for this large a draw in order to fulfill a design that called for 550 veterans was a result of stratification by race, place of service, and site (and affected by the correlation between these variables) in addition to losses of about 15 percent to refusals to cooperate and failure to locate a nominated veteran.

Multiplicity yield is calculated within category by comparing the number of multiplicity nominees to the number of direct hits. The direct hits represent the yield that would occur with the given number of screening interviews if the sample design had been a conventional household survey. Thus N multiplicity/N direct is the increase in yield generated by multiplicity nominations; to state the overall yield of multiplicity sampling including both multiplicity and direct, 1.0 must be added to this figure. In our case, the multiplicity yield was 476/555 = 89 percent (and the overall yield was 1.89). Remember that a small pilot produced an estimated yield of 91 percent. Thus, an inexpensive study was relatively precise for this estimate.

Table 1 compares the yield for white, black, and Chicano subgroups in our sample. The yield for whites is relatively low, at 70 percent. The yield for blacks is almost twice as high as among white veterans (1.85 times as high). Chicanos have the highest yield, 2.44 times that of whites. We shall shortly examine possible explanations of these yield differences. Whatever the explanation, however, these figures have considerable practical significance. They suggest that multiplicity sampling has great promise in surveys of the most difficult to access segments of the United States population—minority groups. It is hard to overstate the importance of improving on our coverage of these subpopulations. Generalizations regarding the black population are frequently based on the relatively small Ns that occur in an overall population survey and thus are subject to considerable sampling error. Or, they are drawn by nonprobability methods and subject to nonrandom error. Obviously, a yield-enhancing method makes it possible to increase N and thus to reduce sampling error. Relative rarity does not, of course, account for all the problems of sampling the black population. Bias in coverage in sample surveys or even in

Table 1. Yield of Eligible Veteran Respondents for 8,698 Completed Telephone Screening Contacts

	Total Contacts (By Race of Phone Respondent)		
	Direct Veteran	Multiplicity Veteran	Yield
All respondents	559	480	85.9%
White	428	300	70.1
Black	107	139	129.9
Mexican-American (Los Angeles)	24	41	170.8

the decennial census has resulted in underestimates of the black population and in systematic errors in generalization (Bridge, 1974; Davis, 1964).

The difficulty in drawing a representative sample of blacks results from at least three factors: (1) greater difficulty in interviewing members of drawn households, (2) greater number of blacks who do not have private telephones and are not therefore drawn in telephone-based surveys, and (3) higher rates of transiency than others, so that persons are not members of households at the time of the survey. We have already noted that multiplicity sampling is likely to be more effective than household sampling in drawing persons who are transient or lack telephones. Therefore, we hypothesize that multiplicity sampling will reduce some of the bias against blacks. However, the method makes it possible to improve coverage, whatever the reason for undercoverage. If substantial amounts of money can be saved in screening, the money is then available to deal with problems of undercoverage, or refusal, or whatever.

Cost Savings

An estimate was made of screening costs as they would have been without the use of multiplicity, and these were compared to actual costs. There are some offsetting cost factors with multiplicity. The method increases somewhat the length of any given contact interview, because of the special information required. All the household respondents must be given the nominating portion of the interview, even though only a small percentage will produce a nominee. If the household screening respondent nominates a veteran, considerable additional time must be expended in getting locational information.

The savings in screening cost were $20 to $24 per interview, or $20,000 to $24,000 for our sample of 1,000. This sample includes both veterans and nonveterans. When cost savings are expressed for the purely veteran sample, the savings per interview rises to $36.00–$44.00 per interview. Our cost savings estimates refer only to screening costs. However, the conduct of an actual multiplicity-selected interview introduces some increase in location costs over the usual cost of contacting the direct household respondent. As we indicated earlier, however, the extra trouble mostly involved a phone call or two. Only occasionally was a fair amount of work required in locating the veteran, re-calling the original household screening contact, spending time locating others in the kin structure, or tracking the veteran through friends. Occasionally, it involved a field visit to an address where the veteran might live or where he last lived. It should be stated, however, that when these complications occurred, the veteran was almost always someone who would have been missed entirely or equally difficult to locate in household survey.

While cost-effective in our study, the application of multiplicity sampling is not invariably appropriate. If the population studied were less rare than the Vietnam era veteran, both additional screening and location cost would offset a substantially lower benefit.

It should also be recognized that sampling variances in mutiplicity estimation are greater than for a simple random sample. Fortunately, in this study, the increase in sampling variances for a representative range of variables is estimated to be under 8 percent. Thus, the increase in variance due to multiplicity weighting was far smaller than the corresponding cost benefit achieved by the method.

Yield, Kinship, and Ethnicity

The yield of multiplicity sampling depends upon which kin are included in the group eligible to nominate a veteran, since different kin categories vary in the likelihood that they will supply a veteran nominee in response to our query. To demonstrate this point empirically requires that we calculate a relative yield ratio between kin categories. We do this by comparing the proportion of all nominations originating for each kin category to the proportions of all eligible kin in that category. The latter estimate is obtained from questionnaire responses of veteran interviewees regarding kin living within their site of residence. It is calculated from data supplied by "direct" veterans only (to avoid having the data of this paper become entangled with the issue of possible multiplicity bias). Thus, the results are fully equivalent to a conventional household survey.

$$\text{relative yield ratio} = \frac{\text{percentage nominated by a kin category}}{\substack{\text{estimated population percentage} \\ \text{of the kin category}}}$$

If the different kin groups were equally likely to nominate veterans, the percentage of nominees (for example, nephews) from any kin group (aunts and uncles) would exactly reflect the proportion of that group in the population.[2] Thus, the relative yield ratio would have

[2] The population here is not a "general" one but is defined in a unique way. The direct veteran group is assumed to be representative of veterans as a whole. Thus, the kin population refers to all persons who have an eligible veteran kin who is a nephew, brother, or son. (Kin who have more than one veteran kin are counted more than once by this definition, since it is the relationship that is being enumerated) A problem with

been 1.00 in that case. Table 2 shows the actual yield ratios for each kin category. The data are presented by racial subcategories, since they show considerable variation in this regard. Yield ratios are not presented for Chicano veterans because the small size of this sample does not permit breakdowns.

The results of Table 2 are intriguing. The most striking finding is the low relative yield for aunts and uncles. Such kin are about one-quarter as likely to nominate a veteran as their size would dictate and are about one-seventh to one-eighth as likely to nominate as are parents. Thus, even though aunts and uncles accounted for about 48 percent of eligible white kin, only 12 percent of nominations came from this source (the figures for blacks are 34 percent and 10 percent respectively). Clearly, the decision to include aunts and uncles is one that we would not make had we these data in hand. The inclusion of nephews increases potential sampling bias relative to the increase in yield. Furthermore, the veteran nephews are disproportionately difficult to locate, thus increasing the cost that this method is designed to reduce.

One possible explanation of these findings is that parents and siblings *overreported* their veteran kin. However, the nominee veterans used in this analysis are only those actually contacted and found to be eligible. Thus, the only explanation for variation in the yield ratios is the tendency to *underreport* eligible veterans. Neither is it possible to

Table 2. Relative Yield by Kin Category of Nominator and Race of Nominee

	Kin Category of Nominator		
Race of Nominee[a]	*Parent*	*Sibling*	*Aunts and Uncles*
White	2.08	1.75	.23
Black	2.07	1.24	.29

[a] The tabular data do not include ratios for the "total" group because the sizes of the black and white groups are completely an artifact of the screening procedure. The data on nominating kin and eligible households can be merged, however, by weighting them by estimates of the population size of the racial groups. For the nine largely urban sites that we have studied around the nation in which we sampled blacks, the black group constituted 20.5 percent of the eligible veteran population (excluding other nonwhites). When the data are weighted by this estimate, the relative yield ratios are: 2.07 for parents, 1.60 for siblings, .24 for aunts and uncles.

this definition is that directly chosen veterans may not be unbiased representatives because of household characteristics noted previously; a perfectly representative group might have somewhat different kinship characteristics. This issue cannot be settled with these data. Note also that we assume that veterans accurately report their kin. Since these data were gathered by enumeration of local kin in the course of a lengthy, face-to-face interview, we feel as justified in the foregoing assumption as one can be under practical circumstances.

explain these data by the fact that certain categories have fewer veteran kin, since by definition the baseline is a relative one: the *percentage* of those with eligible kin who are either parents, siblings, or aunts or uncles.

Why, then is the yield of nephews so low? One explanation is that aunts and uncles are ignorant of the fact that particular nephews are veterans: they have less knowledge than parents and siblings. However, the veteran characteristic is a very public one. While some aunts and uncles may be unknowing, therefore, it is also likely that given the sometimes extensive set of nephews, they simply failed to think about a particular nephew when asked for a veteran nomination, i.e., he was temporarily forgotten, even though his veteran characteristic might have been well known. If it is important to expand nominations by using this kin category then it would seem necessary to enumerate the list of all nephews for each screening respondent to decrease the chance of forgetting. This would be a difficult step to take, however, since it would radically increase the cost of a task repeated many thousands of times in sampling a rare population.

The interpretation of Table 2 is somewhat complicated for parents and siblings by the numerical effects of the low yield of aunts and uncles. Thus, we shall recast it by removing all veterans nominated as nephews and calculating the relative yields for sons and siblings only. Table 3 shows the results. Parents show a higher yield than siblings for both races, but black parents are especially high. Black parents are about 67 percent more likely to nominate a veteran than are black siblings. For whites, the relative increase of parents over siblings is only 18 percent.

What explains these yield differences? As in the case of nephews, we cannot completely discount the possibility that a kin person might be ignorant of veteran status. However, it seems a questionable explanation to apply to kin relationships as close as sibling or son. Of course, even close kin do vary in terms of the amount of actual contact and the salience of that contact. Black sibling networks, in particular, are quite large compared to white ones and are more likely

Table 3. Relative Yield by Kin Category of Nominator and Race of Nominee Excluding Aunt and Uncle Nominations

Race of Nominee[a]	Kin Category of Nominator	
	Parent	Siblings
White	1.11	.94
Black	1.47	.88

[a] The ratio for a combined sample of blacks and whites, computed as stated in the Table 2 note, is 1.16 for parents and .92 for siblings.

to contain step-siblings and half-siblings and, as a function of size, to be characterized by considerable age disparities between the siblings. Thus, when asked for nominations on the occasion of a telephone screening interview, a particular sibling who has served in the military may be momentarily forgotten. Complete enumeration of the sibling structure should reduce this undercoverage, although at the cost of increased screening expense. Thus, the pragmatic sampler may wish to use that procedure optionally. For a draw which is largely white, the additional cost would generate a payoff disproportionately smaller than for a black sample. Another approach worth considering is that of tightening the inclusion rule for siblings. If we eliminate step- and half-siblings from both the nominee group and the kinship size estimates, undercoverage should diminish. The decision to do so, of course, is a serious tradeoff. It is the existence of such siblings that is partly responsible for the high yield of multiplicity sampling among nonwhites. If a reduction in yield means a reduction in sample size, therefore, the decision to eliminate step- and half-siblings will substantially increase sampling error.

Undoubtedly, any procedures for gathering a multiplicity sample would result in some relative yield variation between kin categories. One useful possibility is to adjust the weighting formula for undercoverage. Conventionally, multiplicity weighting by network size assumes that each eligible kin will increase the chance of nomination in equal proportion. If that is not the case for a given kin category, a weighting formula that recognized that fact would increase the accuracy of population estimates. Such a procedure would involve multiplying cases by the reciprocal of the relative yield ratio for their nominating kin.[3]

Earlier, we showed that blacks and Chicanos have considerably higher yields than whites. For ethnicity, the effect of kinship structure can be stated simply: blacks and Chicanos have larger families (and also more complex ones, due to higher rates of family disorganization) and thus more persons available to nominate. This explanation is clearly capable of accounting for the yield differences, since the more kin a household member has, the more likely is one of them to be a veteran. However, it seems likely that some of the yield improvement results from the superior ability of multiplicity sampling to reach difficult-to-access black and Chicano respondents. Additional data on sampling accessibility were gathered and will be analyzed in subsequent reports.

---

[3] It is our opinion that this sort of weighting should not be considered unless the yield ratio is relatively close to 1.0. Otherwise it will exaggerate the influence of a group which might be quite unrepresentative (e.g., it contains a disproportionate number of charming and unforgettable nephews).

In our survey, nominating a veteran requires more than just an eligible kin. The nominee must live in the local area, since our sample is of a geographically delimited area—as are many surveys. The effect of ethnicity on yield is thereby affected. The ratios of black and Chicano to white family size are considerably greater for the local area than for kin in general. One simple way to see this is to ask what percentage of each group has at least one sibling in the local area. The differences are striking. Forty-nine percent of white veterans have no siblings at all in the local area, in contrast with 17 percent of black veterans and only 6 percent of Chicanos.

Summary and Conclusions

Whites are relatively easy to sample as a rule (except in rare subcategories). Blacks and Chicanos, whatever the design, are likely to create cost problems when they are sampled as a stratum within a field survey of households. The findings contained here suggest that these groups have a social characteristic that can provide a solution to the cost problem, namely, their larger local network size. That characteristic makes a multiplicity sample uniquely effective. This social peculiarity may or may not be shared with other minorities. Part of the reason for this network characteristic may be sought in the effect of minority-linked poverty on family size and patterns of migration. But part of the explanation may stem from a general tendency of minority groups to be localized—to not be distant from their families, perhaps because of the psychological importance of homophily. Thus, high local network size may be characteristic even of relatively affluent minorities. (Jews, for example, have relative low family size, but relatively high local network size [Kobrin and Goldschneider, 1978]). If this is so, the promise of multiplicity sampling for studying rare populations may be greater than that suggested by the simple arithmetic of relative fertility.

LOOSER MULTIPLICITY METHODS (SNOWBALL SAMPLES)

As the population becomes rarer, one is tempted to increase the multiplicity net wider to bring in more eligible respondents. Unlike loose snowball sampling, this procedure can retain theoretical rigor if it is possible for the respondent to estimate the size of the network with some degree of accuracy. Thus, there is no theoretical reason why the network must be limited to relatives—it could include friends, co-workers, and neighbors.

The problem, of course, is the difficulty that most respondents would have in giving accurate estimates of the number of others who know them. Note, however, that this is not an absolute difference between these looser methods and those that involve relatives. As we have seen above, the quality of the data on networks is clearly poorer for nephews than for sons and brothers and there are some errors even in these groups.

Response problems do not absolutely rule out the use of looser procedures. If one were able to measure the errors in the respondents' estimates of the size of their networks, this would then become an additional source of sampling variance. For rare populations, the increased sample yield and thus reduction in sampling variance might well outweigh the increase from the response error of size of network.

Once one begins to consider the possibility of such procedures it may be possible to devise questions that improve the accuracy of reporting of network size. From what we know of response errors generally, making the questions as specific as possible and offering aids to memory should help. We believe that more research on the use of more diffuse networks is justified, particularly for very rare populations.

References

Bridge, R. Gary
    1974   Nonresponse Bias in Mail Surveys: The Case of the Department of Defense Post-Service Survey. Santa Monica, Calif.: The Rand Corporation.
Davis, James A.
    1964   "Attrition in the 1962 and 1963 follow-up waves in the NORC panel survey of June, 1961 college students." Working Paper, NORC Survey, September: 431–67.
Fine, M., G. Rothbart, and S. Sudman
    1979   "On finding the needle in a haystack: multiplicity sampling procedures." Annual Meeting of the American Association for Public Opinion Research.
Frankel, Martin R., and Lester R. Frankel
    1977   "Some recent developments in sample survey design." Journal of Marketing Research 4:280–93.
Kobrin, F., and C. Goldschneider
    1978   Ethnic Factors in Family Structure and Mobility. Cambridge, Mass.: Ballinger.
Nathan, Gad
    1976   "An empirical study of response and sampling error for multiplicity estimates with different counting rules." Journal of the American Statistical Association 71:808–15.
    1977   Multiplicity Study of Marriages and Births in Israel. Washington, D.C.: U.S. Department of Health Education and Welfare, National Center for Health Statistics Publication # (HRA) 77–1344.
Rothbart, G. S., M. Fine, and R. S. Laufer
    1978   "Finding and interviewing Vietnam veterans: techniques for reaching rare respondents." Annual Meeting of the American Association for Public Opinion Research.
Sirken, Monroe G.
    1970   "Household surveys with multiplicity." Journal of the American Statistical Association 63:257–66.

1974 "The counting rule strategy in sample surveys." Proceedings of the Social Statistics Section, American Statistical Association:119–23.

1979 "Network sampling in health surveys." Third Biennial Conference on Health Survey Research Methods, Reston, Va.

Sirken, Monroe G., and P. N. Royston

1970 "Reasons deaths are missed in population surveys of population change." Proceedings of the Social Statistics Section, American Statistical Association:361–64.

1973 "Underreporting of births and deaths in household surveys of population change." Proceedings of the Social Statistics Section, American Statistical Association:412–15.

Sirkin, Monroe G., and G. Sabagh

1968 "Evaluation of birth statistics derived retrospectively from fertility histories reported in a national population survey: United States, 1945–64." Demography 5:485–503.

Sudman, Seymour

1976 Applied Sampling. New York: Academic Press.

Trends in Nonresponse Rates, 1952–1979

CHARLOTTE G. STEEH

IN the last decade there has been increasing concern over response rates in sample surveys of the United States household population. Reports of major declines in survey response and criticisms of survey methods led the American Statistical Association in 1973 to sponsor a Conference on Surveys of Human Populations. Lamenting the unavailability of adequate data—particularly from research organizations operating in university settings—the conference concluded that achieving satisfactory completion rates had become more difficult. At the same time it recognized that disagreement existed within the survey research community about the possible causal factors. Opinion was split between those who felt the problem stemmed primarily from an increase in the numbers of respondents who could not be found at home and those who believed the change was due to an increase in refusals. In any case, the conference called for a "more intensive examination of the problem" and recommended the establishment of a full-time research staff whose main task would be

Abstract Reported increases in nonresponse rates to sample surveys have not been systematically documented to date. Data from the National Election Studies and the Surveys of Consumer Attitudes, two well-known continuing studies conducted by the Survey Research Center at the University of Michigan, permit the assessment of long-term trends for the two major components of nonresponse, refusals and other noninterviews, by urban subgroups using time series regression techniques. The analyses clearly demonstrate that there have been substantial increases in total nonresponse due primarily to increases in the percentages of respondents who refuse to be interviewed, and that these trends are related to the level of urbanization.

Charlotte G. Steeh is an Assistant Research Scientist in the Survey Research Center at the University of Michigan. The author wishes to thank Irene Hess and John Scott for sharing their extensive knowledge about SRC surveys, and Howard Schuman, Robert Groves, and Graham Kalton for their comments and advice. The continuing concern of SRC for improving our knowledge of survey methods is demonstrated by its financial and other support of this investigation.

determining precisely the "scale and characteristics" of the difficulties survey research faces (American Statistical Association, 1974).

Shortly after this conference, a Subsection on Survey Research Methods was created within the American Statistical Association and a project for systematically assessing survey practices was designed (Bailar and Lanphier, 1978). Additionally, in 1979 the National Academy of Sciences sponsored a Panel on Missing and Incomplete Data. The plea for empirical documentation of changes in response or nonresponse rates has, however, gone largely unheeded. Some studies, many of them unpublished, have contained hard data presented usually as a preface to a related topic (DeMaio, 1980; Finkner, 1975; House and Wolf, 1978; Juster, 1976; Love and Turner, 1975; Madow and Rizvi, 1979; Marquis, 1977).[1] Only one of these reached conclusions which contradicted the findings of the 1973 ASA conference. On the basis of data from both university and government surveys, Marquis concluded that no decline in response rates has in fact occurred when methodological changes and organizational factors are taken into account.

Since the Survey Research Center (SRC) at the University of Michigan has conducted social surveys for 30 years, including series of similar studies, the records of its field office provide invaluable data for systematically examining the experience of one university-based organization with first contact interviewing situations. The purpose of this paper is to explore the following five issues using data from two personal interview surveys—the National Election Studies[2] and the Surveys of Consumer Attitudes:

1. Whether the two major components of nonresponse—refusals and other noninterviews—have increased over time.[3]

---

[1] See Wiseman and McDonald (1979) for a review of research on response rates which has been completed since 1973. However, very few of the studies listed in Table 1 of their paper deal with change over time.

[2] Since 1970 the National Election Studies have been conducted under the auspices of the Center for Political Studies rather than the Survey Research Center. However, the same field office services both centers.

[3] There is some confusion about the definitions used for various types of nonresponse at the Survey Research Center, as there is in survey research as a whole. Interviewer's manuals from the 1950s through the mid-1960s provided no explanations for the simple classifications which were employed. Since the late 1960s, however, noninterview forms have become increasingly complex and categories of nonresponse less and less comparable. The latest revisions in the noninterview form used for personal interview surveys (1976) make it difficult to divide the nonrefusal component of nonresponse into the standard groups used in the past: the not-at-homes and respondent-absent versus all other reasons (inability to speak English, mental retardation, deafness, for example). Therefore, in this paper these types have been treated as one category representing the nonrefusal component. The 1976 redefinition of refusal includes those respondents who postponed an interview more than twice—a practice

2. Whether one component has increased more than the other.

3. Whether urbanization, conceived as a categorical variable, is related to changes in these nonresponse rates or to their absolute levels at any one point in time, as the ASA conference and other research has suggested (Benus and Ackerman, 1971; House and Wolf, 1978; Juster, 1976; American Statistical Association, 1974).[4]

4. Whether there is any evidence of seasonal effects upon nonresponse rates for the Surveys of Consumer Attitudes.

5. Whether the two surveys differ substantially in the amounts of change or types of relationships which have occurred.

The actual paths of response or nonresponse rates for these surveys have been plotted in previous studies—as one-year or five-year averages for the Surveys of Consumer Attitudes (Benus and Ackerman, 1971; Juster, 1976; Marquis, 1977), and in presidential years for the National Election Studies (House and Wolf, 1978). However, simple time series regression analyses, which easily handle quarterly data, will provide for both the Surveys of Consumer Attitudes and the biennial National Election Studies empirical estimates of *how much*, on the average, nonresponse rates have changed. In addition, it will be possible to specify what forms the changes haven taken. For example, nonresponse rates may have increased by constant amounts over the entire time period (a linear trend), by amounts which are growing larger with the passage of time (an exponential trend), or by rates of increase which are beginning to decline (a growth curve such as the Gompertz curve). Determining which of these trends is appropriate in each case seems a crucial first step toward understanding both the nature of the problem and its seriousness.

The National Election Studies and the Surveys of Consumer Attitudes have many features which make them desirable subjects for an investigation of this type. Each is national in scope and relatively homogeneous in subject matter. In addition, both have respondent eligibility requirements which minimize screening, and data for both are available by primary sampling unit (PSU) from the early 1950s. However, because the sample designs often mixed cross-sections and panels, the time series had to be carefully constructed to include only data which represented a first interview for respondents. Confining the analysis to these cross-sectional samples eliminated the need to use sample weights in calculating the nonresponse rates.[5] Unfortu-

---

which attempts to deal with indirect refusals and which was most probably not followed in the past (Scott, 1975).

[4] Again, see Marquis (1977) for a dissent.

[5] The only exception is the data from the 1970 National Election Study, which included a black supplement with a different probability of selection. Because nonre-

nately, this decision reduced the number of surveys in the time series for the Surveys of Consumer Attitudes from 91 to 45. Since the election studies are conducted every two years, there are only 11 surveys with cross-sectional data.[6] As a result, plots of the actual data points appear relatively smooth.[7]

At the beginning, the appropriateness of linear time series models is assumed, and analysis of covariance is used to test various comparisons across surveys, urban subgroups, and seasons. The dependent variable is the appropriate nonresponse rate and the covariate is time. Each nonresponse rate is calculated as a percentage of the sample units which remain after nonresidential locations, unoccupied dwellings, housing units on military reservations, and nonhousehold living quarters (dormitories, military barracks, transient hotels) have been excluded. For the National Election Studies housing units without United States citizens are also excluded when this information can be determined.[8] The refusal rate plus the other noninterview rate equals the total nonresponse rate.

The categorical variables are simply conceived. For comparisons across surveys, the Surveys of Consumer Attitudes are coded 1 and the National Election Studies, 2. For comparisons across seasons, the winter quarter is designated 1; spring, 2; summer, 3; and fall, 4. The level of urbanization is determined by classifying primary sampling units into three groups.[9] The 12 largest urban areas in the coterminous United States, sampled either as standard metropolitan statistical

---

sponse data for the black supplement were not separately recorded in 1970, as they were in 1964 and 1968, they could not be excluded from the calculation of rates for that survey. However, the supplement constituted only 7.7 percent of the total sample.

[6] A breakdown by type of nonresponse was unavailable for the 1976 preelection survey, and so this study had to be excluded from all analyses. Since data for the new cross-sectional respondents in the 1974 National Election Study could not be recovered, nonresponse rates were substituted from the Generations and Politics Survey which was in the field at almost the same time and had both a totally new sample and an identical definition of respondent eligibility (randomly selected citizens 16 years of age and over). In 1978 the primary sampling units for the election study were congressional districts rather than counties and groups of counties.

[7] An appendix, available from the author on request, describes in detail the decisions which were made as time series were constructed from these data.

[8] Age requirements might also affect the eligibility of a sample unit. Generally the Surveys of Consumer Attitudes have limited respondents to persons 18 and over, while the National Election Studies have used the voting age as a criterion. If a sample unit does not contain anyone meeting the appropriate standard, it is not counted as an eligible unit. The family rather than the household was the sampling unit for the Surveys of Consumer Attitudes prior to 1972.

[9] Data for the Surveys of Consumer Attitudes conducted in the fourth quarter of 1953 and the second quarter of 1954 were not available by PSU and could not be used in the subgroup analysis. Therefore, the time series for the urban subgroups begin in 1954 rather than 1953 and contain 43 instead of 45 surveys.

areas or as consolidated areas made up of two or more SMSAs, comprise the group which is referred to as "large cities." The designation "cities" applies to those PSUs which contain one of the remaining standard metropolitan statistical areas. All PSUs which do not include an SMSA form the "small town" category.[10] The fit of the linear models to the data is gauged by using the standard Durbin-Watson statistic, which tests for random residuals (Chatfield, 1975). The regression coefficients for the election studies are computed on a quarterly, rather than a biennial basis to facilitate comparison with the Surveys of Consumer Attitudes.

Long-Term Trends in Refusal Rates

Figure 1 graphs the overall refusal rates for the Surveys of Consumer Attitudes and the National Election Studies, and Figures 2 and 3 plot the percentages of refusals by the urban subgroups of each survey. These graphs indicate that there have been noticeable increases across the board in refusal rates over the last 28 years. The results of the basic within-class regression analyses, presented in Table 1, confirm these visual impressions. For both surveys and all subgroups the coefficients are highly significant (at or beyond the .0001 confidence level).[11] This means that refusal rates have trends

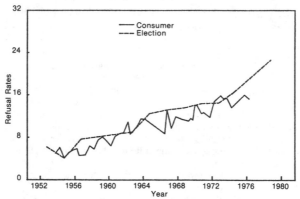

Figure 1. Refusal Rates for the Surveys of Consumer Attitudes and the National Election Studies

[10] It should be noted that "small town" PSUs may be quite populous with cities as large as 49,999.

[11] In time series analyses statistical inference may not be the same as in cross-sectional studies. A particular time series is just one realization or sample from all possible realizations of a stochastic process. The assumption of equal variances for the individual surveys which make up each of the time series presented here appears tenable since the sample designs and sample sizes for both surveys are remarkably constant over time.

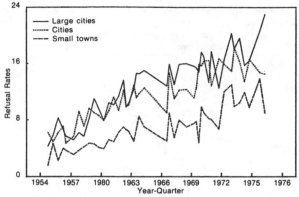

Figure 2. **Refusal Rates for the Surveys of Consumer Attitudes, 1954–1976**

which increase from 8 percentage points for small towns in the Surveys of Consumer Attitudes to 21 percentage points for metropolitan areas in the election studies. It appears as well from the data in Table 1 that the relationship between level of urbanization and amount of change is positive in both surveys so that the largest increases occur in metropolitan centers and the smallest in towns. In addition, the regression coefficients for the National Election Studies are slightly larger than the coefficients for the Surveys of Consumer Attitudes. Furthermore, since none of the Durbin-Watson d statistics is significant at or beyond the .05 level, the residuals appear to fluctuate randomly about the regression lines, and it seems reasonable to assume the adequacy of linear models.

The means listed in Table 1 indicate that the absolute *levels* of refusal rates have been higher in the election studies than in the

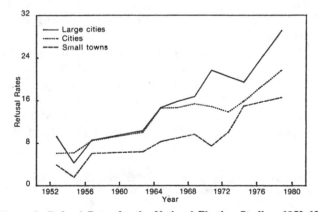

Figure 3. **Refusal Rates for the National Election Studies, 1952–1978**

Table 1. Analysis of Change in Refusal Rates for SRC Surveys, 1952–1978

Urban Category	Regression Coefficient[a]	d	r^2	Total Change[b]	Mean	Intercept
National Election Studies, 1952–1978						
Large cities	.198* (.024)	2.31	.89	20.8	15.5	5.0
Cities	.132* (.015)	1.60	.89	13.9	12.9	5.9
Small towns	.118* (.018)	1.82	.83	12.4	8.6	2.3
Total	.148* (.014)	2.02	.92	15.5	12.3	4.3
Surveys of Consumer Attitudes, 1953–1976						
Large cities	.169* (.011)	1.70	.84	14.7	12.9	4.3
Cities	.127* (.010)	1.97	.80	11.0	11.6	5.1
Small towns	.097* (.009)	2.24	.75	8.4	6.8	1.9
Total	.126* (.006)	1.96	.90	11.5	10.1	3.9

[a]Standard errors are in parentheses.
[b] To obtain total change multiply the regression coefficient by the number of quarters (105 for the election surveys; 91 for the overall Surveys of Consumer Attitudes and 87 for its urban subgroups).
* $p < .0001$.

Surveys of Consumer Attitudes across all subgroups. A positive relationship also exists between these levels in both surveys and the degree of urbanization, with the lowest refusal rates obtained in small towns and the highest in large metropolitan centers. However, the values of the intercepts and the plots of the actual time series (Figures 2 and 3) suggest that this relationship has not been consistently monotonic over time. Refusal rates in large cities and intermediate urban areas appear nearly equal over much of the period for the Surveys of Consumer Attitudes and through 1964 for the election studies. Thus, for refusals, it may be important to distinguish between only two categories of PSU, those which contain an SMSA and those which do not. In any case, the differential rates of increase have insured the divergence of refusal rates for the subgroups of both surveys over time.

Analysis of covariance permits assessment of the significance of these differences by testing the null hypotheses that the regression coefficients and the means are equal among the groups defined by a particular classification.[12] The presence of seasonal effects in the Surveys of Consumer Attitudes can also be determined by testing for differences among four quarterly regressions (Ladd, 1974). The F statistics produced by the analysis of covariance reveal that signifi-

---

[12] When the means of the covariate do not differ across subgroups, as is true in this case, the category means for the dependent variable cannot be adjusted, and the test for equal means reverts to the one-way analysis of variance test. Thus the F statistics are meaningful even though the slopes within the subgroups are significantly different.

cant differences occur between the urban subgroups *within* each survey. All pairs of subgroups have been analyzed separately, and the results, presented in Table 2, indicate that the largest differences occur in both surveys between large cities and small towns. However, for estimates of change the intermediate urban areas are more like the small towns than the large cities. In fact, for the election studies the amounts of change which have occurred in the cities and small towns do not differ significantly. However, the means of the refusal rates for cities more nearly approach those of the metropolitan centers, as Figures 2 and 3 have indicated.

The only other significant differences occur *across* surveys for the means in large cities and small towns ($F = 11.2, p < .01$ for large cities; $F = 8.1, p < .01$ for small towns). From this it would appear that although these subgroups have experienced approximately the same amount of change in each survey, actual refusal rates have been significantly higher in the election studies than in the Surveys of Consumer Attitudes. This conclusion is offered tentatively because the sample designs differ in ways that may affect the comparison of levels across surveys both for refusals and for other noninterviews. The National Election Studies require some screening for citizens—a procedure which would tend to overestimate both nonresponse rates since ineligible housing units cannot be properly eliminated (the number of sample units is too large). On the other hand, the sample unit for the Surveys of Consumer Attitudes until 1972 was the family rather than the household—a procedure which might underestimate nonresponse rates since secondary families may be improperly excluded (the number of sample units is too small). Although the effects of these discrepancies in sample design are impossible to estimate precisely, their probable presence should be taken into account.

In the cases where there are no significant differences in the regression coefficients across the relevant groups—such as for seasons—a common coefficient can be calculated from pooled data. This coefficient is the estimate of increase adjusted for the influence of the

Table 2. F Statistics from Analysis of Covariance Null Hypothesis Tests: Refusal Rates

Survey	Large Cities v. Cities	Large Cities v. Small Towns	Cities v. Small Towns
Differences in slope			
Surveys of Consumer Attitudes	7.7*	24.8*	4.9*
National Election Studies	5.6*	7.4*	.3
Differences in mean			
Surveys of Consumer Attitudes	10.9*	214.8*	188.2*
National Election Studies	6.8*	40.2*	34.1*

* $p < .05$.

categorical variable. Thus the estimates of change for the urban subgroups of the Surveys of Consumer Attitudes, taking season into
account, are .164, .126, and .094, respectively. These differ only
slightly from the unadjusted coefficients listed in Table 1.

Long-Term Trends in Rates of Other Noninterviews

The basic data for the nonrefusal component of nonresponse are
graphed in Figures 4 to 6, and the results of the statistical analyses are
presented in Tables 3 and 4. The large and anomalous increases in
other noninterviews during 1961 for the Surveys of Consumer Attitudes reflect the outcome of a brief experiment which permitted no
more than three call-backs to sample households. Figures 4 to 6 and
the within-class regression coefficients in Table 3 indicate that there

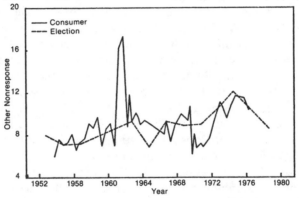

**Figure 4. Other Nonresponse for the Surveys of Consumer Attitudes and the National
Election Studies**

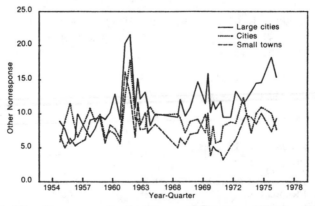

Figure 5. Other Nonresponse for the Surveys of Consumer Attitudes, 1954–1976

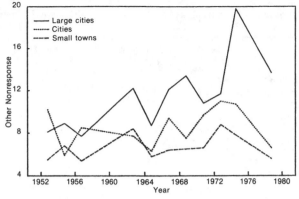

Figure 6. Other Nonresponse for the National Election Studies, 1952–1978

has been almost no increase in the percentages of other noninterviews except in the metropolitan areas of both surveys. The actual changes range from a − .3 percentage point in the small towns for the Surveys of Consumer Attitudes to approximately 8 percentage points in the metropolitan areas for the election studies. As with refusal rates, the changes in the nonrefusal components seem to be somewhat higher for the election studies than for the Surveys of Consumer Attitudes.

The Durbin-Watson d statistics for the large cities and small towns of the Surveys of Consumer Attitudes indicate that the residuals from the linear regressions in these cases are not randomly distributed and that some other regression model might better fit these data. Plots of

Table 3. Analysis of Change in Rates of Other Nonresponse for SRC Surveys, 1952–1978

Urban Category	Regression Coefficient[a]		d	r^2	Total Change[b]	Mean	Intercept
National Election Studies, 1952–1978							
Large cities	.075*	(.023)	2.85	.54	7.9	11.6	7.6
Cities	.010	(.018)	2.06	.03	1.1	8.5	8.0
Small towns	.011	(.011)	2.40.	.10	1.2	6.7	6.1
Total	.029	(.012)	2.45	.40	3.0	8.8	7.3
Surveys of Consumer Attitudes, 1953–1976							
Large cities	.061*	(.019)	1.22*	.21	5.3	11.5	8.4
Cities	.001	(.014)	1.49	.00	.1	8.9	8.9
Small towns	−.003	(.015)	1.16*	.00	−.3	7.6	7.7
Total	.021	(.012)	1.18*	.06	1.9	9.1	8.1

[a] Standard errors are in parentheses.

[b] To obtain total change multiply the regression coefficient by the number of quarters (105 for the election surveys; 91 for the overall Surveys of Consumer Attitudes and 87 for its urban subgroups).

*$p \leq .01$.

Table 4. F Statistics from Analysis of Covariance Null Hypothesis Tests: Other
Noninterviews

Survey	Large Cities v. Cities	Large Cities v. Small Towns	Cities v. Small Towns
Differences in slope			
Surveys of Consumer Attitudes	6.8*	7.1*	—[a]
National Election Studies	5.0*	6.2*	—[a]
Differences in mean			
Surveys of Consumer Attitudes	18.3*	39.2*	6.8*
National Election Studies	8.7*	27.1*	7.7*

[a] Less than .1.
* $p < .05$.

the residuals from the linear regressions do, in fact, reveal cyclical movement. The nonrefusal component of nonresponse in both large cities and small towns appears to have been lower during the 1950s and again during the late 1960s and early 1970s than in the early 1960s and mid-1970s. However, for complex patterns of change which have several cycles, linear regression does provide a reasonable estimate of overall direction.[13]

The lengths of the cycles, roughly gauged from the plots of the residuals, appear similar for both subgroups and suggest a hypothesis for more rigorous testing. The cycles may correspond to changes in respondent selection procedures. From the early 1950s to the mid-1960s, in families with a married head, the respondent was randomly chosen from the head (in this case always defined as the male) or his wife. In all other families the respondent was the head, either male or female. In both cases no substitutions or proxy interviews were permitted. From the mid-1960s to 1972—the period which coincides with a decrease in the rates of other noninterviews—the head of the family unit (again defined as the husband in the case of married couples) became the designated respondent in every instance. More significantly, some substitution was permitted. Under certain conditions—absence of the husband during the entire field period, for example—the wife could be interviewed instead. Beginning in 1972 new selection procedures were instituted: the respondent was selected from the adults in the household on a full probability basis, and proxy interviews were no longer allowed. At this point an upswing in the rates of other noninterviews occurred. It is interesting and perhaps relevant

[13] Since there is no significant trend in the case of small towns—that is, the series is stationary—spectral analysis could be employed to estimate precisely the length of the cycles. However, the series for large cities must have its trend eliminated before further analyses could be undertaken. See Smith (1978) for the use of autoregressive moving average (ARMA) models to estimate the changes in population parameters over time.

that the d's are all insignificant for the National Election Studies, where respondent selection procedures have not varied as much over time as those of the Surveys of Consumer Attitudes.[14]

The means for these series, given in Table 3, suggest that the absolute levels of the nonrefusal components have not differed appreciably across the two surveys. However, examination of the levels within each survey (Figures 5 and 6) reveals more fluctuation across groups than was true of refusal rates. Until the late 1950s there was a tendency in both surveys for the intermediate urban areas to have the highest rates of other noninterviews. Thereafter, in each case the nonrefusal component was consistently largest in metropolitan centers. The expected three-way pattern—highest rates in large cities, intermediate rates in middle-sized cities, and lowest rates in small towns—did not occur until the mid-1960s and is not as regular after that for the Surveys of Consumer Attitudes as for the election studies.

The results of the covariance analyses again reveal that significant differences exist only between pairs of urban subgroups within surveys. The F statistics for these comparisons are listed in Table 4. Here, however, significant differences in slope occur only between the metropolitan centers and each of the other groups. The statistical distinction between the regression coefficients for the intermediate urban areas and for small towns disappears in both surveys. The tests for differences in means yield significant results for all comparisons, which suggests that the urban groups within each survey differ in the level of other noninterviews despite the considerable fluctuation apparent in the time plots. The values of the F statistics suggest that in level as well the metropolitan centers are distinct from the other two groups. The differences *across surveys*—in slopes and means—are all statistically insignificant,[15] and for the Surveys of Consumer Attitudes no seasonal effects can be discerned. The estimates of change adjusted for season are again very close to the original estimates. For the urban subgroups of the Surveys of Consumer Attitudes they are .068, −.001, and .002, respectively.

Methodological Implications

The preceding analyses clearly establish that there have been substantial increases in nonresponse rates since the early 1950s, and that

[14] In the election studies for 1954 and 1962, respondent eligibility requirements were modified most probably to facilitate field procedures for surveys conducted jointly with the Surveys of Consumer Attitudes. In 1962 noncitizens who granted interviews were eliminated at the analysis stage.

[15] Again, the results for the means may be questionable due to the differences in sample design which may affect the level of nonresponse rates but not the slopes.

these increases are due primarily to changes in refusal rates. The increase in refusal rates accounts for 85.7 percent of the increase in total nonresponse for the Surveys of Consumer Attitudes and 83.6 percent of the increase for the election studies. Within the cities and small towns the increases in total nonresponse are almost entirely due to the changes in refusals (respectively 99 percent and 103 percent for the Surveys of Consumer Attitudes, and 93 percent and 91 percent for the election studies). The patterns in large cities are more complex. Although the increases in refusal rates are the primary cause (74 percent for the Surveys of Consumer Attitudes; 73 percent for the election studies), increases in other noninterviews also play a part.

These analyses also indicate that the degree of urbanization may be a major exogenous factor capable of explaining both change over time—since most PSUs have become increasingly urban—and differences among the subgroups at any one point in time. Furthermore, seasonal factors do not appear to affect nonresponse rates in any systematic way. Finally, the forms of change have been predominantly linear, with the increases, where they have occurred, spread evenly over the entire time period. While this is less discouraging than finding that the amounts of increase in nonresponse rates have themselves been increasing over time, it is hardly a hopeful result, especially when forecasts, often the goal of time series analysis, are considered. Therefore, it is crucial to try to determine what survey research methods can do to alter these trends.

In several instances, it is possible to see the operation of methodological factors. The hypothesized effect of respondent selection procedures has already been noted. Methodological changes may also have produced the shift in the relationship between the degree of urbanization and the size of nonresponse rates which occurred during the mid-1960s in both surveys and which seems so theoretically puzzling. As a result of the 1960 census, extensive alterations in SRC's sampling frame were carried out—largely in 1962 and 1963—which may have created more homogeneous urban subgroups.[16] Finally, the 1961 experiment on the Surveys of Consumer Attitudes dramatically demonstrated the impact of repeated callbacks on rates of other noninterviews.

The problems which survey research faces, at least as it is practiced by one university organization, apparently have no easy solutions. Interaction undoubtedly occurs between the quality of the interview-

---

[16] Interestingly, the revisions in SRC's sampling frame after the 1970 census did not have similar effects.

ing staff and the degree of urbanization. Interviewers making personal visits to sample households have a harder time doing their job in urban settings. Potential respondents are less likely to be at home and are more likely to speak foreign languages; neighborhoods are more threatening to enter after dark; and multiple-unit apartment buildings with security arrangements are more prevalent. These factors plus more refusals may make interviewing jobs less rewarding in large cities and increase staff turnover. Consequently, urban areas which require more in the way of interviewer skill and experience probably get less.

There is also the likelihood that respondents are not as willing to be interviewed as in the past for reasons which have little to do with interviewer skills. Heightened concern about privacy and confidentiality, a disillusionment with the uses of survey results, and overexposure to the survey process have, it is theorized, led to higher refusal rates (American Statistical Association, 1974; The National Research Council, 1979). However, the different amounts of change across urban categories require that these causal possibilities be somehow linked to urbanization. In fact, there is empirical evidence which indicates that individuals in urban areas are not as helpful and trusting as people living elsewhere. Some scholars view this attitude as an inevitable concomitant of city life, while others see it as conditioned by the rising crime rates of the 1960s (House and Wolf, 1978).

Since almost no data exist to pinpoint more precisely the causes for increasing refusal rates, methodological innovations must often be tried without full knowledge of the consequences. The effects of one such innovation on the Surveys of Consumer Attitudes can now be tentatively gauged. In the third quarter of 1976 the Surveys of Consumer Attitudes shifted from personal interviewing to telephone interviewing with random digit dialed (RDD) samples. Although the change was not made primarily to lower nonresponse rates, there was some hope based on prior research that this might occur (Groves and Kahn, 1979; Ibsen and Ballweg, 1974; and Kegeles et al., 1969). The cheap and easy access to sample households would maximize callbacks, and the centralization of the interviewing staff would permit greater control over interviewing quality.

In Figure 7 the time series for each component of nonresponse has been extended through the period of telephone interviewing and plotted against the long-term trends derived from personal interviews. Although dissimilarities exist between the area probability samples of personal interviews and the RDD samples used for telephone surveys, they do not appear great enough to prevent linking the data in this

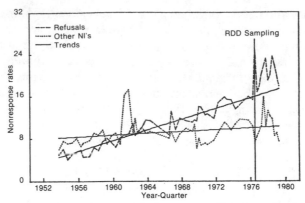

Figure 7. Nonresponse Rates for Personal Interview and Telephone Surveys: Surveys of Consumer Attitudes, 1953–1979

fashion.[17] In fact, survey results, such as the well-known Index of Consumer Sentiment, are usually presented as continuous time series, although complicated weighting procedures attempt to adjust for the differences in sample designs. Figure 7 strongly suggests that a break occurred in the time series for refusals with the introduction of RDD sampling. From the initial RDD survey, refusal rates have been much higher, despite considerable fluctuation, than would have been predicted from trends for personal interviews.[18] On the other hand,

---

[17] The same exclusions from the study populations occur with telephone samples as with area probability samples—businesses, housing units on military reservations, and nonhousehold living quarters. Obviously, all households without telephones also are excluded. Because the sample units are now telephone numbers which can be easily accessed from a central facility, the sample is no longer clustered by primary sampling units. The first stage sample units are instead area code–central office code combinations. Although in theory the denominators of the nonresponse rates should exclude all nonworking telephone numbers, in practice final determinations cannot be made for all numbers which have an ordinary ring but are never answered. In the August 1976 administration of the RDD sample design, the percentage of these numbers was so large (23.1 percent) that they were excluded from the base. Subsequently a screening procedure has reduced this percentage to manageable levels (an average of 3 percent from November 1976 to December 1978), and now all numbers which have never been answered during the study period after repeated callbacks are considered a type of nonresponse. The nonresponse rates for the February, May, August, and November surveys of 1978 and the February and May surveys of 1979 represent the quarterly data points in Figure 7.

[18] These effects have occurred despite monumental effort by the telephone interviewing staff of the Survey Research Center. Until the May 1979 survey, the number of callbacks which could be made to a sample unit was unlimited and sometimes reached 60 or more before the end of the field period. Furthermore, attempts were made in each survey to convert all initial refusals to interviews by recontacting the sample household. To date, this procedure, which places a considerable burden on interviewers, has not reduced refusal rates significantly. Although there have been changes in the definition of refusal from personal to telephone interviewing, they work to the advantage of

telephone interviewing has not reduced the rates of other types of nonresponse.[19]

This particular methodological innovation has had the unfortunate effect of substantially increasing the level of refusal rates. However, when telephone surveys alone are considered, refusal rates appear to have stabilized. Thus, telephone interviewing may have altered a seemingly intractable trend. Had increases in nonresponse been due primarily to changes in the rates of other noninterviews, telephone interviewing might have been more immediately effective. Although the potential for greater control over interviewer quality has not yet produced lower refusal rates, this is probably owing to the impersonality of the telephone as an interviewing medium. Without careful monitoring of interviewer performance, refusal rates may have reached even larger proportions. Because RDD sample designs make calculating nonresponse rates by urban subgroups extremely difficult, future research must determine whether telephone surveys have also lessened the impact of urbanization on nonresponse rates, as one cross-sectional study has suggested (Groves and Kahn, 1979).

Conclusions

These analyses have confirmed that for surveys conducted by an academic organization with interviewing periods of one or two months, full probability sampling at the household level, and very limited use of proxy interviews, there have been substantial increases in refusal rates since the early 1950s. Furthermore, the importance of urbanization for explaining nonresponse patterns in personal interviews has been highlighted. Across two well-known surveys, patterns have been repeated with few significant differences. In both surveys, the increases in the components of nonresponse have differed among the urban subgroups in approximately the same way. Similarly, in both surveys the cross-sectional relationships between urbanization and nonresponse rates have assumed equivalent forms and shifted at roughly the same points in time.

---

telephone interviewing and thus cannot have produced the break which occurs in the time series. For example, respondents who postpone interviews have never been placed in the refusal category, as has been the case in personal interviews since 1976. Furthermore, partial or break-off interviews, a phenomenon peculiar to telephone surveys, have not been classified as refusals. The refusal rates used in this study probably underestimate the actual amount of resistance to telephone surveys.

[19] The so-called Chow test, an F statistic which determines whether regression parameters have changed in moving from one period to another, is highly significant for refusals ($F = 17.9$) and insignificant for other noninterviews ($F = .02$) when the periods are defined by the interviewing mode.

Although these findings are interesting in themselves and may well reflect broad societal changes, researchers will be most concerned about their effect on that important commodity—survey results. The evidence here is mixed but somewhat promising for relational analyses (Goudy, 1976). In general, greater numbers of nonrespondents create problems only when they are systematically distributed with respect to major survey variables. This paper suggests that bias may occur in analyses which depend upon urbanization as a primary explanatory factor. Continued research must establish as precisely as possible the ways in which survey results may be compromised by increasing nonresponse. Heightened awareness of these issues has already fostered experimentation with statistical and sampling methods, as well as with interviewing techniques. Imputation, in particular, offers a cost-effective procedure for overcoming certain sample deficiences introduced by nonresponse. To be most effective, these techniques will require more information about nonrespondents— what demographic and socioeconomic characteristics they exhibit and, if possible, what attitudes they hold—than has yet been provided (Benus and Ackerman, 1971; DeMaio, 1980; Hess, 1962). Given these alternatives, however, the dilemma which increasing nonresponse poses for survey research does not seem so intractable.

References

American Statistical Association
  1974 "The report on the ASA conference on surveys on human populations." The American Statistician 28:30–34.
Bailar, Barbara A., and C. Michael Lanphier
  1978 Development of Survey Methods to Assess Survey Practices. Washington, D.C.: American Statistical Association.
Benus, Jacob M., and Jean Coley Ackerman
  1971 "The problem of nonresponse in sample surveys." Pp. 26–59 in John B. Lansing, Stephen B. Withey, and Arthur C. Wolfe (eds.), Working Papers on Survey Research in Poverty Areas. Ann Arbor: Institute for Social Research.
Chatfield, C.
  1975 The Analysis of Time Series: Theory and Practice. New York: Wiley.
DeMaio, Theresa J.
  1980 "Refusals: who, where and why." Public Opinion Quarterly 44:223–33.
Finkner, A. L.
  1975 "The problem of respondent cooperation and some census bureau experiences." Marketing Research Association. Unpublished manuscript.

Goudy, Willis J.
 1976 "Nonresponse effects on relationships between variables." Public Opinion Quarterly 40:360–69.
Groves, Robert M., and Robert L. Kahn
 1979 Surveys by Telephone: A National Comparison with Personal Interviews. New York: Academic Press.
Hess, Irene, and R. K. Pillai
 1962 "Nonresponse among family heads and wives in SRC surveys." Survey Research Center. Unpublished manuscript.
House, James S., and Sharon Wolf
 1978 "Effects of urban residence on interpersonal trust and helping behavior." Journal of Personality and Social Psychology 36:1029–43.
Ibsen, Charles A., and John A. Ballweg
 1974 "Telephone interviews in social research: some methodological considerations." Quality and Quantity 8:181–92.
Kegeles, S. Stephen, Clinton F. Fink, and John P. Kirscht
 1969 "Interviewing a national sample by long-distance telephone." Public Opinion Quarterly 33:412–19.
Juster, F. Thomas
 1976 "Methodology, data quality and interpretation: some notes on consumer surveys." Paper prepared for the Conference on the Economic and Social Outlook, Ann Arbor, Michigan.
Ladd, George W.
 1964 "Regression analysis of seasonal data." Journal of the American Statistical Association 59:402–21.
Love, Lawrence T., and Anthony G. Turner
 1975 "The census bureau's experience: respondent availability and response rates." Pp. 76–85 in American Statistical Association Proceedings of the Business and Economic Statistics Section 1975. Washington, D.C.: American Statistical Association.
Madow, William G., and M. Haseeb Rizvi
 1979 "On incomplete data: a review." Unpublished manuscript.
Marquis, Kent H.
 1977 "Survey response rates: some trends, causes and correlates." Paper presented at the Biennial Conference on Health Survey Research Methods, Williamsburg, Virginia.
National Research Council
 1979 Privacy and Confidentiality as Factors in Survey Response. Washington, D.C.: National Academy of Sciences.
Scott, John C.
 1975 "Response to fall 1975 omnibus." Memorandum to the Omnibus Steering Committee. Survey Research Center, University of Michigan.
Smith, T. M. F.
 1978 "Principle and problems in the analysis of repeated surveys." Pp. 201–16 in N. Krishnan Namboodiri (ed.), Survey Sampling and Measurement. New York: Academic Press.
Wiseman, Frederick, and Philip McDonald
 1979 "Noncontact and refusal rates in consumer telephone surveys." Journal of Marketing Research 16:478–84.

The Hidden 25 Percent:
An Analysis of Nonresponse on the
1980 General Social Survey

NONRESPONSE can seriously bias survey estimates and distort inferences. The relationship between nonresponse and survey estimates is
simple and well defined, but the actual impact is ill known. For the
sample mean of a particular variable (Y) the association is

$$\overline{Y} = W_1\overline{Y}_1 + W_2\overline{Y}_2 \tag{1}$$

where W_1 and W_2 are the proportion respondents and nonrespondents. The relative bias (RB) of using the response mean to equal the
sample means is

$$RB(\overline{Y}_1) = W_2\frac{(\overline{Y}_1 - \overline{Y}_2)}{\overline{Y}} \tag{2}$$

We can see that the relative bias is serious only when the nonresponse rate (W_2) is large and the difference in the means is great. Given
this simple formula we can easily measure the magnitude of the
nonresponse bias. The problem is that while we know the nonres-

Abstract Methods for estimating nonresponse bias are reviewed and several methods
are tried on the 1980 GSS. The results indicate that various estimating procedures are
inappropriate and that even the more promising techniques can provide faulty estimates
of nonresponse bias. By its nature, nonresponse bias is very difficult to assess accurately and no simple, certain method exists.

Tom W. Smith is Senior Study Director, National Opinion Research Center, University of Chicago. This research was done for the General Social Survey Project directed
by James A. Davis. The project is supported by the National Science Foundation,
Grant No. SOC77-03279. This is an abridged version of GSS Technical Report No. 25
published by NORC, 1981. The author wishes to thank James A. Davis, Howard
Schuman, and Stanley Presser for their comments.

ponse rate, we do not know the nonresponse mean since we have no measure of Y among nonrespondents.

Two alternatives are usually presented in discussing nonresponse—how to minimize nonresponse and how to estimate and correct for differences between the respondents and nonrespondents. In this paper we ignore the first alternative, accepting that a nonresponse rate of .25 is typical for good, state-of-the-art surveys (Smith, 1978; Davis et al., 1980; and Groves and Kahn, 1979). Instead, we will review the various existing approaches to estimating the characteristics of nonrespondents and then apply several of the proposed approaches to nonresponse on the 1980 GSS.

Measuring Nonrespondents and Assessing Nonresponse Bias

Numerous methods have been proposed to estimate the attributes of nonrespondents (Daniel, 1975). Some are appropriate for certain types of surveys (e.g., list samples only) while others can be used with modification across various methods of administration with various sample frames (e.g., from mail lists to RDD telephone). Attention will focus primarily on methods that are appropriate, or at least have been offered as appropriate, for face-to-face, national surveys. Among other things, this eliminates list samples where information about the respondent is known prior to the survey. Our review of nonresponse studies found nine major approaches to assess and adjust for nonresponse:

1. External population checks
2. Geographic/aggregate level data
3. Interviewer estimates
4. Interviewing nonrespondents about nonresponse
5. Subsampling of nonrespondents
6. Substitution for nonrespondents
7. Politz-Simmons adjustment
8. Extrapolation based on difficulty
9. Conversion adjustments

Probably the simplest check is to compare sample estimates (usually distributions) to some universe figures or preferred sample estimates such as the U.S. Census or the Current Population Survey (Crossley and Fink, 1951; Stephen and McCarthy, 1958: Smith, 1979; and Presser, 1981). Strictly speaking, when using such a criterion comparison, one is not checking how much difference comes from nonresponse but how much comes from nonresponse *and* all other sources (item unreliability, interviewer error, etc.). If one shows that differences are within sampling error, then either no noticeable non-response bias exists on the variable being compared or nonresponse bias is being offset by other, countervailing errors. Similarly, a large difference does not specify nonresponse as the cause. This imprecision is, of course, undesirable from the perspective of studying non-response per se, but since one typically wants to know primarily whether the survey is reliable and representative, such general checks often serve the ultimate purpose satisfactorily. Unfortunately, however, superior estimates are often unavailable and are at best usually limited to a few demographics. Since representativeness on one variable is not generalizable to all variables or relationships in question, the usefulness of this approach is limited.

Two related means of assessing bias are the geographic/aggregate-level approach (Houseman, 1953; Dunkelberg and Day, 1973; Hawkins, 1975; DeMaio, 1980; House and Wolf, 1978). Since the geographic location of the sample household is known, one can code for all cases certain aggregate-level data such as (1) region and city type, (2) figures for census tract or other units, (3) interviewer description of neighborhood, and (4) interviewer description of dwelling unit. These can be recorded for all households and they can include many contextual variables that are commonly used in survey analysis. However, they still cover only a small fraction of the variables of interest on a typical survey and suffer from the problem of the nongeneralizability of representativeness across unexamined variables. In particular, they do not apply to individual level attributes. On the other hand, since we have complete and accurate observations, we have a precise measure of nonresponse bias for the covered variables.

Going a step beyond the geographic/aggregate-level approach, interviewers can make observations and estimates about households and individual respondents (DeMaio, 1980; Moser and Kalton, 1972; Lansing et al., 1971). The advantage is that one can expand the range of comparable variables and that one can include individual-level variables. One problem is that it is not possible to get complete information. On the 1980 GSS and the 1968 Michigan election survey no estimates were possible on race for .248 and .215 of nonrespondents, respectively, or on income for .364 and .294. In addition, interviewer estimates are usually more error-prone than directly acquired data. Finally, there is a clear limit to what variables can be checked.

To get into nonrespondents' minds, special field procedures are sometimes used: interviewing nonrespondents, intensive follow-ups on a subsample of nonrespondents, and substituting for nonrespondents. In the nonrespondent interviewing approach refusers are asked a few questions about why they refused to participate and/or a few demographics. The Bureau of Social Science Research (1981) was able in a recent study to get a noninterview interview with 53 percent of refusers, and Wilcox (1977) got some demographics for 29 percent of refusers, for example. The problem of this approach is that it applies only to refusers rather than not-at-homes and others,[1] information is available for only some refusers, and it is difficult to pick up much substantive information pertinent to a study in a necessarily short nonrespondent interview.

The subsampling of nonrespondents is used to get an estimate of nonrespondents by making extraordinary efforts to interview a representative sample of them (Lundberg and Larsen, 1949; Lagay, 1969–70). This method is often used successfully in mail surveys. After several mailings and reminders, a sample of nonrespondents is drawn and this group is approached via some more persuasive medium, such as telephone calls or personal visits (Hansen and Hurwitz, 1946; Kish, 1965:556; Ognibene, 1971). It is difficult to use and not particularly cost-efficient in a first-rate, face-to-face full probability sample. When substantial efforts are made to get all cases, the returns from extraordinary efforts beyond the standard procedures are likely to be small.

Another field procedure that has been proposed is substitution. Under this method alternative households are added to the sample to replace nonrespondent households. While this method is useful to achieve a prescribed sample size, it tends to replace nonrespondents with people who resemble respondents rather than nonrespondents, and this approach does not appear to be widely used to deal with nonresponse bias. However, there are related techniques that do somewhat the same thing. Block quota samples require interviewers to fill a certain quota, for example, so many employed/unemployed females and so many young/old males from a given block. If no one is home, a household refuses, or no one in the household fits the remaining quota slots, then the interviewer proceeds to the next house. In effect, the block quota sampling uses a substitution procedure, passing over unavailable households and substituting available ones instead. The quotas are designed to insure that the hard-to-get groups are represented, so in effect one does not substitute easy for hard households/respondents, but merely gets those easy and hard

---

[1] It might be possible to reach the not-at-homes with a similar nonresponse interview by leaving a mail-back version.

households/respondents that are available at the moment. On its face this sampling approach seems likely to increase nonresponse error, but experiments between full probability and block quota surveys show few differences (Stephenson, 1979).

Another superficially related approach is Kish's replacement procedure (Kish and Hess, 1959; Kish, 1965:560–62), which substitutes previous nonrespondent households (from an earlier and similar survey) for nonrespondents to the current survey, assuming that they are reasonable replacements and that it will be possible to secure interviews in a high percentage of them. Administrative problems and the difficulty of getting a high response rate from the replacement households have severely limited the actual use of this approach. The Current Population Survey does use a related technique, however. Unlike most panel surveys, the CPS does not exclude nonrespondents from subsequent waves. Not-at-homes are continued in the sample and an attempt is made to reach them on all waves despite absences on earlier waves. Refusers are approached a second month, and only after repeated refusals are households dropped from subsequent waves. Thus, each CPS cross-section includes "replacement" households that were nonrespondents on earlier surveys.

Finally, there are several methods for estimating the effects of nonresponse directly from respondents, by the Politz-Simmons approach, by extrapolation based on difficulty, and by convertibility. In the times-at-home or Politz-Simmons approach (Politz and Simmons, 1949; Kish, 1965:559–60; Moser and Kalton, 1972:178–81), respondents are asked how many times they were at home at the time of interview during the last x number of days. This is taken as representing their probability of availability. Respondents are then weighted according to the inverse of the number of days they were home. This method assumes that nonresponse is basically a function of availability (as the block quota samples do) and that weighting adequately adjusts for the probabilities of availability. In two empirical tests (Durbin and Stuart, 1954; Simmons, 1954) this was not found to perform as well as callbacks, however. The technique is still commonly employed; Gallup, for example, included a times-at-home weight as part of its surveys from 1960 to 1967 and since then has included a weight factor that apparently combines a times-at-home weight with a poststratification weight (Gaertner, 1976).

The difficulty method uses some measure of how hard it was to get an interview from a respondent. This might be the number of mailings, visits, or telephone calls, how long it took to get a response, or some measure derived from these indicators of difficulty. While there are numerous variations, the basic approach determines whether a particular variable is related to difficulty (e.g., the proportion employed rising with the number of attempts). If a linear or some other regular relationship is found, then this association is used to impute the distribution of the variable among nonrespondents. This approach has the advantage of allowing an estimate for every variable contained in the survey and thus avoids the problem of nongeneralizability that plagues several of the methods considered above. It rests on the premise that difficulty is related to final nonresponse. If the final nonrespondents differ from the merely difficult, then this procedure will obviously misestimate the attributes of the final nonrespondents. This approach is one of the most frequently employed in estimating nonresponse and has shown some impressive results, especially in mail surveys where known attributes from a list sample could be compared to estimates from the difficulty extrapolations (e.g., Hilgard and Payne, 1944; Crossley and Fink, 1951; Hendrick, 1956; Mayer, 1964; Dunkelberg and Day, 1973; Cranberg, 1975; Filion, 1975–76; Armstrong and Overton, 1977). At the same time, however, there have been a number of criticisms of the method and cautions about its general application. Stephan and McCarthy warn that "great care would have to be exercised in carrying out this extrapolation, and its use is not recommended except under exceptional circumstances" (1958:257). (See also criticism and subsequent rebuttal by Ellis et al., 1970, and Filion, 1976.)

Unlike the difficulty approach, which is aimed at all nonrespondents, the convertibility approach uses converted refusals as estimates for final refusals. Usually the converted are seen as substitutes for the final refusals although it is possible to do an extrapolation with the first group being the respondents who never refused, the converts making the second point, and the final refusers as the last group[2] (Benson et al., 1951; Stinchcombe et al., 1981; Robbins, 1963; O'Neil, 1979; DeMaio, 1980; Andersen et al., 1979). As in the difficulty approach, all variables can be studied and the appropriateness of the technique rests on the supposition that final refusers are like temporary refusers (in the case of the substitution approach) or at least more like temporary refusers than cooperative respondents (in the case of extrapolation).

---

[2] So far this approach uses only two types of respondents, cooperators and converts. This means that there is either no significant difference between the two groups or a linear relationship to extrapolate to final refusers. If temporary refusers were further subdivided into easy or hard to convert, or some other refinement, such as number of attempts needed to convert, then it would be possible for other relationships to emerge. Apparently no one has attempted such a refinement and the usually small number of total converts would make such refined analysis difficult.

In brief, a number of procedures have been proposed to assess the impact of nonresponse. Some methods, such as using geographic/aggregate-level data, allow a complete assessment of nonresponse bias for a limited number of variables; other techniques, such as difficulty extrapolation, permit estimates of nonresponse bias for all variables. None of the methods permit the complete determination of nonresponse bias for all variables.

Analysis of Nonresponse on 1980 General Social Survey

To assess the impact of nonresponse on the 1980 GSS we selected four of the more promising and widely applied techniques: (1) geographic/aggregate-level analysis, (2) interviewer estimates, (3) extrapolation for difficulty, and (4) convertibility. The 1980 GSS was a multistage, full-probability sample of the contiguous United States. Households were sampled according to NORC's equal probability selection procedures and a Kish table was used to choose a respondent from the designated households (King and Richards, 1972; GSS, 1980). Interviewers kept a record of calls, noting each attempt to contact the household or respondent by the date and time of the attempt, method of contact (personal/telephone), and the outcome (not-at-home, temporary refusal, interview, etc.). If a contact could be made, a household enumeration folder was filled out listing all household members along with their relationship to head of household, age, sex, marital status, and location (staying at household/staying elsewhere). If an interview was secured, a questionnaire was completed. For nonrespondents a noninterview report recorded the reason for nonresponse, descriptions of why the nonresponse occurred (e.g., why a person was never found at home), and interviewer estimates of the family income, race of household, number of adults, number of adult males, presence of married couple, and age of head of household.

The 1980 GSS had a net sample of 1,931. There were 1,468 completed cases, 315 refusals, 66 not-at-homes, 78 others (mostly not mentally or physically capable of participating, but also including administrative errors), and 4 lost documents.[3] This gives a response rate of .760, a refusal rate of .163, a not-at-home rate of .034, and an "other" rate of .042 (including the four unclassified cases).

In the subsequent analysis we examine nonresponse in general as

---

[3] These figures differ slightly from those presented in Davis et al., 1980. The difference comes from internal inconsistencies between the record-of-calls and the noninterview report forms.

well as the main types of nonresponse-refusals, not-at-homes, and others. Both past research and findings from this study suggest that these groups are quite different in their motivations for nonresponding, in their demographic profile, and in other notable ways (Stinchcombe et al., 1980; Kish, 1965; O'Neil, 1979; Bebbington, 1970).

Geographical/Aggregate-Level Analysis

The geographic/aggregate-level analysis was restricted to measures of community type and region. As Table 1 shows, there are large differences in the response rates across city types and regions. Response rates are lowest in central cities, rise moderately in suburbs and exurbia within metropolitan areas, and increase substantially in rural areas. This urban-rural difference replicates similar findings from numerous other studies (Lansing et al., 1971; Moser and Kalton, 1972; DeMaio, 1980; House and Wolf, 1978; Groves and Kahn, 1979) and derives mainly from variation in the refusal rate. The not-at-homes follow roughly the same pattern as refusals, and the others

Table 1. Response/Nonresponse by City Type and Region[a]

Response/Nonresponse	Completed Case	Refusal	Not-at-Home	Other	
SRCBELT					
Central city of 12 largest SMSAs	.665	.216	.065	.054	(185)
Central city 13–100 largest SMSAs	.713	.212	.039	.036	(307)
Suburb of 12 largest SMSAs	.697	.211	.038	.054	(185)
Suburb of 13–100 largest SMSAs	.751	.190	.027	.032	(221)
Other urban	.791	.144	.031	.034	(731)
Other rural	.849	.081	.020	.050	(298)
	$\chi^2 = 44.6$ prob. $= .0001$[b]				
REGION					
New England	.716	.230	.041	.014	(74)
Midatlantic	.691	.234	.038	.038	(346)
East North Central	.760	.160	.053	.028	(400)
West North Central	.819	.118	.024	.039	(127)
South Atlantic	.767	.124	.046	.063	(348)
East South Central	.854	.131	.000	.015	(130)
West South Central	.789	.132	.026	.053	(152)
Mountain	.806	.153	.020	.020	(98)
Pacific	.758	.171	.016	.056	(252)
	$\chi^2 = 50.5$ prob. $= .0012$				

[a] Analyses were also conducted on two other community type variables: SIZE—population at local community, and XNORCSIZ—city, suburb, town, rural typology.

[b] Here and elsewhere we used calculations based on SRS assumptions. Since the sample was clustered this underestimates the true sampling variance.

appear to be scattered across city types. Regional response rates tend to be highest in the South and lowest in the Northeast, although the pattern is not completely uniform. Most previous studies have found some regional differences (except House and Wolf, 1978), but there is disagreement on where nonresponse is highest. Love and Turner (1975) found response rates lowest in the Northeast, and results from Schuman and Gruenberg (1970) and Dunkelberg and Day (1973) suggest a similar conclusion, but DeMaio (1980) found that refusals were lowest in the Northeast and highest in the West. As with city size, most variation is in the level of refusals.

Both city type and region exercised independent effects on response rates. When we controlled for city type, the South had a response rate 8.5 percentage points above the Northeast. With region controlled, suburbs and exurbia had a response rate 6.3 percentage points above central cities (Davis, 1975).

Interviewer Estimates

Next, nonresponse bias was examined by having interviewers estimate the following characteristics of the nonresponding households: race, family income, number of adult males, number of adults, presence of married couple, and age of head of household. Estimates were possible in two-thirds to three-quarters of households and were more often available for refusers than for others or not-at-homes (see Table 2). The absence of estimates from a substantial minority of nonrespondents as well as the probable unreliability of some of the estimates necessarily hampers the use of these interviewer estimates to study nonresponse bias.

Looking first at those nonrespondents with available information, we find no significant differences between completed cases and esti-

Table 2. Item Nonresponse Among Completed Cases and Respondents
(Proportion Missing)

		Nonrespondents			
Variables	Completed Cases	All	Refusals	Not-at-Homes	Others
Race	.000	.248	.203	.348	.346
Income	.075	.364	.314	.500	.449
Number of adult males	.000	.296	.273	.379	.321
Number of adults	.000	.303	.283	.379	.321
Married couple	.000	.320	.305	.424	.295
Age of head	.007	.285	.232	.439	.372
	(1,468)	(459)	(315)	(66)	(78)

mated nonrespondents on race, marital status, and number of adult males (see Table 3). Nonrespondent households have, however, older heads of household, fewer adults, and less middle income and poor.

We also discover that the profile of each type of nonrespondent is quite different. Refusers are somewhat more likely to be married, to have a middle income, and to be over 30 years old than respondents. Not-at-homes tend to be isolated individuals, less likely to be married, and more likely to live alone. The others are also isolated individuals, but in addition they are typically old and poor as well. These differences generally follow those in earlier studies.[4]

Table 3. Selected Characteristics Among Completed Cases and Estimatable Nonresponse Cases

						Probability	
						Completed Cases vs. Nonresponse	Completed Cases, Refusals, Not-at-Homes, Others
Variables	Completed Cases	Nonresponse Cases					
		All	Refusals	Not-at-Homes	Others		
Race							
White	.898	.910	.928	.837	.882		
Black	.095	.084	.064	.163	.118	.789	.411
Other	.007	.006	.008	.000	.000		
	(1,468)	(345)	(251)	(43)	(51)		
Income							
Less than $7,000	.204	.226	.153	.212	.605		
$7,000–19,000	.412	.541	.597	.455	.326	.000	.000
$20,000+	.384	.233	.250	.333	.070		
Number of adult males							
None	.193	.251	.223	.244	.377		
One	.695	.684	.725	.634	.547	.066	.167
Two+	.113	.065	.052	.122	.066		
Married couple							
Yes	.606	.641	.721	.447	.455	.243	.000
No	.394	.359	.279	.553	.545		
Number of adults							
One	.252	.359	.305	.488	.491		
Two	.598	.509	.575	.341	.358	.008	.016
Three+	.151	.131	.119	.170	.151		
Age of head							
Under 30	.200	.076	.087	.081	.020		
30–64	.607	.591	.649	.703	.224	.000	.000
Over 65	.193	.332	.264	.216	.755		

[4] Most previous research finds final nonresponse to be highest among the older ages (Lowe and McCormick, 1955; Lansing et al., 1971; Weaver et al., 1975; Hawkins, 1975;

The proportion of nonrespondents with estimates is lowest in large central cities and their suburbs and in rural areas, with smaller central cities, their suburbs, and small towns having estimates for a significantly higher proportion of cases. Missing estimates also appear to be highest in the West and among nonwhite households. These results suggest that the estimated nonresponse households are not typical of all nonrespondents and thus do not give an unbiased estimate of them.

Difficulty

Next, we examined the association between difficulty in completing an interview, as measured by the number of attempts, and respondent characteristics. We believed that difficulty resulted from three factors: availability (essentially the probability of a respondent being home at a given time), contactability (the probability of some other responsible household member being home at a given time), and reluctance (respondent's and/or informant's willingness to cooperate). The following groups were anticipated to have high availability: nonmembers of the labor force (especially homemakers); women; members of the labor force working few hours, not traveling, and not self-employed; widowed people; older people, infirm, and physically restricted; and low socioeconomic status people. Households with high contactability were anticipated to include: married couples and households with more than one adult, young children, and a spouse not in the labor force. Reluctant households were presumed to be urban, fearful of crime, and mistrustful of people. In addition we included race because of its close association with several of the preceding variables.

We tested the relationship between these independent variables and difficulty by using one-way analysis of variance. As Table 4 indicates, the chosen indicators of availability were related to difficulty as anticipated. Availability had a basically linear relationship with labor force participation, socioeconomic status, life stage (age and marital status), health, and sex. It was unrelated to race and self-employment. Too few occupations were identifiable as involving ex-

---

and DeMaio, 1980). Nonresponse was found higher for whites in three studies (Schuman and Gruenberg, 1970; Weaver et al., 1975; and Hawkins, 1975) and not significantly different across races in two studies (DeMaio, 1980; Lansing et al., 1971). Middle income groups are usually found to have the highest nonresponse (Lansing et al., 1971; DeMaio, 1980), but this may well be a function of estimating error. Studies are also divided as to whether nonrespondents vary by sex. Crossley and Fink (1951), Hawkins (1975), and DeMaio (1980) found no difference, but Bartholomew (1961), Lowe and McCormick (1955), and Smith (1979) found an underrepresentation of men.

Table 4. Analysis of Variance of Number of Attempts by Selected Variables[a]

	Probabilities		
Variable	Between Groups	Linearity	Deviation from Linearity
Labor force	.0000	.0000	.0044
Hours	.0000	.0000	.4541
Self-employed	.2345	—	—
Marital status	.0069	.0012	.1774
Age	.0000	.0000	.1569
Health	.0000	.0000	.7900
Education	.0000	.0000	.0300
Prestige	.0000	.0000	.0510
Income	.0000	.0000	.0002
Sex	.0024	.0001	.2876
Adults	.0356	.2475	.0332
Children under 18	.0691	—	—
Number of children	.0009	.0000	.2569
Spouse working	.2371	—	—
SRCBELT	.0031	.0000	.7117
SIZE	.9822	—	—
XNORCSIZ	.0402	.0009	.7209
FEAR	.2214	—	—
TRUST	.4500	—	—

[a] A parallel analysis using nonparametric methods (Davis, 1975) showed similar results except for marital status. The proportion unmarried did not significantly vary but the proportion postmarried varied linearly.

tensive traveling away from home to permit analysis of this factor. Contactability, on the other hand, did not show the anticipated relationships. The presence of a spouse and/or children at home were unrelated to difficulty, and the number of adults had a weak and uninterpretable nonlinear association. Reluctance showed intermediate results. Community type (SRCBELT, XNORCSIZ) showed the expected associations between urbanness and difficulty, but neither fear of crime nor mistrust of people was related to reluctance.

A stepwise multiple regression equation further clarified these relationships. Labor force participation is the strongest correlate of difficulty. High socioeconomic status also meant more difficulty, probably because of more social and occupational activities outside the home. Some of this might result, however, from the growing proportion of people in the upper social rankings "protected" from interviewers by doormen, security systems, and other barriers. The young also proved to be more difficult to reach, probably because of more socializing outside of the home. Urban dwellers were also harder to reach. Part of this difficulty seems to result from the need for more calls to persuade reluctant respondents, but there may also be a greater tendency for urbanites to spend more time away from the homes.[5] Finally, we find that people with children were easier to reach, probably because there is usually someone at home to contact (for details see Smith, 1981).

In order to evaluate the effect of nonresponse on nondemographics we ran attempts by a wide range of attitudes, behaviors, and socio-psychological scales. Only 27.4 percent showed significant variation with number of attempts. Of the significant relationships, most were linear (67.4 percent linear, no significant deviation; 15.2 percent linear, with significant deviation; and 17.4 percent nonlinear).

The hard-to-gets appeared to have three main characteristics— liberal political views (e.g., pro-abortion, civil rights, tolerance), high socioeconomic status (e.g., members of professional groups, never received governmental aid), and active and youthful life style (having received a traffic ticket, members of youth groups, watch less television, favor legalization of marijuana). Of all of these, only the life style variables added explanatory power to the basic demographic model (hours, education, SRCBELT, age, number of children). Favoring the legalization of marijuana and having received a traffic ticket were significantly related, and drinking just missed the cutoff.[6]

While this means that very few nondemographics are independently related to difficulty, many variables (27 percent on the GSS) are closely enough related to the independent variables to vary notably with number of attempts. This means that not only will variables directly related to availability be affected, but many attitudinal and behavioral variables will also be affected. We also took a purposive sampling of 21 bivariate relationships and examined whether they varied by number of attempts. We found few significant differences and no clearly discernible pattern.

Although we can use respondent characteristics to predict difficulty in completing an interview, these characteristics cannot be used to estimate the attributes of nonrespondents. This is because the number of attempts measures primarily how accessible a person is, while the final nonrespondents are made up primarily of refusals, not inaccessibles. The proportion of refusals steadily rises with callbacks as the proportion of not-at-homes falls. After two calls, completed cases

---

[5] Interviewers are just as likely, however, to find an urban respondent at home on the first call as a rural respondent.

[6] In addition, those disagreeing that people shouldn't have children given the state of the world were harder to reach. It is unclear whether this relationship has any substantive meaning.

make up 32.5 percent, refusals 9.9 percent, not-at-homes 50.2 percent, others 6.1 percent, and miscellaneous 1.2 percent. After the final attempt, completed cases have risen to 76.0 percent and refusals to 16.3 percent, while not-at-homes fell to 3.4 percent, others to 4.0 percent, and miscellaneous to 0.2 percent. In brief, repeated callbacks nearly eliminated the not-at-home problem, while both in relative and absolute terms refusals increased. This relationship is also evident in the conversion rates. Only 35 percent of temporary refusals are converted to respondents while 91 percent of not-at-home (excluding those who were both not-at-homes and temporary refusals) were eventually "converted" to respondents. To use a difficulty measure to impute the attributes of final refusals is thus essentially to use the correlates of inaccessibility to predict the correlates of refusal. Given the differences in nonresponse motivations and known demographic profile, this is obviously an improper imputation procedure.

Of course, even if difficulty cannot be used to estimate the values of nonrespondents as a whole, it may be possible that this procedure would improve estimates of the final not-at-homes. We found that for five of seven variables—marital status, community type, region, race, number of adult males—the use of simple difficulty extrapolations did give us improved estimates of not-at-homes. In two cases—number of adults and age of head—the procedure proved inappropriate (for details see Smith, 1981).

Temporary Refusals

Finally, temporary refusals were used as an indicator of final refusals. On the basis of our review of this technique and reasons for refusals in general, we related temporary refusals to (1) mistrust and fear, (2) apathy toward social and political issues (replying DK to questions, not voting, no party identification), (3) negative psychological feelings (unhappiness, dissatisfaction, high anomia), (4) deviant behavior (having been arrested, receiving ticket), (5) attitudes toward science, (6) illness, (7) being too busy (long hours, labor force status), (8) uncooperativeness (interviewer rating and refusal to give family income), (9) place of residence, (10) conservativism, (11) socioeconomic status (education, income, occupational prestige), and (12) standard demographics (age, sex, race).

Only urbanness had a strong relationship to temporary refusals. In the 12 largest central cities 29 percent of the cases were temporary refusals while in rural counties only 11 percent of cases were temporary refusals. Of all other items only refusing to give family income had a significant (prob. = .035) association with reluctance. Of the other variables only being cooperative and being fearful approached significance (prob. < .10). In general, the results show fewer and more modest associations than most previous studies. On the 21 liberalism items (race relations, spending priorities, morality/personal life style, tolerance of Communists and atheists, and abortion) there was not a single significant relationship between conservatism and refusing. This refutes evidence from Hawkins (1975); Schuman and Gruenberg (1970); and Benson et al. (1951), but agrees with Brannon et al. (1973). We find no association with low socioeconomic status as Benson et al. (1951) and O'Neil (1979) found, no tendency to reply "don't know" (Stinchcombe et al., 1981), and no association with race, or number of children (O'Neil, 1979). Our lack of a difference between temporary refusals and age confirms Benson et al., but contradicts O'Neil, who finds the elderly refusing more. In addition our one notable association, between urbanness and refusals, differs from DeMaio (1980), who found no variation between rural and urban. The results do follow Robbins's findings (1963) that there were no significant differences. In general, the discrepancy of results suggests that findings depend on the specialized populations sampled, the survey procedures used, or other variable conditions.

On one hand the lack of associations between the hypothesized variables and temporary refusals is encouraging. If we accept temporary refusals as indicators of final refusals then the lack of significant associations suggests that except for city type, final refusals are not significantly different from completed cases and therefore little bias is introduced. Yet it is somewhat surprising that temporary refusals had such consistently low correlations with variables that might be expected on theoretical grounds to show more substantial relationships. One can hypothesize variables (e.g., willingness to be interviewed) that would have large associations with refusing. In addition it is reasonable to suppose that other variables touching on privacy, misanthrophy, paranoia, and fear, and other sociopsychological attitudes that should be closely related to willingness to be interviewed would show substantial associations. The fact that we were largely unable to find these associations may simply mean that we do not have the right variables, that indicators more closely related to refusing are needed before the anticipated relationships can be detected.[7] It might also be that refusing is really more of a random occurrence, like a transitory mood, and therefore there are no other related variables, but the difficulty of converting temporary refusals and evidence from other studies (Stinchcombe et al., 1981) suggests that this is not the case. Another alternative is that temporary refusals do not adequately indicate attributes of final refusals. Perhaps many of the temporary refus-

[7] This is being tested on the 1982 General Social Survey.

als, but not the final refusals, really represent transitory states. Unfortunately, we cannot fully test these alternatives.

We were able, however, to carry out a more general, less focused comparison between completed cases without temporary refusals (nonrefusals), temporary refusals, and final refusals on the nine variables for which we had aggregate-level data or interviewer estimates. On the three geographic variables, temporary refusals performed well. Estimates using substitution or extrapolation were closer to the true distribution than was the case when assuming no difference (i.e., completed cases equal all cases). On three of the interviewer estimates (number of males, number of adults, race) there are no significant differences between the three groups. While temporary refusals are not really needed for estimating distribution of final refusals, they correctly predict the characteristics of final refusals. For marital status the temporary refusals are in the right direction and provide a better estimate than assuming no difference between nonrefusals and final refusals. On age, however, temporary refusals point in the wrong direction for the old and in the correct direction for the young. Finally, on income temporary refusals do not differ from nonrefusals, while nonrefusals significantly differ from final refusals and temporary refusals differ from final refusals. This may result from the unreliability of the income estimates (see Smith, 1981).

Overall, the evidence is mixed about the appropriateness of using temporary refusals as indicators of final refusals. The fact that temporary refusals perform well on the geographic variables is encouraging both because there are no complications from missing values in these cases and these variables have the strongest theoretical connection with refusals. The evidence is further mixed on whether temporary refusals can best be substituted for final refusals or used to extrapolate to them. In general, the performance of temporary refusals is satisfactory enough to merit further investigation and selective application, but it is clear that neither substitution nor extrapolation of temporary refusals can be used routinely as a sure adjustment for final refusals.

Conclusion

We come close to the conclusion that nothing works in estimating nonresponse bias. Each of the methods we examined proved to be of limited usefulness. The geographic/aggregate-level approach allows definitive measurement of nonresponse bias, but it is limited to readily observable data or data linked from other sources such as the Census. Usually only a few variables of interest are available, and results from them are not necessarily generalizable to other variables (Lagay, 1969–70). Interviewer estimates help to expand the range of variables that can be checked, but (1) missing estimates (typically 25 to 35 percent of cases) prevent complete coverage, (2) the estimated portion of nonrespondents may not be representative of all nonrespondents, (3) some estimates probably have low reliability (e.g., income), and (4) the range of checkable variables is limited. Difficulty extrapolation was found to be inappropriate for nonresponse in general because of the high proportion of refusals among nonrespondents. While probably often useful for imputing to the not-at-homes, evidence in the case of age (and labor force participation) indicates that final not-at-homes arc not always extensions of the hard-to-get. Temporary refusals also gave mixed results in estimating final refusals. Even when temporary refusals are indicative of final refusals the evidence is unclear whether substitution or extrapolation would be most appropriate. In sum, our analysis of nonresponse on the 1980 GSS suggests that there is no simple, general, accurate way of measuring nonresponse bias.

References

Andersen, Ronald, Judith Kasper, and Martin R. Frankel
1979   Total Survey Error: Applications to Improve Health Surveys. NORC Series in Social Research. San Francisco: Jossey-Bass.
Armstrong, J. Scott, and Terry S. Overton
1977   "Estimating nonresponse bias in mail surveys." Journal of Marketing Research 14:396–402.
Bartholomew, D. J.
1961   "A method of allowing for 'not-at-home' bias in sample surveys," Applied Statistics 10:52–59.
Bebbington, A. C.
1970   "The effect of nonresponse in the sample survey with an example." Human Relations 23:169–80.
Benson, Sherwood, Wesley P. Booman, and Kenneth E. Clark
1951   "A study of interview refusals." Journal of Applied Psychology 35:116–19.
Brannon, Robert, et al.
1973   "Attitude and action: a field experiment joined to a general population survey." American Sociological Review 38:625–36.
Bureau of Social Science Research
1980   "Long interviews are not main cause of refusals." BSSR 14 (Fall):1–2.
Cranberg, Gilbert
1975   "Mail survey respondents and nonrespondents." Journalism Quarterly 52:542–43.
Crossley, Helen M., and Raymond Fink
1951   "Response and nonresponse in a probability sample." International Journal of Opinion and Attitude Research 5:1–19.
Daniel, Wayne W.
1975   "Nonresponse in sociological surveys: a review of some methods for handling the problem." Sociological Methods and Research 3:291–307.
Davis, James A.
1975   "Analyzing contingency tables with linear flow graphs: d-systems." In David Heise (ed.), Sociological Methodology. San Francisco: Jossey-Bass.
Davis, James A., Tom W. Smith, and C. Bruce Stephenson
1980   General Social Surveys 1972–1980: Cumulative Codebook. Chicago: National Opinion Research Center.

De Maio, Theresa
   1980 "Refusals: who, where, and why." Public Opinion Quarterly 44:223–33.
Dunkelberg, William C., and George S. Day
   1973 "Nonresponse bias and callbacks in sample surveys." Journal of Marketing Research 10:160–68.
Durbin, J., and A. Stuart
   1954 "Callbacks and clustering in sample surveys." Journal of the Royal Statistical Society (A) 117:387–428.
Ellis, Robert A., Calvin M. Endo, J. Michael Armer
   1970 "The use of potential nonrespondents for studying nonresponse bias." Pacific Sociological Review 13:103–9.
Filion, F. L.
   1975–76 "Estimating bias due to nonresponse in mail surveys." Public Opinion Quarterly 39:482–92.
   1976 "Exploring and correcting for nonresponse bias using follow-ups of nonrespondents." Pacific Sociological Review 19:401–8.
Gaertner, Karen Newman
   1976 "The use of AIPO surveys: to weight or not to weight." In James A. Davis (ed.), Studies of Social Change Since 1948, NORC Report 127A. Chicago: National Opinion Research Center.
Groves, Robert A., Robert L. Kahn
   1979 Surveys by Telephone: A National Comparison with Personal Interviews. New York: Academic Press.
GSS
   1980 "Interviewer procedural manual." Unpublished NORC booklet.
Hansen, M. H., and W. N. Hurwitz
   1946 "The problem of nonresponse in sample surveys." Journal of the American Statistical Association 41:517–29.
Hawkins, Darnell F.
   1975 "Estimation of nonresponse bias." Sociological Methods and Research 3:461–88.
Hendricks, Walter A.
   1956 The Mathematical Theory of Sampling. New Brunswick: Scarecrow Press.
Hilgard, Ernest R., and Stanley L. Payne
   1944 "Those not at home: riddle for pollsters." Public Opinion Quarterly 8:254–61.
House, James S., and Sharon Wolf
   1978 "Effects of urban residence on interpersonal trust and helping behavior." Journal of Personality and Social Psychology 36:1029–43.
Houseman, Earl E.
   1953 "Statistical treatment of the nonresponse problem." Agricultural Economics Research 5:12–18.
King, Benjamin F., and Carol Richards
   1972 "The 1972 NORC national probability sample." Unpublished NORC memo.
Kish, Leslie
   1965 Survey Sampling. New York: John Wiley.
Kish, Leslie, and Irene Hess
   1959 "A 'replacement' procedure for reducing the bias of nonresponse." American Statistician 8 (October):17–19.
Lagay, Bruce W.
   1969–70 "Assessing bias: a comparison of two methods." Public Opinion Quarterly 33:615–18.
Lansing, John B., et al.
   1971 Working Papers on Survey Research in Poverty Areas. Ann Arbor: Survey Research Center.
Love, Lawrence T., and Anthony G. Turner
   1976 "The census bureau's experience: respondent availability and response rates." Proceedings of the Business and Economics Section, American Statistical Association, Washington, D.C.: ASA.

Lowe, Francis E., and Thomas C. McCormick
  1955 "Some survey sampling biases." Public Opinion Quarterly:303–15.
Lundberg, George A., and Otto N. Larsen
  1949 "Characteristics of hard-to-reach individuals in field surveys." Public Opinion Quarterly 13:487–94.
Mayer, Charles S.
  1964 "The interviewer and his environment." Journal of Marketing Research 1 (November):24–31.
Moser, C. A., and G. Kalton
  1972 Survey Methods in Social Investigation, 2nd ed., New York: Basic Books.
Ognibene, Peter
  1971 "Correcting nonresponse bias in mail questionnaires." Journal of Marketing Research 8:233–35.
O'Neil, Michael J.
  1979 "Estimating the nonresponse bias due to refusals in telephone surveys." Public Opinion Quarterly 43:218–32.
Politz, A., and W. R. Simmons
  1949 "An attempt to get the 'not-at-homes' into the sample without callbacks." Journal of the American Statistical Association 44:9–31.
Presser, Stanley
  1981 "A comparison of Harris sample composition with census, IRS, and NORC," In Elizabeth Martin, Diana McDuffee, and Stanley Presser (eds.), Sourcebook of Harris National Surveys: Questions 1963–76. Chapel Hill, North Carolina: Institute for Research in Social Science.
Robins, Lee N.
  1963 "The reluctant respondent." Public Opinion Quarterly 27:276–86.
Schuman, Howard, and Barry Gruenberg
  1970 "The impact of city on racial attitudes." American Journal of Sociology 76:213–61.
Simmons, W. R.
  1954 "A plan to account for 'not-at-homes' by combining weighting and call-back." Journal of Marketing 19:42–53.
Smith, Tom W.
  1978 "Response rates on the 1975–78 General Social Surveys with comparisons to the Omnibus surveys of the Survey Research Center, 1972–1976." GSS Technical Report No. 7. Chicago: National Opinion Research Center.
  1979 "Sex and the GSS: nonresponse differences." GSS Technical Report No. 17. Chicago: National Opinion Research Center.
  1981 "The hidden 25 percent: an analysis of nonresponse on the 1980 General Social Survey." GSS Technical Report No. 25. Chicago: National Opinion Research Center.
Stephan, Frederick F., and Philip J. McCarthy
  1958 Sampling Opinion: An Analysis of Survey Procedure. New York: John Wiley.
Stephenson, C. Bruce
  1979 "Probability sampling with quotas: an experiment." Public Opinion Quarterly 43:477–96.
Stinchcombe, Arthur L., Calvin Jones, and Paul B. Sheatsley
  1981 "Nonresponse bias for attitude questions." Public Opinion Quarterly 45:359–75.
Weaver, Charles N., Sandra L. Holmes, and Norval D. Glenn
  1975 "Some characteristics of innaccessible respondents in a telephone survey." Journal of Applied Psychology 60:260–62.
Wilcox, James B.
  1977 "The interaction of refusal and not-at-home sources of nonresponse bias." Journal of Marketing Research 14:592–97.

Scheduling Telephone Interviews:
A Study of
Seasonal Patterns

GIDEON VIGDERHOUS

BECAUSE telephone interviewing in social surveys has increased substantially in recent years, studies of various methodological problems associated with telephone interviews are increasing (see Colombotos, 1965; Coombs and Freedman, 1964; Rogers, 1976; Groves, 1977; Falthzik, 1972). Among these problems, perhaps the fundamental one is how to maximize the response rate. This problem involves an optimal utilization of all resources, such as human effort, time, and money. Optimizing interviewing schedules means minimizing the number of callbacks by selecting the most appropriate time to reach respondents.

The purpose of this paper is to provide survey analysts with empirical results that should assist them in scheduling telephone interviews. In particular, the following issues will be discussed: (1) On the basis of yearly data, what is the "best" hour of the day to conduct telephone interviews? (2) What is the "best" day of the week and the "best" month of the year to conduct telephone interviews? (3) What is the difference in response rates between the morning, afternoon, and evening hours?

Data Collection

The data collected in this study are based on the monthly telephone interviews conducted by the Canadian Telephone Company (Bell

Abstract What is the best hour, day of the week, or month to conduct telephone interviews? Data in this paper suggest that weekday evening hours during the spring and fall are optimal times for contacting households for personal interviews.

Gideon Vigderhous is Survey Research Advisor at Bell Canada. The author wishes to acknowledge Alfred and Peter Chan for their valuable assistance in conducting this research, and the editor and reviewers for comments on earlier versions of this paper.

Canada) between February 1978 and January 1979, to ascertain the perception of telephone subscribers of the quality of telephone service; the same set of questionnaires was used throughout the whole period. A random sample of residential households were selected from listed and unlisted telephone numbers in the provinces of Ontario and Quebec, which constitute the company's territory. All telephone interviews were conducted between 9 A.M. and 9 P.M., Monday to Friday.[1] The maximum number of callbacks made was six, and the average length of each interview was 10 minutes from the time the first question was asked.

Temporary and Final Nonresponse

In order to study the distribution of different forms of response to telephone interviews, we have to define the following terms: completed response, temporary nonresponse, and final nonresponse. Before discussing this problem in further detail, let us enumerate and define common outcomes of telephone interviews.

1. *Busy:* The number that the interviewer dialed was busy.
2. *Callback:* Interviewer was asked to call back at some other time because the required person was not there or the required person was too busy to answer questions but would like to be called again at another time. (No attempt was made to set a specific time or day.)
3. *No answer:* The dialed number keeps ringing up to six times with no answer.
4. *No responsible party:* Any of the following group of people: (a) child under 18; (b) disabled (deaf); (c) drunk or incapable of reasoning, etc.
5. *Other language:* The interviewer was not able to communicate with the respondent because he was unable to speak the respondent's language.
6. *Partially completed:* Interview has been partially completed and future attempt is made to complete the interview.
7. *Quit:* Respondent refused to proceed with the interview after hearing one or several questions.
8. *Refused to start:* Respondent refused to proceed with the interview even before the first question was asked.
9. *Disconnect:* The particular telephone number has been disconnected.

[1] Because of administrative and organizational difficulties in recruiting interviewers and supervisors to work on weekends and holidays.

10. *Completed:* An interview was considered completed if the interviewer was able to present all the survey questions to the respondent and to record his answers.
11. *Miscellaneous:* Other reasons (e.g., employee of the company, foreign residents, visitor from other province).

This list represents most outcomes of telephone interviews. Outcomes 1–6 are identified as temporary nonresponse, and outcomes 7–9 as nonresponse. During the survey a decision has to be made as to when a temporary nonresponse becomes a nonresponse.

The first general question of interest in analyzing various forms of temporary nonresponse is the proportion of each event as computed from the total number of telephone dialings made in a given study. Table 1 indicates that the most prominent problem of temporary nonresponse is due to "no answer" (about 40–50 percent of the total dialings). The second and third most frequent types of temporary nonresponse are due to "callback" (about 8 percent) and "busy" (about 7 percent). Since these three types of temporary nonresponses are the primary types of temporary nonresponse that possibly result in lowering the response rate, the problem is to minimize these categories. In order to minimize nonresponse, we study the distribution of the type of response by hour of the day, day of the week, and month of the year. Table 1 indicates that the overall response rate to the telephone interviews varied significantly from month to month. In the month of February the response rate to the survey was 63.7 percent and in December, the response rate was 40.8 percent.[2]

"Optimal" Time of Day to Conduct Telephone Interviews

To choose an optimal time for telephone interviews, we could pick the time when either the probability of temporary nonresponse is small or the proportion of successfully completed calls is relatively large. Table 2 shows the distribution of completion ratio over the time of day for the 12-month period. Completion ratio was defined as the ratio of complete dialings to incomplete dialings. A dialing was considered complete if the interviewer was able to present all the survey questions to the respondents. Incomplete dialing signifies that for different reasons the respondent could not be reached or could not respond at that particular time to the telephone survey (see discussion above on temporary and final nonresponse).

[2] Response rate is defined as the proportion of respondents who completed their interview out of the sample selected. For example, in order to calculate the response rate for the month of February, we first compute the number of respondents reached in this month, which is $(.283 \times 5,519) = 1,562$. This implies that it took 5,519 telephone dialings to complete interviews with approximately 1,562 respondents. The response rate is therefore $1,562/2,453 = 63.7$ percent (see Table 1).

Table 1. Outcome of Telephone Interview, by Month (Proportion of Total Dialings)

Outcome	Feb	Mar	Apr	May	Jun	Jul	Aug	Sep	Oct	Nov	Dec	Jan
Busy	.082	.077	.069	.070	.065	.048	.056	.055	.060	.070	.060	.057
Callback	.106	.099	.102	.084	.081	.081	.087	.094	.088	.081	.057	.075
No answer	.406	.421	.420	.460	.501	.490	.480	.441	.438	.422	.461	.440
No responsible party	.052	.048	.048	.046	.047	.058	.059	.062	.062	.065	.072	.066
Other language	.016	.016	.020	.021	.026	.038	.046	.041	.040	.047	.048	.046
Partially complete	.001	.001	.001	.001	.002	.001	.001	.002	.001	.002	.001	.001
Quit	.006	.007	.006	.007	.010	.012	.011	.011	.010	.012	.009	.008
Refused to start	.005	.010	.008	.008	.008	.009	.009	.010	.015	.017	.013	.012
Disconnect	.003	.005	.002	.004	.003	.004	.005	.005	.005	.005	.006	.006
Completed	.283	.290	.294	.269	.237	.240	.238	.258	.269	.261	.208	.268
Miscellaneous	.039	.025	.030	.030	.021	.018	.019	.021	.014	.018	.065	.019
Total dialings	5,519	5,381	5,421	6,134	5,168	5,834	7,023	6,764	6,697	6,845	5,560	6,189
Sample size	2,453	2,427	2,469	2,694	2,191	2,589	3,142	3,216	3,143	3,258	2,833	2,953
% Response rate to the survey	63.7	64.4	64.6	61.3	55.8	54.1	53.1	53.1	44.3	54.75	40.8	56.3

Table 2. Completion Rate of Telephone Interviews by Time of Day and by Month (Proportions of Total Dialings)

Time of Day	Feb	Mar	Apr	May	Jun	Jul	Aug	Sep	Oct	Nov	Dec	Jan	Average
9:00–10:59 A.M.	.284	.353	.310	.394	.269	.218	.229	.239	.310	.273	.227	.244	.279
11:00 A.M.–1:59 P.M.	.351	.333	.340	.293	.259	.266	.199	.291	.322	.310	.268	.387	.302
2:00– 2:59 P.M.	.420	.370	.430	.403	.344	.318	.253	.286	.334	.374	.243	.279	.388
3:00– 3:59 P.M.	.349	.466	.464	.313	.272	.284	.283	.297	.332	.340	.251	.345	.333
4:00– 4:59 P.M.	.553	.514	.443	.373	.305	.369	.373	.387	.352	.391	.324	.302	.391
5:00– 5:59 P.M.	.459	.331	.430	.378	.294	.396	.286	.331	.425	.302	.286	.307	.352
6:00– 6:59 P.M.	.479	.505	.514	.456	.379	.350	.414	.425	.496	.419	.306	.484	.436
7:00– 7:59 P.M.	.543	.401	.457	.388	.340	.346	.451	.432	.444	.323	.357	.404	.407
8:00– 8:59 P.M.	.441	.451	.500	.432	.393	.390	.410	.526	.368	.408	.118	.511	.412

Table 2 shows that the completion ratio is highest from 6:00 P.M. to 6:59 P.M. consistently over the 12 months, with one or two exceptions. We can also look at the distribution of temporary nonresponse such as no answer, callback, and busy. The same preferred hour, 6:00–6:59 P.M., is evidenced by examining the lowest rate of callback and no answer. Generally, Table 2 presents the probabilities that a respondent will be reached at home and will participate in the telephone survey.

Preferred Time, Day, Month for Telephone Interviews— A Log-Linear Analysis

Is there a significant day effect (preferred day) or day-hour interaction besides the hour effect? In other words, what is the effect of the hour of the day when a control for the day of the week is established? Is there any particular hour on a particular day which is significantly different from the others in the response rate? These questions can now be answered using a log-linear analysis. The log-linear technique used in this paper is known as logit analysis, in which the model estimates are derived by the weighted least square solution where the dependent variable is dichotomized (for technical discussion see Green et al., 1977, or Reynolds, 1977). The dependent variable in this study was the proportion of completed telephone interviews, and the object of the analysis was to determine the effect of the hour of the day and day of the week on the completion rate of telephone interviews. An ideal analysis should also take into consideration the effect of the month. However, to incorporate the month of the year into a single model requires a large design matrix, $12 \times 9 \times 5$, which could not be executed because of computer core limitations.

The entire analysis is based on the total number of dialings.[3] A separate analysis is conducted for each month, using the number of completed interviews together with the incomplete (temporary or final nonresponse) calls. Perusal of Table 3 reemphasizes that the hour of the day has the highest weight in predicting the proportion of completed telephone interviews. The next two significant hours are 4:00–4:59 P.M. and 7:00–7:59 P.M. With only a few exceptions, the estimates for those two hours are significant at $p < .05$. In general, most of the evening hours are significant.

---

[3] Total number of dialings was used instead of only the first dialing in the analysis because when the interviews are conducted, arrangement for callbacks are usually in alternating schedules. For instance, if the outcome of the first contact in the morning results in a callback arrangement is usually made for a subsequent recall in the evening. Another problem is that, from a practical point of view, day-shift interviewers usually made the first contact to the respondents.

Table 3. Log Linear Analysis of Completed Telephone Interviews (out of Total Dialings)

					1978							1979
	Feb	Mar	Apr	May	Jun	Jul	Aug	Sep	Oct	Nov	Dec	Jan
Intercept	-1.219	-1.025	-1.206	-1.443	-1.480	-1.623	-1.092	-1.327	-1.289	-1.213	-1.129	-1.608
9:00–10:59 A.M. [a]	—	—	—	—	—	—	—	—	—	—	—	—
11:00 A.M.–1:59 P.M.	.192	-.070	.087	-.021	.023	.160	-.106	.003	.038	.009	.024	.434*
2:00– 2:59 P.M.	.482*	-.067	.322*	.141	.270*	.366*	-.214	.085	.083	.133	.019	.114
3:00– 3:59 P.M.	.208	.273*	.408*	.077	.405	.234	.060	.042	.072	.025	.016	.348*
4:00– 4:59 P.M.	.675*	.391*	.370*	.296*	.144	.517*	.479*	.218*	.124	.100	.101	.204
5:00– 5:59 P.M.	.463*	-.001	.325	-.065	-.086	.571*	.407*	.492*	.295*	.331*	.301*	.203
6:00– 6:59 P.M.	.503*	.340*	.502*	.517*	.357*	.608*	.690*	.857*	.465*	.646*	.401*	.686*
7:00– 7:59 P.M.	.760*	.110	.394*	.382	.461*	.456*	.370*	.668*	.357*	.424*	.276*	.504*
8:00– 8:59 P.M.	.442*	.259	.502*	.282	.398*	.565*	.695*	.571*	.186	.473*	.271*	.723*
Monday	-.092	-.110	.040	.281*	.343*	.219	.088	.166*	.142	.151*	.076	.269*
Tuesday	.021	.062	.038	.383*	.191	.065	-.021	.281*	.265*	.043	.043	.328*
Wednesday	-.031	.103	.155	1.257*	.173	.040	.090	.065	.220*	.178*	.088	.308*
Thursday	.021	-.135	-.021	.157	.096	.268*	.073	.263*	.005	.075	-.123*	.133
Friday [a]	—	—	—	—	—	—	—	—	—	—	—	—
Chi-square	32.89	32.71	33.35	34.72	27.85	34.47	21.48	27.57	28.11	35.90	36.75	32.94
ML Chi-square	32.54	32.75	33.81	34.58	27.96	34.37	21.81	27.46	28.06	35.83	36.44	33.29
d.f.	30	31	32	24	30	29	27	26	32	30	28	32

[a] Referenced.
* Significant at $p < .05$.

Table 4. Log Linear Analysis of Completed Telephone Interviews (out of Total Dialings) Estimate of the Interactions[a]

February			March			May		
4 × 11	−.679		3 × 13	.558		2 × 12	−.909	
3 × 13	−.521					4 × 12	−.942	
						5 × 12	−1.588	
						7 × 12	−.790	
						8 × 12	−.866	
						6 × 13	1.351	
						7 × 13	−.526	
						8 × 13	−.775	
June			July			August		
6 × 10	1.223		4 × 11	−.559		3 × 10	.241	
7 × 12	−.875		4 × 12	.523		6 × 12	−.893	
			7 × 13	−.781		8 × 12	−1.117	
						6 × 13	.745	
						9 × 13	1.203	
September			November			December		
2 × 13	−.288		5 × 11	.346		6 × 10	−2.077	
6 × 10	.463		6 × 11	.499		3 × 11	−.515	
9 × 11	.483					6 × 12	−.392	
7 × 13	−.486					6 × 12	.498	
8 × 13	.515							
9 × 13	−.438							

[a] Months that do not appear suggest that main effect models (without interactions) were satisfactory as determined by the chi-square test. All coefficients significant at $p < .05$.

The preferred day varies from month to month. For instance, during February, March, April, September, and November, there are no significant differences among the days. However, in December, Friday is very different from any other days (see Table 3). Hence, no conclusion can be drawn regarding the importance of the day of the week in scheduling interviews since it depends on which month of the year is under consideration.

In carrying out the above analyses, two reference points are chosen, one for each variable: the period between 9:00 A.M. and 10:59 A.M. is the time, and Friday is the day. The same reference points are chosen throughout the whole analysis. Hence, to interpret a positive coefficient, it means that the contribution toward the predictability of proportion of completed calls is larger for that category than the reference point. For example (see Table 3), the coefficient for the hour 6:00–6:59 P.M. in February is .503, which is essentially the difference between the effect of that hour and the reference hour (9:00–10:59 A.M.). Therefore, each result should be assessed in relation to the reference point or the omitted category.[4]

[4] The conclusions drawn from the log-linear analysis are not affected by the choice of the omitted category.

The chi-square and maximum likelihood chi-square statistics are included as an assessment to the fitness of the log-linear models which may (or may not) include interaction terms, as indicated in Table 4. Interaction terms do not appear uniformly over the months. Some of the reasons may be attributed to seasonal patterns and holiday schedules. For instance, Christmas shopping is affecting the postulated model. However, the fact that interaction changes from month to month leads to another analysis of the monthly effect. Table 5 summarizes the result of the analysis on months.

Because we are mainly interested in the monthly effect, we simplify the analysis by reclassifying the time into three sessions: morning hours (9:00 A.M. to 1:59 P.M.), afternoon hours (2:00 P.M. to 4:59 P.M.), and evening hours (5:00 P.M. to 5:59 P.M.). The results in Table 5 show that January, February, March, and April are the "best" months to conduct telephone interviews; June, July, and August are less preferable, and December is considered to be the worst month. The reference point for a month is January, and for time session it is afternoon. Again, the result supports the argument which states the evening hours are "better." Among the interesting interactions, De-

Table 5. Log Linear Analysis on Completion Rate of Telephone Interviews (Analysis by Total Dialings)

Log Linear Estimates	Monthly Data
1. Intercept	−1.053
2. February	.117*
3. March	.182*
4. April	.159*
5. May	.035
6. June	−.147*
7. July	−.162*
8. August	−.100*
9. September	−.083
10. October	.020
11. November	.024
12. December	−.209*
13. January	Referenced
14. 9:00 A.M.–1:59 P.M.	−.154*
15. 2:00–4:59 P.M.	Referenced
16. 5:00–8:59 P.M.	.214*
Interaction	*Estimates*
3 × 16	−.131*
8 × 16	.258*
9 × 16	.116*
11 × 16	−.159*
12 × 16	−.341*
Chi-square	26.26
ML Chi-square	26.30
d.f.	17

* Significant at 5% level.

cember evening hours carry the largest negative value, implying that evening hours in December are exceptionally low in the response rate.

Another question of interest is to find out which is the "best" season. To do that, we arbitrarily[5] group the months into spring (March, April, May), summer (June, July, August), fall (September, October, November), and winter (December, January, February). Of the four seasons, we learn that spring is probably the "best" time of the year to do the telephone interviews. The months in fall are the second best, and summer mornings are the least favored time.

Summary and Conclusions

The results from this study show that for telephone interviews, evening hours are preferred, with peak hour between 6:00 P.M. and 6:59 P.M. There is no difference on which day of the week. However, it makes some difference on which month of the year the telephone interviews take place. Schedules in spring and fall are generally better than in summer and winter.

A recent study conducted by Weeks et al. (1980) reported results on optimal times to contact sample households in personal interviews. This study, known as the RTI survey, was conducted in March–June 1976; its national probability sample in the United States consisted of 100 district primary sampling units (SMSA's and non-SMSA counties or groups of contiguous counties). Despite the difference in mode of data collection (personal interview versus telephone interview), and differences in location (United States versus Canada), our study is consistent with Weeks et al. (1980) in two of its major conclusions.

1. The evening hours are the "best" hours to find people at home. More specifically, Weeks et al. (1980) reported that the hour at which at least one person aged 14 or older was most likely to be at home was 6:00–6:59 P.M. Our results indicate that the highest completion rates of telephone interviews were achieved at this hour.

2. There is little variation in the proportion of people at home on different weekdays. This result is also consistent with Weeks et al. (1980). Since our study was not carried out during weekends and holidays, no comparison can be made of the effect of Saturday compared to other days of the week on the overall response rate.

Despite these conclusions, our study did not take into consideration the cost factor. It is probably unfeasible to conduct interviews only in

---

[5] The grouping of the months into seasons depends on the climate where the telephone interviewing takes place.

a single hour of the day, because a considerable amount of telephone equipment would be idle for the rest of the day. Nevertheless, it is evident that there is no reason to distribute evenly the interviewing effort during the various hours of the day. Given the cost factor involved in conducting interviews and the expected response rate, one should concentrate on the late hours of the day rather than the early hours. It is not always feasible to choose the "best" month of the year to conduct public opinion surveys. However, if such an option is available, this study indicates which month to avoid in order to maximize response rate.

References

Braun, Peter
   1976 "Interviewer success rates in a national survey." New Surveys
        2:10–17.
Colombotos, J.
   1965 "The effects of personal vs. telephone interviews on socially accept-
        able responses." Public Opinion Quarterly 29:457–58.
Coombs, L., and R. Freedman
   1964 "Use of telephone interviews in a longitudinal fertility study." Public
        Opinion Quarterly 28:112–17.
Falthzik, A. M.
   1972 "When to make telephone interviews." Journal of Marketing Re-
        search 9:451–52.
Green, P. E., F. J. Carmone, and D. P. Wachspress
   1977 "On the analysis of qualitative data in marketing research. Journal of
        Marketing Research 14:52–59.
Groves, R.
   1977 "A comparison of national telephone and personal interview surveys:
        some response and non-response differences." Paper presented at
        the annual meetings of AAPOR.
Kruskal, J. B.
   1965 "Analysis of factorial experiments by estimating montone
        transformation of data." Journal of the Royal Statistical Society,
        Series B, 27:251–63.
Rogers, T.
   1976 "Interviews by telephone and in person: quality of response and field
        performance." Public Opinion Quarterly 40:51–65.
U.S. Department of Commerce
   1973 "Who's home when." Working paper 37, January 1973, Bureau of the
        Census.
Weeks, M. F., B. L. Jones, R. E. Folsom, Jr., and C. H. Benrud
   1980 "Optimal times to contact sample householders." Public Opinion
        Quarterly 44:101–14.

USING DUAL FRAME DESIGNS TO REDUCE NONRESPONSE IN TELEPHONE SURVEYS

MICHAEL W. TRAUGOTT
ROBERT M. GROVES AND
JAMES M. LEPKOWSKI

Abstract   This article reports on the results of a series of experiments designed to improve response rates for telephone surveys. In three surveys telephone households were selected using both standard random digit dialing (RDD) techniques and lists of telephone numbers purchased from a commercial firm. In the RDD portions of the samples "cold contact" interviewing methods were used; in the list frame portions advance letters were mailed, and the listed household name was used in the introduction. Experiments were designed to test the effects on response rates of the advance letters and use of the listed household name as a means of establishing rapport. The advance letters increased response rates, but no difference could be attributed to the use of names. The mixture of RDD and list sampling techniques is also used to evaluate the effects of relative response rates on substantive findings. The cost consequences of these dual frame designs are assessed along a number of dimensions, and the cost and error components of these designs are discussed.

Survey nonresponse error is partially a function of achieved response rates. The researcher's ability to increase response rates, in turn, depends on a number of survey design features—the topic of the survey,

MICHAEL W. TRAUGOTT is Research Scientist in the Center for Political Studies, ROBERT M. GROVES is Associate Research Scientist in the Survey Research Center, and JAMES M. LEPKOWSKI is Assistant Research Scientist in the Survey Research Center, all at the University of Michigan. The data utilized in this paper were collected in conjunction with a contract with the *Detroit News*. Support for consideration of dual frame telephone survey designs was obtained from the U.S. Bureau of the Census. However, all of the analyses and interpretations presented here are the sole responsibility of the authors. The research assistance of Judy Connor and Kim Fridkin Kahn is gratefully acknowledged, as is the computing support of the University of Michigan. A version of this paper was presented at the annual meeting of the American Association for Public Opinion Research, St. Petersburg, Florida, 16–18 May 1986.

the population studied, the efforts at refusal conversion, the duration of the interviewing period, information known about the sample persons, and a host of other factors. Inevitably, decisions regarding response rate goals require a balancing of the expected costs of these design attributes and the likely nonresponse error reduction which may result from them.

When names, addresses, and telephone numbers are available on a frame, two techniques can be used to improve cooperation—advance letters or telephone calls informing sample persons that they have been selected for a study and indicating the need for cooperation in order to achieve accurate results. Brunner and Carroll (1967) found that an advance telephone call for a personal interview actually led to lower response rates. Groves and Magilavy (1981) observed that advance telephone calls for a telephone survey had no effect on final response rates in an RDD survey. Dillman, Gallegos, and Frey (1976) found that overall response rates were increased by about five percentage points using an advance letter, but that the content of the letter had little influence on the magnitude of the response rate increase. Sykes and Hoinville (1985) found no effect in a telephone survey in Great Britain. Brunner and Carroll (1969) found large increases in response rates to a telephone survey (30 percentage points) with a letter sent on university stationery, but a decline in response rates (6 percentage points) using one from a market research company.

Response rates are also sensitive to the amount of effort used to contact sample households, but even this may be affected by characteristics of the sampling frame. The use of callbacks is a minimum condition for increasing response rates (Traugott, 1987), and refusal conversion techniques are also important for this purpose. In some surveys the number of callbacks is a fixed design feature, determined prior to the interviewing period. In other designs the maximum number of callbacks is determined by the length of the survey period. Since the time spent screening ineligible sample units detracts from time available for interviewing, the percentage of units on the sampling frame that are eligible can also affect response rates. In this way, the choice of sampling frame can have a consequence for nonresponse error.

The achievement of high response rates is a goal linked not only to improved estimation of descriptive statistics but also increased confidence in measured relationships. While there has been considerable research on increasing response rates, there has been little on their effects on measured relationships between variables. This is ordinarily complicated by an inability to measure relationships for nonrespondents. The literature that does exist compares relationships between variables among cooperative and reluctant respondents (O'Neil, 1979; Smith, 1984).

Telephone surveys based upon random digit dialed (RDD) samples have offered substantial advantages in reducing data collection costs relative to personal interview surveys, in large part because travel costs can be eliminated and the number of interviewers required to complete a given sample size is often smaller. The RDD method has, however, also resulted in a reduction in survey response rates (Groves and Kahn, 1979). In some part these reduced rates may be attributed to "cold contacts" with respondents about whom the interviewers know little. In addition, the lower response rates may be attributed to features of the RDD sampling frame, including the relatively high percentages of nonworking and nonresidential numbers that are part of this frame. The time requirements for screening out such sample numbers reduces the time available to pursue eligible numbers.

This article summarizes a series of experiments conducted across three telephone surveys designed to measure cost and nonresponse advantages of a sampling frame based on telephone directories (termed the "list frame") in comparison with RDD samples.[1] In contrast to prior uses of directories as the sole frame or as a "seeding" mechanism for RDD work (Sudman, 1973), these experiments explored their use in a dual frame design, jointly employing RDD and directory based methods. The research reported here focuses not on the statistical design issues involved in dual frame telephone surveys but on those properties of the list frame that make it a desirable companion to the RDD frame.

The major test described in this paper involved a comparison of the response rate among list frame households sent an advance letter with the rate for those in which cold contacts were made. Following previous results it was hypothesized that the use of the letter would increase response rates. A subsidiary experimental treatment involved the use upon initial contact of the name in the directory listing for a portion of the households that were sent the letter. Assuming that personalized approaches emphasize the unique attributes of the sample person, it was hypothesized that the use of names in conjunction with the letter would further increase response rates.

Because of the anticipated higher proportions of working household numbers on the list frame, and possible differences in cooperation

1. The first two of these three surveys used the same basic dual frame sample design, while the third used a two-phase design described in Lepkowski and Groves (1986b). There were other elements of each study which differed. The first survey was conducted between 18 October and 10 November 1985, involved 753 interviews which averaged 23 minutes in length, and achieved an overall response rate of 61%. The second survey was conducted between 14 February and 3 March 1986, involved 668 interviews which averaged 13 minutes in length, and achieved an overall response rate of 61%. The third survey, conducted between 24 May and 15 June 1986, involved 789 interviews which averaged 22 minutes in length, and achieved an overall response rate of 63%.

among respondents with listed and unlisted numbers, it was hypothesized that response rates would be higher in the list frame than in the RDD frame, for an equivalent level of effort at contacting respondents. The effects of these design features on survey costs, measured as efficiency in obtaining interviews, were evaluated under controlled conditions in a fixed field period and achievement of a designated final response rate. Examples are also presented of differences in observed bivariate relationships among respondents who were sent a letter (the "high response" sample) and those who were not (the "low response" sample).

Elements of the Dual Frame Design for Telephone Households

Dual frame designs utilize two sets of materials (frames) to identify the target population. Separate samples are taken from the frames and then combined in analysis, using appropriate weights, to estimate the overall population parameters. Two frames are desirable when, in combination, they offer better survey cost and error properties than one frame alone (Hartley, 1962). Dual frame designs that jointly use area frames and telephone frames have been proposed to reduce sampling and measurement error, compared to surveys using area frames only, for the same cost (Groves and Lepkowski, 1985; Biemer, 1983; Lepkowski and Groves, 1986a).

Dual frame designs can also be employed in household surveys using the telephone as the only mode of data collection. In a dual frame design for telephone surveys, a list frame sample is selected from a set of numbers based upon telephone directories, and then it is combined with a sample selected from an RDD frame. Typically the RDD frame sample is generated from a computer tape of existing central office codes or prefixes. The names and addresses of potential respondents are available for the list frame sample cases, providing an opportunity to contact these cases with an advance letter describing the study and eliciting their cooperation. The rate of working household numbers on the list frame might also exceed that on the RDD frame, offering lower costs for screening eligible numbers. Dual frame designs for telephone surveys offer both the prospect of reduced nonresponse error *and* lower cost relative to single frame RDD telephone surveys.

The purpose of a dual frame design for telephone household surveys is thus to build upon the relative strengths of the two frames, minimize their respective problems, and provide data of superior quality, given the fixed resources which can be devoted to sampling and interviewing. In terms of survey errors, an RDD sample will provide complete coverage of all telephone households, including unlisted numbers, but at the cost of generating and pursuing about 35%–45% nonworking and non-residential numbers among all sample numbers (Groves, 1978). A list frame, on the other hand, will minimize problems of pursuing non-working and nonresidential numbers. At the same time, a telephone directory is out of date even as it is printed, excludes unlisted numbers by definition, and may erroneously contain some nonresidential num-bers in the residential section. In terms of sampling errors, the RDD design increases sampling variance from clustered sample selections compared to independently selected element samples, while the list frame has the potential for decreasing sampling variance based upon stratified element selection.

In terms of survey costs, the comparison of the two frames is more complex. The two-stage RDD cluster design proposed by Waksberg and Mitofsky (Waksberg, 1978) requires a screening of "primary" numbers as a first stage of sample selection. This step can essentially be eliminated with the list frame sample. However, the list frame in-volves a purchase cost which is much higher initially. In addition, in the list frame design described below, preparation of advance letters, including printing, signatures, and postage, also increases costs.

In the first two of the experiments reported here, an RDD sample of Michigan telephone households was drawn using a geographic division of the state into three strata.[2] Then a list sample was purchased from Metromail Corporation of Lincoln, Nebraska, for the same three strata, based upon a file of continuously updated keypunched tele-phone directory listings of residential households. The file is supple-mented with additional information which permits sorting by zip code and address. A systematic sample was drawn from this version of the file for the state of Michigan. Finally, all telephone numbers in the RDD first stage clusters which had a working primary number were also sent to the Metromail Corporation to determine their listed status. It was necessary to match the potential RDD sample numbers to the list frame in order to determine probabilities of selection and, hence, appropriate weights for estimation.

---

2. This is the standard design employed in the surveys conducted for the *Detroit News* to provide for analyses corresponding to important elements of their circulation area. It divides the state into three regions consisting of the city of Detroit, the surrounding suburbs in Wayne, Oakland, and Macomb counties, and the rest of the state. Taking equal numbers of cases from each stratum provides the basis for reliable comparisons between strata; the resulting data are weighted to conform to their appropriate propor-tions of the Michigan population to generate statewide estimates. Each survey involved a different questionnaire, and the average interview lengths varied from 13 to 23 minutes.

List Frame Characteristics

One important issue regarding the list frame is its coverage—the proportion of all working household numbers that appear on the list. This proportion can be assessed in two ways: (1) matching all RDD numbers to the list in order to ascertain the degree of correspondence, or (2) asking respondents in the RDD sample whether their number is listed in the current telephone directory. Both of these approaches were followed in this investigation, primarily to assess whether respondent reports of list frame status were accurate.[3] Table 1 shows the proportion of all telephone household numbers that were listed for each of the strata as well as the total for the state in the first sample.

Using the matching procedure, 61% of the numbers generated by the RDD procedure were found to be on the file of listed numbers as well. With 39% of all household numbers in the state not appearing on the list frame, it is possible that severe coverage biases might result from its use alone for inference to the telephone household population. The stratum-specific results reflect the general observation of a number of studies that the rate of listed numbers is higher in less urban areas. These findings are likely the net effect of several influences, including the relative frequencies of subscribers requesting that their numbers not be listed in the directory, the transiency rate since the publication of the last directory, and the success of Metromail in updating directory information for each exchange.

As an alternative means of assessing the list status of telephone households, self-reported listed rates were computed for the interviews completed from both frames in the first survey. As indicated in Table 2, about three-quarters of the respondents (73%) drawn from the RDD frame indicated that their telephones were listed, and one-fifth (22%) said they were unlisted. Four percent indicated their number was too recently assigned to be listed in the current directory. When these numbers were matched against the list frame, high levels of correspondence were found, although significant discrepancies remained. Of the respondents who reported their numbers were listed, for example, only 81% were found on the list. At the same time, 9% of the numbers reported as "unlisted" were found on the list. Finally, 15% of the numbers reported to be too recent to be listed were nevertheless found on the list.

Among the list sample cases, virtually all of the respondents (95%) described their number as listed, although 4% said it was unlisted.

---

3. The exact question wording was: "As far as you know, is the number I dialed listed in the current telephone book? [If no] Why isn't it listed?"

Table I. Proportions (and Standard Errors) of RDD Sample Cases on List Frame for Households and Other Numbers by Stratum

| Stratum | Working Residential Numbers | | Other Numbers[a] | |
	Proportion on List	N	Proportion on List	N
Detroit	0.430	193	0.033	183
	(0.036)		(0.013)	
Suburbs	0.512	205	0.114	149
	(0.032)		(0.030)	
Outstate	0.722	205	0.205	122
	(0.036)		(0.058)	
State total	0.611	603	0.149	454
	(0.022)		(0.033)	

NOTE: Unweighted for joint list frame–RDD frame probabilities.
[a] Includes working nonresidential and nonworking numbers.

Table 2. Self-reported Directory Status of Households with Completed Interviews

Self-reported Directory Status	List Frame Cases (N = 399)	RDD Frame Cases (N = 354)
Currently listed	95%	73%
Unlisted	4	22
Too recent to be listed	1	4
Don't know	—[a]	1

[a] Less than 0.5%.

There are two explanations for the discrepancies between known appearance on the Metromail list and the survey responses to these questions. The first is that the respondent's number is published in the current local directory, and the Metromail file is out-of-date or in error. The second is that the respondent misreported the listing status, either because the number is published under a prior subscriber's name in the current directory, or because he or she is unaware of the listed status in their name, misunderstood the question, or, less likely, deliberately distorted the truth. In any case, the data suggest that respondents' self reports of listing status are not reliable enough to be used in the determination of sample weights.

Results of the Letter Experiments

Two treatments involving the letter were administered in the experiments. The first was the use of the advance letter, which was sent to a portion of the list frame respondents. For each survey, between 600 and 700 copies of the letter were prepared using word processing software which inserted the respondent's name and address above a standard body of text. Following Dillman (1978), they were typed on University of Michigan stationery, signed by the study director, inserted in envelopes prepared with the same word processing software, and stamped with commemorative stamps rather than a metered machine. This treatment was applied in the first survey and replicated in the second.

The second treatment involved the use of the subscriber's family name in the initial interviewer contact with the household, which was applied to approximately half of the list frame sample sent the letter. Because a Computer Assisted Telephone Interviewing (CATI) system was used, it was a straightforward procedure to use alternate introductory screens upon contact with the household. For those who were not sent a letter, a standard introduction noting the affiliation of the interviewer and the purpose of the call was used. For those who were sent a letter, two different introductions were used. One inquired whether they recalled receiving the advance letter. The other asked if this was the particular household sampled, using the surname on the letter, and if they recalled receiving a letter.[4] This experiment was conducted in all three surveys.

---

4. The exact wordings of the introduction for regular RDD respondents was

> Hello, my name is. . . . I'm calling from the University of Michigan in Ann Arbor. Here at the university, we are currently working on a study for the Survey Research Center. First of all I need to be sure I've dialed the right number. Is this . . . ?

For list frame respondents who were sent a letter, one of the two following forms of introduction was used:

> Hello, my name is. . . . I'm calling from the University of Michigan in Ann Arbor. Recently we mailed you a letter about a study we are working on here at the Survey Research Center. Did you receive that letter?

or

> Hello, my name is. . . . I'm calling from the University of Michigan in Ann Arbor. Is this the . . . household? Recently we mailed you a letter about a study we are working on here at the Survey Research Center. Did you receive that letter?

Whether the name was correct or not, the interview proceeded. In the first survey, 71%

Table 3 shows the unweighted allocation of sample cases to each of the experimental treatments, the weighted response rates which resulted in the statewide sample, and their standard errors. In order to rule out interaction effects, it is best to review the results by evaluating first the effects of the use of the name, second the effects of using the letter, and third the differences between the RDD and list frames. In the first survey there was among list frame respondents who received a letter an unanticipated negative difference of 6.2 percentage points in the response rate when the directory name was used. This was not a statistically significant difference, and the experiment was replicated in the second survey, where an equally small difference of 5.4 percentage points was observed in the opposite but expected direction. In the third replication of the experiment, the difference was only 1.1 percentage points. We conclude from this that the use of a directory name in conjunction with an advance letter has no effect on response rates.

The use of the advance letter was evaluated in two surveys. As the results in Table 3 show, among list frame cases the advance letter had a significant positive effect on response rates in both surveys. In the first, response rates increased 13.4 percentage points among the list frame respondents when the advance letter was used. In the second survey, the increase was 8.5 percentage points.

Because of modifications to the sample design, there are sufficient data to compare the list frame response rates to the RDD response rate only in the first survey. In general, a higher response was achieved from the list frame sample than from the RDD sample. Within the RDD frame, response rates were greater among those numbers which appeared on the list frame as well (13.2 percentage points higher, standard error 4.9). Reasons for unlisted status—such as transiency status and concern with safety or privacy—are probably correlated with the likelihood of cooperation with a survey request.

The Cost Effectiveness of the Dual Frame Design

While the results presented above indicate the effects on response rates of using the list sample, a separate question is whether survey costs can be reduced by the use of the list sample as well. The potential

of the list frame households where no name was used acknowledged receipt of the letter. For those where the name was used, 75% of them acknowledged receipt of the letter. The set of 52 respondents who said they did not receive a letter or could not remember whether they did is somewhat larger than the 30 letters which were returned by the postal service. On the third survey, 61% of the list frame respondents where no name was used acknowledged receipt of the letter, relative to 66% where the name was used. On the first survey, for cases using the listed name, 96% of the names were correct. On the third survey, 94% indicated it was the correct household.

Table 3. Response Rates (and Standard Errors) by Experimental Treatment for Three Telephone Surveys in the State of Michigan

Condition	First Experiment	N	Second Experiment	N	Third Experiment	N
RDD frame						
	0.616	603	—		—	
	(0.021)					
On list	0.663	336	—		—	
	(0.025)					
Not on list	0.531	267	—		—	
	(0.042)					
List frame						
No letter	0.560	85	0.694	234	—	
	(0.072)		(0.036)			
Letter	0.694	529	0.779	456	0.724	656
	(0.026)		(0.023)		(0.020)	
With name in introduction	0.664	267	0.805	220	0.729	330
	(0.036)		(0.030)		(0.029)	
Without name in introduction	0.726	262	0.751	236	0.718	326
	(0.035)		(0.034)		(0.029)	
Comparisons						
Letter–no letter	0.134*		0.085*		—	
	(0.078)		(0.044)			
With name–without name	−0.062		0.054		0.011	
	(0.050)		(0.045)		(0.042)	

*$p < 0.05$.

savings could result from a combination of factors, including fewer calls made to nonworking or nonresidential numbers and more easily obtained cooperation due to the use of an advance letter. The calculation of savings, whether actual or potential, is complicated by the need to have appropriate cost accounting and to make assumptions about the applicability of the current design to other surveys.

In principle, there are three cost factors which are affected by the use of the list sample: the cost of list purchase, mailing expenses, and greater efficiency in interviewing. While these cost factors can be modeled (Groves and Lepkowski, 1986), exact costs are difficult to calculate for a given application because of such factors as variations in survey designs and administration and an inability to account precisely for real costs.

The first factor includes two components: the cost of purchasing a sample of numbers from the list and the cost of matching the RDD sample numbers against the list frame to determine membership on both frames. In each case these are added costs compared to the typical RDD design. In the first dual frame survey, the total cost of list frame processing was $1,610, which included selection of a sample of 750 listed numbers for $625 and an additional $985 to match 30,000 telephone numbers in the second-stage clusters of the RDD Waksberg-Mitofsky sample design against the telephone numbers in the list frame to determine which RDD frame cases could also have been selected from the list frame. The cost of the list frame sample and the matching operation depend upon the firm from which the list sample is purchased and their charging algorithms, the size of the sample, and its geographical dispersion.[5]

A second cost factor involves the added expense of preparing and distributing the advance letters to the sample households. Names and addresses of list frame selections were transferred to a microcomputer, and a program with a mail-merge capability was used to produce letters and address envelopes. The cost of supplies (including stationery and postage) and labor to generate and send the letters amounted to approximately $0.52 per letter.

The third cost factor concerns the efficiency of conducting the interviews with the list sample respondents. Greater cooperation was expected from the list frame households because they had received ad-

5. For the list frame sample, the cost is usually computed as a charge to access the computer file and to pass the number of records from Michigan in the file plus a charge per each sample selection. The matching cost involves a similar access charge plus an additional charge per 1,000 matches. Limiting the selection to a smaller geographic area reduces the passing charges for both operations; extending the selection to a larger area (e.g., the coterminous United States) greatly increases the passing charge. The illustrative costs presented here should not be used to estimate a single charge per list frame sample selection or per completed interview for other survey designs.

vance letters. In addition, list frame telephone numbers were known to have been working residential numbers recently, and, hence, there is a greater chance for them to be working residential numbers at the time of calling than for the RDD numbers. A reduced number of calls is expected to be placed to list frame cases relative to RDD cases as a result of a higher density of residential numbers among the list frame cases. Only about 60% of the RDD numbers, selected at the second stage of the sample, were found to be residential; in contrast, about 88% of the list frame numbers were residential. Therefore there were fewer unproductive calls during the survey period and an increase in the efficiency of the interviewing.

In our study it was impossible to calculate the overall savings in dollar terms attributable to these efficiency factors because accounting algorithms and procedures were not in place to measure costs separately for each experimental treatment group. However, the savings can be estimated by calculating the ratio of the total number of calls made to various types of sample selections to the number of completed interviews obtained from those selections. A comparison of this ratio for list frame and RDD frame numbers indicates how much could be saved by the increased efficiency which the list sample provides in contacting potential respondents and obtaining interviews from them.

Data on calls per completed interview for the first survey are presented in Table 4. In every case the ratio of calls to completed interviews was higher in the RDD sample than it was in the list sample. Across the entire sample, an average of 3.1 more calls were required to obtain an RDD sample interview than one from the list frame, an increase of 39.7%. This relationship can be observed in each stratum as well, and the differences were much greater in the Detroit metropolitan area than outstate. The magnitude of these differences ranged from 1.38 to 5.55 calls, representing relative increases in effort ranging from 17.3% to 60.5%.

Response Rate Effects on Substantive Conclusions

While considerable research has been devoted to finding ways to increase survey response rates, relatively little is known about the effects of differential response on observed relationships among variables in the resulting data (Goudy, 1976; O'Neil, 1979). Another benefit of the dual frame design is that it permits a routine test of the effects of relative response rates by comparing estimates of theoretically relevant relationships among respondents who were on the list and received an advance letter (and who were more cooperative) with those

Table 4. Ratio of Total Calls to Completed Interviews by Selected Experimental Treatment and by Stratum

Condition	Detroit	Suburbs	Outstate	State Total
List frame				
Letter	9.36	7.17	7.97	7.84
No letter	9.30	12.83	8.23	8.23
RDD frame	14.91	11.51	9.35	10.95
Comparison				
Letter–RDD	−5.55*	−4.34*	−1.38	−3.11*
Standard error	1.83	1.26	1.24	0.86
Percent relative change[a]	−59.3	−60.5	−17.3	−39.7

[a] $100 \times$ (Letter − RDD) / Letter.
*$p < 0.05$.

among all respondents (both list and RDD) who did not receive a letter.[6]

As examples of these possibilities, consider first the robustness of the relationship between education and knowledge of apartheid among white respondents.[7] It was expected that higher levels of education would be associated with greater levels of knowledge. In each subsample, the proportion of college-educated respondents was the same. Among those who were sent a letter, 54% had *heard about* apartheid, while 48% of those who were not sent a letter had heard about apartheid. Further, in each subsample the relationship between education and hearing about apartheid was the same as well (tau beta = 0.36 and 0.28, respectively).

On the other hand, the relationship between education and being able to *define* apartheid for those white respondents who had heard about it changes between the two groups, as shown in Table 5. For the sample respondents who received the letter, there is no relationship

6. We assume that the letter does not influence the response itself but only the rate at which list frame households respond. Under this assumption the difference in estimates between those list frame respondents receiving a letter and those not receiving a letter is interpreted as nonresponse bias.
7. The exact question wordings were

Have you heard or read about the policy of apartheid? [If yes] Can you tell me what it is?

1. A form of racial discrimination against blacks
2. Other policy
5. No
8. Don't know

Table 5. The Effects of Relative Response Rates, Indicated by Advance Letter Treatment, on the Relationship Between Education and Ability to Define "Apartheid," Whites Only

Education	Received Letter and Defined "Apartheid"				Did Not Receive Letter and Defined "Apartheid"			
	Correctly	Incorrectly	Can't Define	N	Correctly	Incorrectly	Can't Define	N
High school or less	82%	1	17	53	62%	14	23	40
Some college or more	83%	4	13	107	92%	5	3	71
Total sample	83%	3	14	160	81%	9	10	111
	tau beta = .02				tau beta = .37			

between education and an ability to define apartheid correctly (tau beta = 0.02). But there is a relationship among the sample who did not receive the letter (tau beta = 0.37). Using this definition of knowledge, in effect, an increase in response rates results in the disappearance of a positive relationship observed at lower response rates.

A second example is presented in Table 6, which shows the relationship between party identification and approval of Ronald Reagan's handling of his job as president.[8] Here the hypothesis is that respondents who identify with the president's political party will be more likely to evaluate him positively than those who identify with the other party. The distribution of partisanship was different in each subsample, with more Democrats than Republicans among respondents who had not been sent a letter but more Republicans than Democrats among those who had. However, approval ratings in each subsample were approximately the same—76% among those who were sent a letter and 72% among those who were not. As the data in Table 6 illustrate, the basic relationship between partisanship and presidential approval is unchanged, but the magnitude is considerably stronger among the subsample who received a letter (tau beta = 0.49) than those who did not (tau beta = 0.29).

From the above analyses one can see that the effects of nonresponse rate differences on substantive conclusions can vary across analyses within the same survey. The impact of nonresponse rates depends on relationships between the motivation for failure to respond and the substantive variables being measured. Thus, there is no reason to suspect uniform effects over all survey statistics. Indeed such variation has plagued researchers' attempts to understand how nonresponse alters survey results. The two examples above are presented to illustrate the ability of the dual frame design to offer insight into the effect of higher response rates on substantive conclusions from the survey. Since each implementation of the dual frame survey provides a portion of the sample with higher response rates based upon more rigorous methods, and a complement with standard RDD methods of cold contact, the investigator can compare results from each of the portions. In short, an added attraction of the design—a feature that can inform the researcher about data quality—is its imbedded experiment affecting nonresponse rates.

Summary and Conclusions

The experimental results show higher response rates and greater interviewer productivity with the use of a telephone directory frame, and

8. The exact question wording was: "In general do you approve or disapprove of the way Ronald Reagan is handling his job as President?"

Table 6. The Effects of Relative Response Rates, Indicated by Advance Letter Treatment, on the Relationship Between Party Identification and Approval of Presidential Performance, Whites Only

Party Identification	Received Letter			Did Not Receive Letter		
	Approve	Disapprove	N	Approve	Disapprove	N
Republicans	95%	5	128	86%	14	87
Independents	81%	19	38	77%	23	35
Democrats	46%	54	105	57%	43	104
Total sample	76%	24	271	72%	28	226
	tau beta = .49			tau beta = .29		

they suggest the utility and advantages of pursuing dual frame designs for telephone surveys. That is, although the list frame covers only about three-quarters of the telephone household population, it can be combined with an RDD sample to produce a survey design that offers higher response rates and more attractive costs.

These findings do not indicate what allocation of sample to the two frames should be used in the dual frame design. An allocation which minimizes the total survey budget can be made an explicit design criterion. The list frame has increased costs for acquisition and mailing which are offset by decreased costs due to improved screening efficiency and lower costs per interview taken. At the same time, the RDD component provides coverage for unlisted numbers which is unavailable in the list frame, although it involves higher screening costs and, therefore, higher costs per interview.

One way to approach these issues is through the evaluation of the cost and error components of surveys which employ a dual frame design (Groves and Lepkowski, 1986). For a given level of available resources, the increased efficiency of the dual frame design will permit a researcher to increase overall sample size or increase the intensity of interviewing efforts at nonresponse reduction. These improvements in data quality can be achieved without appreciable increases in overall survey costs, and they can have an effect upon substantive conclusions as well.

The analysis also suggests that variations in levels of response can affect the existence and magnitude of relationships observed in the resulting data. This is an important question which warrants additional research in order to increase our understanding of the links between data costs and quality.

Finally, the findings presented here may stimulate investigations of other telephone household sample designs which allow even higher proportions of the sample cases to be sent advance letters. Lepkowski and Groves (1986b) describe a two-phase telephone sample design which allowed 62% of the sample cases to be sent an advance letter. In the dual frame design used in the first two experiments described previously, approximately 50% of the sample cases were sent an advance letter. Other sample designs and other uses of the names and addresses available from a list frame may also be possible.

References

Biemer, Paul (1983)
  "Optimal dual frame design: Results of a simulation study." Proceedings of the Survey Research Methods Section, American Statistical Association, 630–635.

Brunner, G. Allen, and Stephen J. Carroll, Jr. (1967)
    "The effect of prior telephone appointments on completion rates and response
    content." Public Opinion Quarterly 31:652–654.
——— (1969)
    "The effect of prior notification on the refusal rate in fixed address surveys."
    Journal of Advertising Research 9:42–44.
Dillman, Don A. (1978)
    Mail and Telephone Surveys. New York: John Wiley and Sons.
Dillman, Don A., Jean G. Gallegos, and James H. Frey (1976)
    "Reducing refusal rates for telephone interviews." Public Opinion Quarterly
    40:66–78.
Goudy, Willis J. (1976)
    "Nonresponse effects on relationships between variables." Public Opinion
    Quarterly 40:360–369.
Groves, Robert M. (1978)
    "An empirical comparison of two telephone sample designs." Journal of Marketing
    Research 15:622–663.
Groves, Robert M., and Robert L. Kahn (1979)
    Surveys by Telephone. New York: Academic Press.
Groves, Robert M., and James M. Lepkowski (1985)
    "Dual frame, mixed mode survey designs." Journal of Official Statistics 1:264–286.
——— (1986)
    "An experimental implementation of a dual frame telephone sample design."
    Proceedings of the Survey Research Methods Section, American Statistical
    Association, 340–345.
Groves, Robert M., and Lou J. Magilavy (1981)
    "Increasing response rates to telephone surveys: A door in the face or foot in the
    door?" Public Opinion Quarterly 44:346–358.
Hartley, H. O. (1962)
    "Multiple frame surveys." Proceedings of the Social Statistics Section, American
    Statistical Association, 203–206.
Lepkowski, James M., and Robert M. Groves (1986a)
    "A mean square error model for dual frame, mixed mode survey design." Journal
    of the American Statistical Association 81:930–937.
——— (1986b)
    "A two phase probability proportional to size design for telephone sampling."
    Proceedings of the Survey Research Methods Section, American Statistical
    Association, 357–362.
O'Neil, Michael (1979)
    "Estimating the nonresponse bias due to refusals in telephone surveys." Public
    Opinion Quarterly 43:218–232.
Smith, Thomas (1984)
    "Estimating nonresponse bias with temporary refusals." Sociological Perspectives
    27:473–489.
Sudman, Seymour (1973)
    "The uses of telephone directories for survey sampling." Journal of Marketing
    Research 10:204–207.
Sykes, Wendy, and Gerald Hoinville (1985)
    Telephone Interviewing on a Survey of Social Attitudes: A Comparison with
    Face-to-Face Procedures. London: Social and Community Planning Research.
Traugott, Michael W. (1987)
    "The importance of persistence in respondent selection for preelection surveys."
    Public Opinion Quarterly 51:48–57.
Waksberg, Joseph (1978)
    "Sampling methods for random digit dialing." Journal of the American Statistical
    Association 73:40–46.

THE QUESTIONNAIRE

More development time is probably spent on the questionnaire than on any other aspect of the typical survey. In part this is because the questionnaire is the least transferable feature of a survey. The sample design and interviewing procedures on one study can frequently be used as is or with minor modification on other studies. When it comes to the questionnaire, however, researchers generally must start from scratch. The resulting lack of standardization contributes to the claim that question writing is an art.

Even so, it has been possible to develop generalizations about the effects of different question types and orders. These generalizations rest on evidence gathered using "split ballot" experiments. In such experiments, random subsamples of a single survey are administered different forms of a questionnaire. Differences in results that exceed sampling error can then be attributed to the differences in the questionnaire forms.

Split ballot experiments date back to the early days of polling when the questionnaire was referred to as the "ballot," usage still customary at the Gallup organization today. The most influential reports of this early work were Hadley Cantril's *Gauging Public Opinion* (1944) and Stanley Payne's *The Art of Asking Questions* (1951).

The major aim of research from this period was to demonstrate the existence of wording or order effects. Almost all the early investigations looked only at marginals, or the overall distribution of responses. The impact of questionnaire changes on relationships between variables went unexamined. In addition, the issue of why effects occurred received little attention.

The focus of more recent work has shifted to the consequences of response effects for relationships between variables and to a search for the factors that underlie the effects. Evidence has mounted that the effects tend to be restricted to marginals and that they only occasionally alter associations among attitudes or between attitudes and demographic characteristics. This is reassuring news in terms of the robustness of conclusions about associations. But the other side of the coin, that subgroups of respondents defined by demographic or attitudinal characteristics are generally affected in similar ways, means that only modest progress has been made in understanding the causes of questionnaire effects.

The first three articles in this section address issues of question wording in the measurement of attitudes. Smith looks at the impact of the word "welfare" as opposed to "assistance to the poor," Presser and Schuman examine the effects of offering a middle alternative, and Alwin and Krosnick compare ratings with rankings. The next two papers, by Sigelman and by Schuman, Kalton, and Ludwig, explore the impact of question sequence or context. The final three papers, by Bradburn and Miles, by Schwarz, Hippler, Deutsch, and Strack, and by Bachman and O'Malley, analyze question variations in asking about the frequency of behaviors and feelings. The response effects turned up in each of these articles suggest that survey respondents pay careful attention to the questions they are asked. It is thus essential for survey researchers both to exercise care in writing questions and to be sensitive to the exact wording of questions in interpreting survey results.

General guides to issues in the questionnaire literature can be found in Schuman and Presser, 1981; Sudman and Bradburn, 1982; and Converse and Presser, 1986. Promising developments in the application of cognitive psychology to the understanding of questionnaire effects are described in Hippler, Schwarz, and Sudman, 1987. Finally, an excellent early POQ paper that is rarely cited but still repays reading is Gallup, 1947.

References

Cantril, Hadley (1944)
   Gauging Public Opinion. Princeton: Princeton University Press.
Converse, Jean M., and Stanley Presser (1986)
   Survey Questions: Handcrafting the Standardized Questionnaire. Beverly Hills, CA:
   Sage Publications.
Gallup, George (1947)
   "The quintamensional plan of questionnaire design." Public Opinion Quarterly
   11:385–393.
Hippler, Hans-J., Norbert Schwarz, and Seymour Sudman (1987)
   Social Information Processing and Survey Methodology. New York:
   Springer-Verlag.
Payne, Stanley (1951)
   The Art of Asking Questions. Princeton: Princeton University Press.
Schuman, Howard, and Stanley Presser (1981)
   Questions and Answers in Attitude Surveys: Experiments on Question Form,
   Wording, and Context. New York: Academic Press.
Sudman, Seymour, and Norman M. Bradburn (1982)
   Asking Questions: A Practical Guide to Questionnaire Design. San Francisco:
   Jossey-Bass.

THAT WHICH WE CALL
WELFARE BY ANY OTHER NAME
WOULD SMELL SWEETER
AN ANALYSIS OF THE
IMPACT OF QUESTION WORDING
ON RESPONSE PATTERNS

TOM W. SMITH

Abstract Responses to survey questions are dependent on the words used in the questions. Sometimes the alteration of words can completely change the response distribution without obviously changing the meaning or intent of the question. This situation occurs when "welfare" is used instead of "poor." In all contexts examined "welfare" produced much more negative and less generous responses than "poor." In addition the two terms appear to tap slightly different dimensions with "welfare" accessing notions of waste and bureaucracy that are untapped or tapped much less by "poor."

Although the order of words in a question and the alteration of "small, simple" words in the query and response categories can alter the perceived meaning and response distribution of a question (Schuman and Presser, 1981; Payne, 1951), it is generally believed that abstract "concept" words that specify the object being evaluated or the state along which the object is being evaluated are particularly susceptible to variation. Fee (1979, 1981), for example, has shown that abstract words in common use in the mass media often mean very different things to different people. "Big government," for example, tapped four major definitional clusters: (1) welfare-statism, (2) corporatism, (3) federal control, and (4) bureaucracy. Similarly Smith (1981) found that "confidence" was defined in four distinct ways as (1) trust, (2) capability, (3) attention to common good, and (4) following respondent's self-interest.

TOM W. SMITH is Senior Study Director at the National Opinion Research Center, University of Chicago. This research was done for the General Social Survey project directed by James A. Davis and Tom W. Smith. The project is supported by the National Science Foundation, Grant No. SES-8118731.

Since the same word can conjure significantly different meanings to different respondents, it is not surprising that different words designed to tap the same object or feeling state can actually serve as significantly different stimuli and trigger different response patterns. Smith (1981) and Lipset and Schneider (1983) have shown that using different descriptors for institutions being ranked on confidence can significantly vary the level of confidence. For example, 46% have a great deal of confidence in "colleges" while only 29% have such confidence in "professors" and 48% have a great deal of confidence in "the military" while only 21% rank "military leaders" as high.

A recent experiment on the General Social Survey (GSS) comparing three different versions of spending priorities scales revealed systematic differences by question form and some large differences between particular referents used (Smith, 1984). The largest observed difference in support for spending was between the traditional category "welfare" and the two variant forms "assistance for the poor" and "caring for the poor." Two of the three forms used in the 1984 experiment (excluding "caring") were again employed on the 1985 survey and again showed a large effect. When we compared these results to other surveys that (1) employed some type of program priority question and (2) inquired about "welfare" (or some variation that used this term) and about "the poor," "the unemployed," or "food stamps" (in one variation or another), we found that the effects were large, similar in magnitude, and persistent across time and survey organization. As Table 1 shows, on average support for more assistance for the poor is 39 percentage points higher than for welfare. Similarly, support for the unemployed always exceeds support for welfare (averaging 12 percentage points), although the margin is somewhat variable. Only support for food stamps is as low or lower than support for welfare.

The welfare/poor contrast is consistently replicated across various other questions as well. The feeling thermometer in Table 2 shows that people on welfare are rated more coolly (negatively) than blacks, poor people, or working men (by 9.9, 19.5, and 25.8 degrees, respectively). Similarly, Table 3 shows that people on welfare are more likely blamed for having too much influence than blacks, poor people, or workingmen (by 0.8%, 24.8%, and 26.2%, respectively). (See also Jaffe, 1978.)

In sum, "welfare" consistently produces much more negative evaluations than "the poor."

One common explanation for the low level of public support for welfare (and by extension for its low standing versus help for the poor) is that welfare is associated with minorities in the public mind. Wright (1977) argued that "welfare," like law and order or local/community control of schools, is a code word for racism. He showed that next to spending for "improving the condition of blacks," spending on "wel-

Table I. Percentages Favoring More Assistance/Spending for Welfare/Poor

Source	Date	Poor	Welfare	Unemployed	Food Stamps
MAP[a]	1968	61.0	32.0	—	—
		N.A.	N.A.	—	—
Harris[b]	12/72	62.0	22.0	—	—
		N.A.	N.A.	—	—
HF[c](Gallup)	1976	—	28.8	34.7	—
		—	(625)	(625)	—
HF[d](Gallup)	1976	—	25.3	45.7	25.6
		—	(524)	(524)	(524)
Yank.[e]	1/76	51.0	17.5	—	—
		(951)	(951)	—	—
Harris[f]	3/76	—	51.2	69.1	—
		—	(1517)	(1515)	—
MAP(Yank.)[e]	1982	59.0	25.0	—	—
		N.A.	N.A.	—	—
ISR[g]	Fall/1982	—	19.3	26.3	14.5
		—	(1407)	(1408)	(1407)
GSS[h]	3/84	69.3/64.0	24.6	—	—
		(473)(427)	(471)	—	—
GSS[i]	3/85	64.7	19.3	—	—
		(762)	(719)	—	—

[a] MAP = Monitoring Attitudes of the Public by Institute of Life Insurance. Percentages wanting government to do more for "the poor" and "people on welfare."
[b] Percentages for increase for "helping the poor" and "people on welfare."
[c] HF = Hopes and Fears surveys conducted by Gallup. Percentages for increase for "welfare program to help low-income families," "program to help the unemployed," and "program to provide food stamps to low-income families to help them buy food."
[d] Percentages for increase for "welfare program to help low-income families," "program to help the unemployed," and "program to provide food stamps to low-income families to help them buy food."
[e] Yank. = Yankelovich, Skelley, and White. Percentages for more spending for "help for the poor" and "welfare."
[f] Percentages saying abolishment of programs would be a very serious loss for "jobs for unemployed" and "welfare."
[g] ISR = Institute for Social Research, University of Michigan election study. Percentages saying spending too little for "welfare," "unemployment compensation," and "food stamps."
[h] Percentages saying spending too little for "caring for the poor"/"assistance to the poor" and "welfare."
[i] Percentages saying spending too little for "assistance to the poor" and "welfare."

fare" was most strongly associated with race of respondents. Replication of his finding using the 1984 and 1985 GSS confirms this pattern. But "welfare" is no more associated with race than "assistance to the poor" is. Similarly, a comparison between spending on welfare and the poor and 20 racial items from the 1984 and 1985 GSS showed that for both items more spending was associated with more tolerant racial attitudes, but there were no differences in the magnitude of the associa-

Table 2. Feeling Thermometer (Mean Degrees) Towards Groups[a]

	1972	1974	1976	1980	1984
Poor people	73.6	77.2	71.5	75.2	71.2
People on welfare	—	—	54.4	52.2	52.8
Blacks	64.0	65.5	60.8	64.2	64.2
Workingmen[b]	78.6	—	75.3	82.8	—

SOURCE: 1972, 1974, 1976, 1980, 1984 American National Election Studies, Institute for Social Research, University of Michigan.

[a] "Here is a card on which there is something that looks like a thermometer. We call it a ''feeling thermometer'' because it measures your feelings towards these people. Here is how it works. If you don't feel particularly warm or cold towards a person, then you should place him in the middle of the thermometer, at the 50 degree mark. If you have a warm feeling toward a person, or feel favorably toward him, you would give him a score somewhere between 50° and 100°, depending on how warm your feeling is toward that person. On the other hand, if you don't feel very favorable toward a person—that is, if you don't care too much for him—then you would place him somewhere between 0 and 50 degrees. Of course, if you don't know too much about a person, just tell me and we'll go on to the next name. We'd also like to get your feelings about some groups in American society, using the feeling thermometer just as we did for the leaders. If we come to a group you don't know much about, just tell me and we'll move on to the next one." Above is 1974 version. Small variations occur in other years.

[b] In 1980, workingmen and workingwomen.

Table 3. Comparisons of Group Influence: Percentage Having Too Much Influence

	1972	1974	1976
Poor people	5.4 (2164)	3.7 (2469)	6.5 (2396)
Blacks	27.2 (2158)	29.8 (2464)	30.6 (2392)
People on welfare	27.3 (2146)	30.1 (2468)	32.6 (2390)
Workingmen	3.2 (2160)	— —	4.4 (2394)

SOURCE: 1972, 1974, 1976 American National Election Studies, Institute for Social Research, University of Michigan. "Some people think that certain groups have too much influence in American life and politics, while other people feel that certain groups don't have as much influence as they deserve. On this card [1976:Here] are three statements about how much influence a group might have. For each group I read to you, just tell me the number of the statement that best says how you feel."

tions by descriptor (1984: welfare = 0.228, poor = 0.237, 1985: welfare = 0.254, poor = 0.246—average gammas). While this could be interpreted to mean that both "poor" and "welfare" are equivalent racist code words, we doubt Americans are such accomplished cryptographers that these and dozens of other words are merely ciphers for racism. In any event, the fact that *no* difference in racial association appears between the two terms indicates that racial connotations with the term "welfare," as opposed to "poor," do not explain the large difference in support that these two terms elicit. (See also AuClaire, 1984.)

A second explanation suggests that "welfare" is seen as a wasteful program that encourages sloth and sponging. The perception of public assistance as a boon to the lazy and cheats has long existed. Back in the nineteen thirties the WPA (Works Progress/Projects Administration) was derisively referred to as standing for "We Piddle Around." Schiltz (1970) has shown that the public has consistently labeled public assistance as wasteful, excessive, and disproductive. The negative connotation that "welfare" carries is apparent from such terms as "welfare queen" and "welfare Cadillac."[1]

To examine whether such connotations are influencing the public's evaluation of "welfare" vs. the "poor," we studied the relationship of these spending items to measures of political orientation and attitudes towards social welfare and redistributive actions of government. Overall, the "poor" spending items have stronger associations than "welfare" in 18 of 21 comparisons on the 1984 and 1985 GSS, averaging gammas in 1984 of 0.287 for "assistance to the poor," 0.265 for "caring for the poor," and 0.204 for "welfare" (see Table 4). In general, the "welfare" associations are similar in direction and slightly smaller in magnitude than the "poor" associations. The one notable and instructive difference is on taxes. Those who oppose more spending for the poor tend to rate their tax load as more onerous than those who favor more welfare spending. (The insignificant association in 1985 is an outlier since on four of six surveys tax is significantly associated to welfare spending and gamma averaged −0.125.) For spending for the poor the associations are reversed. Those who oppose more spending for the poor are slightly less likely to rate their taxes as too high. This suggests that "welfare" triggers more concerns about the cost of public assistance service and perhaps more of a concern with waste, especially in the sense of fraud and program abuse.

1. A survey of nine dictionaries reveals that use of the term "welfare" to refer to government or private activity concerning the disadvantaged dates only from 1904 and that the use of the term to refer to relief payments was not recognized until the mid-1960s. No dictionary indicated any recognition of any negative connotations associated with the term.

Table 4. Association between Welfare/Poor Spending and Other Variables (Gammas/Probability)

	Welfare		Assistance to the Poor		Caring for the Poor
	1984	1985	1984	1985	1984
Political Items					
Party identification (PARTYID)	.212	.228	.331	.340	.322
	(.003)	(.000)	(.000)	(.000)	(.001)
Political ideology (POLVIEWS)	.128	.220	.285	.385	.188
	(.044)	(.000)	(.001)	(.000)	(.009)
Redistribution and Entitlement Items					
Govt do more (HELPNOT)	.302	—	.289	—	.316
	(.000)		(.003)		(.000)
Govt health care (HELPSICK)	.280	—	.288	—	.353
	(.000)		(.000)		(.000)
Govt help poor (HELPPOOR)	.355	—	.506	—	.464
	(.000)		(.000)		(.000)
Govt equalize incomes (EQWLTH)	.235	—	.366	—	.349
	(.000)		(.000)		(.000)
Govt care for all (GOVCARE)	−.374	—	−.396	—	−.376
	(.000)		(.000)		(.001)
Must look out for self (EQUAL1)	−.113	—	−.051	—	.034
	(.628)		(.424)		(.542)

Profits benefit all (EQUAL2)	−.068 (.615)	—	−.275 (.012)	—	−.137 (.049)
Govt run economy (EQUAL3)	.181 (.050)	—	.257 (.000)	—	.386 (.000)
Govt meet needs (EQUAL4)	.257 (.002)	—	.356 (.000)	—	.437 (.000)
Welfare disincentive (EQUAL5)	−.203 (.005)	—	−.281 (.005)	—	−.170 (.057)
All can live well (EQUAL6)	−.297 (.000)	—	−.284 (.003)	—	−.293 (.024)
Profits fairly divided (EQUAL7)	−.091 (.326)	—	−.273 (.000)	—	−.254 (.045)
Success is earned (EQUAL8)	.049 (.289)	—	−.110 (.175)	—	.055 (.853)
Own efforts count (USCLASS4)	.073 (.228)	—	.259 (.015)	—	.236 (.001)
Decent life for all (USCLASS5)	.263 (.000)	—	.387 (.000)	—	.369 (.000)
Taxes too high (TAX)	−.186 (.016)	−.003 (.544)	.176 (.005)	.123 (.005)	.037 (.428)
Anomia Items					
Aver. man worse off (ANOMIA5)	.170 (.024)	.188 (.001)	.380 (.000)	.268 (.000)	.289 (.001)
Future bleak (ANOMIA6)	−.047 (.267)	.073 (.082)	.368 (.000)	.200 (.007)	.189 (.006)
Officials don't care (ANOMIA7)	−.196 (.035)	.084 (.015)	.240 (.026)	.213 (.006)	.279 (.012)

While items explicitly tapping concerns about government waste were lacking, we looked at three anomia items. On the "poor" spending items, opposition to more spending was associated with socially integrated (nonanomic) responses. This association prevails because those with lower SES are both more alienated and more in need (and in favor) of these types of governmental benefits. Support for more welfare spending was either less strongly associated or the relationship actually reversed. We believe that the association with welfare is attenuated and/or reversed because some alienated people see "welfare" as a waste rather than a potential benefit and therefore shift their positive support for the poor to a negative vote on welfare.[2]

We have considerably less information about the differences between support for "welfare" and references to the unemployed. It is well established, however, that Americans are much more in favor of workfare programs than welfare (Schiltz, 1970; Erskine, 1975). For example, in a 1968 Gallup Poll 31.9% endorsed welfare payments of up to $3200 for families of four while 77.2% backed the government guaranteeing enough work for a family wage earner to earn up to $3200. The unemployment references may benefit from both avoiding the negative connotation of welfare as well as gaining some positive association with workfare programs.

Food stamps are ranked at a low level comparable to welfare. While one might assume that the program's face association with preventing hunger might encourage public support, it does not apparently have any more appeal than welfare. Like welfare it may be tarred by images as a wasteful, mismanaged program open to abuse.

Overall the term "welfare" obviously carries more negative connotations than does "poor." If we think of a continuum in which the least favorable descriptor might be "loafers and bums" and the most favorable terms might be the "truly needy" or "widows and orphans," it would appear that "welfare" would fall nearer the loafer end (maybe rather close to it) while "poor" would be towards the "truly needy."

Poor also seems to be a more valid measure of support for the welfare state, in particular of support for programs to equalize conditions and provide for the care of people. Welfare clearly taps these same concerns but perhaps not as cleanly. It seems to conjure up a second concept of waste and perhaps an antibureaucratic image as well. Welfare receives more negative ratings because of these additional associations and shows lower associations with questions dealing with redistribution and entitlements. Presumably welfare would correlate more highly than poor with questions on government waste and red tape.

These large differences have important linguistic lessons for writing survey questions. The welfare/poor distinction illustrates the major

2. Welfare may also suffer by emphasizing the program rather than the problems. On this point see Smith (1984).

impact that different words can have on response patterns. It argues for more systematic investigation of the impact of such wording differences and is another example in favor of using multiple measures of phenomena. It also serves as a stark warning about the possible policy and scientific misapplication of survey data. Taking the welfare item alone might lead a social scientist to conclude that the public was callous towards the poor and perhaps backed a social Darwinism approach to poverty. It might lead a politician to decide that public assistance programs, lacking public support, could (and should?) be cut with impunity. Opposite errors could be made if only the "poor" item was used. An investigator might conclude that concern about ending poverty was the public's top concern, while welfare administrators might think there was strong public support for their programs. In truth the situation is much more complex and even both items reveal only small slices of the public's attitudes towards public assistance.

References

AuClaire, Philip A. (1984)
    "Public attitudes toward social welfare expenditures." Social Work 29:139–44.
Erskine, Hazel (1975)
    "Government role in welfare." Public Opinion Quarterly 39:257–74.
Fee, Joan Lesley Flynn (1979)
    "Symbols and attitudes: How people think about politics." Ph.d. dissertation, University of Chicago.
Fee, J. F. (1981)
    "Symbols in survey questions: Solving the problem of multiple word meanings." Political Methodology 7:71–95.
Joffe, Natalie (1978)
    "Attitudes toward public welfare programs and recipients in the United States." In Lester M. Salamon (ed.), Welfare: The Elusive Consensus. New York: Praeger.
Lipset, Seymour M., and William Schneider (1983)
    The Confidence Gap—Business, Labor, and Government in the Public Mind. New York: The Free Press.
Payne, Stanley L. (1951)
    The Art of Asking Questions. Princeton: Princeton University Press.
Schiltz, Michael E. (1970)
    Public Attitudes Toward Social Security, 1935–1965. Washington, DC: U.S. Government Printing Office.
Schuman, Howard, and Stanley Presser (1981)
    Questions and Answers in Attitude Surveys: Experiments on Question Form, Wording, and Context. New York: Academic Press.
Smith, Tom W. (1981)
    "Can we have confidence in confidence? Revisited." in D. F. Johnston (ed.), Measurement of Subjective Phenomena. Washington, DC: U.S. Government Printing Office.
Smith, Tom W. (1984)
    "A preliminary analysis of methodological experiments on the 1984 GSS." GSS Technical Report No. 49. Chicago: National Opinion Research Center.
Wright, Gerald, Jr. (1977)
    "Racism and welfare policy in America." Social Science Quarterly 57:718–30.

The Measurement of
a Middle Position
in Attitude Surveys

STANLEY PRESSER AND HOWARD SCHUMAN

MANY SURVEY QUESTIONS require respondents to choose between two contrasting opinion alternatives. Frequently there is a logical middle position that some respondents might prefer to either end of the implicit attitude dimension. For instance, whether one is liberal or conservative could be answered by "middle-of-the-road"; whether laws on marijuana should be more strict or less strict implies the possibility of "same as now"; whether the U.S. government provides too much or too little aid to another country can lead to the answer "right amount." Survey investigators must decide whether such a middle alternative should be built explicitly into a question , or merely accepted when offered spontaneously, or even discouraged altogether.

Abstract Five split-ballot experiments, plus replications, were carried out in several national surveys to compare the effects of offering or omitting a middle alternative in forced-choice attitude questions. Explicitly offering a middle position significantly increases the size of that category, but tends not to otherwise affect univariate distributions. The relation of intensity to the middle position is somewhat greater on Offered forms than on Omitted forms (less intense respondents being more affected by question form than those who feel more strongly), but in general form does not alter the relationship between an item and a number of other respondent characteristics. Finally, in one instance there is evidence that form can change the conclusion about whether two attitude items are related, but the results are of uncertain reliability.

Stanley Presser is Research Associate, Institute for Research in Social Science, and Visiting Assistant Professor of Sociology, The University of North Carolina. Howard Schuman is Professor of Sociology and Program Director, Survey Research Center, The University of Michigan. This research was supported by grants from the National Science Foundation (Soc76–15040) and the National Institute of Mental Health (MH–24266). We are grateful to Jean M. Converse and Jacob Ludwig III for commenting on an earlier draft. At various points, Otis Dudley Duncan, Graham Kalton, and William M. Mason provided valuable help with problems related to our analysis, though the authors alone are responsible for any errors. An earlier version was presented at the 1978 American Statistical Association Meetings.

Our primary concern is whether such decisions by survey investigators have consequences for the conclusions drawn from attitude surveys. After documenting the fact that the presence or absence of an explicit middle alternative generally affects the proportion of such responses, we consider two types of possible consequences. First, is the univariate distribution of the other alternatives altered significantly by the movement of respondents into or out of a middle position? Second, does the relation of an item to other variables change importantly depending upon whether a middle alternative is offered?

Related to these practical questions are theoretical issues having to do with the nature of the middle position in a set of attitudinal alternatives. Three hypotheses are implied by the way the middle position is handled in the wording of questions. First, when survey investigators decide against offering an explicit middle alternative, they are usually assuming that the middle category consists largely of responses from those who lean toward one or the other polar alternatives, though perhaps with little intensity. Thus it is legitimate to press respondents to choose one of these alternatives, rather than allowing them to take refuge in a middle position. Second, some investigators omit the middle alternative in the belief that it tends to attract people who, having no opinion on the issue, find it easier to choose a seemingly noncommittal position than to say "don't know." Third, investigators who do offer a middle alternative are probably assuming that respondents who opt for it really do favor the middle position, and if forced to choose a polar alternative will contribute some form of random or systematic error to the distribution.

As part of a larger project on the effects of question form and wording (Schuman and Presser, 1977), we designed a series of middle alternative experiments to address these issues. Our main method of investigation is what has traditionally been called the "split-ballot." Two forms of an item, administered to random subsamples of the same survey, are compared in each experiment: on the Offered form a middle alternative is explicitly read to respondents; on the Omitted form, no middle alternative is presented, although it is accepted if given by the respondent.[1]

---

[1] An "If Volunteered" middle alternative response box was included on Omitted forms, and interviewers were instructed to accept that answer if given spontaneously. This instruction may reduce slightly the size of the form effect, compared to the effect produced if interviewers had been encouraged to try to force respondents into one of the polar alternatives, accepting another response only as a last resort. The practice we followed deliberately confines the experiments to question form differences, since variations in interviewer practices would involve other factors difficult to standardize.

Figure 1 presents the exact wording for all our experiments. The Marijuana item was adapted from a 1972 Gallup survey, the Local Education item comes from the Institute for Social Research (ISR) Election Studies, and the Divorce item appears regularly in the National Opinion Research Center (NORC) General Social Survey. The other two questions (Vietnam and Liberal/Conservative) were modeled on frequently asked questions about those subjects. The five experiments (plus replications) were carried out as part of Survey Research Center and NORC national surveys: 1974 and 1978 face-to-face surveys, a 1976 survey conducted partly face-to-face and partly by phone (see Groves and Kahn, 1979) and 1976, 1977, and 1978 telephone surveys. (Letters and digits are used to indicate the survey organization and time of survey, e.g., SRC–74F indicates the 1974 fall survey carried out by the Survey Research Center.)[2]

Effects of the Middle Alternative on Middle Responses

The only previous middle alternative split-ballot experiments that we know of were carried out in the 1940s. In their compilation of wording experiments, Rugg and Cantril (Cantril, 1944:33–34) provide the marginals for two such comparisons. In one, offering the middle category increases the choice of it by about 30 percent; in the other, by only 3 percent. Tamulonis (1947:68–73) presents four additional examples, all of which show substantial shifts in the middle position, ranging from 16 percent to 52 percent. Finally, Stember and Hyman (1949–50) report a middle alternative split-ballot experiment that shows an increase in the middle position of 16 percent.

The results of our own 10 experiments are presented in Table 1.[3] Each of the 10 shows a highly significant increase ($p < .001$) in the middle category when it is offered explicitly, with the increases rang-

---

[2] Questionnaire forms were randomized by cover sheet instructions so that the randomization occurs within interviewer. (For the 1974 survey there were actually three forms, but except for the Liberal/Conservative experiment as described below, two of the forms were identical for the middle alternative experiments.) Response rates for the surveys varied from about 50 percent to 75 percent. The lower figures were on the telephone surveys, most of which were composed of recontact samples from earlier face-to-face studies. Thus their response rates are a function of the original response rate, the proportion giving telephone numbers, and the recontact response rate. A comparison of the results based on the lower response rates with those from the studies with higher response rates turned up no differences. Likewise, the experimental comparison of mode of administration (telephone vs. face-to-face) in the 1976 survey showed no differences for the middle alternative experiment.

[3] Table 1 and all succeeding tables omit responses coded "other" and N.A., which together average (over the 10 experiments) less than 2 percent of the total. In no case is the difference by form in this missing data component greater than 1.7 percent, and it averages less than 1 percent.

Omitted Forms

In your opinion, should the penalties for using marijuana be <u>more</u> strict or <u>less</u> strict than they are now?

| 1. MORE STRICT | 5. LESS STRICT | 3. <u>(IF VOLUNTEERED)</u> ABOUT SAME AS NOW |

Looking back, do you think our government did <u>too much</u> to help the South Vietnamese government in the war, or <u>not enough</u> to help the South Vietnamese government?

| 1. TOO MUCH | 5. NOT ENOUGH | 3. <u>(IF VOLUNTEERED)</u> RIGHT AMOUNT |

On most political issues, would you say you are on the <u>liberal</u> side or on the <u>conservative</u> side?

| 1. LIBERAL | 5. CONSERVATIVE | 3. <u>(IF VOLUNTEERED)</u> MIDDLE-OF-ROAD, HALF-WAY BETWEEN |

Do you feel that the federal government has too much or too little control over local education?

| 1. TOO MUCH | 5. TOO LITTLE | 3. <u>(IF VOLUNTEERED)</u> RIGHT AMOUNT |

Should divorce in this country be easier or more difficult to obtain than it is now?

| 1. EASIER | 2. MORE DIFFICULT | 3. STAY AS IT IS |

Figure 1. Middle Alternative Split Ballots

ing from 11 to 20 percentage points in seven of the cases. The other three cases all involve the question on Liberal/Conservative self-identification and reveal a much larger increase of 22 to 39 percentage points, possibly because on this issue the offered "middle-of-the-road" response is a socially well-crystallized one. If this last explanation is correct, then the fact that the middle category on the Liberal/Conservative Omitted form is not much larger than it is for that form of the other items demonstrates how readily most respondents accept the constraints of the Omitted form.

Effects of the Number of Other Categories on the Frequency of Middle Responses

Do respondents who move into the middle position when it is offered actually lean toward one of the polar alternatives? If so, then

Offered Forms

In your opinion, should the penalties for using marijuana be <u>more</u> strict, <u>less</u> strict, or <u>about the same</u> as they are now?

| 1. MORE STRICT | 5. LESS STRICT | 3. ABOUT SAME AS NOW |

Looking back, do you think our government did <u>too much</u> to help the South Vietnamese government in the war, <u>not enough</u> to help the South Vietnamese government, or was it about the <u>right amount</u>?

| 1. TOO MUCH | 5. NOT ENOUGH | 3. RIGHT AMOUNT |

On most political issues, would you say you are on the <u>liberal</u> side, on the <u>conservative</u> side, or <u>middle-of-the-road</u>?

| 1. LIBERAL | 5. CONSERVATIVE | 3. MIDDLE-OF-ROAD |

Do you feel that the federal government has too much, too little, or the right amount of control over local education?

| 1. TOO MUCH | 5. TOO LITTLE | 3. RIGHT AMOUNT |

Should divorce in this country be easier to obtain, more difficult to obtain, or stay as it is now?

| 1. EASIER | 2. MORE DIFFICULT | 3. STAY AS IS |

Figure 1. (continued)

we should be able to decrease the size of the Offered middle category (and therefore the size of the form effect) by providing alternatives between the polar positions and the middle point. However, if such respondents truly subscribe to the middle ground, then offering intermediate categories should have no impact on the size of the Offered middle category.

We were able to test this with data from one of our experiments. In SRC–74F, in addition to asking the two forms of the Liberal/ Conservative item already presented, we included a third form with a 5-point scale: "On most political issues would you say you are liberal, somewhat liberal, middle-of-the road, somewhat conservative, or conservative?" Although the size of the middle category on this 5-point Offered form (41.4 percent) is still much larger than on the Omitted form (16.2 percent), it is significantly smaller than on the 3-point Offered form (53.7 percent). Offering the "somewhat liberal"

Table 1. Response by Question Form

	Omitted	Offered
Marijuana (SRC-1974F)		
More strict	61.0%	55.8%
Less strict	27.0	19.8
About same as now	7.9	19.6
Don't know	4.0	4.7
	99.9%	99.9%
	(1014)	(489)
Marijuana (SRC-1976W)		
More strict	54.6%	43.5%
Less strict	31.6	30.9
About same as now	9.3	22.4
Don't know	4.6	3.3
	100.1%	100.1%
	(637)	(612)
Marijuana (SRC-1977S)		
More strict	49.1%	41.8%
Less strict	41.8	30.6
About same as now	6.1	25.8
Don't know	2.9	1.8
	99.9%	100.0%
	(603)	(562)
Vietnam (SRC-1974F)		
Too much	64.1%	56.2%
Not enough	9.9	8.4
Right amount	15.4	26.1
Don't know	10.5	9.4
	99.9%	100.1%
	(986)	(479)
Vietnam (SRC-1978W)		
Too much	68.4%	57.8%
Not enough	13.0	10.9
Right amount	8.4	22.5
Don't know	10.1	8.7
	99.9%	99.9%
	(621)	(550)
Liberal/Conservative (SRC-1974F)		
Liberal	33.1%	16.9%
Conservative	44.4	24.5
Middle of road	16.2	53.7
Don't know	6.3	4.8
	100.0%	99.9%
	(507)	(497)
Liberal/Conservative (SRC-1976S)		
Liberal	29.2%	15.8%
Conservative	50.4	27.3
Middle of Road	12.0	50.8
Don't know	8.3	6.0
	99.9%	99.9%
	(1562)	(1489)

Table 1. (continued)

	Omitted	Offered
Liberal/Conservative (SRC-1978W)		
Liberal	28.9%	27.1%
Conservative	59.5	40.8
Middle of road	5.4	27.5
Don't know	6.2	4.6
	100.0%	100.0%
	(627)	(564)
Local Education (SRC-1976W)		
Too much	53.6%	44.7%
Too little	18.2	15.6
Right amount	13.7	28.8
Don't know	14.5	10.8
	100.0%	99.9%
	(627)	(617)
Divorce (NORC-1978W)		
Easier	28.9%	22.7%
More Difficult	44.5	32.7
Stay as is	21.7	40.2
Don't know	4.9	4.3
	100.0%	99.9%
	(760)	(770)

and "somewhat conservative" categories reduces the number of respondents who move into the middle position though it also draws
significantly from the "liberal" and "conservative" categories.[4] It is
possible that the provision of even more intermediate categories
around the midpoint (say, a 7-point scale) would further reduce the
size of the middle category, and such experiments would be useful.
For the present it appears that at least some respondents who choose
the middle category on our 3-point Offered forms do lean toward one

[4] The entire 5-point response distribution is:

1. Liberal	9.6%
2. Somewhat liberal	11.1
3. Middle of road	41.4
4. Somewhat conservative	18.8
5. Conservative	12.9
6. DK	6.1
	99.9%
	(488)

The Liberal/Conservative Offered form in SRC–78W also contained these same five
categories, which have been collapsed in Tables 1 and 4. (The 78W uncollapsed
frequencies, using the category numbers above, are (1) 66, (2) 87, (4) 137, and (5) 93.) In
SRC–76S the Liberal/Conservative Offered form contained only three positions.

of the polar positions, but most continue to choose the middle position even when intermediate categories are offered.[5]

Effects of the Middle Alternative on Other Categories

Depending on the item, between 11 and 39 percent of the total sample would take the middle position on the Offered form but move into other categories on the Omitted form. How do these individuals respond on the Omitted form? One hypothesis is that they give responses on the Omitted form much like other respondents. If this happens, the marginals for the Omitted and Offered forms, *excluding all middle responses,* will not differ beyond sampling error.

Data in Table 1 allow one to test this null hypothesis for all the experiments, and in no case can it be rejected. The chi-square (with two degrees of freedom) produced by comparing each pair of Offered and Omitted forms excluding all middle responses is never significant.[6] Thus, apart from the size of the middle category itself, one would draw the same conclusions from the marginals for one form as from the marginals for the other form. Moreover, the same holds for the experiments presented three decades ago by Rugg and Cantril (1944), Tamulonis (1947), and Stember and Hyman (1949–1950): not one of their comparisons reveals a significant change in univariate distributions once middle responses are excluded. These findings are striking in consistency, for they suggest that moving substantial numbers of respondents between middle and other (mainly polar) positions does not generally change the relative distributions among the latter.[7]

The overall tests just reported may obscure one finer implication of the middle option—its effect on the Don't Know (DK) category. It is sometimes claimed that the middle category will attract persons who

[5] After this paper was substantially complete we learned of another analysis of middle alternative experiments by Kalton et al. (1979). They suggest that the increase in the size of the middle category on Offered forms like those used here may be partly due to the fact that the middle option is listed at the end of the question. To determine if respondents are affected by such a position effect (or "recency" bias), we have just carried out two experiments varying the order of presentation of the middle alternative in the Offered form of the Vietnam and Divorce items. The first yielded negative results, the second positives ones, more people choosing the middle position when it was listed last. Thus *some* of the form difference analyzed here may be due to the placement of the middle option, not simply whether it is offered.

[6] If all DK's are also excluded, then, with one exception, the comparisons continue to be nonsignificant. The exception is the 1978 Liberal/Conservative experiment in which $\chi^2 = 5.20$, df $= 1$, $p < .05$, comparing the liberal to conservative ratio by form. There is no hint of the same difference in either of the other two Liberal/Conservative experiments and so we regard it as a chance finding.

[7] However, some of the Kalton et al. (1979) experiments, which use items about health, do show form effects on the polar ratio. Thus our findings here cannot be generalized to all other items. The exceptions demonstrate how unwise it is ever to assert the null hypothesis with regard to question form effects.

might otherwise say DK but prefer to give a more substantive-sounding response. One implication of this hypothesis is that the proportion of DK responses should go down on the form that includes an explicit middle category. A review of Table 1 shows that a decrease in DK does occur for 9 of the 10 comparisons, which would have happened on a chance basis less than 2 times out of 100. At the same time, all the individual differences are quite small, the largest (and the only one that is significant) being 3.7 percent and the average being less than 2 percent. Thus there is evidence that offering the middle position is linked to frequency of DK, but also that the connection is quite weak. Moreover, the correct interpretation of the DK difference by form is not necessarily that explicit middle alternatives attract DK respondents. It is equally possible that question forms omitting a middle alternative increase DK levels by forcing persons who hold the middle position to say DK when they find it impossible to choose one of the specified alternatives. Distinguishing between these two possibilities would be theoretically interesting, but the tiny number of respondents involved means that neither process is an important factor in producing the form differences in the size of the middle alternative itself.

Effects of the Middle Alternative on Associations

Although form differences in marginals are of some importance, the more critical issue for survey research is whether associations of variables differ significantly in nature or magnitude depending upon omission or inclusion of a middle alternative. For example, is education related differently to the "same" item when it omits rather than offers a middle alternative? If so, investigators will have to take account of this aspect of form in designing, analyzing, and reporting survey questions and responses. On the other hand, if no important differences in relations occur, inclusion or exclusion of a middle alternative can be treated as a matter of administrative convenience. This type of issue has not been thoroughly studied before: Rugg and Cantril (1944) do not proceed beyond the examination of marginals referred to above; Tamulonis (1947) does raise the issue but summarizes her results in a generalized fashion that makes their evaluation difficult; and the Stember and Hyman (1949–50) analysis is limited to a single item and its relation to the special problem of interviewer effects.

RELATIONS TO BACKGROUND VARIABLES

We investigated several ways in which Omitted and Offered forms might produce different results in associations with other variables.

Our first hypothesis about form differences in response was that they should be related to education. We expected less educated respondents to be more influenced by whether or not a middle alternative was offered, on the assumption that a middle position among the better educated would be more "crystallized" and thus insisted upon regardless of question wording. If this were true, then the shift of a disproportionate number of the less educated from the polar positions to the middle position on the Offered form would also alter the correlation between education and middle vs. polar positions on that form.

In fact, there is little evidence for this hypothesis. Conclusions about the relation of education to the middle category of a particular item are generally unaffected by whether or not that category is explicitly offered. A representative example is presented in Table 2. As may be observed there, the less educated are more apt to be "middle of the roaders" but this is equally true on both forms of the Liberal/Conservative question.[8]

On other items, the simple bivariate relation between education and the middle response is reversed (e.g., on Marijuana it is the more

Table 2. Liberal/Conservative by Education by Form (SRC–1974F)

	Education		
	0–11	*12*	*13+*
Omitted form			
Liberal	25.0%	31.1%	45.7%
Middle of road	23.4	20.1	10.8
Conservative	51.6	48.8	43.5
	100.0%	100.0%	100.0%
	(124)	(164)	(186)
	$\chi^2 = 19.77$ df $= 4, p < .001$		
Offered form			
Liberal	10.4%	14.5%	25.8%
Middle of road	64.9	63.8	44.6
Conservative	24.6	21.7	29.6
	99.9%	100.0%	100.0%
	(134)	(152)	(186)
	$\chi^2 = 21.75$, df $= 4, p < .001$		
	Three-way interaction: $\chi^2 = 0.44$, df $= 4$, n.s.		

[8] In testing for the difference in association between two tables, i.e., for three-variable interactions, we have used the method developed by Goodman (1971) for the analysis of multiway contingency tables. All chi-squares reported are likelihood ratio statistics computed with the computer program ECTA. The probability levels reported must be regarded as approximations, since we have used SRS tests even though our samples involve some clustering. We computed more exact sampling errors (taking into account clustering) for all bivariate results (form by response) from our first survey; in no case did this change an inference.

educated who are apt to be in the middle), but the reversal is obtained on both question forms. Thus the important point is that findings about the association between education and the middle position on an item are typically invariant with respect to question form.

We were also able to test variants of the education hypothesis by measuring information about, and interest in, the general kinds of political issues that served as the content of these experiments. The measure of information consisted of three items asking for identification of public figures (e.g., William O. Douglas), and the indicator of interest was a single question asking how much attention the respondent paid to national and international news. Although these tests were restricted to the three experiments in SRC–74F, they showed little evidence of an interaction between form, response, and information or interest.[9]

Holding aside the middle category, the relations of polar categories to these variables also do not typically differ by form. For example, if one repercentages the figures in Table 2, excluding all middle responses, then the better educated are more likely to identify as liberal, the less educated as conservative, irrespective of item form. Thus, in general, form does not affect inferences about the relation between attitudinal items and a number of different background variables.

INTENSITY AND CHOICE OF THE MIDDLE ALTERNATIVE

Our second hypothesis about form differences in response was that persons feeling less intense about an issue should be attracted to the middle alternative, hence the Offered form should more completely remove such respondents from polar categories. An implication of this reasoning is that intensity of opinion should be more sharply related to middle vs. polar positions on the Offered form than on the Omitted form.

We tested this hypothesis by including intensity measures with three of our experiments—the two Marijuana replications and the initial Vietnam experiment. After each of these questions was answered, respondents were asked either, "How strongly do you feel about this issue: quite strongly or not so strongly?" or, for the second Marijuana replication, "How important is a candidate's position on penalties for marijuana use when you decide how to vote in an election—is it one

---

[9] We also examined three other background variables widely used in survey analysis (sex, age, and race) and generally found them to be related to response in the same way on the two question forms. For presentation of many of these results for most of the experiments, see Presser (1977).

of the most important factors you would consider, a very important factor, somewhat important, or not too important?'' As can be seen in Table 3, in each case the difference in the relation to intensity is as expected: stronger on the Offered form. Although the size of these form differences is not great (in no single case is it clearly significant), the results are consistent in direction in three independent surveys.

The tendency for low intensity to be somewhat more strongly related to the middle position on the Offered form than on the Omitted can be stated in another way: the form effect is larger among less intense respondents than among more intense individuals. We interpret this to mean that people who have more definite or "crystallized" opinions on an issue are less likely to be influenced by variations in the categories offered.[10] But though our original hypothesis receives support, it should be noted that even respondents who claim high intensity show some form effect.

Table 3. Response (Polar Alternatives vs. Middle) by Item Intensity by Form

	Omitted Form		Offered Form	
Intensity	Polar Alternatives	Middle Alternative	Polar Alternatives	Middle Alternative
Marijuana (SRC–1976W):				
Very strongly	410	34	356	74
Not so strongly	137	24	99	61
	$\chi^2 = 6.61$, df $= 1$,		$\chi^2 = 27.05$, df $= 1$,	
	$p < .02$, $Q = .36$		$p < .0001$, $Q = .50$	
	Three-way interaction: $\chi^2 = 0.93$, df $= 1$, n.s.			
Marijuana (SRC–1977S):				
One of most important + Very important[a]	163	7	159	17
Somewhat important + Not too important[a]	369	29	241	124
	$\chi^2 = 2.18$, df $= 1$,		$\chi^2 = 41.16$, df $= 1$,	
	n.s., $Q = .29$		$p < .0001$, $Q = .66$	
	Three-way interaction: $\chi^2 = 3.24$, df $= 1$, $p < .10$			
Vietnam (SRC–1974F):				
Very strongly	515	70	234	51
Not so strongly	206	77	69	69
	$\chi^2 = 29.84$, df $= 1$,		$\chi^2 = 46.46$, df $= 1$,	
	$p < .0001$, $Q = .47$		$p < .0001$, $Q = .64$	
	Three-way interaction: $\chi^2 = 3.03$, df $= 1$, $p < .10$			

[a] The third and fourth intensity categories were collapsed because they showed no difference in the way they affected the response-form relation; the first and second categories were collapsed partly for the same reason and partly because of the small number of cases in the first category.

[10] The argument of Sherif and Sherif (1969), that attitudes are usefully seen as configurations of latitudes of acceptance and rejection, applies here. Their finding, that the more ego-involved (i.e., intense) have smaller latitudes of acceptance and larger latitudes of rejection, leads to the same conclusion that the less intense should be more affected by the presence of a middle category.

ASSOCIATIONS BETWEEN ATTITUDES

Our final hypothesis involves the issue of whether form affects conclusions about the nature of relations between attitudes themselves. If correlations between attitudes are generally larger for those who feel more intensely (e.g., Jackman, 1977), then our finding that the average intensity of those in the polar categories is higher on the Offered form than on the Omitted one implies that correlations between *polar* opinions should be larger for Offered forms than for Omitted forms.[11] We tested this notion for the three instances where there was a relation between experiments on at least one form.[12] In all three cases the difference is in the expected direction: the association between polar positions is stronger on the Offered form. In only one of these instances does the response-by-response-by-form interaction reach significance, but it is an important case since an investigator would draw quite different conclusions from the two forms about the relation of liberal/conservative self-identification to judgment of whether the U.S. gave too much or too little aid to the South Vietnamese government.

To test further the reliability of this finding, the Vietnam and Liberal/Conservative experiments were repeated in SRC–78W. The results shown in Table 4 replicate those found in 1974. On the Omitted versions there is no difference in opinion on Vietnam between liberals and conservatives, but on the Offered forms liberals are more likely to say "too much aid," while conservatives say "not enough."[13] Thus the relation that might be expected on some ideological grounds occurs on only one form. What seems to be happening is that among liberals the switch to the middle position on Vietnam comes disproportionately from the "not enough aid" category, whereas among conservatives it comes disproportionately from the "too much aid" response. It may be that respondents are somewhat uncomfortable holding these combinations of attitudes (Liberal with Not Enough Aid and Conservative with Too Much Aid), which are in some sense counter to conventional expectations, and thus are more likely to opt

[11] We also examined whether correlations between *middle* vs. combined polar positions on different items are affected by form. In a preliminary analysis of our first set of experiments we reported that a "generalized set" might be implicated in the form effect because choosing the middle position on the Offered Vietnam item was more strongly related to choosing the middle position on another Offered item than on the corresponding Omitted forms (see Presser and Schuman, 1975:21). Analysis of the other experiments failed to replicate this finding.

[12] In the only other case where two experimental items can be intercorrelated (Marijuana and Local Education) there is no relation on either form. Since none of the items were originally designed to be associated, this case does not seem an appropriate test.

[13] In both years, the Liberal/Conservative Offered form had five points which have been collapsed to three in these analyses.

Table 4. Vietnam Response by Liberal/Conservative Response by Form (SRC–1978W)

	Liberal	Middle	Conservative
Omitted forms			
Too much aid	76.7%	71.4%	76.9%
About right	7.0	21.4	9.0
Not enough	16.3	71.1	14.0
	100.0%	99.9%	99.9%
	(172)	(28)	(321)

$$\chi^2 = 6.10, \text{df} = 4, \text{n.s.}$$
Due to association between polar positions:
$$\chi^2 = 0.33, \text{df} = 1, \text{n.s.}$$

	Liberal	Middle	Conservative
Offered forms			
Too much aid	72.0%	59.4%	58.9%
About right	22.0	28.0	24.2
Not enough	6.1	12.6	16.8
	100.1%	100.0%	99.9%
	(132)	(143)	(202)

$$\chi^2 = 11.62, \text{df} = 4, p < .03$$
Due to association between polar positions:
$$\chi^2 = 10.19, \text{df} = 1, p < .002$$
Three-way interaction:
$$\chi^2 = 11.81, \text{df} = 4, p < .02$$

for the middle position on the Offered form as a way to resolve the "inconsistency."[14] However, two still more recent attempts to replicate this form difference were not successful, for reasons that even after considerable effort remain unclear. These lack of replications throw doubt on the original findings, and the general point about whether form can affect associations between attitude items is thus uncertain.

Conclusion

Offering an explicit middle alternative in a forced-choice attitude item increases the proportion of respondents in that category. On most issues the increase is in the neighborhood of 10 to 20 percent, but it may be considerably larger. Although there is a very slight decrease in the proportion of spontaneous "don't know" responses when the middle alternative is offered, almost all the change in the middle position comes from a decline in the polar positions. The decline tends to affect the polar positions proportionately, so that item form is usually unrelated to the univariate distribution of opinion once middle responses are excluded from analysis.

[14] Whatever its interpretation, it should be noted that people affected by form are not contributing random error to the association as might have been assumed, but instead join these issues together in a way opposite to that of people unaffected by form. For a similar finding for respondents affected by no opinion filters see Schuman and Presser (1978).

Intensity appears to be one factor that partly distinguishes those affected by form from those not affected. The relation of intensity to the middle response is somewhat greater on the Offered form than on the Omitted. A number of other respondent characteristics, by contrast, are generally unrelated to the form effect, and conclusions about the link between such variables and attitudinal items are unaffected by form. Finally, one inference about the association between the polar opinion categories of two different items was significantly affected by question form in two independent surveys. The unusual and uncertain nature of this result, however, suggests the need for further work to discover how frequently, and under what circumstances, such effects occur.

Susceptibility to constraint by question form has sometimes been seen in terms of cognitive limitations or passivity in the interview situation (see, for example, Schuman and Duncan, 1974:240). This interpretation, however, appears inconsistent with our finding that the form effect is essentially unrelated to measures of cognitive sophistication such as education and information. An alternate interpretation focuses on what is communicated by question form. There are investigators who purposely omit a middle alternative in order to force respondents into one of the polar positions, and it is not unreasonable to assume that respondents who feel constrained by question form are in some sense aware of this intention. Question form probably structures these respondents' decision-making. Particularly for a respondent with a weak opinion leaning in one direction, the answer to the question, "Which of the offered alternatives am I closest to?" will differ depending on whether an investigator presents only the two polar options, or those two plus a middle position. Thus some respondents may simply make different assumptions about the information being requested, depending on which question form is asked.

If this analysis is correct, then it provides support for Stanley Payne's advice about whether middle alternatives should be included in survey questions. Writing in *The Art of Asking Questions,* Payne advised: "If the direction in which people are *leaning* on the issue is the type of information wanted, it is better not to suggest the middle ground. . . . If it is desired to sort out those with more definite convictions on the issue, then it is better to suggest the middle-ground" (1951:64, emphasis in original).[15]

[15] It might seem as though both these objectives could be accomplished by initially asking an Offered form of an item, then following it up with a probe to those choosing the middle alternative: "If you had to choose, which way would you lean . . .?" When we tried this in two experiments (Vietnam and Liberal/Conservative) and added the follow-up choices to the original choices, the resulting distribution was not significantly different from the distribution that occurred on the parallel Omitted form of the same item. However, in one of the two cases (Vietnam) the division of opinion to the

References

Cantril, Hadley
1944   Gauging Public Opinion. Princeton: Princeton University Press.
Goodman, Leo A.
1971   "The analysis of multidimensional contingency tables: stepwise procedures and direct estimation methods for building models for multiple classifications." Technometrics 13:33–61.
Groves, Robert M., and Robert L. Kahn
1979   Surveys by Telephone: A National Comparison with Personal Interviews. New York: Academic Press.
Jackman, Mary
1977   "Prejudice, tolerance, and attitudes toward ethnic groups." Social
Science Research 6:145–69.
Kalton, Graham, Julie Roberts, and Tim Holt
1979   "The effects of offering a middle response option with opinion questions." SCPR Working Paper No. 19. Social and Community Planning Research, London.
Payne, Stanley L.
1951   The Art of Asking Questions. Princeton: Princeton University Press.
Presser, Stanley
1977   "Survey question wording and attitudes in the general public." Unpublished Ph.D. dissertation, The University of Michigan.
Presser, Stanley, and Howard Schuman
1975   "Question wording as an independent variable in survey analysis: a
first report." Proceedings of the Social Statistics Section, ASA,
16–25.
Schuman, Howard, and Otis Dudley Duncan
1974   "Questions about attitude survey questions," pp. 232–51 in Herbert
L. Costner (ed.), Sociological Methodology 1973–74. San Francisco:
Jossey-Bass.
Schuman, Howard, and Stanley Presser
1977   "Question wording as an independent variable in survey analysis."
Sociological Methods and Research 6:151–70.
1978   "The assessment of no opinion in attitude surveys," pp. 241–75 in
Karl Schuessler (ed.), Sociological Methodology 1979. San Francisco: Jossey-Bass.
Sherif, Muzafir, and Carolyn Sherif
1969   Social Psychology. New York: Harper & Row.
Stember, Herbert, and Herbert Hyman
1949–   "How interviewer effects operate through question form." Interna-
1950   tional Journal of Opinion and Attitude Research 3:493–512.
Tamulonis, Valerie
1947   "The effect of question variations in public opinion surveys." Mas-
ter's thesis, University of Denver.

---

follow-up, taken by itself, was significantly different from that obtained by the initial
Offered question. Thus it is not clear that the two methods of forcing respondents to
choose a polar alternative will necessarily yield the same results.

The Measurement of Values in Surveys: A Comparison of Ratings and Rankings

DUANE F. ALWIN AND JON A. KROSNICK

To MANY social psychologists the concept of values is crucial to the understanding of human behavior. Values are generally defined as standards of desirability invoked in social interaction to evaluate the preferability of behavioral goals or modes of action (Williams, 1968). According to this perspective, values are assumed to be central to the cognitive organization of the individual and to serve as a basis for the formation of attitudes, beliefs, and opinions (see Rokeach, 1970).

Survey researchers have generally measured values using standardized techniques of ordering (or ranking) a set of competing alternatives provided by the investigator. Other methods have been used, but rankings have been the method of choice most frequently. However, rankings

---

Abstract Social values are most commonly measured using ranking techniques, but there is a scarcity of systematic comparisons between rankings and other approaches to measuring values in survey research. On the basis of data from the 1980 General Social Survey, this article evaluates the comparability of results obtained using rankings and ratings of valued qualities. The comparison focuses on (1) the ordering of aggregate value preferences and (2) the measurement of individual differences in latent value preferences. The two methods are judged to be similar with respect to ordering the aggregate preferences of the sample, but dissimilar with regard to the latent variable structure underlying the measures.

Duane F. Alwin is Research Scientist and Professor of Sociology, Survey Research Center, Institute for Social Research, The University of Michigan. Jon A. Krosnick is Assistant Professor of Psychology, The Ohio State University. This article is a revised version of a paper presented at the annual meetings of the American Association for Public Opinion Research, May 17–20, 1984. An earlier version of the paper was reprinted as Technical Report No. 40, General Social Survey, NORC, Chicago. The research was supported by a grant from the National Institute of Mental Health (MH-37289). An important debt is owed NORC and the staff of the General Social Survey for cooperation in conducting this research. The authors wish to thank Frank Andrews, David Jackson, Melvin Kohn, and Tom Smith for helpful comments on earlier drafts and Lynn Dielman and Marion Wirick for help in manuscript preparation. Address all correspondence to Duane F. Alwin, Survey Research Center, Institute for Social Research, P.O. Box 1248, Ann Arbor, MI 48106.

have a number of problems tied to their degree of difficulty, and some have suggested that other techniques, such as ratings, could serve as effective alternatives. In this article, we compare the rating and ranking approaches to measuring values using data on parental orientations toward children from a randomized split-ballot experiment carried out in the 1980 General Social Survey. Before reporting our findings, we place the work in context by reviewing the literature that has discussed the relative advantages and disadvantages of rating and ranking techniques for measuring values.

The Measurement of Values: Ratings vs. Rankings

Value researchers have consistently argued on theoretical grounds that ranking techniques provide the most appropriate conceptual mapping to conceptions of values. For example, Rokeach (1973:6) points out that values are often thought to be inherently comparative and competitive, and thus the "choice" nature of the ranking task fits nicely with this conceptualization. Also, Kohn (1977:19) observes that the ranking approach to measuring values is demanded by their very nature, in that "a central manifestation of value is to be found in *choice*." This point of view is validated to some extent by the sheer prevalence of the use of rankings to measure values (e.g., Allport et al., 1960; Kluckholn and Strodtbeck, 1961; Lenski, 1961; Bengston, 1975).

Despite these arguments regarding the conceptual mapping of ranking techniques to the concept of values, this approach has a number of significant practical drawbacks when used in survey research. First, rankings are often difficult and taxing for respondents, demanding considerable cognitive sophistication and concentration. This is particularly problematic when the list of concepts to be ranked is lengthy (Rokeach, 1973:28; Feather, 1973:228). Second, the use of ranking techniques is time-consuming and may therefore be more expensive to administer (Munson and McIntyre, 1979:49). Third, since rankings often require the use of visual aids, or "show-cards," it is difficult to gather such information using telephone methods of data collection (Groves and Kahn, 1979:122-33). And finally, the sum of the ranks for any individual respondent equals a constant, so there is a linear dependency among the set of ranked items (Clemans, 1966; Jackson and Alwin, 1980). Consequently, it may not always be possible to employ conventional statistical techniques in the analysis of the latent content of ranked preference data.

In contrast to rankings, rating scales are easy to present to respondents. Munson and McIntyre (1979:49) estimate that ranking tasks take three times longer than similar rating tasks and involve a considerable decrease in respondent burden. Also, ratings can readily be administered over the telephone and do not involve the linear dependency problem inherent in rankings. So ratings have none of the major disadvantages of rankings and might therefore be a good substitute for survey measurements of values.

However, ratings have two potential drawbacks which should be evaluated before they are employed. First, since ratings require less effort, the quality of data may be reduced relative to rankings. And as Feather (1973:229) points out, making the task easier may also reduce respondents' willingness to make more precise distinctions about the relative importance of valued qualities. Thus, although easier to administer and perform, ratings may compromise the level of precision of the data.

A second potential drawback of ratings is their susceptibility to problems of response style or response sets (Berg, 1966; Block, 1965; Phillips, 1973). When the rated qualities are all considered good or socially desirable, ratings tend to fall within a rather restricted range of the available scale points (Feather, 1973). The particular center or anchor-point of an individual's ratings may be due to extremity response style (Hamilton, 1968), individual interpretations of the meaning of judgment categories (Cronback, 1946, 1950; Messick, 1968), or group response sets (Cunningham et al., 1977). Variation across persons in such response tendencies may lead to correlated response patterns, or what Costner (1969) referred to as differential bias, producing spuriously positive correlations among ratings due to the common method of measurement (see also Alwin, 1974; Andrews, 1984). These positive correlations may complicate the analysis of the latent structure of value preferences.

EMPIRICAL COMPARISONS OF RATINGS AND RANKINGS

The major research comparing ratings and rankings as measures of values has focused on Rokeach's rankings of "instrumental" (modes of behavior) and "terminal" (end-states of existence) values using his *Value Survey* (Rokeach, 1967) and rating techniques adapted from it. This research has shown the following: (1) the aggregate or average preference orders measured by ratings and rankings have generally been found to be quite similar (Feather, 1973, 1975; Moore, 1975); (2) individual-level preference orders tend to be much less similar across ratings and rankings (Moore, 1975; Rankin and Grube, 1980), primarily because in using ratings respondents can score valued qualities equally; (3) over-time relationships among identical measures are slightly higher for rankings than for ratings, although the differences tend to be small (Munson and McIntyre, 1979; Rankin and Grube, 1980; Reynolds and Jolly, 1980); and (4) the predictive validity of ratings is somewhat higher than that of rankings (Rankin and Grube, 1980).

This research suggests that rating and ranking techniques may be interchangeable for the purpose of measuring aggregate preference orderings. However, there are other purposes for which researchers may wish to assess the value-preferences of respondents in surveys, and the validity of various measurement approaches depends on the extent to which these objectives are accomplished.

Another important purpose for measuring values is to study their latent content as reflected in their covariance or correlational structure (e.g. Kohn, 1969; Rokeach, 1973). Past research has failed to focus explicitly on differences in the covariance structures of measures produced by ratings and rankings. Although some of the research cited above deals superficially with this issue, there is a virtual absence of research that has compared the covariance properties of ratings and rankings and the consequences of these differences for analysis of the comparative measurement differences between the two techniques. This is especially remarkable since the major anlaytic technique used to decompose measures of value preferences and to ascertain their underlying latent dimensionality, namely factor analysis, depends intimately on the covariance structure of the measures of preferences.[1]

In the following analysis of value measures, we compare the results obtained with a rating technique to those obtained using a more conventional ranking procedure. We first examine measures of the relative importance of value-preferences in the aggregate in order to verify in our data the finding in the literature that ratings and rankings provide similar pictures of relative preference orders. Second, we compare the intercorrelations among rated items with those among rankings. These analyses illustrate some major differences in the covariance properties of measures obtained via the two procedures. Third, we examine results obtained from the factor analysis of the two types of measures, and we examine these differences in light of the differences in their covariance properites. And fourth, we examine the relationships of the latent factors identified through factor analyses with criterion variables thought to be related to these values.

Data

The 1980 General Social Survey (see NORC, 1982) conducted an experimental comparison of three forms of a measurement technique

---

[1] One study referred to by Munson and McIntyre (1979) factor-analyzed rating and ranking measures of Rokeach's terminal and instrumental values. Three times as many factors were apparently required to account for the correlations among ratings compared to the number required for correlations among rankings. This suggests that the latent structure of the two types of measures are quite different. One problem with generalizing much from

prominent in the literature on the measurement of parental valuation of child qualities (see Kohn, 1969). Two forms were quasireplications of the ranking method originally used by Kohn, and a third form used a rating scale format.

The question used in prior GSS surveys and for one ranking form (Form X) of the current experiment is as follows:

a. The qualities listed on this card may all be important, but which *three* would you say are the *most desirable* for a *child* to have?
b. Which *one* of *these three* is the *most* desirable of all?
c. All of the qualities listed on this card may be desirable, but could you tell me which *three* you consider *least important*?
d. And which *one* of these three is *least important* of all?
   (1) that he has good manners
   (2) that he tries hard to succeed
   (3) that he is honest
   (4) that he is neat and clean
   (5) that he has good sense and sound judgment
   (6) that he has self-control
   (7) that he acts like a boy (she acts like a girl)
   (8) that he gets along well with other children
   (9) that he obeys his parents well
   (10) that he is responsible
   (11) that he is considerate of others
   (12) that he is interested in how and why things happen
   (13) that he is a good student.

On the second ranking form (Form Y), "a child" was substituted for "he" in the usual NORC format in order to remove any gender connotation in the list of qualities. Schaeffer (1982) has recently demonstrated very little difference in the mean rankings using these two forms, and our results were the same for both, so we combine them for presentation below.[2]

The rating form (Form Z) of the values measure asked the following question:

Please look at the qualities listed on this card. All of the qualities may be desirable for a child to have, but could you tell me whether the quality is extremely important, very important, fairly important, not too important, or not important at all?

The list of qualities presented was the same as those presented with the Form X ranking version, that is, phrased with the pronoun "he."

The population sampled in the 1980 NORC survey was the total

---

this type of comparison is that the ordinary factor analysis of rankings is inappropriate without modifying the common factor model to accommodate the ipsative properties of the data (See Jackson and Alwin, 1980).

[2] We also confirmed this finding using more appropriate Hotelling T-tests (see Anderson, 1958) on the vectors of means between forms and found no significant difference.

noninstitutionalized English-speaking population of the continental United States, 18 years of age or older. The 1980 sample was produced by full-probability cluster sampling methods.[3] One-third of the sample each received (on a random basis) one of the following three forms:

1) Form X—The standard reduced-ranking form using the "he" pronoun.
2) Form Y—The standard reduced-ranking form using "a child."
3) Form Z—The use of five-point rating scales for each quality separately.

For the analyses reported below, the 13 valued qualities measured using Form X and Y were scored as follows:

5—The trait or quality most valued of all
4—One of the three most valued qualities, but not the most valued
3—Neither one of the three most nor one of the three least valued qualities
2—One of the three least valued, but not the least valued quality
1—The quality least valued of all

In Form Z the response categories are scored as follows:

5—Extremely important
4—Very important
3—Fairly important
2—Not too important
1—Not at all important

These coding schemes are relatively arbitrary and may not necessarily represent interval-level metrics. However, we are convinced by O'Brien's (1979) analysis that the assumption of interval-level scoring is robust with respect to monotonic transformations of the scale units which preserve the ordinal character of the data.

Results

THE IMPORTANCE OF CHILD QUALITIES

Consistent with earlier research (e.g., Feather, 1973), we found that ratings and rankings produce very similar results when considered in

---

[3] The sampling details are given in NORC (1982:207–212). Earlier analyses of these measures in the pre-1980 GSS data restricted the analysis to parents (Kohn, 1976; Alwin and Jackson, 1982b). Consistent with this previous research we present results for the subsample of parents only, defined as respondents who reported ever having had children, regardless of whether they were currently living with them. In addition, we exclude cases for which there is not complete data on the 13 parental value items. In the ranking forms this necessitated deleting 13 percent of the cases, and in the rating form 3 percent of the cases were deleted.

terms of their measurement of the relative importance of the child qualities. Table 1 presents the mean ranks and ratings for each quality studied
and the percentage of respondents choosing a particular quality as "most
important" (in Forms X and Y) and "extremely important" (in Form Z).
Using either technique, the quality estimated to be the most valued in the
population is "honesty" and the quality estimated to be the least valued is
"acting like a child should." The rank-order of the remaining qualities in
terms of their overall relative importance is very similar. The Spearman
rank-order correlation between the mean rankings and mean ratings in
Table 1 is .966.

Table 1. Descriptive Statistics for Ratings and Rankings of Child Qualities by Experimental Condition: NORC General Social Survey, 1980

	Form			
	Ranking (n=655)		Rating (n=318)	
Quality	Mean Reduced-Rank Score	% Ranking Quality Among 3 Most Important	Mean Rating	% Rating Extremely Important
Manners	2.05	24.5	3.13	29.6
Tries hard	1.97	17.2	3.05	29.2
Honest	3.12	66.1	3.64	66.0
Neat & clean	1.48	6.4	2.93	24.8
Good sense	2.46	41.1	3.31	40.3
Self-control	2.01	13.7	3.22	35.5
Role	.84	3.4	2.71	24.8
Gets along	1.96	13.6	2.96	24.2
Obeys	2.38	31.6	3.30	44.7
Responsible	2.35	34.2	3.29	38.1
Considerate	2.21	25.3	3.29	36.8
Interested	1.64	16.9	3.00	27.0
Studious	1.65	5.8	2.88	23.6

The ranking technique produced sharper distinctions among the various qualities. Table 1 shows that ratings tend to be somewhat skewed,
with the bulk of respondents responding positively, as suggested in the
existing literature. For most rated qualities, at least one-quarter of the
respondents selected the "extremely important" category, and in several
cases, the figure is upwards of 40 percent. These results stand in clear
contrast to the ranking of child qualities, wherein the procedure requires
that some qualities be ranked below others. Here the percentage of respondents choosing qualities among the "three most important" is quite
variable over items, suggesting the greater differentiation of preferences
by the ranking approach.

CORRELATIONS AMONG VALUE ITEMS

Rankings have built-in negative correlations among them since the rankings for any given respondent sum to a constant (see Cattell, 1944; Horst, 1965; Clemans, 1966; Jackson and Alwin, 1980; Alwin and Jackson, 1982a; 1982b). And as discussed above, ratings of value preferences may have built-in positive correlations among them due to response biases (e.g., Bentler, 1969). This difference between the covariance

Table 2. Bivariate Correlations Among Child Qualities for Ratings and Rankings: NORC General Social Survey, 1980

Quality	1	2	3	4	5	6	7	8	9	10	11	12	13
1. Manners	1.0	.385	.204	.517	.183	.320	.400	.444	.444	.304	.259	.249	.389
2. Tries hard	-.067	1.0	.352	.455	.336	.311	.427	.351	.336	.307	.176	.378	.492
3. Honest	-.030	-.166	1.0	.166	.388	.321	.182	.146	.279	.359	.288	.268	.261
4. Neat & Clean	-.092	-.090	.005	1.0	.306	.378	.539	.525	.412	.286	.320	.314	.535
5. Good sense	-.186	-.025	-.204	-.152	1.0	.484	.276	.329	.210	.446	.380	.442	.334
6. Self-control	-.106	-.141	.003	-.145	-.043	1.0	.355	.326	.406	.418	.331	.387	.446
7. Role	-.088	-.020	-.053	-.105	-.128	-.046	1.0	.457	.486	.198	.135	.339	.577
8. Gets along	-.020	-.084	-.093	-.139	-.101	-.044	-.100	1.0	.377	.348	.372	.368	.502
9. Obeys	.043	-.195	-.109	.089	-.278	-.054	-.006	-.057	1.0	.310	.290	.248	.485
10. Responsible	-.236	-.072	-.049	-.203	.065	-.014	-.087	-.066	-.259	1.0	.514	.430	.409
11. Considerate	-.162	-.131	-.063	-.137	-.010	-.061	-.151	.010	-.052	.002	1.0	.380	.359
12. Interested	-.185	.002	-.193	-.190	.025	-.083	-.229	-.025	-.186	.032	-.005	1.0	.409
13. Studious	-.073	-.043	-.093	-.084	-.080	-.053	-.143	-.028	.051	-.060	-.073	-.147	1.0

NOTE: Form X and Y $N=655$ (below diagonal).
Form Z $N=318$ (above diagonal).

properties of ratings and rankings is illustrated in Table 2. The correlations among the (nonipsative) rating scales are all positive and show considerable intercorrelation in all cases, whereas the intercorrelations among ranked items tend toward zero, and in most instances are negative. As indicated in the foregoing, these covariance properties are directly linked to fundamental differences between the measuring procedures themselves. Consequently, it is difficult to compare the two techniques without taking into account these inherent sources of differences in their covariance structures. Therefore, the factor analysis of ratings must allow for positive correlations due to correlated response errors, and the factor analysis of rankings must take into account the negative correlations of ranked qualities.

ANALYSIS OF LATENT STRUCTURE

The Factor Analysis of Rankings. To analyze the factor structure of the ranking data, we applied the Jackson-Alwin ipsative common factor model (see Jackson and Alwin, 1980; Alwin and Jackson, 1982a; 1982b), which imposes a set of constraints to produce the negative correlations among disturbances which are inherent in ipsative data.[4] For purposes of comparison, we also evaluated a "nonipsative" factor model, which assumes the disturbances in the factor model are uncorrelated. For the purpose of estimating these parameters, we have arbitrarily constrained the variance of the latent factor to unity. Parameter estimates were obtained using maximum-likelihood confirmatory factor analysis (Jöreskog and Sörbom, 1981), and the results are presented in Table 3.

Table 3. Parameter Estimates of a Single-Factor Model for Rankings of Child Qualities Using Ipsative and Nonipsative Factor Models: NORC General Social Survey, 1980

Parameter	Nonipsative Model	Ipsative Model
Factor loadings		
Manners	-.300*	-.281*
Tries hard	.091*	.086
Honest	-.110*	-.095
Neat & clean	-.304*	-.280*
Good sense	.360*	.339*
Self-control	.033	.033
Role	-.103*	-.092
Gets along	.014	.013
Obeys	-.391*	-.385*
Responsible	.312*	.307*
Considerate	.097*	.097*
Interested	.326*	.309*
Studious	-.025	-.051
Factor variance	1.000[a]	1.000[a]
Disturbance variances		
Manners	.595	.609
Tries hard	.636	.647
Honest	.758	.753
Neat & clean	.598	.620
Good sense	.712	.726
Self-control	.418	.420
Role	.861	.860
Gets along	.401	.400
Obeys	.581	.580
Responsible	.493	.493
Considerate	.467	.466
Interested	.855	.858
Studious	.491	.484

Goodness of Fit
Ipsative model: $L^2 = 100.750$, df=53, $L^2/df= 1.90$
Nonipsative model: $L^2 = 1290.931$, df=54, $L^2/df=23.91$

[a] Fixed parameter.
* Factor loading is at least twice its standard error.

[4] The rationale for this model and the details involved in its estimation may be found in Alwin and Jackson (1982a).

The relative sizes of the factor loadings shown in Table 3 are consistent with the notion of a single underlying self-direction/conformity factor in these data, and there is strong similarity between the two factor solutions in this regard. These numbers resemble those obtained both by Kohn (1976) and by Alwin and Jackson (1982b). Negative loadings are associated with conformity items, such as obedience, manners, and cleanliness. Positive loadings are associated with self-direction items, such as good sense and sound judgment, responsibility, and curiosity.[5]

We also examined the residual covariances among the variables under the two models. In virtually every case, the residual covariances are negative in the nonipsative model, suggesting the need for negatively correlated disturbances. Because the ipsative model incorporates such correlations, no such pattern is obvious from the inspection of the residual covariances of that model. Also, because the ipsative common factor model does not ignore the "built-in" negative correlations among disturbances, the fit of this model to the data is literally more than 10 times better than the fit of the nonipsative model (see Table 3). The fit of the ipsative factor model is acceptable ($L^2/df=1.90$), whereas the fit of the nonipsative model is clearly unacceptable ($L^2/df=23.91$).[6]

The Factor Analysis of Ratings. We analyzed the factor structure of the rating data using two types of common factor models: (1) a model based upon preliminary exploratory factor analyses specifying two latent factors, and (2) a model that incorporates these two factors and a general method factor, uncorrelated with the other two, upon which all items had equal loadings.[7] This third factor was included to incorporate explicitly the spurious positive correlations which might result from differential response bias (Costner, 1969; Bentler, 1969; Alwin, 1974; Andrews, 1984).

Table 4 displays the factor pattern coefficients in standard form for the

---

[5] Because of the properties of the common factor model for rankings, the factor pattern coefficients must sum to zero. Therefore, the coefficients in Table 3 *cannot* be interpreted in absolute terms; they simply reflect the relative ordering of items in relation to one another (see Jackson and Alwin, (1980:222-23).

[6] We use the notation L^2 to refer to the sample estimate of the population likelihood-ratio χ^2 value for the model. We should point out that the use of L^2 as an estimate of χ^2 depends upon its maximum likelihood properties. In order for L^2 to estimate χ^2, the variables must have multivariate normal distributions. This assumption is likely to be violated in the case of rankings (but not necessarily for ratings) since rankings are often relatively skewed. We acknowledge this distributional requirement and therefore place less weight on the statistical tests in evaluating the fit of the models to the data. The Bentler-Bonett normed fit index for this model using the null model suggested by Jackson and Alwin (1980:235) is .66. By this criterion this may not appear to be a very good fit to the data, but given the difficulty of modeling ipsative data (see Alwin and Jackson, 1982b:211-12), it is not clear what an acceptable alternative would be.

[7] The results obtained by relaxing this constraint are not very different from those reported here.

two-factor model, along with the estimated factor intercorrelations and disturbance variances. As in the case of rankings, the rating data tend to cluster in a manner consistent with Kohn's conceptual framework. That is, the conformity-related characteristics of children tend to cluster together—obedience, good manners, neatness and cleanliness—and self-direction qualities also tend to cluster—curiosity, consideration, self-control, responsibility, and good judgment. However, instead of the clusters being opposed at polar ends of the same continuum as in the case of rankings, here the clusters are positively correlated ($r=.65$), which is

Table 4. Parameter Estimates for Two- and Three-Factor Models for Ratings of Child Qualities: NORC General Social Survey, 1980

Parameter	Two-Factor Model		Three-Factor Model		
	I	*II*	*I*	*II*	*III*
Factor Loadings					
Manners	.411*	.000ᵃ	.340*	.000ᵃ	.587*
Tries hard	.402*	.095	.149	-.197*	.587*
Honest	-.009	.266	-.363*	-.187	.587*
Neat & clean	.608*	-.038	.513*	.078	.587*
Good sense	.000ᵃ	.423*	.000ᵃ	.153*	.587*
Self-control	.175*	.321	.071	.079	.587*
Role	.945*	-.238*	.490*	-.182	.587*
Gets along	.425*	.090	.463*	.247*	.587*
Obeys	.431*	.035	.280*	.000ᵃ	.587*
Responsible	-.046	.503*	-.067	.328*	.587*
Considerate	-.030	.411*	.000ᵃ	.511*	.587*
Interested	.125	.396*	.064	.160*	.587*
Studious	.544*	.107	.377*	.053	.587*
Factor covariances	1.000ᵃ		1.000ᵃ		
	.648*	1.000ᵃ	-.223	1.000ᵃ	
			.000ᵃ	.000ᵃ	1.000ᵃ
Disturbance variances					
Manners		.632			.633
Tries hard		.632			.566
Honest		.748			.499
Neat & clean		.453			.433
Good sense		.570			.612
Self-control		.596			.614
Role		.414			.393
Gets along		.566			.495
Obeys		.612			.616
Responsible		.456			.482
Considerate		.592			.442
Interested		.619			.638
Studious		.419			.445

Goodness of fit
Two-factor model: $L^2=142.962$, df=53, L^2/df=2.70
Three-factor model: $L^2=120.750$, df=54, L^2/df=2.24

ᵃ Fixed parameter.
* Factor loading is at least twice its standard error.

clearly inconsistent with the structure of ranking data. The fit of this model is only marginally acceptable; the ratio of the L^2 to degrees of freedom is 2.70.

Some of the lack of fit evident here may be due to this model's failure to explicitly take into account the effects of correlated response bias; we therefore estimated the parameters of a three-factor confirmatory factor model designed to account for these effects. The results for this three-factor model (shown in Table 4) and the improved goodness-of-fit measures demonstrate the importance of positing such a general method factor for rating data. The loadings on the method factor are statistically significant, and the improvement in fit of this model as compared to the two-factor model is significant ($\Delta L^2=22.21$, df=1).[8] Moreover, the correlation between the latent self-direction and conformity factors is now negative ($r=-.22$), rather than highly positive, although this correlation is not statistically significant. Thus, by including this method factor we improve the fit to the data and reduce the correlation between the two substantive latent factors to what we would expect on the basis of the ranking results. So by modeling the methodological properites of value ratings, we have found evidence of a latent structure in these data similar though not identical to that of the ranking data.

CRITERION-VALIDITY OF RATINGS AND RANKINGS

Even though the results of the factor analysis of ratings and rankings are different, we have identified concepts of self-direction and conformity as "latent" dimensions in both types of data. It is therefore worthwhile to examine the correlations between the latent dimensions and theoretically relevant predictor variables. For this purpose, we correlated the parental values factors with a set of predictors used in previous studies, namely, parental occupational prestige, education, and income. These socioeconomic indicators were chosen because their relationship to parental values has been the focus of much previous research (e.g., Lynd and Lynd, 1929; Duvall, 1946; Miller and Swanson, 1958; Lenski, 1961; Kohn, 1969, 1976, 1977, 1981; Alwin and Jackson, 1982b; Alwin, 1984).

The measurement of these variables in the 1980 NORC survey is as follows:

1. *Respondent's occupational prestige*—measured in the metric of Hodge-Siegel-Rossi scores (Siegel, 1971) assigned to 1970 U.S. Census detailed occupation codes.

---

[8] This is not a hierarchical test, since the models are not nested, but the improved fit is evident from the reduction in the ratio of L^2 to degrees of freedom. The Bentler-Bonett normed fit index for these models, using a null model which posits only random variance in the measures, are .91 and .93 for the two- and three-factor models, respectively.

2. *Respondent's education*—measured as the number of years of formal schooling completed.
3. *Family income*—measured as the total family income, from all sources, before taxes in the year preceding the survey. Our analysis assigns the midpoints of 12 income categories using $100 units.

Past research indicates that the contrast between self-direction and conformity, as measured by the latent factors identified above for the ranking data, correlates positively with these socioeconomic variables. On this basis we would expect the self-direction dimension of the ratings to correlate positively and the conformity dimension to correlate nega-

Table 5. Zero-order Correlations of Latent Factors with Criterion Variables: NORC General Social Survey, 1980

	Predictor		
Model	*Education*	*Occupational Prestige*	*Income*
1. Rankings—single-factor nonipsative model			
I. Self-direction/conformity	.591*	.422*	.344*
2. Rankings—single-factor ipsative model			
I. Self-direction/conformity	.624*	.448*	.367*
3. Ratings—two-factor model			
I. Self-direction	.053	-.045	-.058
II. Conformity	-.355*	-.321*	-.319*
4. Ratings—three-factor model			
I. Self-direction	.036	.210*	-.062
II. Conformity	-.532*	-.267*	-.401*
III. Differential bias	-.060	-.181*	-.120

* Coefficient is greater than twice its standard error.

tively with these variables. We estimated the relationships of these predictor variables with the latent self-direction/conformity factors underlying the rating and ranking data using linear structural equation (LISREL) models (Jöreskog and Sörbom, 1981).

As anticipated, the self-direction/conformity factor underlying the rankings shows strong correlation with these indicators of socioeconomic position. Table 5 presents the zero-order correlations of the latent factors underlying our models for rankings and ratings with the set of theoretically relevant parental characteristics. The two factor models we have contrasted for ranking data, the ipsative common factor model and the nonipsative model, are quite similar in the magnitudes of correlations with these socioeconomic factors. The relationships are slightly higher for the ipsative factor model than for the nonipsative model, but the differences here are small. This is an important result because there has been no research to date that has reported an empirical comparison of these two models.

In the rating data (see the results for the three-factor model) the "conformity" latent variable correlates negatively with the measures of socioeconomic position, as anticipated. The "self-direction" latent variable assessed by the ratings correlates positively with occupational prestige, but, contrary to our expectations, it is essentially uncorrelated with education and income. This is a striking difference between the results obtained using ratings and rankings. The comparable relationships for the two-factor version of the model are generally weaker, which again demonstrates the value of positing a general method factor for the rating data.

Summarizing these results, the latent factor underlying the ranking data is correlated with theoretically relevant predictor variables in a manner consistent with previous research. While the results for the rating data are not in dramatic contrast to these findings, generally weaker relationships are involved, as evidenced both by the weaker correlation between the latent self-direction and conformity dimensions and the correlations with the predictor variables. Moreover, the major difference between the results for ratings and rankings is the lack of correlation of the rating self-direction factor with the socioeconomic indicators. Thus, one would reach different substantive conclusions using ratings compared to the use of rankings.

Summary and Conclusions

Although ranking methods tend to be preferred for measuring social values, the empirical evidence available from past research suggests that rating techniques may be used just as effectively. In our analyses of parental values for children, we found that ratings and rankings produced similar results in terms of ordering the relative importance of value choices in the aggregate but are dissimilar with regard to latent structure. The main reason for the observed differences seems to be the different constraints introduced by the two techniques in the measurement process. The ranking technique forces value-choices to be generally negatively correlated, whereas the rating approach encourages positive correlations. As a consequence, the latent variable structures for the two sets of measures are quite different.

However, even after we took the method-induced positive and negative correlations between the items into account in our analyses, the latent structures of the rating and ranking items were different. A single bipolar factor was found to represent the latent content underlying the ranking measures, whereas two separate and distinct substantive factors were found underlying the rating data. Although these two factors corresponded to the two concepts contrasted in the bipolar factor for rankings, the correlation between the two rating factors was not as strongly negative as the ranking analysis suggests it would be. The two types of measures produce different correlations between values and theoretically relevant predictor variables. All of these differences mitigate against the conclusion that ratings and rankings are interchangeable in the measurement of values.

Value researchers have consistently argued that the ranking technique is uniquely suited to the measurement of values, owing to the inherent comparative nature of values. From this point of view the present findings may be interpreted as support for this premise. However, these results are also consistent with a somewhat different interpretation; that is, rankings may impose a somewhat artificial contrast on the data and, as a result, measure both the latent dimension of contrast as well as the ability to see logical contrasts in the list of ranked qualities. It seems worthwhile to ask, in part because of our results using ratings, whether the ranking approach may in fact create artificial contrasts among the latent content of the measures.

Recall that the correlation between self-direction and conformity in the ranking data is in theory -1.0, since the two concepts define a bipolar factor. The latent variable underlying the set of rankings of child qualities has therefore been thought of as a continuum that distinguishes between the two extremes on a standard of desirability, i.e., the contrast between self-direction and conformity (Kohn. 1969). If one assumes that self-direction and conformity are contrasting values, as would be expected on the basis of the ranking data, the results for the rating data—that self-direction and conformity are only slightly related in a negative way—may seem incongruous. And if the values in question are in fact contrasting in this sense, one would expect the self-direction cluster of the ratings to correlate more strongly than it does with the socioeconomic predictor variables. Perhaps instead, self-direction and conformity are in actuality not contrasting values, in the sense that there is not a strong negative correlation between them. Is it not possible that the ranking technique essentially forces a contrast between them by asking respondents to make choices that they may not otherwise make? Since the conformity factor underlying the rating measures correlates nearly as strongly with the socioeconomic predictors as the contrast between self-direction and conformity in the ranking data, the correlation between the latent factor underlying the rankings and the socioeconomic predictors may be solely due to an association between the latter variables and values for conformity.

Although we raise these two differing interpretations of the differences between the rating and ranking results, it is not possible on the basis of our present analysis to choose between them. To conclude that ratings and rankings measure somewhat different things when viewed in terms of the latent content involved does not necessarily lead to the additional conclusion that one is the more valid approach to measuring values. Until further research evidence is developed on these issues, particularly with respect to the extent to which rankings impose contrasts which do not occur using other methods, such a conclusion would be premature.

It may be difficult to generalize from these findings to the measurement of other kinds of value phenomena. One's choice of measurement approach should depend upon theoretical considerations, as much as on knowledge of the properties of various measurement techniques. The problems we have addressed in this paper are closely tied to a well-defined set of theoretical issues, and our analysis informs the choice of measurement strategy in this context. To the degree that other theoretical problems are similar to those studied here, there may be some correspondence between the measurement issues involved. More generally, in the absence of a priori theoretical knowledge about the content one wishes to measure, generalizations about the relative advantages of various measurement strategies are difficult. We look forward to further research that will bring more theory-based evidence to bear on the relative advantages and disadvantages of these and other approaches to the measurement of values.

References

Allport, G.W., P.E. Vernon, and G. Lindzey
    1960   A study of Values. Boston: Houghton Mifflin.
Alwin, D.F.
    1974   "Approaches to the interpretation of relationships in the multitrait-multimethod matrix." In H.L. Costner (ed.), Sociological Methodology 1973-74. San Francisco: Jossey-Bass.
    1984   "Trends in parental socialization values: Detroit, 1958 to 1983." American Journal of Sociology 90:359-82.
Alwin, D.F., and D.J. Jackson
    1979   "Measurement models for response errors in surveys: issues and applications." Pp. 68-119 in K.F. Schuessler (ed.), Sociological Methodology 1980. San Francisco: Jossey-Bass.
    1982a "Adult values for children: an application of factor analysis to ranked preference data." Pp. 311-29 in R.M. Hauser, D. Mechanic, A.O. Haller, and T.S. Hauser (eds.), Social Structure and Behavior: Essays in Honor of William Hamilton Sewell. New York: Academic Press.
    1982b "The statistical analysis of Kohn's measures of parental values." Pp. 197-223 in K. G. Jöreskog and H. Wold (eds.), Systems Under Indirect Observation: Causality, Structure, and Prediction. Amsterdam: North-Holland.
Anderson, T.W.
    1958   An Introduction to Multivariate Statistical Analysis. New York: Wiley.

Andrews, F.M.
   1984   "Construct validity and error components of survey measures: a structural modeling approach." Public Opinion Quarterly 48:409-42.
Bengtson, V.L.
   1975   "Generation and family effects in value socialization." American Sociological Review 40:358-71.
Bentler, P.M.
   1969   "Semantic space is (approximately) bipolar." Journal of Psychology 71:33-40
Berg, I.A.
   1966   Response Set in Personality Assessment. Chicago: Aldine.
Block, J.
   1965   The Challenge of Response Sets New York: Appleton-Century-Crofts.
Cattell, R.B.
   1944   "Psychological measurement: ipsative, normative and interactive." Psychological Review 51:292-303.
Clemans, W.V.
   1966   "An analytical and empirical examination of some properties of ipsative measures." Psychometric Monographs 14.
Costner, H.L.
   1969   "Theory, deduction, and rules of correspondence." American Journal of Sociology 75:245-63.
Cronbach, L.J.
   1946   "Response sets and test validity." Educational and Psychological Measurement 6:475-94.
   1950   "Further evidence on response sets." Educational and Psychological Measurement 10:3-31.
Cunningham, W. H., I. C. M. Cunningham, and R. T. Green,
   1977   "The ipsative process to reduce response set bias." Public Opinion Quarterly 41:379-84.
Duvall, E. M.
   1946   "Conceptions of parenthood." American Journal of Sociology 52:193-203.
Feather, N.T.
   1973   "The measurement of values: effects of different assessment procedures." Australian Journal of Psychology 25:221-31.
   1975   Values in Education and Society. New York: The Free Press.
Groves, R.M., and R. L. Kahn
   1979   Surveys By Telephone: A National Comparison with Personal Interviews. New York: Academic Press.
Hamilton, D.L.
   1968   "Personality attributes associated with extreme response style." Psychological Bulletin 69:192-203.
Horst, P.
   1965   Factor Analysis of Data Matrices. New York: Holt, Rinehart and Winston.
Jackson, D.J., and D.F. Alwin
   1980   "The factor analysis of ipsative measures." *Sociological Methods and Reseach* 9:218-38.
Jöreskog, K.G., and D. Sörbom
   1981   LISREL—Analysis of Linear Structural Relationships by the Method of Maximum Likelihood. Version V. Chicago: National Educational Resources, Inc.
Kluckholn, F.R., and F.L. Strodtbeck
   1961   Variations in Value Orientations. Evanston IL: Row, Peterson and Co.
Kohn, M. L.
   1969   Class and Conformity: A Study in Values. Homewood, IL: Dorsey.
   1976   "Social class and parental values: another confirmation of the relationship." American Sociological Review 41:538-45.
   1977   "Reassessment 1977." In Kohn, Class and Conformity: A Study in Values. 2nd ed. Chicago: University of Chicago Press.

1981 "Personality, occupation, and social stratification: a frame of reference." In D. J. Treiman and R. V. Robinson (eds.), Research in Social Stratification and Mobility, Vol 1. Greenwich, CT: JAI Press.

Lenski, G.
1961 The Religious Factor. Garden City, NY: Doubleday.

Lynd, R., and H. Lynd
1929 Middletown: A Study in Contemporary American Culture. New York: Harcourt-Brace.

Messick, S.
1968 "Response sets." In D.L. Sills (ed.), International Encyclopedia of the Social Sciences, Vol 13. New York: Macmillan.

Miller, D.R., and G.E. Swanson
1958 The Changing American Parent. New York: John Wiley.

Moore, M.
1975 "Rating versus ranking in the Rokeach Value Survey: an Israeli comparison." European Journal of Social Psychology 5:405-08.

Munson, J.M., and S. H. McIntyre
1979 "Developing practical procedures for the measurement of personal values in cross-cultural marketing." Journal of Marketing Research 16:48-52.

National Opinion Research Center
1982 General Social Surveys, 1972-82: Cumulative Codebook. Chicago: National Opinion Research Center, University of Chicago.

O'Brien, R.
1979 "The use of Pearson's correlation with ordinal data." American Sociological Review 44:851-57.

Phillips, D.L.
1973 Abandoning Method. San Francisco: Jossey-Bass.

Rankin, W.L., and J.W. Grube
1980 "A comparison of ranking and rating procedures for value system measurement." European Journal of Social Psychology 10:233-46.

Reynolds, T.J., and J.P. Jolly
1980 "Measuring personal values: an evaluation of alternative methods." Journal of Marketing Research 17:531-36.

Rokeach, M.
1967 Value Survey. Sunyvale, CA: Halgren Tests, 873 Persimmon.
1970 Beliefs, Attitudes and Values. San Francisco: Jossey-Bass.
1973 The Nature of Human Values. New York: Free Press.

Schaeffer, N.C.
1982 "A general social survey experiment in generic words." Public Opinion Quarterly 46:572-81.

Siegel, P.M.
1971 "Prestige in the American occupational structure." Ph.D. dissertation, University of Chicago. Proceedings of the Association for Consumer Research.

Williams, R.M.
1968 "Values." In D.L. Sills (ed.), International Encyclopedia of the Social Sciences. New York: Macmillan.

Question-Order Effects
on Presidential Popularity

LEE SIGELMAN

SOCIAL scientists are becoming increasingly sensitive to the potential contamination of survey data by response effects. This paper explores a type of response problem about which relatively little is known: the effect of question order (see especially Sudman and Bradburn, 1974). The paper centers on a question that has been asked in Gallup Polls for more than 40 years: "Do you approve or disapprove of the way that —— is handling his job as President?"

A question-order effect is said to operate when responses are influenced by the question's placement within a survey. Most research on order effects pertains to the situation in which people's responses to one item in a survey are consciously or unconsciously influenced by their responses to a previous item; had the order of the items been reversed, or had the first one not been asked, their responses to the later question would have been different. This can happen, for example, as the result of what Bradburn and Mason

---

Abstract A methodological experiment is conducted on the same question that is used virtually every month in the Gallup Poll to measure presidential popularity. The point of the experiment is to determine whether presidential popularity is affected by the placement of the question within the survey, in response to a recent charge that alternations in the order in which this question has been asked invalidate time-series analyses of presidential popularity. The primary finding is that the order in which the question is presented does not significantly affect the direction of response (the balance between approval and disapproval), but it does affect opinionation (the willingness to make a directional response, whether positive or negative). This effect is found to be particularly pronounced for less educated respondents. The implications of these findings for time series analysis of presidential popularity are spelled out.

Lee Sigelman is Associate Professor in the Department of Political Science, University of Kentucky. The data analyzed in this study were collected and made available by the University of Kentucky Survey Research Center. The author bears sole responsibility for the analyses and interpretations presented here. Thanks are due to Michael Baer and Carol Sigelman for helpful comments.

(1964) called a "consistency effect," meaning that responses to a given question are brought into line with responses to an earlier question.

Recently, Darcy and Schramm (1979) have expressed concern that the Gallup presidential popularity question may be affected by question-order bias. Prior to 1956, this question was asked toward the end of the Gallup interview schedule, but since 1956 (except for several surveys conducted during the Johnson administration) it has been the very first question Gallup respondents are asked. The problem, as Darcy and Schramm see it, is that when the question was asked toward the end of the interview, a previous question may have influenced people's responses to it. To illustrate, they cite the January 1968 Gallup Poll, in which before being asked the presidential popularity question respondents were asked about Vietnam, wage and price controls, and their preferences for the presidential nomination. These questions may, they argue, have stacked the deck against President Johnson, so that his popularity appeared lower than it would have if none of the preceding questions had been asked. "Without evidence to the contrary," Darcy and Schramm (1979:544) conclude, "it seems reasonable to assume that presidential approval items preceded by politically charged items are not comparable to presidential approval items not so preceded."

This argument is plausible, but Darcy and Schramm present no hard evidence in support of it. Rather, they simply assume ("without evidence to the contrary") that a consistency effect invalidates comparison of presidential popularity across pre- and post-1955 surveys. In light of the lack of hard evidence one way or the other, the operation of a consistency effect on the Gallup presidential popularity question is taken here as a proposition to be tested rather than as an accomplished fact.

Hypotheses

In testing this proposition, it is useful to think of presidential popularity as a vector composed of two elements: *opinionation,* or the willingness to evaluate the president, whether positively or negatively; and *direction,* or the balance between positive and negative evaluations. The consistency effect to which Darcy and Schramm refer relates to the impact that preceding survey items can have on the direction of people's evaluations. *H1: When the Gallup presidential popularity question is preceded by negatively charged items, presidential popularity tends to be biased downward.*

If this hypothesis is correct, placing the presidential popularity question first in the Gallup interview schedule may seem to be the ideal solution. However, there is more to order effects than just the consistency problem, for bias could also occur if a question is asked too soon. Survey researchers have often been counseled against asking sensitive, unpleasant, or embarrassing questions in an interview before rapport and trust have developed between respondent and interviewer (see Warwick and Lininger, 1975:150). Asking such questions prematurely can lead respondents to shade their answers in a direction they perceive to be socially desirable (Sudman and Bradburn, 1974:50–51). Problems may arise if respondents are called on to express a judgment before they have "warmed up"—before their critical faculties have been fully engaged. In this situation, too, the tendency may be to respond in a safe, stereotypical fashion. Since the president occupies a high place in the American normative order (see Greenstein, 1965), safety and social desirability both seem more likely to produce "approve" than "disapprove" responses to the Gallup question. This type of problem actually has the same implication for presidential popularity as the consistency effect referred to in H1. *H2: When the Gallup presidential popularity question is asked very early in an interview, it tends to elicit more favorable evaluations than when it is asked late.*

An additional possibility is that the placement of a question might affect people's very willingness to express an opinion. This seems most likely in the same types of circumstances discussed in the preceding paragraph. That is, asking a touchy question very early in an interview could prompt a socially desirable response, as H2 predicts, but it could also prompt a noncommittal response—a refusal to offer any evaluation at all, pro or con. Similarly, asking a fairly complex evaluative question before respondents are warmed up could lead to a higher rate of "don't know" responses than would be given if the very same question were asked later in the interview, after such questions had become routine. In hypothesis form: *H3: When the Gallup presidential popularity question is asked very early in an interview, it tends to elicit less opinionation than when it is asked late.*

Data and Methods

Testing of these hypotheses was made possible by the cooperation of the University of Kentucky Survey Research Center, which agreed to use a split-ballot format for the Fall 1979 administration of its continuing series of statewide telephone surveys in Kentucky. Between November 6 and November 28, 1979, interviews were conducted with 746 Kentuckians. Telephone numbers were randomly selected from all telephone directories used in the state, but then the last digit of each number was randomized before calls were placed to insure that new and unlisted numbers could be sampled. Sampling error for a random sample of this size is approximately 4 percent.

Two different versions of the questionnaire were alternated from one telephone call to the next. Each version contained the very same 48 questions, in which respondents were asked, among other things, about what they perceived to be the most pressing social problem as well as about energy problems, gasoline costs, home heating costs, nuclear power, pollution, drugs, and the bribing of politicians. While none of these questions referred directly to the president, most were "politically charged," as Darcy and Schramm use the term, in a negative direction. In fairness to Darcy and Schramm, the implicit bias of these items seems less extreme than that of the items in the 1968 Gallup Poll they cited; in this sense the Kentucky survey poses a "weak test" of H1.

The only difference between the two versions of the questionnaire was the placement of the presidential popularity question: on Version A, it was the very first opinion question, preceded only by three short information items concerning the respondent's place of residence; on Version B, it was the thirty-third question, asked after all the other questions referred to in the preceding paragraph. Overall, 293 (44.1 percent) of the 665 interviewees who provided useable responses said they approved of President Carter's performance in office, 269 (40.5 percent) said they disapproved, and 103 (15.5 percent) offered no opinion; of those who expressed an opinion, 52.1 percent approved and 47.9 percent disapproved of Carter's performance.

Findings

Table 1 reveals that, contrary to both H1 and H2, there was virtually no difference in the direction of evaluations of the president

Table 1. The Effect of Question Order on Direction and Opinionation of Responses

	Version A	Version B
Direction[a]		
% Approve	52.8% (143)	51.5% (150)
% Disapprove	47.2% (128)	48.5% (141)
Opinionation[b]		
% Opinionated	80.4% (271)	88.7% (291)
% Not opinionated	19.6% (66)	11.3% (37)

NOTE: See text for question wording. In Version A, the presidential popularity item was the first opinion question; in Version B it was the thirty-third question.

[a] $Z = .309$, n.s.

[b] $Z = 2.964$, $p < .01$.

from Version A to Version B. A small discrepancy did emerge, with 52.8 percent of the opinionated respondents supporting Carter when the question was asked at the outset and 51.5 percent supporting him when the question was asked later; but as the z-statistic for difference of proportions indicates, this difference was much too slight to be attributed to anything but chance. Accordingly, both H1 and H2 were rejected.

This is not to say that there were no order effects at all, for as Table 1 indicates, there was a statistically significant difference between Versions A and B in respondents' willingness to express an evaluation of President Carter's performance in office. When the presidential popularity question was the first opinion item in the interview, 80.4 percent of the respondents offered an opinion and 19.6 percent did not. But when the same question was the thirty-third item in the interview, the percentage of opinionated respondents rose to 88.7 percent and the "don't knows" dropped to 11.3 percent—a difference that is easily significant at the .01 level. Thus, while question order seems to have had virtually no effect on the direction of people's evaluations of the president, it does, as H3 predicted, seem to have affected their willingness to express an opinion.

Taking the analysis one step farther, let us see whether order effects had a disproportionate influence on any particular type of respondent. The research literature suggests that response effects are especially pronounced among less educated respondents (Sudman and Bradburn, 1974), presumably because such individuals are generally less informed and are thus more susceptible to influence by contextual factors. In order to explore this possibility, respondents were divided into two categories, depending on whether their formal education had ended after no more than 12 years or had continued beyond high school.

This proved to be very revealing. Just as in the sample as a whole, question order had no significant effect on the direction of the evaluations expressed by either type of respondent (see Table 2). However, Table 2 clearly differentiates between more and less educated respondents with respect to the effect of question-order effect on opinionation. Among more educated respondents, there was no question-order effect on opinionation: Versions A and B elicited almost identical rates of "don't know" response—15.8 percent and 16.8 percent, respectively. However, fully 20.5 percent of the less educated respondents offered no opinion of President Carter's performance when the question was first on the survey, but only 8.4 percent declined to offer an opinion when the question was asked later—a difference that was significant at the .01 level.

Table 2. Effect of Question Order on Direction and Opinionation of Responses, by Level of Education

	Version A		Version B	
Direction				
Less educated respondents[a]				
% Approve	53.9%	(96)	54.1%	(106)
% Disapprove	46.1%	(82)	45.9%	(90)
More educated respondents[b]				
% Approve	48.2%	(41)	45.7%	(43)
% Disapprove	51.8%	(44)	54.3%	(51)
Opinionation				
Less educated respondents[c]				
% Opinionated	79.5%	(178)	91.6%	(196)
% Not opinionated	20.5%	(46)	8.4%	(18)
More educated respondents[d]				
% Opinionated	84.2%	(85)	83.2%	(94)
% Not opinionated	15.8%	(16)	16.8%	(19)

[a] $Z = .038$, n.s.
[b] $Z = .333$, n.s.
[c] $Z = -3.270$, $p < .01$.
[d] $Z = .196$, n.s.

Discussion

It may be that a consistency effect would have emerged if the presidential popularity question had been preceded by items that were even more politically charged than those in the Kentucky survey. But for the present it would seem at the very least that unless the implicit bias of other items is quite extreme, evaluations of presidential performance are fairly impervious to a consistency effect.

Perhaps the most ironic twist to these findings is that even though question order had no significant directional impact on people's evaluations of the president, a post-1955 president could still cite these findings to support a claim that his standing with the public is higher than the Gallup popularity figure suggests. There are two keys to such an argument. First, presidential popularity is customarily discussed in terms of the precentage of all Gallup Poll respondents—those who express an opinion and those who do not— who approve of the president's performance. This is how presidential popularity is usually treated in the press, where Gallup press releases are given headlines like "Carter Popularity Falls to 32 percent"; it is also how scholarly researchers typically treat presidential popularity in their time-series analyses (see Mueller, 1973). Second, according to the evidence that was presented earlier, question order does affect opinionation. Thus, even though there was no significant difference between Version A and Version B respondents in the balance of positive and negative evaluations, presidential popularity as traditionally measured was nonetheless 3 percent to 4 percent higher in Version B than in Version A because people were about 8 percent more judgmental in Version B than in Version A. Therefore, it would be legitimate to conclude on the basis of this evidence that by asking the question first, Gallup deflates presidential popularity below what it would be if the question were asked later. The other side of the coin is that by asking the question first, Gallup also deflates presidential *un*popularity. But as long as attention centers primarily on presidential popularity rather than presidential unpopularity, this latter implication seems less significant than the former.

In this light, what can be said about Darcy and Schramm's contention that presidential popularity figures from Gallup Polls conducted before 1956 and at various points between 1965 and 1968 are not strictly comparable to figures from other Gallup Polls? On balance, it would appear that Darcy and Schramm were right, but for the wrong reason. Their argument concerned the effect of question order on the direction of evaluations, but in the Kentucky survey no such effect emerged. However, the significant effect of question order on opinionation itself poses a threat to comparability: as shown in the previous paragraph, the primary impact of placing the question first in a survey was to cut down on opinionation, but the by-product was to lower presidential popularity. The implication is that presidential popularity would have been higher in a given post-1955 Gallup Poll if the question had been asked later in the interview, simply because opinionation would have been higher; in like manner, presidential popularity would have been lower in a given pre-1956 Gallup Poll if the question had been asked first.

How serious this question-order effect is for researchers depends in large measure on how time-series analyses are conducted. If separate regression equations are estimated for each presidential administration, as has sometimes been done (e.g., Kernell, 1978), the problem should be very minor. For each administration except Johnson's, the only effect on the regression equation would be on the intercept value; because question order was constant within administrations other than Johnson's, there could be no possible question order effect on other regression statistics.

If attention centers on the Johnson administration, or if researchers wish to estimate a single equation across all administrations, the question-order problem becomes somewhat more complex. But contrary to the impression left by Darcy and Schramm, even in these circumstances the problem is not insuperable, for experimental evidence like that presented above could be used as a guide for adjusting popularity figures to enhance comparability across surveys. Specific numerical examples of such adjustment procedures could be given, but at this point it seems prudent to defer any such illustrations until data become available from a national survey in which various question orderings have been tried and sets of preceding items that are either positively or negatively charged have been included. For the present, it can be said that the size of any adjustment should be a function of: (1) the size of the opinionation effect, here estimated to be approximately 12 percent for less educated respondents and essentially nonexistent for more educated ones; (2) the size of the consistency effect, here estimated to be inconsequential for both groups; (3) the size of the social desirability effect, also estimated to be inconsequential for both groups; (4) the size of the gap between more and less educated respondents in the direction of their evaluations of the president; and (5) the relative sizes of the more and less educated groups in the sample. The sheer magnitude of any such adjustments would not be great—almost always 5 percent or less—but this is put into perspective by the fact that in all the years that Gallup has asked the presidential popularity question the *mean* absolute monthly change in percent approval is between 3 percent and 4 percent (*Gallup Opinion Index,* 1975).

The more general lesson to be learned from the present study is that greater attention must be given to question-order effects. Particular attention must be paid to the effect of question order on opinionation. It seems likely that the potential biasing effect of question order is less pronounced than that of some other sources of response bias, but the evidence presented above indicates nonetheless that question order can have a significant impact on survey responses. It is also true that strategies can be devised to offset the biases that are introduced by question order, but the application of such strategies presupposes an awareness that question order problems exist. Failure to seek out and neutralize such effects can only result in uncertainty about what threats to validity might be lurking and what their effects on research findings might be.

References

Bradburn, Norman H., and William M. Mason
   1964   "The effect of question order on responses." Journal of Marketing Research 1:57–61.
Darcy, R., and Sarah Slavin Schramm
   1979   "Comment on Kernell." American Political Science Review 73:543–45.

Gallup Opinion Index
  1975   Report No. 125 (November–December).
Greenstein, Fred I.
  1965   "Popular images of the president." American Journal of Psychiatry
         122:523–29.
Kernell, Samuel
  1978   "Explaining presidential popularity." American Political Science Re-
         view 72:506–22.
Mueller, John
  1973   War, Presidents and Public Opinion. New York: Wiley.
Sudman, Seymour, and Norman M. Bradburn
  1974   Response Effects in Surveys. Chicago: Aldine.
Warwick, Donald P., and Charles A. Lininger
  1975   The Sample Survey: Theory and Practice. New York: McGraw-Hill.

Context and Contiguity
in Survey Questionnaires

HOWARD SCHUMAN, GRAHAM KALTON,
AND JACOB LUDWIG

THE IMPORTANCE of context effects in survey questionnaires has been pointed up in several recent reports.[1] In the present paper we start from one of the most firmly established such effects and address a further important issue: to what degree are context effects due to placing questions in contiguous positions, with no intervening items, as against having them simply appear in the same questionnaire. Looked at from a practical standpoint, can investigators reduce context effects by interposing neutral items between questions that are known or thought likely to influence one another?

We focus on a pair of items concerning Communist and American reporters where the context effect has been shown to be both strong and stable over time:

Communist reporter item: Do you think the United States should let Communist newspaper reporters from other countries come in here and send back to their papers the news as they see it?

[1] A review of the literature on context effects is included in Schuman and Presser (1981), chap. 2.

Abstract Previous experiments have shown an order effect for two adjacent items, one concerning the admittance of American reporters to Russia and the other concerning the admittance of Communist reporters to the U.S. The experiment reported here found that this effect remained when the two items were separated by a series of 17 other unrelated questions.

Howard Schuman is Director of the Survey Research Center and a Professor of Sociology, Graham Kalton is a Research Scientist in the Survey Research Center and a Professor of Biostatistics, and Jacob Ludwig is a doctoral student in sociology, all at The University of Michigan. This paper is based on research carried out with the aid of a grant (SES–80–16136) from the National Science Foundation. The authors wish to acknowledge helpful comments by Otis Dudley Duncan.

American reporter item: Do you think a Communist country like Russia should let American newspaper reporters come in and send back to America the news as they see it?

Hyman and Sheatsley (1950) conducted the first split-ballot experiment with these items in 1948, asking the Communist reporter question followed by the American reporter question for one half the sample and reversing the question order for the other half. They found a highly significant question order effect, with respondents more likely to allow Communist reporters into the United States after having answered the American reporter question, and less likely to want American reporters admitted to a Communist country after having answered the Communist reporter question. Recently Schuman and Presser (1981) replicated the experiment, again finding a sizable order effect. Although the effect diminished over time, it remained in 1980 quite large relative to other context effects reported in the literature, and its significant interaction with time (1950 vs. 1980) added to its importance for trend analysis. Furthermore, the basic effect is readily interpretable in both years as due to context making salient a norm of reciprocity that exerts a pressure toward consistency in response to the two items. In sum, the items are good candidates for a further experiment on contiguity.

A new split-ballot experiment was carried out in September 1981, using three randomly assigned forms in a Survey Research Center national telephone survey.[2] Responses to the Communist reporter item are presented in Table 1, with the results for the standard

Table 1. Percent Yes to the Communist Reporter Question by Context and Contiguity

Order	A Com./Amer.	B Amer./Com.	C Amer./(17 items)/Com.
Percent	44.4%	70.1%	66.4%
(Sample size)	(117)	(107)	(107)

A vs. B: $X_1^2 = 15.20$, $p < 0.001$[a]
B vs. C: $X_1^2 = 0.34$, n.s.
A vs. C: $X_1^2 = 10.95$, $p < 0.001$[a]

[a] The overall χ^2 for the table is $\chi_2^2 = 18.11$; $p < 0.001$. For an approximate multiple comparisons test based on the Bonferroni inequality, the p-values may be increased by a factor of 3; the A vs. B contrast remains significant at the $p < 0.001$ level and the A vs. C contrast is significant at the $p < 0.005$ level.

[2] The initial question appeared two-thirds of the way through a half-hour interview. The sample consisted of 335 RDD interviews and had a response rate of 70.6 percent. (An additional sample of reinterviews done at the same point with respondents originating from an RDD sample of six months earlier showed results essentially the same as those in Table 1.)

experimental design shown in the first two columns (A and B).[3] In both cases the items were asked one immediately after the other, varying only in which item came first. As can be seen, the previously discovered context effect is replicated, the size of the effect (26 percent) being close to the figure of 20 percent obtained in 1980 by Schuman and Presser (1981). The third column (C) presents the result for the contiguity variation: the American reporter item appears first, followed by 17 mainly demographic items, and then finally the Communist reporter item.[4]

The results involving the new variation are clear-cut. The original context effect is successfully replicated not only in contiguous positions but in similarly ordered but separated positions. There is a slight trend for the context effect on the dispersed form (C) to be smaller than on the adjacent form (B) having the same order, but the difference is trivial and falls well within the range of sampling error. The full cross-tabulations (see Appendix) also show very similar distributions for forms B and C. Overall, the evidence from this experiment is that the context effect is not diminished by separating the key items within the same questionnaire.

We do not wish to claim that separating items that are subject to a context effect will never reduce or eliminate the effect. If the effect is weak to begin with, or perhaps involves subtle wording connotations that can persist only in short-term memory, it may be possible to decrease it by interposing a number of unrelated items. But this experiment indicates that at least in some cases context effects are not necessarily a function of question contiguity in any simple sense, nor are they always reducible by the simple stratagem of dispersing items throughout a questionnaire. Since for the reporter items it can also be argued that the effects are not artifacts in the sense of one context being more valid than another (Schuman, 1982), we are forced to regard the problem of context as a matter of real substantive importance, rather than a technical issue of interest only to questionnaire specialists.

[3] Only the effects of question order on the Communist item are shown in Table 1, since only it appears in the second position both contiguously (form B) and noncontiguously (form C). However, for forms A and B, there is also a difference due to context for the American item (76 percent yes and 55 percent yes, respectively), similar in direction and size to that reported by Schuman and Presser (1981). Full cross-tabulations are presented in the Appendix.

[4] In addition to standard demographic items (e.g., age, marital status), there were also several questions dealing with racial attitudes. Some of the demographic items had contingent follow-ups, so that many respondents experienced more than 17 questions between the two reporter items. None of the 17 items had content in any way related to reporting, to Communism, or to the Soviet Union.

Appendix

The following tables contain cross-tabulations of responses to the two reporter questions, given separately for each experimental form. Cell entries are raw frequencies. Note that N's for each form are slightly lower than those reported in Table 1, due to missing data on the American reporter question.

	A. *Com./Amer.*		B. *Amer./Com.*		C. *Amer./(17 items)/Com.*	
ORDER	COMMUNIST		COMMUNIST		COMMUNIST	
	Yes	No	Yes	No	Yes	No
AMER. Yes	52	11	67	10	65	12
AMER. No	0	52	5	18	5	21

References

Hyman, H. H., and P. B. Sheatsley
  1950 "The current status of American public opinion." Pp. 11–34 in J. C. Payne (ed.), The Teaching of Contemporary Affairs. Twenty-first Yearbook of the National Council of Social Studies.
Schuman, H.
  1982 "Artifacts are in the mind of the beholder." The American Sociologist 17:21–28.
Schuman, H., and S. Presser
  1981 Questions and Answers in Attitude Surveys: Experiments on Question Form, Wording, and Context. New York: Academic Press.

Vague Quantifiers

NORMAN M. BRADBURN AND CARRIE MILES

I N surveys we frequently ask respondents to make judgments about "how much," "how often," "how strongly," and the like. Such judgments are most often made in terms of sets of ordered categories such as "very often, pretty often, or not too often," "sometimes, often, never," "too little, about right, too much," or "below average, average, above average." While we assume that the quantifiers involved are ordered in their intensity, we know little about the characteristics of such quantifying adverbs. For example, do these imprecise quantifiers have some common meaning that is more precise than is apparent on the surface? Do they mean the same thing to each respondent or are variations in meaning patterned in some discoverable way? Does the meaning depend not only on the quantifier itself but also on the context in which it is used—for example, on the word it modifies or on the other quantifiers used in the set? Previous research gives us some clues to the types of problems that are apt to arise, although it does not give us full understanding.

An early study on quantifying meaning (Mosier, 1941) noted that the meaning of a word varied for each individual and in each context in which the word was used. He postulated that word meaning had two components: one constant, anchoring meaning in the vicinity of a particular point on a continuum, and one variable, representing fluctuations in meaning that stemmed from the individual usage of the

Abstract   The responses to many survey questions are often made in terms of vague quantifiers such as "very," "pretty," or "not too." We know little about the characteristics of such quantifying terms. This article reviews several theoretical approaches to the problem of quantifying meaning based on studies from experimental psychology. It also reports data from a pilot study that tries to make more precise quantitative estimates for three common vague quantifiers.

Norman M. Bradburn is Senior Study Director, National Opinion Research Center. Carrie Miles is a graduate student in the Department of Behavioral Sciences, University of Chicago. This research was partially supported by NSF Grant No. GS 43245 and by Bio-Medical Grant No. 5–S07–RR05783–02.

speaker and the context. If measured over a large group of speakers, the mean of the distribution represents the constant; individual responses to meaning are arranged in a normal distribution around that point. Data from Mosier's study and from Jones and Thurstone (1955) support this interpretation.

Mosier's 1941 study also included a set of words modified by adverbial intensifiers—for example, "very," "quite," "completely," "extremely." These intensifiers seem to shift the meaning of the base word toward the extremes of the continuum.

Simpson (1944) attempted to quantify meaning along slightly different lines. Dealing with frequency words, Simpson asked his subjects to indicate the proportion of times out of 100 the stimulus word represented. Subjects were asked, for example, to what proportion "sometimes" referred. Hakel (1968) repeated the study with some variation and obtained results that correlated highly with Simpson's. Hakel noted that "variability is rampant. One man's 'rarely' is another man's 'hardly ever.' " But he found that there was considerable stability in overall distributions. Wide individual variability may not be incompatible with stable group variation.

Cliff (1959) studied the effect of adding words that act like multipliers, similar to Mosier's intensifiers. These words, such as "quite," "very," and "unusually," have no value of their own but act to "stretch" the meaning of the words they modify. Cliff's subjects rated sets of modified evaluative adjectives on an unfavorable-neutral-favorable continuum. The results supported Cliff's hypothesis that the "common adverbs of degree multiply the intensity of the adjectives they modify" (p. 43). For example, he found that "very" multiplied the unfavorable-favorable scale value of an adjective or adverb it modified by about 1.317; "slightly" modified the adjective by about .55. If these results have applicability to the responses of subjects in survey conditions, then one might expect respondents to consider "very often" to be 1.317 times as frequent as "often." If one could confirm such values, one might use information about the scale intervals to construct continuous rather than merely ordered scales, assuming that individual variation is not too great.

The view that meaning is precise and may be specified as a point on a continuum or intersection of continuums is explicit in these studies. That view has been challenged by Parducci (1968), Chase (1969), and Pepper and Prytulak (1974), who point out that the context of words is important in establishing their meanings. Chase devised two scales using Hakel's terms, one composed of low-frequency terms (seldom, not often, once in awhile, occasionally, generally) and the other of higher-frequency terms (occasionally, now and then, about as often as not, usually, very often). Thirty-four students rated their use of 10 different study methods using each of these scales. Chase hypothesized that if people actually responded to the meaning of the words, the responses based on the high-frequency scale would be quite different study methods using each of these scales. Chase hypothfact, Chase found that the differences between the two scales were small. He concluded that "respondents get a good deal of meaning from scale adjectives because of the adjectives' relative position in a group of response categories, rather than in terms of a 'standard' definition of a given word out of context of other category levels" (p. 1043).

In the Pepper and Prytulak study, subjects provided numerical definitions of terms used in contexts which varied in frequency. In a "low-frequency" context, one of five terms—very often, frequently, sometimes, seldom, almost never—was embedded in the following paragraph:

The *Standard Daily* reported that during 1951 California (frequency term) had sizable earthquakes. One would estimate that during 1951 there were sizable earthquakes on about — days out of every 100.

Since earthquakes (and airplane crashes, the other low-frequency event) are not common occurrences, these were held to be low-frequency events. "High-frequency" events, such as the occurrence of shooting in Hollywood westerns, and "moderate-frequency" events, such as a student's missing breakfast, were also included. The results of this study showed that subjects did indeed perceive the frequencies of these events as the experimenters had expected. Further, they indicated that the numerical estimate for each term increased as the expected frequency for each term increased. Thus the mean response for "sometimes" in the shooting in Hollywood westerns context is higher than the mean response for "very often" in the context of earthquakes. In short, "often" for an improbable event is less than "often" for a highly probable event. A related study by Bass, Cascio, and O'Conner (1974), however, failed to find differences in the values assigned to quantifiers when the context was varied according to the importance of the topic about which opinions were solicited. A critical difference here may have been between quantifiers applied to events or behavior and quantifiers applied to attitudes or beliefs.

Another approach to the study of meaning looks at individual differences rather than contextual differences. Goocher (1965), drawing on Helson's (1964) adaptation level theory, predicted a negative relationship between a favorable attitude toward or participation in an activity and the frequency term selected to describe the median frequency of the occurrence of that event. Data from this study suggest that subjects who engage less in an activity or have a less favorable attitude toward it are more likely than involved or favorable subjects to describe the actual median frequency of the occurrence of the event as "often" or "frequently." This difference appears to result from differences in the perceived median for the activity. Those who do not engage in the activity or do so very infrequently appear to believe that the median frequency is lower than it actually is; thus they describe the actual median with higher level quantifiers. People who are actively engaged in the activity or are favorable to it perceive the median as higher than it actually is, and thus use lower level quantifiers. For example, respondents who dislike eating alone describe eating alone three times a week with adverbs that denote greater frequency than subjects who like eating alone, and respondents who "rarely" eat alone describe eating alone three times a week with adverbs that denote greater frequency than those who "often" eat alone.

Data to begin an exploration of vague quantifiers in surveys comes from an experimental survey conducted for methodological purposes (for a complete description of the study see Blair et al., 1977). In this survey we asked respondents about a series of feeling states they might have experienced during the recent past. For example, we asked how often during the past few weeks respondents had felt particularly excited or interested in something and how often they had felt bored. Respondents were asked to answer in terms of a four-point scale that was labeled "never, not too often, pretty often, or very often." At the conclusion of the set of ten questions, five reflecting positive states and five reflecting negative states, we asked respondents about the meaning of the response category they had chosen for the positive and negative items, those that were least often reported as "never" having been experienced—that is, "particularly excited or interested in something" and "bored." For example, we asked those who reported that they had felt excited or interested in something during the past few weeks "very often" exactly how many times a day or week they meant when they said "very often"; we asked the same individuals how often they meant by the response category they had used for the item about feeling bored. Thus each individual was asked about one response category for one positive and one negative item. While it would have been nice to have estimates for each degree of "often" from each respondent, we felt that this would be too much to ask of the respondents, at least in this survey.

In general, interviewers reported that giving a more precise meaning to degrees of "often" was difficult for respondents and that they were reluctant to give responses. However, only between 5 and 6 percent finally said they did not know or otherwise refused to give a response.

The mean frequencies and the standard deviations for each of the response categories are given in Table 1. Respondents reported in their own terms. The responses were then converted into the number of times per month (taking a month as equal to four weeks if the responses were given in terms of times/week and twenty-eight days if given in terms of times/day). Respondents who reported that they "never" felt excited or bored are, of course, omitted from this table.

If we take these estimates of frequency as rough estimates of the distance between the response categories or the degree to which the modifying terms change the meaning of "often," we see that, although the categories are ordered as we would suppose, the distance between the categories is not the same. It is further from "not too often" to "pretty often" than it is from "pretty often" to "very often." If we think of "times per month" as our metric for excited or interested in something, the distance between "not too often" and "pretty often" is 6.30 times per month, while the distance between "pretty often" and "very often" is only 4.78 times per month. For bored, it is 9.57 times per month between "not too often" and "pretty often," while "very often" is only 3.67 times per month greater than "pretty often."

Perhaps a better way of looking at these data is to consider the category "pretty often" as equivalent to "often" unmodified. (There is evidence from Hakel, 1968, that this is not an unwarranted assumption.) Then we might think of the modifier "not too" as multiplying the meaning of "often" by .51 for excited and .30 for bored, while the effect of the modifier "very" is to multiply the meaning of "often" by 1.37 for excited and 1.27 for bored. Or, to put it in round numbers, "not too often" is about 50 to 70 percent less than "often," and

Table 1. Means and Standard Deviations of Responses to "How Often Is . . . Often?"
(Times/Month)

Response Categories	Excited	Bored
Means		
Not too often	$6.65_{(327)}$[a]	$4.15_{(552)}$
Pretty often	$12.95_{(495)}$	$13.72_{(127)}$
Very often	$17.73_{(247)}$	$17.39_{(99)}$
Standard deviations		
Not too often	8.57	5.71
Pretty often	12.11	10.64
Very often	15.00	13.09

[a] Numbers in parentheses are sample sizes.

"very often" is about 30 percent more. The value of about 1.3 for "very" is similar to that obtained by Cliff (1959).

Note also that there is some support for the hypothesis that the meaning of quantifiers may change in relation to the overall frequency of the event. For the sample as a whole, being excited or interested in something is more frequent than is being bored. Ninety-eight percent of the sample reported feeling excited or interested in something at least once during the past few weeks, while only 70 percent reported feeling bored at least once. When we look at the meaning assigned to the phrase "not too often," we see that it is 2.5 times a month less for bored than for excited or interested. For the other two categories, however, there is very little difference between the frequency estimates given for the two feeling states. Pepper and Prytulak (1974) found that the meaning of specific frequency terms was lower for rare events than for more common events. Since we are not dealing with events whose occurrence is as discrepant as Pepper and Prytulak's (e.g., earthquakes and shooting in westerns), we should not expect to find differences as substantial as they did.

Another way of exploring the relationship between the frequency of the occurrence of events and the meaning given to vague quantifiers is to look at the relationship between scores on two scales, one made up of responses to all the items related to positive feelings and one made up of responses to all the items related to negative feelings. This type of scale, which was developed in other contexts (see Bradburn, 1969), is constructed by giving equal weights to each of the different response categories—for example, zero for "never" through a score of three for "very often"—and summing across the five positive items or five negative items. Thus for each scale the scores could range from zero to 15. If there is a relationship between the frequency of occurrence of a feeling state and the meaning assigned to the quantifiers, we would expect that those who are high on the positive or negative effect scale would report, for example, that "very often" means more times a month than would those who are low on the positive or negative affect scale.

In general, the data shown in Tables 2 and 3 support this hypothesis, although the differences in assigned frequencies are not large for the category "not too often." For the meaning of "very often," those who score high on Positive Affect (scores from 11 to 15) report a mean frequency of 19.3 times a month as compared with a mean frequency of 12.3 times a month by those who score low on Positive Affect (scores from 0 to 8). Not only are those high on the Positive Affect Scale more likely to have reported that they felt excited or interested in something "very often," but also they appear to mean

Table 2. Mean Times/Month "Excited" by Positive Affect

	Positive Affect					
	Low (0–8)		Medium (9–10)		High (11–15)	
Response Category	$\bar{x}$	S.D.	$\bar{x}$	S.D.	$\bar{x}$	S.D.
Not too often	$6.7_{(266)}$[a]	8.9	$7.4_{(43)}$	7.3	—	—
Pretty often	$11.0_{(142)}$	9.8	$12.9_{(251)}$	9.7	$15.7_{(100)}$	18.6
Very often	$[12.3]_{(19)}$	12.2	$14.9_{(60)}$	16.3	$19.3_{(164)}$	15.2

[a] Numbers in parentheses are sample sizes.

more times a month by that response category than those lower on the scale. Similar differences are found for the frequencies assigned to the categories "pretty often" and "very often" among those who differ in scores on the Negative Affect Scale. Note, however, that for all these estimates the standard deviations are quite large.

Having demonstrated some of the differences in the values assigned to the response categories that we typically treat as equal interval categories, how might we use this information in our analysis? One way might be to use the empirical estimates of frequency to weight responses differentially instead of equally. Ideally we would like each respondent to have given a separate estimate of the frequency he or she would assign to each response category for each item. Then we could weight by individual meaning. But here we do not have such complete individual estimates, so we can only use average values. Given the large standard deviations of these estimates, we should not be surprised if the use of average values does not alter the interpretations very much.

As an example of how such a procedure might go, let us look at the relationship between the Positive and Negative Affect Scales and overall ratings of life satisfaction and happiness under different weighting schemes for the various response categories. Table 4 presents data for the Positive and Negative Affect Scales constructed

Table 3. Means Times/Month "Bored" by Negative Affect

	Negative Affect					
	Low (0–4)		Medium (5–6)		High (7–15)	
Response Category	$\bar{x}$	S.D.	$\bar{x}$	S.D.	$\bar{x}$	S.D.
Not too often	$3.6_{(168)}$	3.5	$4.3_{(292)}$	6.9	$4.8_{(88)}$	4.6
Pretty often	—	—	$8.9_{(32)}$	8.7	$15.3_{(91)}$	10.8
Very often	—	—	—	—	$17.3_{(92)}$	13.3

[a] Numbers in parentheses are sample sizes.

Table 4. Correlations and Regression Coefficients for Positive Affect, Negative Affect and Life Satisfactions Using Different Values for "How Often"

Response Categories (Values of "Often")	Correlations				Regression Coefficients	
	Positive Affect/ Negative Affect	Positive Affect/ Life Satisfaction	Negative Affect/ Life Satisfaction	R^2	Betas (S.E.)	
					Positive Affect	Negative Affect
Valued equally	−.079	.317	−.338	.199	.292 (.009)	−.315 (.009)
Valued by frequency	.265	.380	−.363	.218	.306 (.002)	−.282 (.002)
Valued by ratios (Pretty often = 1)	−.266	.381	−.363	.219	.307 (.024)	−.281 (.022)

under different assumptions about the values to be assigned to the frequency categories. The table gives the correlations and the results of a regression of the life satisfaction ratings on Positive and Negative Affect. In the first set of figures the values of 0, 1, 2, and 3 were assigned to the response categories "never," "not too often," "pretty often," and "very often," respectively. The correlation between Positive and Negative Affect is low and negative, while each scale correlates with overall ratings of life satisfaction to about the same degree, although, of course, in opposite directions. The R^2 is .199.

The second set of figures shows the values derived from the respondents' mean reports about how often was meant by each of the response categories, the figures reported in Table 1. The effect of using these values is to give greater weight to the top two response categories and to weight the response "not too often" less for negative affect items than for positive affect items. Using these values to construct the scales changes the correlation between the scales substantially (from −.079 to −.265) and raises slightly the respective correlations with the overall ratings of life satisfaction. The R^2 is also increased slightly, from .199 to .218, but there is very little change in the beta coefficients. We should note, however, that the beta coefficients have now changed around somewhat, so that the beta for Positive Affect is now slightly higher than the beta for Negative Affect and the standard errors are slightly smaller.

In the third set of figures, the values derived from the respondents' mean reports of how often was meant by each of the response categories were also used to construct the scales, but in this transformation the ratios of the mean frequency estimates, instead of the frequency means themselves, were used. In this case "pretty often" was taken as the standard and set to one. "Not too often" thus became .50 for the positive feeling state items and .31 for the negative feeling state items; the value for "very often" became 1.37 for the positive items and 1.27 for the negative items. Using the ratios instead of the frequencies produces nearly identical correlations among the scales and virtually the same R^2 and beta weights for the variables, but it has the effect of substantially increasing the standard errors of the betas. Other transformations, using ratios based on "not too often" as one or using the logarithms of the values, produce substantially the same pattern of correlations and the same R^2.

We conclude from this exercise that using information from estimates of the "oftenness" of different degrees of often does improve the explanatory power of the affect items a little and is worthy of further exploration. Although use of the mean values does not improve things greatly, the variance in the values is very large, and it is likely that substitution of individual estimates, which were not available in this study, would improve things to a considerable extent.

If one needs to rely on individual estimates for the more exact meaning of vague quantifiers, why not just ask for exact estimates in the first place and avoid the problem? We do not typically do this because of the difficulty respondents have with the task. While it is relatively easy for respondents to report how many times in the past week they have been to a movie or how many hours they watched television yesterday, they seem to have a great deal of difficulty in putting precise numbers on subjective states and on events of relatively low salience. It would thus place too great a burden on respondents to have to make precise estimates for each item in a typical survey questionnaire. It does seem possible, however, that respondents could be asked to make one overall numerical estimate for frequency terms within the context of an interview. Further exploration of the benefits of using one-time individual estimates in the interpretation of data will determine whether or not it is worth putting even this increased burden on respondents.

References

Bass, B. M., W. F. Cascio, and E. J. O'Connor
   1974   "Magnitude estimations of expressions of frequency and amount." Journal of Applied Psychology 59:313–20.
Blair, E., S. Sudman, N. M. Bradburn, and C. Stocking
   1977   "How to ask questions about drinking and sex." Journal of Marketing Research 14:315–21.
Bradburn, N. M.
   1969   The Structure of Psychological Well-Being. Chicago: Aldine.

Chase, C. I.
1969 "Often is where you find it." American Psychologist 24:1043.
Cliff, N.
1959 "Adverbs as multipliers." Psychological Review 66:27–44.
Goocher, B. E.
1965 "Effects of attitude and experience on the selection of frequency adverbs." Journal of Verbal Learning and Verbal Behavior 4:193–95.
Hakel, M. D.
1969 "How often is often?" American Psychologist 23:533–34.
Helson, H.
1964 Adaptation Level Theory. New York: Harper & Row.
Jones, L. V., and L. L. Thurstone
1955 "The psychophysics of semantics: an experimental investigation." Journal of Applied Psychology 39:31–36.
Mosier, C. I.
1941 "A psychometric study of meaning." Journal of Social Psychology 13:123–40.
Parducci, A.
1968 "Often is often." American Psychologist 23:828.
Pepper, S., and L. S. Prytulak
1974 "Sometimes frequently means seldom: context effects in the interpretation of quantitative expressions." Journal of Research in Personality 8:95–101.
Simpson, R. H.
1944 "The specific meanings of certain terms indicating differing degrees of frequency." Quarterly Journal of Speech 30:328–30.

Response Scales: Effects of
Category Range on Reported Behavior
and Comparative Judgments

NORBERT SCHWARZ, HANS-J. HIPPLER,
BRIGITTE DEUTSCH, AND FRITZ STRACK

IN SURVEY research as well as laboratory experiments category scales are frequently used to assess quasi-objective data such as frequency of church attendance, hours of television watched, and the like. Although a few practical guidelines are available (Payne, 1951; Sudman and Bradburn, 1982), the selection of the range of categories to be presented to respondents is usually left to the intuition of the researcher. Moreover, previous research has mostly concentrated on response biases without considering the cognitive processes underlying the use of category scales.

In the present paper we want to employ an information-processing perspective to explore the impact of the range of response categories provided to respondents on their behavioral reports and subsequent judgments. Central to the present perspective is the assumption that response scales are not simply "measurement devices" that respondents

Abstract   Effects of the range of response categories provided in a closed answer format on behavioral reports and subsequent judgments were explored. Respondents reported their daily use of television along a scale that either ranged from "up to a half hour" "to more than two and a half hours" or ranged from "up to two and a half hours" to "more than four and a half hours." The former subjects reported less use of television than the latter and estimated the average use of TV to be lower. Moreover, the former subjects evaluated TV to be more important in their lives (Experiment 1) and reported less satisfaction with the variety of their leisure-time activities (Experiment 2). These results indicate that subjects inferred the average amount of television watching from the response alternatives provided them and used it as a standard of comparison in evaluating their behavior and its implications.

Norbert Schwarz is Assistant Professor of Psychology, and Brigitte Deutsch is Research Associate, Universität Heidelberg. Hans-J. Hippler is Project Director, Zentrum für Umfragen, Methoden und Analysen (ZUMA), and Fritz Strack is Assistant Professor of Psychology, Universität Mannheim. Experiment I was supported by ZUMA, Mannheim, as part of a larger study on response effects in surveys; Experiment II was supported by grant Schw 278/2-1 from the Deutsche Forschungsgemeinschaft to Norbert Schwarz and Fritz Strack. The authors want to thank George W. Bohrnstedt, Detlev Kommer, Seymour Sudman, and Robert S. Wyer, Jr. for their helpful comments on an earlier draft of this article. Address correspondence to Norbert Schwarz, Psychologisches Institut, Universität Heidelberg, Hauptstr. 47-51, D-6900 Heidelberg, Federal Republic of Germany.

use to report their behaviors. Rather, respondents may consider the range of behaviors described in the response alternatives to reflect the researcher's knowledge of or expectations about the distribution of these behaviors in the "real world." If so, respondents may use the range of behaviors described in the response alternatives as a frame of reference in estimating and evaluating their own behavior.

In selecting response categories, researchers are generally advised to "make sure that all reasonable alternative answers are included. Omitted alternatives and answers lumped into an "Other" category will be under-reported" (Sudman and Bradburn, 1982. 21).

Moreover, Payne (1951) reported that "given a list of numbers (respondents) are prone to choose those near the middle of the list" (p. 80). He suggested that for knowledge questions that may involve guessing "it may be a wise precaution to set up any list of figures for a test of knowledge with the correct figure at one of the extremes" (p. 82). Indeed, most questions about behavioral frequencies are likely to involve guessing because records of the frequency with which respondents engage in "usual" behaviors are usually not available and respondents provide an estimate rather than an exact report. On the other hand, several studies (e.g., Carp, 1974; Payne, 1946, 1951; Quinn and Belson, 1969) indicated that respondents are particularly likely to endorse the first category of a list of three or more categories (verbal rating scales/ evaluative items) provided them.

In the present studies we explore how respondents' reported estimate of the frequency with which they engage in a mundane behavior (watching TV) is affected by the range of the response categories provided in a closed answer format. In addition, we hypothesize that respondents will use the presumably "usual" behavior, inferred from the range of specific values stated in the response scales, as a standard of comparison in making judgments to which social comparisons are relevant (cf. Suls and Miller, 1977). Two experiments were designed to test these expectations.

Experiment I: Effects on Reported Behavior, Estimated Behavior of Others, and Importance of TV

In the first study, effects of category range on behavioral reports and estimates of the behavior of others were investigated. Respondents were asked to estimate the amount of television they watch along a category scale that ranged, in half-hour steps, either (a) from "up to a half hour" to "more than two and a half hours" or (b) from "up to two and a half hours" to "more than four and a half hours." It was hypothesized that respondents presented the high category range beginning with "up to two and a half hours" would report more TV consumption than respondents presented the low category range beginning with "up to a half hour." Previous research indicated that the average TV consumption in the Federal Republic of Germany is slightly more than two hours (Darschin and Frank, 1982). Thus, both versions of the response scale conform with Payne's (1951) suggestion to place the "true" response at the extreme of the list. In the present study, the "true" response was presented as the first value of the high category list and as the last value of the low category list. If respondents extract information about the real world from the range of the response categories provided, those presented the high category range list should estimate the average TV consumption to be higher as well. Moreover, they may use the inferred average behavior as a standard of comparison in evaluating how important TV is in their own leisure time.

METHOD

The first experiment was carried out in March/April 1983 as part of a larger survey (quota sample) with 132 German adults (more than 18 years of age). Quotas were based on an intersection of age, sex, and years of education. Respondents were randomly assigned to conditions and had to report how many hours they watched TV daily, using one of the two previously described scales, ranging in half-hours steps either from "up to a half hour" to "more than two and a half hours" or from "up to two and a half hours" to "more than four and a half hours." Subsequently, they estimated the daily TV consumption of the average citizen in an open answer format and evaluated how important a role TV played in their own leisure time on a scale from 0 (not at all important) to 10 (very important).

RESULTS AND DISCUSSION

An examination of respondents' behavioral reports indicates that those who were presented the low range scale tended to choose categories in the middle of the list, whereas respondents who were presented the high range scale tended to endorse the first category provided (see Table 1). To assess the impact of the response scale on subjects' reports, their responses in both conditions were coded as either (a) two and a half hours or less or (b) more than two and a half hours. The range of the response scale affected respondents' behavioral reports as expected. Specifically, only 16.2 percent of the respondents who were presented the low category range reported watching TV for more than two and a half hours, while 37.5 percent of the respondents presented the high category range did so, chi^2 (1) = 7.7, $p < .005$. Moreover, respondents presented the low category range subsequently estimated the average TV consumption of German citizens to be 2.7 hours, whereas respondents presented the

Table 1. Reported Behavior, Estimated Behavior of Others,
and Importance of TV as a Function of Category Range

	Reported Behavior		
Low Category Range		High Category Range	
Up to 1/2h	7.4% (5)	Up to 2 1/2h	62.5% (40)
1/2h to 1h	17.7% (12)	2 1/2h to 3h	23.4% (15)
1h to 1 1/2h	26.5% (18)	3h to 3 1/2h	7.8% (5)
1 1/2h to 2h	14.7% (10)	3 1/2h to 4h	4.7% (3)
2h to 2 1/2h	17.7% (12)	4h to 4 1/2h	1.6% (1)
More than 2 1/2h	16.2% (11)	More than 4 1/2h	0.0% (0)
	100% (68)		100% (64)
Estimated TV use of average citizen	2.7h		3.2h
Importance of TV	4.6		3.8

NOTE: N = 132. Importance of TV was assessed on a 10-point bipolar scale (1 = not at all, 10 = very important).

high category range estimated it to be 3.2 hours, $F(1,127) = 8.8$, $p < .004$, indicating that they based these estimates in part on the frequencies suggested by the range of the scales. Consistent with the comparison information derived from these scales, respondents presented the low category range (suggesting to them that other people watch little TV) evaluated TV to be *more* important in their *own* leisure time, $M = 4.6$, than respondents presented the high category range, $M = 3.8$, $F(1,127) = 7.92$, $p < .006$. Note that this was true even though the former reported watching *less* TV than the latter.

In summary, the data provide strong support for the assumption that the range of categories presented as part of a closed format question would affect respondents' behavioral reports as well as related judgments. However, in the present study respondents were explicitly asked to estimate average TV consumption. This task might have directed their attention to the category range for appropriate hints, resulting in a high salience of the category range. As a result, the effect of category range on the evaluation of TV importance might be more pronounced than it would have been otherwise. This possibility was explored in a second study.

Experiment II: Effects on Leisure Time Satisfaction

Two procedures were used in this study to guard against artifactual effects of making the response range salient. First, respondents estimated the average TV consumption after rather than before giving evaluative judgments. Second, for half of the respondents the category scale and the evaluative judgment were separated by filler items to render the category range less salient. Finally, a control condition was run in which subjects were not presented a category scale but reported TV consumption in response to an open ended question. In summary, the present study followed a 3 × 2 factorial design with scale (low or high category range, open question) and filler items (present, absent) as between-subjects factors.

Respondents' satisfaction with the variety of their leisure-time activities (rather than importance of TV) was assessed as an evaluative judgment in this study. Since watching a lot of TV is socially undesirable in West Germany (Mueller, 1980), it was hypothesized that respondents would report higher satisfaction with the variety of their leisure-time activities when the response scale suggests that other people watch more TV than when it suggests others watch less TV.

METHOD

In a survey embedded in a larger questionnaire, 79 German employees, recruited during office hours and randomly assigned to conditions, reported their daily TV consumption on one of the two previously described category scales, or in response to an open question. Subsequently, they reported their satisfaction with the variety of their leisure-time activities on a scale from 1 (very dissatisfied, I wish there were more variety) to 11 (very satisfied, I don't want more variety). For some respondents the two questions were separated by several filler items regarding their mass media consumption while for others they were not. Finally, respondents estimated the TV consumption of the average German citizen.

RESULTS AND DISCUSSION

As in Experiment I, the ranges of the response scales affected subjects' reports of their own use of TV. Using two and a half hours as a cut-point, 19.2 percent of the control group respondents reported watching TV for more than two and a half hours per day while none (0 percent) of the respondents presented the low category range and 29.6 percent of those presented the high category range reported doing so, $chi^2 (2) = 8.68, p < .02$. As in the previous study, respondents presented the low category range preferred the middle categories while those presented the high category range preferred the first category presented, as shown in Table 2.

Moreover, the type of scale used by subjects to report their behavior affected their evaluation of their leisure-time activities, $F(2,73) = 3.13, p < .05$. Specifically, planned comparisons indicated that respondents who reported their TV consumption on the high range category scale,

Table 2. Reported Behavior, Leisure Time Satisfaction, and Estimated Behavior of Others as a Function of Category Range

Reported Behavior					
Low Category Range		High Category Range		Open Answer Format	
Up to 1/2h	11.5% (3)	Up to 2 1/2h	70.4% (19)	Up to 1/2h	0.0% (0)
1/2h to 1h	26.9% (7)	2 1/2h to 3h	22.2% (6)	1/2h to 1h	19.2% (5)
1h to 1 1/2h	26.9% (7)	3h to 3 1/2h	7.4% (2)	1h to 1 1/2h	15.4% (4)
1 1/2h to 2h	26.9% (7)	3 1/2h to 4h	0.0% (0)	1 1/2h to 2h	46.2% (12)
2h to 2 1/2h	7.7% (2)	4h to 4 1/2h	0.0% (0)	2h to 2 1/2h	0.0% (0)
More than 2 1/2h	0.0% (0)	More than 4 1/2h	0.0% (0)	2 1/2h to 3h	19.2% (5)
	100% (26)		100% (27)		100% (26)
Estimated TV use of average citizen	2.8h		3.7h		3.7h
Leisure time satisfaction	8.2		9.6		8.8

NOTE N = 79. Leisure-time satisfaction was assessed on an 11-point bipolar scale (1 = very dissatisfied, I wished there were more variety, 11 = very satisfied, I don't want more variety).

suggesting to them a high average TV consumption, subsequently reported more satisfaction with the variety they had in their leisure time, $M = 9.6$, than respondents presented the low category range, $M = 8.2$, $t(73) = 2.50$, $p < .02$. Control group subjects responding in an open answer format reported intermediate satisfaction, $M = 8.8$, that did not significantly differ from either of the experimental groups, t's (73) = 1.34 and 1.15, respectively, n.s. Finally, these effects were not affected by the presence of filler items, $F < 1$ for main effect and interaction.

As expected, the type of scale presented also affected respondents' estimates of the TV consumption of the average German citizen, $F(2,73) = 6.17$, $p < .003$. Specifically, respondents presented the low category range estimated the average consumption to be lower, $M = 2.8$, than both control group respondents and respondents presented the high category range, M's = 3.7, t's (73) = 3.0 and 3.12, respectively, $p < .004$. The latter groups did not differ from one another, suggesting that the information transmitted by the high category range was similar to control group respondents' spontaneous assumptions concerning the typical use of TV. Again, the results were not affected by the presence of filler items, $F < 1$ for the main effect and $F(2,73) = 1.11$, n.s. for the interaction.

In summary, the data replicated the results of the first study and supported the hypothesis that respondents derived comparison information from the category range they were presented and used this comparison information in making satisfaction judgments. Moreover, the effects on satisfaction judgments were obtained without any attempt to direct respondents' attention to the presumed typical behavior; that is, their estimates of the "typical" behavior were not assessed until after satisfaction judgments had been reported. Finally, neither the effects of response range on satisfaction judgments nor its effects on estimates of others' behavior were affected by the introduction of filler items, suggesting that the effects are rather robust.

General Discussion

The present studies demonstrate that response scales serve informative functions. Specifically, the response categories provided in a closed answer format inform the respondent about the researcher's knowledge of or expectations about the real world. The response categories suggest a range of "usual" or "expected" behaviors, and this information affects respondents' behavioral reports as well as related judgments. Specifically, respondents seem to use the frame of reference provided by the scale in estimating their own behavior and they seem reluctant to report behaviors that are unusual in the context of the response scale, e.g., because they constitute the extreme categories.

In addition, respondents use the presumably "usual" behavior suggested by the response scale as a standard of comparison in related judgments. In line with this assumption, respondents' evaluations of the importance of TV in their own lives as well as of the variety of their leisure-time activities were affected by the comparison standards suggested by the scales. Because the impact of the information provided by the scale should be the more pronounced the less other relevant comparison information is available to respondents, effects of category range are likely to be obtained in content domains for which direct access to comparison information is difficult. The effects should be much smaller, however, for content domains in which the behavior of others is highly visible. This implication remains to be tested in future research.

Turning to the applied implication of the results, researchers should consider the use of open answer formats in obtaining data on behavioral frequencies. As Sudman and Bradburn (1982: 115) have noted, "There is no difficulty in coding such responses, since the data are numerical and can easily be processed without need for additional coding." Precoding the question, on the other hand, may introduce systematic bias in respondents' behavioral reports and related judgments, because response scales are not only measurement devices but serve informative functions as well.

References

Carp, F.M.
   1974   "Position effects on interview responses." Journal of Gerontology 29:581–587.
Darschin, W., and B. Frank
   1982   "Tendenzen im Zuschauerverhalten. Teleskopie-Ergebnisse zur Fernsehnutzung im Jahre 1981." Media Perspektiven 4:276–284.
Mueller, Albrecht
   1980   "Einstellungen der Fernsehzuschauer zur weiteren Entwicklung des Mediums Fernsehen." Media Perspektiven 3:179–186.
Payne, Stanley L.
   1946   "Some opinion research principles developed through studies of social medicine." Public Opinion Quarterly 10:93–98.
   1951   The Art of Asking Questions. Princeton: Princeton University Press.
Quinn, S.B., and W.A. Belson
   1969   The Effects of Reversing the Order of Presentation of Verbal Rating Scales in Survey Interviews. London: Survey Research Center.
Sudman, Seymour, and Norman M. Bradburn
   1982   Asking Questions. San Francisco: Jossey-Bass.
Suls, J.M., and R.L. Miller (eds.)
   1977   Social Comparison Processes: Theoretical and Empirical Perspectives. New York: Hemisphere Publishing.

When Four Months Equal a Year: Inconsistencies in Student Reports of Drug Use

JERALD G. BACHMAN AND PATRICK M. O'MALLEY

THE basic finding presented in this brief report, already implied by the title, can be summarized in a sentence: Among high school seniors who report any drug use during the past year, reported use during the past month is generally inconsistent with reported use during the past year; either the annual frequencies are too low, the monthly frequencies are too high, or both. Although phenomena of this sort are not new to the literature of survey methodology, we considered an early presentation of these findings useful for several reasons: (1) the effects are quite large, (2) they show an impressive degree of consistency across different drugs and different levels of use, and (3) they are based on large and nationally representative samplings of an important area of behavior—young people's use of drugs.

In what follows we first present an overview of our sample and

Abstract In this analysis of the high school senior classes of 1976 through 1979, reports of frequency of drug use during the past month are roughly three times larger than would be estimated based on reports of use during the past year; this phenomenon appears fairly consistently for alcohol, marijuana, and 10 other categories of illicitly used drugs. The underreporting of events that are more distant in time has been observed in a wide range of surveys, and these findings are general and stable enough to fit in very well with that explanation. The authors conclude that self-reports of frequency of drug use during the past year, and also during the lifetime, are in many cases systematically underreported, that percentages reporting *any* use during a given interval are likely to be more accurate and, further, that analyses of *trends* are likely to be largely valid, since biases are likely to be fairly constant from year to year.

Jerald G. Bachman is Program Director and Patrick M. O'Malley is Study Director at the Survey Research Center of the Institute for Social Research, The University of Michigan. This work was supported by Research Grant No. R 01 DA 01411-06 from the National Institute on Drug Abuse, U.S. Public Health Service. The authors thank Pamela R. E. Kittel for her assistance in the preparation of this report and Willard L. Rodgers for his helpful comments on an earlier draft of this paper.

survey procedures, we then report in some detail the pattern of inconsistencies that emerges when self-reports of drug use for the past month and the past year are compared, we consider several possible explanations for the discrepancies, and we note some ways in which the present findings match and extend findings in other survey areas—particularly studies of accuracy in reporting health-related events. (This report does not attempt any overall description of recent levels and trends in drug use, or the correlates of drug use, since all these aspects of the data have been treated extensively in other reports. See Johnston et al., 1979a, 1979b; Bachman et al., 1981.)

Methods

Our data are obtained from the Monitoring the Future project, an ongoing study of high school seniors conducted by the Institute for Social Research under a grant from the National Institute on Drug Abuse. The study design has been described extensively elsewhere (Bachman and Johnston, 1978; Johnston et al., 1977, 1979a; Bachman et al., 1980); briefly, it involves nationally representative surveys of each high school senior class, beginning in 1975, plus follow-up surveys mailed each year to a subset of each senior class sample.

SAMPLE AND QUESTIONNAIRE ADMINISTRATION

The present report relies primarily on the survey of high school seniors during the spring of 1979. A three-stage national probability sample (Kish, 1965) led to questionnaire administrations in 111 public high schools and 20 private ones, and yielded a total of 16,654 respondents (reflecting a response rate of approximately 80 percent of all seniors included in the sample).

The questionnaires were administered by professional interviewers from the Institute for Social Research during school hours, usually in a regularly scheduled class period. Special procedures were employed to ensure confidentiality, and these procedures were carefully explained in the questionnaire instructions and reviewed orally by the interviewers when they administered the questionnaires. The instructions also stressed the voluntary nature of participation and suggested leaving blank any question that might be objectionable to the respondent or her/his parents.

DRUG USE MEASURES

Although the Monitoring the Future project has a primary focus on drug use and related attitudes, a much broader range of topics are of relevance to the project and are included in the questionnaire content. Items specific to drug use occur near the middle of the question sequence, after respondents have dealt with a variety of other matters. All items employ closed-ended response alternatives in order to facilitate optical scanning of the completed forms.

Use of alcohol, use of marijuana, and ten other categories of illicit drug use were measured by questions having the following format:

On how many occasions (if any) have you used (name of drug category) . . .

    a. . . . in your lifetime?
    b. . . . during the last 12 months?
    c. . . . during the last 30 days?

Seven response categories were available: 0 occasions, 1–2 occasions, 3–5, 6–9, 10–19, 20–39, 40 or more.

This format for self-reports of drug use was designed to meet a number of criteria: (1) it is simple and straightforward for respondents; (2) it is suited to the closed-ended optically scanned questionnaire method; (3) the response scale is roughly logarithmic (on the assumption that people can make more accurate recollections about the exact number of relatively rare events than about the exact number of more frequent events); and (4) it is broadly applicable to three different time intervals (lifetime, year, month) and a variety of different drugs (ranging from the frequently used alcohol to the rarely used heroin). Although the use of a seven-point scale causes some roughness and inaccuracy for our present purposes, we think it will be clear in what follows that the basic findings are not fundamentally distorted by scale limitations.

Results

The relationship between annual and monthly self-reports of frequency of alcohol use is evident from the percentage distribution shown in Table 1. Note that the cell entries are percentages based on the total sample (excluding cases with missing data or logically impossible answers). Thus, for example, the entries in the second row of the table indicate that 9.4 percent of the total sample reported drinking alcohol on one or two occasions during the last year but not drinking at all during the last month, whereas another 2.8 percent reported alcohol use on one or two occasions in the last year *and* in the last month. To put it another way, just under one-quarter of those who reported drinking on one or two occasions in the past year also reported some use during the past month—a minority, but a some-

Table 1. Twelve-Month Versus Thirty-Day Self-Reported Frequency of Alcohol Use (N = 15,461)

Number of Uses in Last Year Interval (Midpoint)	Number of Uses in Last 30 Days							Row %	Mean Ratio[a]
	0 (0)	1–2 (1.5)	3–5 (4.0)	6–9 (7.5)	10–19 (14.5)	20–39 (29.5)	40+ (–)		
0 (0)	12.0%[b] (Inap.)[c]							12.0	—
1–2 (1.5)	9.4 (0.0)[c]	2.8 (12.0)						12.3	(2.8)
3–5 (4.0)	4.0 (0.0)	6.8 (4.5)	0.6 (12.0)					11.3	(3.3)
6–9 (7.5)	1.6 (0.0)	5.8 (2.4)	3.3 (6.4)	0.5 (12.0)				11.2	(3.6)
10–19 (14.5)	0.9 (0.0)	4.2 (1.2)	6.9 (3.3)	3.5 (6.2)	0.4 (12.0)			16.0	(3.4)
20–39 (29.5)	0.3 (0.0)	1.3 (0.6)	4.5 (1.6)	4.9 (3.1)	2.7 (5.9)	0.2 (12.0)		13.9	(3.0)
40+	0.1 (Inap.)	0.5 (Inap.)	2.6 (Inap.)	5.7 (Inap.)	7.7 (Inap.)	3.9 (Inap.)	2.7 (Inap.)	23.4	—
Column %	28.4	21.5	17.9	14.6	10.8	4.2	2.7	100.0	
Overall Mean Ratio for Rows Shown									(3.2)

[a] This is the mean for each row of actual versus "expected" monthly use (see note c).

[b] Table entries are percentages of total sample, excluding those with missing or logically inconsistent data on the alcohol questions. (Due to rounding, percentages and totals do not match exactly).

[c] Entries in parentheses show a ratio consisting of actual reported monthly use (midpoint) divided by "expected" monthly use, the latter defined as reported annual use (midpoint) divided by 12.

what larger minority than might be expected if the monthly and annual data were strictly "proportionate." If we move further down the table to those who reported 10–19 uses in the past year, the lack of proportionality becomes much clearer. Assuming that their 10–19 uses were spread more or less equally across the 12 months of the year, we would expect that most respondents would report their usage during the past month to be 1–2 occasions, while some would report none and others would report more. In fact, however, among all seniors who reported 10–19 uses of alcohol in the past year, more than two-thirds reported using alcohol three or more times during the past month, and only a handful reported no use. The same pattern of "too much" use during the past month can be seen for the other levels of annual use (except, of course, that we cannot make appropriate extrapolations for the row involving 40 or more uses).

The same general sort of inconsistency is evident if we extrapolate from annual to monthly reports by reading down the columns in Table 1 rather than reading across the rows; however, the scale limitations are more severe. Thus, among those reporting 1–2 uses of alcohol during the past 30 days, we might reasonably expect most to report yearly use totaling one to two dozen occasions. In fact, however, the majority report fewer than 10 uses during the past year. Similarly, we might expect most of those who report 3–5 uses in the past month would also report 40 or more uses over the whole year, but only a small minority (about one in seven) do so; the majority report fewer than 20 uses during the year. For the next category of monthly use, 6–9 occasions, we would expect the large majority to report more than 40 occasions for the year, but well under half do so. In short, when we try to extrapolate from monthly use, we find that seniors' reports of alcohol use throughout the year are far "too low."

Before we try to sort out whether the monthly reports of alcohol use are too high or the annual reports are too low, let us first attempt to quantify the extent of the discrepancy for alcohol reports and then consider whether there is a similar phenomenon for reported use of marijuana and other illicit drug use.

QUANTIFYING THE DISCREPANCY

The parenthetical entries in Table 1 represent an attempt to quantify the discrepancies described in the rather general terms above. We must stress that this is a fairly rough procedure that we have found useful for the present analysis and reporting. Because our drug use measures involve intervals rather than exact numbers, a really precise quantification is not possible; fortunately, such precision is not necessary for our purposes here.

As a first step in quantifying the discrepancy, we chose to treat each of the response intervals in terms of its midpoint; of course, no midpoint is possible for the top category—40 or more occasions. Then, for each of five levels of yearly use (midpoints ranging from 1.5 to 29.5) we computed a set of "discrepancy ratios" in which the reported "actual" monthly use is divided by an "expected" monthly use, defined as one-twelfth of the reported annual use (in all instances using midpoints of the scale intervals). Thus, for example, the third row of Table 1 refers to those who reported 3–5 uses of alcohol during the past year; from the midpoint of 4.0 we extrapolate an "expected" monthly use of .33; those who reported 1–2 uses during the past month are assigned a ratio value of 4.5 (the midpoint monthly use, 1.5, divided by the "expected" monthly use, .33); those who reported 3–5 uses during the past month are assigned a ratio value of 12.0 (4.0 divided by .33). Discrepancy ratios such as those illustrated above are shown in parentheses for most combinations of annual and monthly use in Table 1. It is important to understand that this procedure excludes those who reported zero use during the past year and those who reported 40 or more occasions of alcohol use during the past year. Thus any respondent who reported from one to 39 occasions of alcohol use during the past year can be assigned a ratio (ranging from 0.0 to 12.0); furthermore, means of those ratios can be computed for each row in Table 1 as well as for the total of all respondents who fall in the 1–39 range of uses during the past year.[1]

[1] Representing each interval by its midpoint seemed the simplest approach for these computations, if not necessarily the most elegant. An alternative would be to use a different sort of midpoint derived from a log transformation of each interval. Thus, for example, the interval 1–2 woud have a midpoint of 1.41 by this method. The *ratios* shown in Table 1 would be affected only trivially by this approach, and the overall mean ratio for the alcohol data would remain unchanged at 3.2; accordingly, the log transformation approach was not pursued further for this report.

Much more elaborate alternatives to simple midpoints would make use of the actual distributions of responses obtained for each item; however, this would vastly complicate the process of applying the procedure to other drugs (with other distributions), and thus it was not considered worth pursuing here. We did, however, carry out several additional sets of calculations, using the alcohol data shown in Table 1, in order to satisfy ourselves that the discrepancy data reported here are robust and not attributable primarily to our use of midpoints. As one example, we continued to use the midpoint for annual reports (which is in all likelihood somewhat higher than would be obtained if we had asked for exact reports rather than using intervals), but at the same time we used the one-third point for monthly reports (e.g., a value of 7 for the category of 6 to 9 uses, which is very likely somewhat too low). By slightly overestimating the annual reports and slightly underestimating the monthly reports, we reduced the overall mean discrepancy ratio for alcohol from 3.2 to 2.9. Carrying this approach to the limit would involve using the bottom of each category of monthly reports (e.g., treating all reports of 6 to 9 uses in the past month as if they represented only 6 uses); and under that extreme assumption, the overall mean discrepancy ratio for alcohol is 2.3. Thus, even when we make the most exaggerated assumptions to try to reduce the effect, we still find monthly alcohol use reports to be more than twice what would be expected based on reports of annual use.

An examination of the mean discrepancy ratios for each row in Table 1 reveals a considerable consistency; whether we consider respondents whose reported use of alcohol in the past year is 1–2, or 6–9, or 20–39, their *average* reports of monthly use are roughly three times as large as would be extrapolated based on their reported annual use. A grand mean of discrepancy ratios based on all respondents reporting 1–39 occasions of alcohol use during the past year (just under two-thirds of the total sample) shows a ratio of 3.2. In other words, with the rate of use reported for the past month, on the average, it would take less than four months to accumulate the amount of alcohol use reported for the entire preceding year.

CONSISTENCY ACROSS DIFFERENT DRUGS

Table 2 presents results for that class of illicit drugs most widely used among high school students, marijuana and hashish (which we will henceforth denote simply as marijuana). It is of interest to note both the differences and similarities between the marijuana use data in Table 2 and the alcohol use data in Table 1. Perhaps the most important difference is that about half of all seniors reported no use of marijuana during the past year, in contrast to only 12 percent reporting no use of alcohol. On the other hand, at the top end of the scale of annual use there are fewer differences, and there are actually more seniors reporting very frequent use of marijuana (20 or more times per month) than is true for alcohol. The fact that so many seniors report no use of marijuana in the past year means that there is a much smaller proportion who fall in the range of 1–39 occasions of use during the past year. Accordingly, we can compute ratios of "actual" versus "expected" monthly use for only about one-third of all seniors. Nevertheless, those discrepancy ratios show an impressive similarity to the ones obtained for alcohol use. Again we find that average reports of use in the past month are about three times what would be expected based on use reported for the past year; the overall ratio is 3.0.

The computation procedures used in Tables 1 and 2 were applied also to 10 other categories of illicitly used drugs, and the results are displayed in Table 3. First it should be noted that the large majority of seniors in 1979 reported no illicit drug use other than marijuana; for most drug categories shown in Table 3, fewer than 10 percent of seniors reported any use during the past year. Most of the mean ratios in Table 3 are thus based on rather small proportions of seniors, although the actual numbers of cases remain fairly substantial for all drugs except heroin. The mean discrepancy ratios for the other drugs

Table 2. Twelve-Month Versus Thirty-Day Self-Reported Frequency of Marijuana Use (N = 15,879)

Number of Uses in Last Year Interval (Midpoint)	Number of Uses in Last 30 Days							Row %	Mean Ratio[a]
	0 (0)	1–2 (1.5)	3–5 (4.0)	6–9 (7.5)	10–19 (14.5)	20–39 (29.5)	40+ (—)		
0 (0)	49.4%[b] (Inap.)[c]							49.4	—
1–2 (1.5)	7.7 (0.0)[c]	2.1 (12.0)						9.8	(2.6)
3–5 (4.0)	3.3 (0.0)	2.9 (4.5)	0.4 (12.0)					6.6	(2.7)
6–9 (7.5)	1.4 (0.0)	2.0 (2.4)	1.3 (6.4)	0.3 (12.0)				5.0	(3.3)
10–19 (14.5)	1.1 (0.0)	1.6 (1.2)	2.3 (3.3)	1.4 (6.2)	0.3 (12.0)			6.7	(3.3)
20–39 (29.5)	0.5 (0.0)	0.4 (0.6)	1.1 (1.6)	1.3 (3.1)	1.8 (5.9)	0.3 (12.0)		5.4	(3.7)
40+ (—)	0.3 (Inap.)	0.4 (Inap.)	0.8 (Inap.)	1.4 (Inap.)	4.4 (Inap.)	4.8 (Inap.)	5.1 (Inap.)	17.2	—
Column %	63.6	9.4	5.9	4.5	6.5	5.1	5.1	100.0	
Overall Mean Ratio for Rows Shown									(3.0)

[a] This is the mean for each row of actual versus "expected" monthly use (see note c).

[b] Table entries are percentages of total sample, excluding those with missing or logically inconsistent data on the marijuana questions. (Due to rounding, percentages and totals do not match exactly).

[c] Entries in parentheses show a ratio consisting of actual reported monthly use (midpoint) divided by "expected" monthly use, the latter defined as reported annual use (midpoint) divided by 12.

Table 3. Mean Ratios of Reported Monthly Use Versus the "Expected" Monthly Use Based on Extrapolations from Reported Annual Use: Twelve Types of Drugs

	Class of 1979					Mean Ratio, Classes of 1976–1979
	Number of Uses Reported in Last Year[a]					
Type of Drug	0	1–39	40+	N for Ratio	Mean Ratio	
Alcohol	12.0	64.6	23.4	9996	3.2	3.3
Marijuana	49.4	33.4	17.2	5315	3.0	3.2
LSD	93.4	6.5	0.1	1051	2.5	2.4
Other psychedelics	93.3	6.6	0.1	1054	2.2	2.4
Cocaine	88.0	11.4	0.6	1828	2.9	2.7
Amphetamines[b]	81.8	16.7	1.5	2674	3.1	2.9
Quaaludes[b]	94.2	5.7	0.1	919	2.6	2.5
Barbiturates[b]	92.6	7.2	0.2	1156	2.7	2.6
Tranquilizers[b]	90.4	9.4	0.2	1489	2.6	2.6
Heroin	99.5	0.5	0.0	77	2.7	2.7
Other narcotics[b]	93.8	6.1	0.1	958	2.6	2.6
Inhalants (4 forms)	94.7	5.1	0.2	660	2.4	2.6

[a] Table entries are percentages of total sample reporting each level of use.
[b] The question covers illicit use only, i.e., "without a doctor telling you to take them."

show considerable consistency with the overall findings for alcohol and marijuana; however, the findings for the class of 1979 (next to last column in the table) do show a degree of variability which we were inclined to attribute largely to random "noise." Accordingly, we repeated the calculations using comparable data from the classes of 1976 through 1978, and have entered the mean ratios for all four years in the last column of Table 3. A much clearer pattern then emerges: alcohol and marijuana both show discrepancy ratios slightly larger than three, whereas the ratios for other illicit drugs are somewhat lower, with most lying within a range of 2.5 to 2.7. Thus for alcohol and marijuana it takes just under four months to equal a year, whereas for the other illicit drugs it takes somewhat less than five. There is, thus, a systematic difference between the more "popular" drugs and those less commonly used; but perhaps the more impressive finding is the extent to which the pattern is largely similar whether one is dealing with marijuana or cocaine or heroin.

Discussion

We think the findings presented above are basically quite solid, but the following attempts to explain those findings are necessarily much more tentative. At the broadest level, we can distinguish two explanations which may underlie the discrepancies between monthly and annual reports of drug use: either the discrepancies are genuine, and/or the reports are inaccurate.

Let us first consider the possibility that some or all of the discrepancy is genuine. This might be the case if there were a very marked acceleration of drug use during the senior year of high school, with each new month involving more use than the last. There is indeed some such acceleration during the high school years, with each new grade level involving somewhat more overall use than the previous one (Abelson et al., 1977; Johnston et al., 1979b); nevertheless, the increase is moderate from year to year and could not begin to account for the size of discrepancy we have been observing.

Another possible explanation of a genuine discrepancy is the often observed tendency for seniors to become increasingly exuberant as the time approaches for their liberation from high school. If in fact a greater than average amount of partying during the spring months is an important contributor to actual and reported levels of drug use for the 30 days preceding the survey, then it should follow that the kind of discrepancy we have observed would be most evident for those classes of drugs likely to be included at parties. Alcohol and marijuana would certainly head the list of such drugs, and they have two of the largest discrepancy ratios shown in Table 3. But the ratio for amphetamines is just about as large as that for marijuana, and the ratio for heroin is only slightly lower. Thus, the considerable degree of consistency in discrepancy ratios across both party drugs and nonparty drugs tends to undermine this explanation as a means of accounting for most or all of the discrepancy between "actual" and "expected" monthly use.

On the basis of the brief overview above, we conclude that to a large degree the discrepancies we have observed are not genuine, but rather reflect some considerable inaccuracies in reporting. Ideally, we would examine this possibility by comparing respondent reports with external validity data; unfortunately, no such data exist for individual respondents in the Monitoring the Future study (as is the case in most other drug use surveys).

But in another area of study such validity data are available, and the findings seem highly relevant to those reported here. Cannell and his colleagues (Cannell et al., 1965; Cannell and Fowler, 1963; Oksenberg and Cannell, 1977), as well as a number of other investigators (see Cannell et al., 1977, for a summary), have analyzed the reporting of health events in interviews and have been able to relate such reports to objective records of those events. One of the conclusions from such analyses bears repeating here: "Perhaps the best documented phenomenon of underreporting of health events as well as of a wide variety of other types of events and behaviors, is the decrease in the reporting of events as time elapses. This is characteristic of studies of consumer purchases, reports of income, behavior of children as reported by parents, and so forth" (Cannell et al., 1977:7). Oksenberg and Cannell also note that underreporting increases as the time between an event and the interview increases, adding: "This generalization will surprise no one, but what is unexpected is the *rapidity* with which the failure to report the event increases with time" (p. 2). Indeed, there is evidence of considerable underreporting of health events (physician visits, illness incidents, etc.) over intervals as short as two or three weeks; and for intervals longer than six months the underreporting can exceed 50 percent.

A further bit of data is available from Delbert Elliott, who has found that reports of delinquent behavior do not increase proportionately to the time interval involved; for example, the average number of delinquent acts reported during a four-month interval is nearly identical to the average number reported during an eight-month interval (personal communication).

The above findings from other areas of survey research, as well as our own findings, are clearly consistent with the explanation that forgetting increases over longer time intervals. There is thus a good deal of indirect evidence to suggest that much of the discrepancy reported here is due to an *underreporting* of drug use over the past 12 months. We suspect that estimates are far more accurate for the shorter and more recent interval of the past month; nevertheless, it seems likely that even for a 30-day interval there are difficulties in recall, and some respondents may underestimate while others may actually overestimate by "telescoping" their recollections of events during the past several months.

One of the reasons why events in the past are underreported in surveys may be that many individuals are simply not sufficiently careful or motivated in their role of respondent (Cannell et al., 1977). Such individuals may fail to search memory adequately; furthermore, in the case of relatively frequent events that could not be recalled in detail, they may make careless and imprecise *estimates* of the total number of occurrences over longer intervals (Cannell, personal communication).[2] We did not have any direct evidence of respondent motivation in the Monitoring the Future survey; however, we considered it possible that students with higher grade-point averages, in contrast to their less academically successful classmates, might be better motivated or otherwise more "skillful" and consistent in the

[2] As a reviewer of an earlier draft pointed out, one of the reasons why estimates for annual use tend so much to the low side may be that respondents feel uncomfortable or threatened by reporting the total number of drug-using incidents that correspond to 12 times the monthly level of use. Such resistance to admitting the full extent of annual use may, of course, be unconscious as well as conscious. It may be especially likely to happen when the same categories are used for monthly and yearly estimates.

role of questionnaire respondent. When we tested this assumption empirically, we found that the expected pattern of findings emerged clearly for alcohol use and marijuana use (using data from seniors in 1979). For reports of alcohol use, the mean "expected" versus "actual" ratios are 2.86 for students with (self-reported) grades averaging A, 3.17 for B students, and 3.64 for students with grades averaging C or lower. For reports of marijuana use, the corresponding ratios are 2.48, 2.87, and 3.47. In each case the A students' mean discrepancy ratio is about one-fourth of a standard deviation lower than that of the C students, an effect that is statistically trustworthy ($p < .01$), yet not really massive in size. For the other drug categories shown in Table 3, a comparison of ratios for different grade levels produced no consistent pattern at all, perhaps because of the much smaller numbers of cases involved in each subgroup and/or because the use of the other drugs is sufficiently rare (especially among the A students) that the drug users are in no sense "typical" or "representative" of others in that grade category. Thus the present evidence on respondent motivation or "skill" in reporting annual and monthly drug use is quite limited; nevertheless, the findings for the most widely used drugs—alcohol and marijuana—provide some modest support for the hypothesis that inaccurate reporting is a primary cause of the discrepancies.

What implications does all this have for interpretations of drug use data from the Monitoring the Future project? Obviously, it means that drug use during the past year, and presumably also lifetime drug use, are in many cases systematically underestimated. But we suspect that other aspects of the data are less subject to error. In particular, we think it likely that a respondent will remember having used a particular class of drug at least once, even though the number of times (beyond one or two) may be less clearly recalled. If this assumption is correct, then there may be relatively little recall error involved when data are presented in terms of percentages of respondents who report any use of a drug during the past year or during their lifetime. Additionally, our examinations of four separate years of senior class data indicate that the patterns of inconsistency reported here occur quite regularly from one year to the next; therefore, analyses of *trends* are likely to be largely valid, since the biases will be fairly constant from year to year.

References

Abelson, H. I., P. M. Fishburne, and I. H. Cisin
1977 National Survey on Drug Abuse: 1977 (Vol. I, Main Findings). National Institute on Drug Abuse. Washington, D.C.: U.S. Government Printing Office.

Bachman, J. G., and L. D. Johnston
  1978 The Monitoring the Future Project: Design and Procedures. Monitoring the Future Occasional Paper 1. Ann Arbor: Institute for Social Research.
Bachman, J. G., L. D. Johnston and P. M. O'Malley
  1980 Monitoring the Future: Questionnaire Responses from the Nation's High School Seniors, 1978. Ann Arbor: Institute for Social Research.
  1981 "Smoking, drinking and drug use among American high school students: correlates and trends, 1975–1979." American Journal of Public Health 71:59–69.
Cannell, C. F., G. Fisher, and T. Bakker
  1965 "Reporting of hospitalization in the health interview survey." Vital and Health Statistics, U.S. Public Health Service, Series 2, No. 6.
Cannell, C. F., and F. Fowler
  1963 "A study of the reporting of visits to doctors in the National Health Survey." Survey Research Center, University of Michigan (mimeo).
Cannell, C. F., K. H. Marquis, and A. Laurent
  1977 "A summary of studies of interviewing methodology." Vital and Health Statistics, U.S. Public Health Service, Series 2, No. 69.
Johnston, L. D., J. G. Bachman, and P. M. O'Malley
  1977 Drug Use Among American High School Students, 1975–1977. National Institute on Drug Abuse. Washington, D.C.: U.S. Government Printing Office.
  1979a Drugs and the Class of 1978: Behaviors, Attitudes and Recent National Trends. National Institute on Drug Abuse. Washington, D.C.: U.S. Government Printing Office.
  1979b Drugs and the Nation's High School Students. Five Year National Trends, 1979 Highlights. National Institute on Drug Abuse. Washington, D.C.: U.S. Government Printing Office.
Kish, L.
  1965 Survey Sampling. New York: John Wiley & Sons.
Oksenberg, L., and C. Cannell
  1977 "Some factors underlying the validity of response in self-report." Survey Research Center, University of Michigan (mimeo).
Sudman, S., and N. M. Bradburn
  1974 Response Effects in Surveys. Chicago: Aldine.

MODE OF ADMINISTRATION

The largest difference among the three main modes of administration is usually cost. It is much more expensive to conduct a survey face-to-face than by telephone, and telephone studies are, in turn, considerably more costly than self-administered surveys sent through the mail. At the same time, the modes differ in many other ways, including the speed of data collection, the kinds of information that can be collected, and the quality of the results. Research on mode of administration has been fueled by a concern to understand the trade-offs among these factors.

In interpreting the findings of studies that compare different modes it is important to recognize that mode can operate in two different ways: indirectly through sample composition, by influencing how many and which individuals cooperate, and directly, by affecting how questions are answered.

On the first point, the conventional wisdom has been that response rates will be lower in mail surveys than in interviewer-administered ones. Yet the work of Dillman (1978) and others has shown that changes in various aspects of mail survey administration (e.g., follow-up mailings) can reduce, if not eliminate, the response-rate gap. The Wiseman study reprinted here found no significant response-rate differences between the three modes when individuals assigned to the mail mode received prior telephone notification that they would shortly be receiving a questionnaire.

Until recently, some researchers also assumed that people would be more willing to cooperate with a request for an interview over the telephone than in person. To the extent that refusals are due to fear of crime or concerns about invasion of privacy, phone interviewing might seem to have an advantage over in-person interviewing in which an interviewer is admitted to a respondent's home. Yet the experimental evidence shows that this is not true. In the study by Wiseman, as well as those by Rogers and Groves included in this section, response rates were no higher on the phone than in person. In fact, in the Groves study and others not reprinted here, response rates were somewhat lower on the telephone than they were face-to-face.

Turning to the impact of mode on how questions are answered, the readings included here suggest only a modest effect. Although there are some noticeable differences (e.g., on open questions and those with "socially desirable" responses), overall the response distributions between modes are quite similar. This is consistent with the findings of most other work on this topic (e.g., Cannell and Fowler, 1963; Locander, Sudman, and Bradburn, 1976; and Groves and Kahn, 1979).

An important recent innovation in mode of administration is Computer Assisted Telephone Interviewing (CATI), in which questions are displayed on a computer terminal and answers are entered directly into a machine-readable file via the terminal. Among other advantages, this makes it possible to tailor questions to respondents based on their prior answers, to alert the interviewer to answers inconsistent with previous ones, and to eliminate coding errors for closed items. In an experimental comparison of CATI and traditional phone interviewing, Groves and Mathiowetz (1984) found somewhat smaller interviewer variance with CATI, possibly because of the greater standardization it imposes on interviewers.

Another important recent development in research on mode involves dual-frame, mixed-mode designs, in which different modes are used to interview samples drawn from different frames (Groves and Lepkowski, 1985). This makes it possible to combine the cost advantages of one method (typically telephone) with the coverage advantages of another (usually in-person). (An example of a dual-frame, single-mode design is presented in the Sampling section of this volume.)

A final area of mode research, broadly construed, goes under the rubric of "house effects": differences attributable to the organization that conducted the survey. Consistent with the results of Cantril (1945) published in POQ four decades ago, Smith, in the study reprinted here, suggests that such effects are not a large problem for major survey research organizations.

References

Cannell, Charles F., and Floyd J. Fowler (1963)
    "Comparison of a self-enumerative procedure and a personal interview: A validity study." Public Opinion Quarterly 27:250–264.
Cantril, Hadley (1945)
    "Do different polls get the same results?" Public Opinion Quarterly 9:61–69.
Dillman Don A. (1978)
    Mail and Telephone Surveys: The Total Design Method. New York: Wiley.
Groves, Robert M., and Robert L. Kahn (1979)
    Surveys by Telephone: A National Comparison with Personal Interviews. New York: Academic Press.
Groves, Robert M., and James M. Lepkowski (1985)
    "Dual frame, mixed mode survey designs." Journal of Official Statistics 1:264–286.
Groves, Robert M., and Nancy Mathiowetz (1984)
    "Computer assisted telephone interviewing: Effects on interviewers and respondents." Public Opinion Quarterly 48:356–369.
Locander, William, Seymour Sudman, and Norman M. Bradburn (1976)
    "An investigation of interview method, threat, and response distortion." Journal of the American Statistical Association 71:269–275.

METHODOLOGICAL BIAS IN PUBLIC OPINION SURVEYS

BY FREDERICK WISEMAN*

Statistically designed sample surveys have enabled pollsters to gauge public opinion on a wide range of issues. In such surveys, selection of a data collection technique is generally based on four criteria: (1) cost; (2) completion time; (3) response rate; and (4) response bias. Typically, more weight is placed on the first three factors and, as a result, adequate attention has not been given to the latter consideration. The study described in this paper looks at one type of response bias—that which results from the use of a specific data collection method. More specifically, this research uses a controlled experimental design in order to determine whether responses given in a public opinion polling are influenced by the method used to collect the data. Three methods are investigated: (1) mail questionnaire; (2) telephone interview; and (3) personal interview.

METHODS

Residents of a suburban Boston community were polled on nine current issues, both local and national. In order to determine the influence of the data collection technique, three experimental groups were formed and asked identical questions. Members of the first group received a mail questionnaire, while those in the second and third groups had telephone and personal interviews, respectively. If there were no technique bias, then one would expect identical results (except for random variation) in each of the three experimental groups.

Critical to the reasoning above is the assumption that the experimental groups are equivalent samples from a common population. A two-stage sampling process was used in an attempt to satisfy this requirement. In stage one, the population was divided into twelve mutually exclusive and collectively exhaustive clusters, and a random selection of a street within each cluster was made. In stage two, those residing on each of the selected streets were sequentially assigned to groups in the following order: mail—telephone—mail—personal. Approximately the same number of potential respondents was obtained for each of the twelve street listings.

As can be seen, there were twice as many potential mail respondents

* Frederick Wiseman is Assistant Professor of Marketing at Northeastern University.

as potential telephone or personal interview respondents. This particular sample allocation was made because of (1) the belief that the response rate from the mail questionnaire would be significantly lower than that from the other two methods; and (2) the desire to obtain approximately the same number of completed interviews for each of the three data collection techniques. To improve upon the mail questionnaire response rate, a follow-up postcard was sent three days after the original mailing. In addition, on an experimental basis, approximately 25 percent of this group received a prior telephone notification. This brief notification informed potential respondents that they would be receiving a questionnaire in the mail within the next few days and that their cooperation in filling it out would be greatly appreciated.[1]

RESULTS

The response rates achieved for each of the three techniques are given in Table 1.[2]

As can be seen from Table 2, the number of completed interviews using the mail questionnaire was considerably larger than that for either the personal or the telephone interview. This particular result was unexpected and was primarily due to the relatively large number of questionnaires returned from those households which had received prior telephone notification.

Sample Validation. Socioeconomic and demographic data were obtained for each of the respondents. No statistically significant differences were found among the groups on any of the following characteristics: sex, marital status, age, occupation, income, and religion.

TABLE 1

COMPLETION RATES FOR EACH DATA COLLECTION TECHNIQUE

Data Collection Technique	Attempts	Completions
Mail questionnaire		
Prior notification[a]	75	50 (67%)
No prior notification	245	107 (47%)
Telephone interview	160[b]	102 (64%)
Personal interview	160	96 (60%)

[a] The position of the stamp on the self-addressed return envelope made it possible to identify all returns coming from households receiving prior notification.

[b] Not included are 56 households for which there was no telephone number.

[1] Both these procedures have been found to have a positive effect on the response rate. See, for example, Morton L. Brown, "Use of a Postcard Query in Mail Surveys," *Public Opinion Quarterly*, Vol. 29, 1965, pp. 635-637; and James E. Stafford, "Influence of Preliminary Contact on Mail Returns," *Journal of Marketing Research*, Vol. 3, 1965, pp. 410-411.

[2] Telephone and personal interviews were obtained by students in an advanced undergraduate marketing research course.

TABLE 2

SURVEY RESULTS BY DATA COLLECTION TECHNIQUE

	Percent Yes Answers[a]			
Issue	Mail	Telephone	Personal	X^2
1. In favor of Congress's decision to eliminate funds for the SST	74	73	75	.2
2. In favor of an all-volunteer army within two years	71	77	81	3.0
3. In favor of a reduction in the size of the Massachusetts House of Representatives	81	76	79	.7
4. In favor of legalizing marijuana	39	43	42	.8
5. In favor of making birth control devices readily available to un-married people	83	67	72	8.0[b]
6. In favor of legalizing abortion	89	62	70	29.5[c]
7. In favor of the Court's decision in finding Lt. Calley guilty	64	58	53	2.6
8. In favor of giving state aid to Catholic schools	37	32	34	.6
9. In favor of lowering the legal drinking age to eighteen	60	62	67	1.7

[a] Excluding "Don't know" responses.
[b] Significant at the .05 level.
[c] Significant at the .01 level.

Thus, the previously described sampling process did, in fact, generate equivalent groupings of respondents. No differences in response patterns were found between those receiving and those not receiving prior notification in the mail questionnaire group.

Survey Results. The results of the public opinion polling are shown in Table 2. Significant technique bias was present on only two of the nine questions: "Do you believe that birth control devices should be readily available to unmarried people?" and "Should abortion be legalized in Massachusetts?" These issues are both personal, and, in each instance, the largest percentage of socially undesirable responses was obtained in the mail questionnaire while the smallest percentage was obtained in the telephone interview.

Further analysis of the two significant questions revealed that the response bias was related to the religious preference of the respondent.

On the birth control issue, 75 percent of the Catholics who received a mail questionnaire were in favor of making birth control devices readily available to unmarried people, compared with only 44 percent of those Catholics receiving either a telephone or personal interview. On the abortion issue, Jewish members of the sample varied most depending on which method was used to collect the data. Ninety-eight percent of

Jews receiving the mail questionnaire agreed with the proposition, compared with approximately 73 percent of those responding to one of the other data collection methods. Again, the largest percentage of socially undesirable responses was obtained with the mail questionnaire.

The problem of respondents not revealing socially undesirable traits or characteristics has been previously discussed by Edwards[3] and, more recently, by Dohrenwend.[4] The results of the present research suggest that research techniques affording greater privacy of response are more likely to reduce this problem than those affording less privacy.

A possible solution to the problem when personal interviews are used is to employ a data collection technique for which the probability of respondents' giving untruthful answers is relatively small. Such a technique is the randomized response model which was first proposed by Warner.[5] This promising technique, based on probability theory, has been empirically tested in a recently completed North Carolina abortion study. Results and discussion of this research, together with the methodological framework of the model itself, can be found in Greenberg et. al.[6]

CONCLUSION

The major finding obtained from this research is that responses given in a public opinion polling are not always independent of the method used to collect the data. Response bias is likely to be a problem in telephone and personal interviews whenever the question being asked is one for which there exists a socially undesirable response. The significance of this result is twofold: (1) pollsters must be especially careful in designing sample surveys in which the objective is to measure public sentiment on sensitive issues; and (2) new data collection techniques, such as the randomized response model, must be developed so as to reduce the probability that respondents give socially desirable responses when, in fact, they do not hold such viewpoints.

[3] A. L. Edwards, *The Social Desirability Variable in Personality Assessment and Research,* New York, Dryden Press, 1957.

[4] Barbara Snell Dohrenwend, "An Experimental Study of Directive Interviewing," *Public Opinion Quarterly,* Vol. 34, 1970, pp. 117-125.

[5] S. L. Warner, "Randomized Response: A Survey Technique for Eliminating Evasive Answer Bias," *Journal of the American Statistical Association,* Vol. 60, 1965, pp. 63-69.

[6] B. G. Greenberg, R. R. Kuebler, Jr., J. R. Abernathy, and D. G. Horvitz, "Application of the Randomized Response Technique in Obtaining Quantitative Data," *Journal of the American Statistical Association,* Vol. 66, 1971, pp. 243-250.

INTERVIEWS BY TELEPHONE AND IN PERSON: QUALITY OF RESPONSES AND FIELD PERFORMANCE*

BY THERESA F. ROGERS

A small carefully controlled field experiment tests the effects of alternative interviewing strategies on the quality of responses and on field performance. Measures include ability to answer complex knowledge and attitudinal items, response validity, and willingness and consistency in providing personal information. Field performance is assessed by examining differential length of the interview, number of contacts required, suitable times for interviewing, respondent preferences for interview strategy, and interviewer effects.

Theresa F. Rogers is a Senior Research Associate at the Bureau of Applied Social Research, Columbia University.

F
OR MANY YEARS, it was assumed that the best way to conduct an interview was in person. In the last decade, however, there has been a shift to the use of the telephone, and now telephones are being used for local and long-distance interviews with specialized and nonspecialized populations, and in large and small surveys using schedules of varying length and complexity.[1]

The administrative and cost advantages please the researcher and the client: the telephone is efficient in reaching people and cheaper. But some nagging questions remain. How good are telephone interviews? Can the interviewer ask complex questions and get the answers just as well on the telephone as in person? Does the telephone present special interviewing problems—different in kind and degree from interviewing in person?

This paper reports a small carefully controlled experiment to measure the effects of alternative interviewing strategies on the quality of respon-

* An earlier version of this article was presented at the Thirtieth Annual Conference of the American Association of Public Opinion Research, 1975. The research was supported by Grant No. GI 32437, Research Applied to National Needs Directorate of the National Science Foundation. Any opinions, findings, conclusions or recommendations expressed are those of the author and do not necessarily reflect the views of NSF. The author is grateful to Ken Lenihan, Laurie Bauman, Nathalie Friedman, and Allen Barton for comments on an earlier draft of this article.

[1] The results of a recent survey of academic research organizations which have used the telephone for interviewing are reported in *Survey Research*, Vol. 5, No. 1, 1973, pp. 9–13. A selected bibliography on telephone interviewing appears in *Survey Research*, Vol. 5, No. 2, 1973, pp. 13–14.

ses and on field performance. Quality of response is measured by ability to answer complex items, willingness to provide personal information, response validity, and consistency of information. Measures of field performance include the response rate, the length of the interview, number of contacts required, preferable times for interviewing, respondent preferences for interviewing strategy, and interviewer effects.

The experiment was part of a resurvey of New York City residents to examine the perceptions and responses of local citizens to an experimental program in decentralizing city services.[2] The initial interviews were conducted in person in 1972; the follow-up data were collected in 1974 either by telephone or in person.

Subjects for the experiment were drawn from all respondents interviewed in Washington Heights (Manhattan) and the Grand Concourse (Bronx) in 1972. Those who did not have working telephones or did not speak English were eliminated.[3] From the remaining pool we chose a stratified sample based on ethnicity (white, black, Hispanic) and age (eighteen to thirty-five, thirty-six to fifty-nine, sixty or older) to minimize the variation. In all, 95 white, 95 black, and 57 Hispanic respondents were chosen for study and then randomly assigned to be interviewed by telephone or in person.[4] Randomization worked well: assignment to an interview by telephone or in person according to race, age, sex, and education was practically identical. The response rate for this reinterview experiment was 82 percent; the response rate for the original sample interviewed in 1972 was 73 percent.[5]

Every respondent received a letter in advance explaining the purpose of the interview and asking for his or her cooperation. The interview schedule was 35 pages long and consisted of both open and closed items. Everyone included in the experiment was interviewed with the same

[2] The respondents were residents of seven community planning ditricts in New York City. They were somewhat more likely than the population of New York City to be black, to have incomes lower than $15,000, and to be renters. See Nathalie Friedman and Naomi Golding, "Urban Residents and Neighborhood Government: A Profile of the Public in Seven Urban Neighborhoods of New York City," in *Information Requirements for Local Units of Government*, State Charter Revision Commission, New York City, 1974.

[3] Shortly before the field work began, we checked respondents' telephone numbers with the local telephone information service. If a respondent's telephone had been disconnected or changed to an unlisted number, we excluded that person from the experiment.

[4] Because this was a reinterview study, specific respondents were sought out and contacted by name after assignment to the experiment. Fewer Hispanics than blacks or whites were assigned because proportionately fewer Hispanics were in the study population; about one-half had been interviewed in Spanish, which made them ineligible for the experiment, and they were less likely to have telephones.

[5] For the 1972 survey, one-fourth of the households were chosen by probability sampling and three-fourths by quota; selection of the respondent within the household was by quota. There were no notable differences between the probability sample and the quota sample of households on a wide range of respondent characteristics; the completion rate for the probability sample was 73 percent. For a discussion of the problems of reinterviewing an urban sample see Theresa F. Rogers, "Reinterviewing New Yorkers: Movers, Stayers, Non-Locatable," forthcoming, 1976.

schedule. The field work was carried out between March and July, 1974.

The results indicate that the quality of data obtained by telephone is comparable to that obtained by interviews in person. Respondents can and do answer complex items on the telephone; they reveal sources and amount of income; they report years of schooling and whether they voted in recent elections. A consistency check on the reporting of education and a validity check on voting show no inherent superiority of one interviewing strategy over another.[6] If anything, the data suggest that those interviewed in person are somewhat more likely to give socially desirable answers than those interviewed by telephone. However, item by item, differences by method are all small, and the chi-square test shows no statistical significance. The percentage differences—never more than 10 percent—show that telephone data on reported education were more consistent, and on voting, more accurate, but face-to-face interviewing was more successful in obtaining income. Items on familiarity with and assessment of neighborhood services and conditions show the telephone equal to the interview in person.

A comparison of interviewing methods from the perspective of field operations shows that the telephone is highly desirable. Response rates, ability to conduct a long interview (50 minutes), number of contacts required, and suitable times for interviewing all compare favorably. From the perspective of the respondents themselves, interviewing method is irrelevant. Finally, the interviewer's style, whether judged "cool" (task-oriented) or "warm" (person-oriented) appears to intrude somewhat on the quality of response whether obtained in person or on the telephone, and the data suggest it may be less of a factor on the telephone.

PREVIOUS STUDIES

The telephone has become such an attractive way to interview that the researcher is virtually compelled to weigh its suitability when planning a survey. Many studies report the successful use of the telephone,[7] but few have randomly assigned respondents to one or the other method and then compared the results. Notable exceptions are Wiseman,[8] Colombotos,[9]

---

[6] Reported voting was checked against official records.

[7] Studies have underscored the advantages of using the telephone for making appointments, locating the hard to reach, screening for the proper respondents (S. Sudman, "New Uses of Telephone Methods in Survey Research," *Journal of Marketing Research,* Vol. 3, 1966, pp. 163–67), for brief reinterviews on health matters (S. Kegeles, C. Fink, and J. Kirscht, "Interviewing a National Sample by Long-distance Telephone," *Public Opinion Quarterly,* Vol. 33, 1969, pp. 412–19), for gathering data on fertility (L. Coombs and R. Freedman, "Use of Telephone Interviews in a Longitudinal Fertility Study," *Public Opinion Quarterly,* Vol. 28, 1964, pp. 112–17), and for sampling (M. Hauck and M. Cox, "Locating a Sample by Random Digit Dialing," *Public Opinion Quarterly,* Vol. 38, 1974, pp. 253–60).

[8] F. Wiseman, "Methodological Bias in Public Opinion Surveys," *Public Opinion Quarterly,* Vol. 36, 1972, pp. 105–8.

[9] J. Colombotos, "Personal Versus Telephone Interviews: Effect on Responses," *Public Health Reports,* Vol. 84, 1969, pp. 773–82.

and Hochstim.[10] Wiseman collected data by mail, on the telephone, and in person on nine public opinion issues. The results were comparable by method on 7 out of 9 items. On two items, however—attitudes toward legalizing abortion and making birth control information available to the unmarried—more liberal responses were obtained by mail. Little difference was evident in comparisons between telephone and in person responses. Hochstim, using the same three methods in two short surveys, reported no sacrifice in the quality of data depending on method. The two differences reported did not favor interviewing in person. Women were less likely to be candid about drinking patterns in person than by mail or telephone, and their responses to a question on husband-wife discussions of women's medical problems were less likely to be affirmative when interviewed in person than by either of the other methods. The data from these studies suggest that a mail questionnaire is the most neutral data gathering instrument, and the face-to-face interview may be the most vulnerable to bias. Colombotos' study of physicians, however, showed that those interviewed in person were no more likely to give socially acceptable responses than those interviewed by telephone. The present study adds to what is known about the strengths and weaknesses of alternative interviewing strategies by comparing their suitability under controlled conditions, along dimensions not previously examined.

QUALITY OF DATA

Complex Knowledge and Attitudinal Items

The interview schedule included a number of items which measured the respondent's familiarity with specific local services and his or her assessment of these services. In 1972 when all interviews were conducted in person, the respondent was handed a card to facilitate remembering the answer categories.[11]

The longest item of this kind, the rating of 15 local services (sanitation, health, addiction, recreation, etc.) on a five-point scale was repeated in 1974 but without the use of a card. Interviewers found the item not to their liking: they had to recite the answer categories many times while at the same time motivate the respondent to think about his answers. Respondents seemed to have coped well.

Comparing the responses elicited by telephone and in person suggests that interviewing strategy is interchangeable (Table 1). Respondents are slightly less likely to say "don't know" or "no such service in the neighborhood" by telephone, but the differences are trivial. Moreover, there is no evidence of respondent bias in the evaluation of these services.

[10] J. R. Hochstim, "A Critical Comparison of Three Strategies of Collecting Data from Households," *Journal of the American Statistical Association*, Vol. 62, 1967, pp. 976–89.

[11] In the past, the telephone was considered inappropriate for interviewing when experience indicated the need to present cards to the respondent (Sudman, *op. cit.*).

TABLE 1
RESPONSES BY INTERVIEWING METHOD: KNOWLEDGE AND ATTITUDINAL ITEMS

	Telephone (N = 85)	In Person (N = 98)
Rating of 15 local services		
Percent who rated 4 or more services:		
Excellent/good	73%	69%
Bad/very bad	31	32
Percent who said at least once:		
No such service	35	42
Don't know	75	84
Knowledge of local groups and organizations		
Percent who said they know of:		
Community School Board	53	48
Community Planning Board	33	28
Office of Neighborhood Government	12	18
Place in the neighborhood which helps people		
deal with city offices & services	38	41

NOTE: In all tables except in Table 2, the "no answer" and "don't know" responses were excluded in testing for the statistical significance of the differences between interviewing methods and between interviewer styles. Frequencies are reported in parentheses. The symbol * for one item in Table 8 indicates the only difference which is statistically significant (chi-square).

Respondents are just as likely to say a particular service is good or bad, whether interviewed by telephone or in person.

Four additional items inquired specifically into the respondent's knowledge of neighborhood groups and organizations, for example, Community School Board, Office of Neighborhood Government. Again, respondents were no more likely to say that they knew of such facilities when queried by telephone, suggesting that interviewing strategy has no bearing on the attempts by respondents to impress the interviewer with the breadth of their knowledge or to give the "right" answer.

Previous research indicates that sensitive information—for example, contraceptive use[12] and drinking patterns[13]—is accessible by telephone. We tested accessibility to three other kinds of personal data, namely, income, voting, and level of education.

Personal Income

The items requesting income information included a six-part question on sources of income, e.g., social security, welfare, pensions, etc. Early in the field work one respondent interviewed by telephone spontaneously remarked to the interviewer, "I don't think I would have told you I'm on

[12] Coombs and Freedman, *op. cit.*
[13] Hochstim, *op. cit.*

welfare, if you'd come to my house. I'd be too embarrassed." At the time, her comment suggested that telephone interviews could elicit a socially undesirable answer such as this one better than face-to-face interviews, but later, cross-tabulation of responses by interviewing strategy revealed no special merit to either method. Virtually the same proportion of people on the telephone and in person said that they had received welfare payments during the past year (Table 2).

The reporting of last year's income, either a precise amount or within a category, is accessible by both methods. A total of 80 percent interviewed by telephone and 88 percent interviewed in person reported income. The 8 percent differential in favor of face-to-face interviewing is not statistically significant. Moreover, we might add two supplementary pieces of information. First, all three ethnic groups in the sample—blacks, Hispanics and whites—appear to be as willing to provide income data by telephone as in person. Second, respondents who refused to report their income when interviewed in 1972 are not the same ones who refused in 1974; 79 percent cooperated both times, 17 percent cooperated one time, but not another; 4 percent refused both times.

Accuracy on Voting

As a test of response validity, reported voting in the 1973 New York City mayoral election and in the 1972 presidential election was checked against actual voting.[14] The results reveal that 74 percent of the respondents were accurate in reporting that they had voted in the mayoral election, and a comparable proportion, 71 percent, accurately reported voting in the presidential election.[15] The direction of the bias was toward

TABLE 2
RESPONSES BY INTERVIEWING METHOD: FAMILY INCOME

	Telephone (N = 85)	In Person (N = 98)
Percent who acknowledged income from welfare	5%	6%
Reporting of family income		
Provided information	80%	88%
Refused	11	6
Don't know	9	6
	100%	100%

[14] The validation data were extracted from the record books of the New York City Board of Elections.

[15] It proved impossible to check the voting behavior of 14 respondents for various reasons: the election book was unavailable; the respondent moved to another election district between the election and the interview; the respondent did not answer the question on voting.

social acceptability—respondents claimed that they *had* voted rather than not. For example, of the 44 respondents inaccurate on voting in the mayoral election, 39 said they had voted, but really had not; 5 said they did not vote, but the record shows that they did. The accuracy of self-reporting in our sample is in line with that of middle-class populations and welfare recipients.[16]

Voting data obtained by telephone are slightly more likely to be accurate than those obtained by a face-to-face interview, and this is true for both the mayoral and the presidential election[17] (Table 3). In general, whites seem to be more candid about voting than blacks or Hispanics. Moreover, when interviewing strategy is introduced, the data suggest that the telephone may be the better way to collect such information. For example, 92 percent of the whites accurately reported voting by telephone in contrast to 80 percent when interviewed face-to-face. Blacks are slightly more likely to be candid on the telephone than in person (69 percent vs. 58 percent), and method does not matter with Hispanics.

Consistency on Education

Both in 1972 and in 1974 respondents were asked, "How many years of school did you finish?" Eleven categories ranging from "never attended school" to "graduate or professional school" were offered, and interviewers field-coded the responses. The result, excluding respondents who completed additional years of schooling between the two interviews and those who answered "technical or business school," is that one out of

TABLE 3
RESPONSES BY INTERVIEWING METHOD: REPORTED VS. ACTUAL VOTING

1973 NYC Mayoral Election	Telephone (N = 81)	In Person (N = 90)	Total (N = 171)
Accurate	79%	71%	74%
Voted	44	37	40
Didn't vote	35	33	34
Inaccurate	21	30	26
Yes, no record	20	26	23
No, yes on record	1	4	3
Percent nonvoters admitting not voting	64	57	60

[16] Summary data for five studies appears in Carol H. Weiss, "Validity of Welfare Mothers' Interview Responses," *Public Opinion Quarterly,* Vol. 32, 1968, p. 625.

[17] For brevity, Table 3 presents data only on the mayoral election, but the pattern is virtually identical for the presidential election.

three was inconsistent.[18] The fact that 14 percent deflated their educational attainment in 1974, as compared with 1972, and 20 percent inflated it, suggests that respondents do not necessarily bias their answers to enhance their status. What it does suggest is that while many answer categories may appeal to the analyst, the request for such precise information cannot really be met by the respondent.

In all likelihood, the analyst will group the data, but this accommodation will not necessarily eliminate the error. Comparing 1972 and 1974 responses shows 18 percent off more than one category. Moreover, although one might think the better educated respondent would be more likely to be consistent, there is no support for this belief. As Table 4 shows, it is the high-school graduate who is most likely to be consistent (83 percent).

Examining the cases assigned to the experiment on interviewing method, we find no real differences in consistency of reporting education, whether respondents were reinterviewed on the telephone or in person. While 71 percent reinterviewed on the telephone gave identical responses, the figure is 62 percent for those reinterviewed in person (Table 5). Whites are more likely to be consistent than blacks, regardless of method, and these racial differences are the sharpest found in the study. On the telephone, 50 percent of the blacks are consistent and 81 percent of the whites; in person, the figures are 48 percent and 73 percent, respectively. With the limited number of cases it is hard to tease out an explanation, but the data suggest that blacks who spent their childhood in a large city

TABLE 4

PERCENT OF TOTAL SAMPLE REPORTING EDUCATION IN 1974 EXACTLY AS REPORTED IN 1972, BY LEVEL OF EDUCATION*

	(N)
Never went to school	70% (10)
4 years or less	53 (41)
5, 6, or 7 years	59 (103)
Finished 8th grade	56 (97)
One year of high school	49 (51)
2–3 years of high school	50 (167)
High school graduate	83 (219)
Technical/business school	27 (33)
Some college	65 (97)
Finished college	50 (32)
Graduate or professional school	76 (33)

* The data in Table 4 use the entire sample reinterviewed in 1974, but the pattern is similar for those in the interviewing experiment. To have confidence in the finding, however, it was necessary to test it against the entire sample.

[18] Respondents who said "technical or business school" were omitted because of the ambiguity of the category. Although it is intended to identify respondents who have had some post-high-school training other than college, it actually may be a substitute for high school or equivalent to some college training.

TABLE 5
RESPONSES BY INTERVIEWING METHOD: CONSISTENCY IN REPORTING EDUCATION

	Telephone *(N = 58)*	*In Person* *(N = 66)*
Consistent, 1972 and 1974	71%	62%
Overreported, 1974	19	21
Underreported, 1974	10	17
	100%	100%

and those who were born in New York State are more likely to be consistent than blacks who come from elsewhere.

FIELD PERFORMANCE

It is one thing to report that the quality of data obtained by telephone is comparable to that obtained in person, but another to ask what modifications might be desirable in field operations when different interviewing strategies are under consideration. Will interviewing strategy, for example, make a difference in the response rate? Does it require modification in the desired length of the schedule or in planning the optimum times for contacting the respondent? Interviewer costs are clearly lower by telephone, and respondents can be interviewed by either method, but do respondents in fact have a preference for one or another interviewing strategy? Finally, what evidence is there of interviewer effects, and if there are any, are they muted or sharpened by method of interviewing?

Response Rate

Of the 247 respondents randomly assigned to an interview by telephone or in person, 183 were actually interviewed. Of the 64 who were not, 25 were ineligible because they had moved outside the study area, were ill or had died, or because they spoke only a foreign language. This reduced the target to 222, yielding a completion rate of 82 percent. The 18 percent missed either refused (9 percent), were not locatable (5 percent), or were not at home at any time (4 percent).

A case by case review of the 20 refusals indicates that method of interviewing was not the stumbling block. Although one might think that the presence of the interviewer at the respondent's home could help to convince him of the importance of the interview,[19] neither face-to-face nor telephone contact converted firm refusals to completed interviews. Offering the option of a later contact by either method provided one

[19] J. B. Lansing and J. N. Morgan, *Economic Survey Methods.* Ann Arbor, Institute for Social Research, University of Michigan, 1971, pp. 111–13.

more opportunity to try to convince the respondent of the need for his cooperation, but it still proved irrelevant to the firm refusal.

The volunteered comments of the refusing respondents suggest what the deterrents were. The typical reasons, in their words, were:

I didn't like the questions last time . . . How long have you lived here? How many children do you have?

My son is a lawyer, and he said, "Mom, don't bother."

I work too hard, I have no time for a telephone or a personal interview.

Switchers from One Method to Another

Respondent requests for a change in interviewing method were minimal. Only 12 of the experiment interviews could not be completed in the assigned method, and for 11 this meant a switch from a telephone to a face-to-face interview. The Hispanics numbered high among the switchers (8 out of 11 from telephone to in-person) for the simple reason that their telephones were not in working order, although they had been when case assignments were made. Of the remaining three, one was hard of hearing, another asked that the telephone not be used because his wife was ill, and a third insisted on seeing the interviewer. The one switcher from a face-to-face to a telephone interview was an older white woman who refused to let a stranger into her house. The responses of the switchers ($N = 12$) and the nonswitchers ($N = 171$) reveal no differences in quality of response, and accordingly, they were combined in the analysis.

Contacting the Respondent

Three considerations in contacting the respondent were tested against interviewing strategy, namely, preferred time of day, days of the week, and number of contacts required to conduct the interview.[20]

Time of day. Although we anticipated that telephone interviewing would permit more flexibility in the time of day when interviews were conducted, method appears to make absolutely no difference. Interviews, whether by telephone or in person, were most likely to be conducted in the evening (53 percent), then the afternoon (34 percent), and least likely in the morning (13 percent) (Table 6).

Day of the week. The findings on best days of the week are also somewhat surprising. Although we suggested in the interviewer training sessions that weekends might be particularly good, Monday through

[20] A contact was defined as speaking to the respondent or a member of his or her household, or sending the respondent a personal letter from the supervisor, if he or she had expressed disinterest or reluctance to be interviewed.

TABLE 6
RESPONSES BY INTERVIEWING METHOD: FIELD PERFORMANCE

	Telephone (N = 85)	In Person (N = 98)
Time of day interview conducted		
Evening	55%	52%
Afternoon	33	35
Morning	12	13
	100%	100%
Day of the week[a]		
Sunday	5%	11%
Monday	24	15
Tuesday	22	24
Wednesday	14	20
Thursday	19	11
Friday	11	5
Saturday	6	14
	101%	100%
Number of contacts		
One	34%	29%
Two	27	31
Three or more	40	41
	101%	101%
Average length of interview	49 min.	51 min.

[a] Data for Friday should be discounted, because interviewers reported to the study office weekly on Friday.

Thursday were the most productive days, both for telephone and in-person interviewing; Saturday and Sunday were moderately successful for interviewing in person, but not by telephone.[21] It should be added that interviewers were paid per interview rather than hourly, and this fact strengthens the finding on when to contact prospective respondents.

Number of contacts. The need to contact a respondent more than once may increase his hesitation, surely discourages the interviewer, and usually raises field costs. Our experience was that only 1 out of 3 interviews could be conducted on the first contact, and 2 out of 5 required at least three contacts (Table 6). Here again, interviewing method makes no difference but interviewing costs can skyrocket in a survey in which the primary method of data collection is an in-person interview.

Length of Interview

Sustaining a respondent's interest in a one-hour telepone interview has been achieved in a survey of physicians[22] and undoubtedly with other

[21] No comparison is made for Friday, because interviewers reported to the study office weekly on that day.

[22] Colombotos, *op. cit.*

elites who routinely use the telephone in their work. To date, however, telephone interviews with more broadly based samples tend to be short.[23]

Our schedule was estimated to take about 40 minutes, but the average length was closer to 50 minutes. Again, interviewing strategy was no barrier. Telephone interviews averaged 49 minutes and those conducted face to face, 51 minutes (Table 6). Moreover, only 3 of the 183 interviews required more than one session for completion.

But does the respondent's sex, age, ethnicity, or education affect the length of time needed to complete an interview, if it is conducted on the telephone rather than in person? A comparison of the two methods shows no difference by sex; a face-to-face interview takes about five minutes longer with the poorly educated or older person and with the white respondent, but again these are trivial differences.

Preference for Interviewing Method

At the very end of the interview, respondents who had been interviewed by telephone were reminded that they had been interviewed in person two years before, and they were asked: "Do you prefer being interviewed in person or by telephone?" To our knowledge, this is the first time respondents have been asked this question, and either method turns out to be acceptable to half of them: 50 percent have no preference; 26 percent favor an interview in person; and the remaining 24 percent, a telephone interview (Table 7).

TABLE 7
PREFERENCES FOR INTERVIEWING METHOD*

	No Preference	In Person	By Telephone	Total (N)
Ethnicity				
Blacks	61%	25%	13%	99%(36)
Hispanics	50	40	10	100 (10)
Whites	40	21	38	99 (37)
Age				
18–35	43	40	16	99 (30)
36–59	59	17	24	100 (29)
60 or older	48	17	35	100 (23)
Employment status				
Employed full-time	44	31	25	100 (52)
Other	62	17	20	99 (29)

* Only respondents reinterviewed by telephone; of these, 50 percent had no preference, 26 percent preferred an in-person interview, and 24 percent preferred a telephone interview.

[23] J. Schmiedeskamp, "Reinterviews by Telephone," *Journal of Marketing,* Vol. 26, 1962, pp. 28–34; Hochstim, *op. cit.;* Kegeles *et al., op. cit.;* Coombs and Freedman, *op. cit.; Survey Research,* Vol. 5, No. 1, 1973.

The convenience of being interviewed by telephone and reluctance to open the door to a stranger are the most frequently given reasons for preferring the telephone interview. ("I've got my feet propped up and I'm comfortable." "I don't open my door to no stranger!") Ease of communication attracts those who prefer an interview in person. For example, "I can understand and give better answers in person."

Of the several respondent characteristics checked against preferred method, three merit comment. First, blacks are more likely than whites or Hispanics to be indifferent to interviewing method, and whites are most likely to want to be interviewed by telephone. Second, the older the respondent is, the more likely he is to prefer a telephone interview, but the differences by age are not as sharp as those by ethnicity. Third, contrary to what we thought, respondents who work full-time are not more likely to prefer a telephone interview.

Interviewer Effects

From what is known in general about interviewing, it would seem that a respondent and an interviewer might be less engrossed in an interview conducted by telephone than in person. By telephone the interviewer is merely a voice; she or he has not taken the trouble to go to the respondent's home, so how important can the interview really be? The lack of visual cues may make the interview more mechanical, with neither interviewers nor respondents as motivated as they might be to accomplish the task of complete and accurate information. The present study shows that data collected by telephone are as complete and accurate as in-person data. What remains to report are the consequences of interviewing style, because the results suggest that two quite different styles which obtain in person also are in evidence on the telephone.

After the data were collected, interviewers assigned to the experiment were classified into those whose style was person-oriented and friendly ("warm") and those whose style was task-oriented and businesslike ("cool").[24] Analysis shows that there appears to be such a thing as a "warm" telephone interview, and what is more, this style may be a handicap for obtaining full and accurate information on the telephone as it has been in person.[25]

---

[24] Twelve interviewers interviewed both in person and by telephone for the experiment. The field supervisor and the assistant supervisors independently rated each of these interviewers and agreed completely on the interviewing style of 11 of them. It is these interviewers, five of whom were rated "cool" and six "warm," who provide the data for analysis of interviewing styles. These 11 interviewers completed 86 percent of the interviews assigned to the experiment. Interviewers included whites, blacks, and Hispanics between twenty-five and thirty-five years of age who were college educated.

[25] Although previous research on the effects of interviewing style conflict somewhat, the balance of evidence is that a warm and friendly interviewing style increases response bias.

Most of our interviewers were relatively inexperienced, and interviewer training stressed the need to be professional and task-oriented. Still, it was the judgment of the supervisory staff that some interviewers were probably more task-oriented than others. Two days of training combined with weekly conferences could not alter their basic personality styles even for this specific task. Once in the field and reinforced by success in gaining the respondent's cooperation, it is our view that they may have adopted interviewing skills which fit their personality and rejected those that did not.

The data, of course, do not permit a refined test of the effects of interviewer behavior, but they suggest a pattern. Holding constant method of interviewing, in 11 of the 14 comparisons presented in Table 8, warm interviewers tend to be less successful than those rated cool.[26] Only one difference is statistically significant, but the consistency of the direction of the bias lends support to previous research which shows that interviewer style can influence data collection. There is a slight tendency

TABLE 8
Interviewing Method and Interviewer Style

Percent of Respondents	Telephone		In Person	
	Warm	Cool	Warm	Cool
	(N)	(N)	(N)	(N)
Consistent in reporting education	63% (24)	72%(25)	52% (25)	72% (32)
Willing to report family income	70 (33)	86 (37)	84 (45)	95 (38)
Accurate in reporting voting	71 (31)	82 (39)	64 (42)	78 (36)
Rating 4 or more local services excellent/good	79 (34)	72 (40)	80 (45)	59 (39)
Rating 4 or more local services bad/very bad	29 (34)	30 (40)	29 (45)	38 (39)
Saying "don't know" at least once when rating local services	85 (34)	67 (40)	93 (45)	69* (39)
Saying "no such service" at least once when rating local services	32 (34)	37 (40)	42 (45)	44 (39)

* Statistically significant ($p < .01$).

See Herbert H. Hyman, *et al., Interviewing in Social Research,* Chicago, University of Chicago Press, 1954; Richard J. Hill and Nason Hall, "A Note on Rapport and the Quality of Interview Data," *Southwestern Social Science Quarterly,* Vol. 44, 1963, pp. 247–55; Barbara S. Dohrenwend, John Colombotos, and Bruce P. Dohrenwend, "Social Distance and Interviewer Effects," *Public Opinion Quarterly,* Vol. 32, 1968, pp. 410–22; James A. Williams, Jr., "Interviewer Role Performance: A Further Note on Bias in the Information Interview," *Public Opinion Quarterly,* Vol. 32, 1968, pp. 287–94; Carol H. Weiss, "Interaction in the Research Interview: The Effects of Rapport on Response," *Proceedings of the Social Statistics Section,* American Statistical Association, 1970, pp. 17–20.

[26] Re-examination of the 20 refusals suggests that warm interviewers were somewhat more likely than those judged cool to have been refused an interview, but the few cases involved make this finding only a trace of a suggestion for future research.

for the differences in interviewing style to be larger in person than on the telephone, suggesting that the telephone can mediate this effect to some extent. For example, on the telephone warm interviewers obtained consistent education data 63 percent of the time, while cool interviewers were successful with 72 percent of their respondents. In person, the figures are 52 percent and 72 percent, respectively. Face-to-face interaction, then, seems to encourage bias and may be a barrier to obtaining high-quality data.

SUMMARY

The results of this experiment show that the quality of data obtained by telephone on complex attitudinal and knowledge items as well as on personal items is comparable to that collected in person. Moreover, field techniques for contacting the respondent and for conducting an almost hour-long interview need not be modified. Using cards to facilitate collecting certain kinds of data may be helpful, but it is by no means essential.

The problem of the personal involvement of the interviewer remains. We suggest that in training sessions, data such as those presented in this paper could be used to illustrate the consequences of alternative interviewing styles to demonstrate to interviewers the costs of a warm and friendly style while asking and recording information. Work satisfaction and encouragement to perform an often difficult and responsible task might better be built into training by addressing this problem directly and then offering alternative sources for motivation and satisfaction. These might include fuller participation in the research process by contributing field observations to the analysts, by exchanging experiences with other interviewers, by attempting to increase interviewer convictions about the importance of the study, and, of course, by higher pay.

Actors and Questions
in Telephone and Personal Interview Surveys

ROBERT M. GROVES

OTHER researchers have compared results of personal interview surveys and telephone surveys (Hochstim, 1967; Rogers, 1976), and the strategy can be used to guide researchers facing a choice of survey mode. Such comparisons also permit closer inspection of specific differences between modes that contribute any discrepant results. In that regard, two components of the survey interview can be studied—the actors in the situation (the interviewer and the respondent) and a set of questions that direct the interaction (the questionnaire). These components are of interest because they are sources of different types of errors in survey data. For example, the refusal of a selected respondent to cooperate yields potential nonresponse bias, and inadequate thought given to his answers can produce response errors. The questionnaire can contain poorly constructed questions that yield erroneous reports on issues of interest. When contemplating a change from personal to telephone interviews, the researcher should give attention to any changes in the actors' behavior or in the form of the questionnaire that are required by the nature of telephone interviewing.

This paper addresses some differences between personal and tele-

Abstract This paper concentrates on two aspects of telephone survey administration: (1) the respondent's reactions to the request for an interview and to the interview itself, and (2) the properties of questions using response cards in personal interviews and adaptations of these questions for telephone use.

Robert M. Groves is a Study Director at the Survey Research Center and an Assistant Professor in the Department of Sociology, University of Michigan. Research for this study was supported by NSF (SOC 76–07519). An earlier version of this paper was presented at the 1977 annual meeting of AAPOR. A full report of the study, entitled *Comparing Telephone and Personal Surveys,* is forthcoming (Groves and Kahn in press).

phone interviews in the actors' behavior and in the form of the questioning. In examining the attitudes and behaviors of respondents, we will focus on those characteristics that may imply that the modes differ in the amount of nonresponse and response bias, and when possible, we will search for possible causes of those differences. The data we use come from a project which conducted two national telephone surveys (of a total of 1,734 respondents), one using a stratified random sample with phone numbers spread over the entire United States, the other using the 74 counties and metropolitan areas in the Survey Research Center's national household sample. The telephone interviewing was conducted simultaneously with the field work of the 1976 SRC Spring Omnibus Survey, a biannual, multipurpose personal interview survey (with a total of 1,548 respondents). The project supplemented the variety of questions asked of the Omnibus national probability household sample with measures thought to be differentially sensitive to interviewing methods and representatives of types of measures used in much social science research. The same questions were asked of the personal interview sample by SRC field interviewers and of the two different national telephone samples by a centralized telephone staff.[1]

Other reports from this project have noted the tendency toward faster-paced interviews and more succinct answers to open-ended questions on the telephone (Groves and Kahn, forthcoming). Consistent with the Colombotos findings (1964), there were no differences between modes in tendencies to provide socially desirable answers. On those items where external data sources provided validity checks (voting behavior questions), no differences between modes were found. This is similar to the results of the Rogers study (1976) in New York City and to those of Locander et al. (1974).

This paper concentrates on two aspects of telephone survey administration that deserve more systematic study than this first experimental experience provided. We present these results in hopes of stimulating such research. The first aspect could generally be classified as the selected persons' reactions to the request for an interview and to the interview experience itself. In this discussion we attempt to collect information that identifies areas where changes in interviewer behavior may produce better data. The second topic arises from attempts to adapt to telephone use questions utilizing response cards in personal interviews. In that presentation we use the differences between modes to discuss the properties of response cards and of their verbal analogs used on the telephone.

---

[1] Objective selection of one adult (18 years old or older) within sample households was accomplished using techniques similar to those of Kish (1949).

Reactions of the Respondent to the Survey

The response rate for the total telephone sample lies between 59 percent and 70 percent, depending on whether unanswered numbers are included in the denominator, although there is evidence that the true rate is closer to 70 percent than to 59 percent.[2] The response rate for the personal interview survey was 74.2 percent, at least four percentage points higher than the telephone rate. In general the number of callbacks on the telephone exceeded that in the persoanal interview survey.[3] Although we initially suspected that our inexperience with the methodology depressed the telephone response rate, SRC national telephone surveys conducted since this initial experiment generally have replicated this finding.

The response rate comparison identifies one possible weakness in our use of the telephone to collect data—greater bias due to nonresponse. We introduced into the questionnaire an item that measured the respondent reactions to the interview directly. Although this item can address only the feelings of those consenting to an interview, it may provide some insight into the lower response rate on the telephone survey.

Table 1 presents the responses to a question about how the respondent might prefer to answer the questions in the survey—in person (face-to-face), on the telephone, or by mail. The question was asked with the same wording in telephone and personal interviews. The top portion of the table shows that a large proportion of personal interview respondents are satisfied with the mode they are experiencing (78.4 percent), but that a much smaller proportion of telephone respondents favor the telephone mode (39.4 percent). There are three possible interpretations of these differences: (1) the stimulus of the mode which they are experiencing differs by mode, that is, the telephone respondents actually don't enjoy the experience as much as personal interview respondents enjoy a personal interview; (2) the willingness of the respondents to reveal that they prefer another mode differs by mode; for example, the physical presence of the personal interviewers makes their respondents more reticent to reveal that they prefer another mode; or (3) the commitment of the respondent who

---

[2] We define the response rate as number of completed interviews divided by number of eligible sample units. In telephone sample designs like ours, the working status of unanswered numbers cannot be determined with certainty. Later experimental investigations have shown that the vast majority of unanswered numbers dialed 17 or more times during the field period are nonworking.

[3] One finding with contrasting implications is that the telephone surveys had slightly higher response rates in large metropolitan areas than did the personal interview survey. This may suggest a mixed-mode design with telephone interviews in urban areas and personal interviews in more rural areas.

Table 1. Preference for Questioning Mode, Respondents in Phone Households, by Interview Type[a]

	Personal Interviews		Telephone Interviews	
Preference				
Face-to-face Interview		78.4%		22.7%
Telephone Interview		1.7		39.4
Mailed questionnaire		16.9		28.1
Mixed opinion		1.5		1.8
Don't know		1.5		8.0
Total		100.0%		100.0%
Missing data		14		69
Total N		1,437		1,696
Reason for choice				
Reasons for face-to-face		47.3%		23.2%
More personal, like to see person I'm dealing with	17.6%		11.6%	
Can give better answers	10.7%		5.2%	
Reasons against face-to-face		0.7%		6.9%
R rarely home, may be busy	0.4%		2.5%	
R may not let stranger in HU	0.1%		1.8%	
Some interviewers are pushy, R wouldn't feel comfortable	0.2%		1.1%	
Reasons for telephone interview		1.0%		24.3%
Easier, quicker to do	0.0%		10.6%	
Doesn't require visit by interviewer	0.3%		3.2%	
Reasons against telephone interview		20.0%		2.8%
Don't know who you are talking to	6.8%		1.0%	
Don't like to talk on phone	6.0%		0.7%	
Reasons for mailed questionnaire		15.8%		27.8%
Gives you more time to think about questions	7.6%		17.8%	
Can fill out at your convenience	5.9%		6.9%	
Reasons against mailed questionnaire		14.5%		12.9%
Wouldn't fill it out	12.4%		10.9%	
Get too much junk mail	0.8%		0.4%	
Other		0.6%		2.1%
Total		99.9%		100.0%
Missing data		26		34
Total N		1,400		1,694

[a] Data weighted by reciprocal of selection probability.

agrees to the interview differs by mode; for example, only those strongly attracted to personal interviews may consent to them; telephone respondents might be less committed to any mode, and since the interview requires little intrusion into their home, they might grant the interview. No doubt to some extent all these influences are acting to create the results shown in Table 1. For whatever reason, however, telephone survey respondents are much more willing to report preferences for personal or mailed questionnaires.

In the lower part of Table 1 are the reasons for the mode preference. They were arrived at by coding answers to the open-ended item that asked respondents why they made the choice of mode; the reasons are divided in categories for and against each mode. The reason given most frequently in personal interviews was positive feelings about the face-to-face interview (47.3 percent); the most prevalent reason by the telephone respondents was associated with preferences for mailed questionnaires (27.8 percent). Under each category of reasons are the two or three specific reasons mentioned most often. The single reason most frequently mentioned for preferring personal interviews was seeing the person who was asking the questions and having the personal contact that is part of the interview. Telephone respondents most often praised mailed questionnaires because they allow more time to think about the questions.[4]

Another measure of respondents' reactions to the interview, which was introduced at the end of the questionnaire, asked whether the respondent felt uneasy about discussing such topics in the interview as their income, racial attitudes, income tax returns, questions about their health, their job, voting behavior, and their political opinions. Table 2 presents the proportion of respondents in the two different modes of interview who admitted uneasiness about discussing the topics. Larger proportions of telephone respondents felt uneasy about each of the topics mentioned; the largest differences appear for questions about the financial status and political opinions of the respondents. Over one-quarter of the telephone respondents (27.9 percent)

Table 2. Percentages of Respondents Who Reported Feeling Uneasy About Discussing Specific Topics, by Mode of Interview[a]

Topic	Telephone	Personal Interview (Phone Households)
Income	27.9%	15.3%
Racial attitudes	9.2	8.8
Income tax return	14.1	8.6
Health	3.0	1.6
Job	3.1	1.9
Voting behavior	9.1	8.0
Political opinions	12.1	8.5

[a] Data weighted by reciprocals of selection probabilities.

[4] This question of preference was added to a recent SRC personal interview survey in a different context and yielded the same finding—that the telephone interview mode was preferred less than the personal interview mode. In that application, however, the differences between modes were somewhat smaller.

admitted feeling uncomfortable about answering questions about their income, and this report is consistent with the higher missing data rates for income in the telephone data.[5]

We have examined data concerning respondent reactions to the interview in an attempt to understand the lower response rates of the national telephone interview survey. Many of the reports of lack of personal contact and uneasiness about discussing sensitive topics may relate to several constraints of telephone surveys without previous household contact. In personal interview surveys, sample households receive precontact letters and have a chance to observe as well as hear the interviewer before consenting to the survey request. The unanticipated telephone call and immediate request for an interview provides the respondent less time and information to judge the wisdom of complying with the request.

Overcoming these constraints requires work on filling the audio medium with analogs of the information exchange that occurs in the personal interview. This requires attention to the initial moments of contact with the respondent. Respondent trust in the interviewer and the impression that the interview will be an enjoyable experience must be developed at that time and maintained throughout the interview. We implemented an introduction and respondent selection technique that started the actual interview very quickly after the telephone conversation began. It may be preferable to delay the request for an interview somewhat, to devote the initial dialog to detailed descriptions of the survey, the survey organization, the role of the respondent, and the proposed uses of the data. Example questions could be used to inform the respondent about the nature of the interaction that is desired. A preinterview contact might be used to simulate the effect of the precontact letter. These and other approaches are worthy of study in order to improve the response rates of national telephone surveys.

Adapting Show-card Questions for Telephone Survey Use

In this section we will discuss differences in questions using response cards in personal interviews and attempt to associate those differences with the nature of measurement employed. Two methods of adaptation were employed for different show-card questions. In one method, major categories of the scale were verbally presented; the respondent chose one, and on the basis of that choice, a set of more

---

[5] Some of the greater expressed uneasiness about discussing their income may arise from the request for a dollar amount on the telephone instead of a selection of a category as in the personal interview.

specific alternatives was presented for respondent selection. This resulted in a process of "unfolding" the respondent's answer. Two scale questions used the unfolding technique—the probability of the respondent buying a car in the next 12 months, and one version of a life satisfaction item. In the other method, the nature of the scale was verbally communicated by describing what certain points on the scale meant, and then the respondent was asked to choose a numbered point on the scale. Three questions—personal and family income, political attitude thermometer items, and one version of the life satis-faction scale—used this technique.

In examining the results for questions which asked the telephone respondent to give a numbered point on the scale in response to the question, it seems clear that labeling a point on the response card can encourage its choice by a respondent. Figure 1 presents a histogram for the political thermometer items for Jimmy Carter; on the left side of the figure the results for the telephone survey are plotted; on the right, those for the personal interview survey appear. The labeled points on the response card given to the respondent were 0, 15, 30, 40, 50, 60, 70, 85, and 100 degrees. The ranges and points mentioned in the telephone interviews were 0–50 degrees, 50 degrees, and 50–100 degrees. On neither of the modes are all possible points from 0 to 100 degrees mentioned, but the clustering of respondents on points differs across mode. In telephone interviews respondents tend to give numbers divisible by ten (10, 20, 30, 40, 50, and so on) or numbers representing quarters of the 0 to 100 range (25, 50, 75, 100). The large remainder of their answers are divisible by five (15, 35, 45, 55, and so on). There also seems to be some tendency to become more precise for numbers above 90 degrees. In total, however, the percentage of telephone respondents who provide numbers not divisible by five or ten is only 3.0 percent. In personal interviews the clustering of an-swers is almost completely dominated by the labeling of points on the show card. Only 2.7 percent of respondents provide answers outside those nine points.

The largest single difference between the two modes on the distri-bution of thermometer scores arises from the absence of a label for the points at 75 and 80 degrees on the show card. If we collapse over all numbers between 70 and 85, however, the differences in mode are smaller (26 percent for the telephone and 32 percent for the personal interview in that range). Most of the other differences are found for points divisible by five or ten that are not labeled on the show card.

Five questions measuring the respondent satisfaction with different parts of his life were asked in different ways on half-samples within both modes. The one that utilized a satisfied-dissatisfied scale asked the respondent for a numbered point on the scale after the three

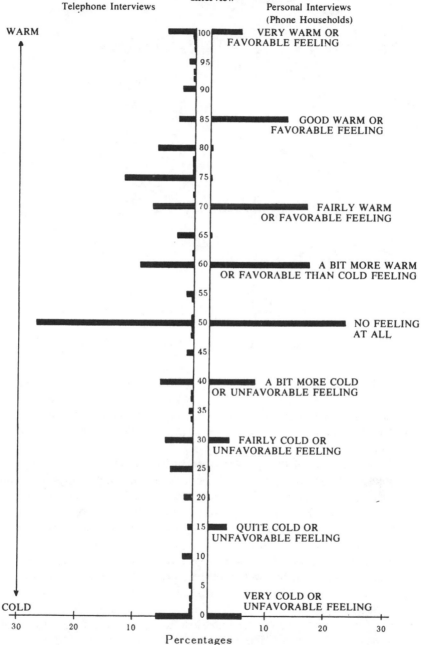

Figure 1. Histogram of Responses for Carter Feeling Thermometer Item by Mode of Interview[a]

Telephone Interviews

Personal Interviews
(Phone Households)

WARM

VERY WARM OR
FAVORABLE FEELING

GOOD WARM OR
FAVORABLE FEELING

FAIRLY WARM
OR FAVORABLE FEELING

A BIT MORE WARM
OR FAVORABLE THAN COLD FEELING

NO FEELING
AT ALL

A BIT MORE COLD
OR UNFAVORABLE FEELING

FAIRLY COLD OR
UNFAVORABLE FEELING

QUITE COLD OR
UNFAVORABLE FEELING

COLD

VERY COLD OR
UNFAVORABLE FEELING

Percentages

[a] Data weighted by reciprocals of selection probabilities. Incorporating design effects that reflect the complexities of the sample designs, we estimate standard errors of .031 on differences of proportions in the two modes.

Figure 2. Response Distribution for Delighted-Terrible Scale on "Your Life as a Whole"
by Mode of Interview[a]

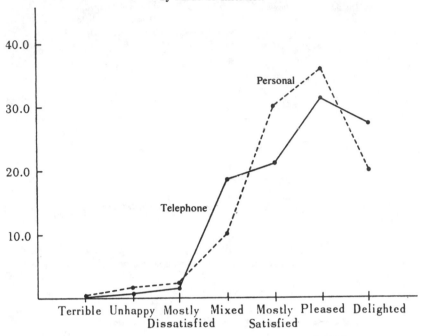

[a] Data weighted by reciprocal of selection probabilities.

labeled points were described. The response distributions are generally the same, the largest difference being a greater tendency for
telephone respondents to answer "completely satisfied" (41.9 percent of the telephone respondents and 35.1 percent of the personal
respondents do so).

The other form of the questions unfolded the respondents' original
response in terms of "good, bad, or mixed" into a seven-point scale
(see Figure 2). Those who originally replied "mixed" were not asked
for a more specific response. Figure 2 presents the marginal distribution on a measure about "Your Life as a Whole" using this technique. In addition to application of the unfolding technique in this
case, there is another difference between this scale and the satisfied-
dissatisfied scale. In this delighted-terrible scale, all seven points are
given labels, so neither the telephone nor the personal interview
respondent answered in terms of a number. The differences between
modes for this version of the question are somewhat larger than for
the other version. Since the response "mixed" was not followed by
an interviewer probe for a more specific answer, respondent desires

to complete the interview may have caused some telephone respondents to choose that answer.[6]

The larger proportion answering "mixed" on the telephone is not, however, the only difference between modes of interview. In addition, the distributions across the three responses on the positive side of the scale also differ. In the telephone interviews these responses were read to those who replied that their feelings were on the "good" side in response to the initial question. In the personal interview the respondent was faced with all seven alternative answers at the same time, and the interviewer verbally described the end and middle points of the scale only in the introduction of the question series. The proportion choosing "delighted" is much larger on the telephone (27.3 percent) than in person (20.4 percent). Conversely, those answering "mostly satisfied" appear disproportionately smaller on the telephone. We have already noticed some tendency for the telephone respondents to choose the extreme satisfaction point in the other scale used. The larger proportions of "delighted" responses on the telephone may be other evidence for higher optimism and satisfaction in this group of telephone respondents. Alternatively, the differences on the delighted-terrible scale may also be the result of the telephone interviewer verbally presenting the three alternatives "mostly satisfied," "pleased," and "delighted" for each of the five items. The word "delighted" may not be frequently used by some respondents to characterize their own feelings, and they may not readily choose it from among printed alternatives. Hearing another person offer that as an alternative may reduce this avoidance somewhat. Finally, we note that in both telephone and personal interviews, smaller proportions of respondents choose "delighted" than the end point of the other scale "completely satisfied."

Since these two scales were used for five different items, the data set offers an opportunity to investigate whether the relationships among the scale items are similar in the two modes of data collection. We examine two measures: (1) the number of times respondents gave the same answer to different items in the scale (estimating tendencies of response set), and (2) empirical estimates of association among

---

[6] Another response card question using an unfolding technique on the telephone asked the respondent to judge the probability that he would purchase a car in the next 12 months. A follow-up question probed for a more specific answer to all the initial responses. Among those initially choosing the middle alternative on the telephone, the follow-up question formed three equal-sized groups. Conversely, personal interview respondents, faced with all eight responses simultaneously, tend to choose the middle point more than the two adjacent answers. This suggests that asking follow-up questions to unfold initial responses may yield a larger spread across the final response categories.

responses to the different items. Tables 3 and 4 measure the number of times among the five items that each response was chosen. For example, 97.0 percent of the telephone respondents never chose the response "terrible" for any of the five items, 3 percent chose it once. Two summary statistics can be examined from these tables, the proportion of respondents who never choose one of the alternatives, and the proportion of respondents who choose one of the responses many times (we use three of the five items as the criterion). For the delighted-terrible scale the largest difference between modes is centered on the "mixed" category, which more personal respondents fail to choose (69.1 percent) than telephone respondents (56.0 percent). On the positive side of the scale ("mostly satisfied," "pleased" and "delighted") personal interview respondents exhibit more avoidance of the term "delighted" than telephone respondents. When we look at the percentage of respondents who gave the same answer three or

Table 3. Number of Times Same Response Category Was Chosen for Five X Version Life Satisfaction Measures by Response Category for Phone and Personal Interview in Phone Households

Response	Sample Type	Number of Times Response Chosen %						Total[a] %	% with 3 or More Times
		None	1	2	3	4	5		
Terrible	Phone	97.0	3.0					100.0	
	Personal	93.9	5.9	.1				99.9	
Unhappy	Phone	95.8	3.8	.2	.1			99.9	.1
	Personal	91.7	7.4	.8	.1			100.0	.1
Mostly dis-satisfied	Phone	91.8	7.6	.5	.1			100.0	.1
	Personal	87.2	10.4	2.2	.1			99.9	.1
Mixed	Phone	56.0	24.9	11.5	5.5	1.9	.2	100.0	7.6
	Personal	69.1	23.6	5.3	1.8	.3		100.1	2.1
Mostly satisfied	Phone	42.5	27.4	16.6	8.9	3.6	1.1	100.1	13.6
	Personal	30.8	29.7	26.2	10.5	2.2	.5	99.9	13.2
Pleased	Phone	31.8	30.4	20.3	11.9	4.5	1.2	100.1	17.6
	Personal	20.9	31.4	24.6	13.2	7.9	2.0	100.0	23.1
Delighted	Phone	40.5	23.5	16.0	10.3	5.8	3.9	100.0	20.0
	Personal	47.9	25.1	12.6	7.5	5.1	1.7	99.9	14.3
No feelings	Phone	98.1	1.7	.1	0	.1		100.0	—
	Personal	98.8	.9	.1	.1			99.9	—
NA	Phone	95.5	3.0	.9	.4	.2	—[b]	100.0	—
	Personal	97.5	2.1	.1	.1	.1	—[b]	99.9	—
Total phone									59.0
Total personal									52.9

[a] N for phone = 824, N for personal = 677.
[b] Records with NA on all 5 items deleted from table.

Table 4. Number of Times Same Response Category Was Chosen for Five Y Version Life Satisfaction Measures by Response Category for Phone and Personal Interviews in Phone Households

Response	Sample Type	Number of Times Response Chosen %						Total[a] %	% with 3 or More Times
		None	1	2	3	4	5		
Completely dis-	Phone	93.2	5.8	.7	.1	.1		99.9	.2
satisfied	Personal	89.8	8.4	1.2	.4	0	.1	99.9	.5
2	Phone	94.4	4.6	1.0				100.0	.0
	Personal	90.8	7.5	1.3	.3			99.9	.3
3	Phone	84.5	13.5	1.7	.4			100.1	.4
	Personal	82.0	14.9	2.7	.4			100.0	.4
Neutral	Phone	64.2	23.8	8.3	2.9	.6	.2	100.0	3.7
	Personal	61.7	26.4	8.6	2.1	.9	.3	100.0	3.3
5	Phone	55.1	29.2	12.0	3.3	.4		100.0	3.7
	Personal	53.3	32.2	11.1	2.8	.4	.1	99.9	3.3
6	Phone	43.4	26.0	18.8	8.0	3.2	.6	100.0	11.8
	Personal	38.0	28.7	19.5	10.0	3.2	.6	100.0	13.8
Completely	Phone	20.3	21.4	20.3	17.5	12.6	8.0	100.1	38.1
satisfied	Personal	26.3	21.9	18.2	16.5	10.6	6.5	100.0	33.6
No feelings; never	Phone	97.6	2.2	.2				100.0	—
thought	Personal	99.1	.7	.1				99.9	—
NA	Phone	95.3	3.0	.6	.5	.6	—[b]	100.0	
	Personal	97.3	2.2	.3	0	.1	—[b]	99.9	—
Total phone									57.9
Total personal									55.2

[a] N for phone = 843, N for personal = 760.
[b] Records with NA on all 5 items deleted from table.

more times for the given items, only three response categories show non-negligible differences—"mixed," "pleased," and "delighted." About 5 percent more personal interview respondents than telephone respondents chose "pleased" three or more times. Overall on the five different items, more telephone respondents (59 percent) chose the same answer three or more times in this version of the scale than did personal interview respondents (52.9 percent).

The differences in response behavior for the satisfied-dissatisfied scale are much smaller across the two modes. The largest discrepancies occur in the category "completely satisfied." Telephone respondents seem to choose this category more frequently than personal interview respondents, but even this difference is smaller than many of those for the delighted-terrible scale. That single category is the only one of the seven to have non-negligible differences across mode

(38.1 percent on the telephone, 33.6 percent in person). In total, however, the proportion of respondents who chose any answer three or more times is quite similar regardless of which mode is being examined (57.9 percent in telephone to 55.2 percent in person). The smaller method effect for this scale than for the delighted-terrible scale may reflect the different methods of adapting the scales to telephone use.

Table 5 presents Goodman-Kruskal gamma measures for inter-associations among the five life-satisfaction items separately for the two different scales utilized. For both scales the two modes of inter-view produce similar interrelationships; 7 out of 10 pairs of the gam-mas lie within .10 of each other for the delighted-terrible scale, and all 10 of the satisfied-dissatisfied pairs of gammas do so. Although there is a balancing of differences between modes over the 10 measures of inter-association, the direction of the difference does seem to be systematic across the pairs of items; for example, for 9 of the 10 pairs of measures, the direction of difference is the same for both the delighted-terrible scale and the satisfied-dissatisfied scale, and in al-most all cases the relationships between the attitude about "your health" and the other four are stronger in the telephone interview

Table 5. Interitem Association for Life Satisfaction Measures[a] for Phone and Personal Interview Samples

	Sample Type	Health	Marriage	Living	Life
Delighted—terrible					
Measure	Phone	.3456	.4180	.4883	.1774
House	Personal	.1861	.4208	.4947	.2902
Health.	Phone		.3471	.4095	.4096
	Personal		.2676	.2290	.3316
Marriage	Phone			.4159	.5100
	Personal			.4566	.4648
Living	Phone				.5077
	Personal				.4909
Satisfied—dissatisfied					
Measure	Phone	.2148	.3065	.3708	.2462
House	Personal	.2411	.3602	.4544	.3228
Health	Phone		.3547	.2598	.3793
	Personal		.3337	.2173	.3750
Marriage	Phone			.3574	.5835
	Personal			.4148	.5323
Living	Phone				.4469
	Personal				.4159

[a] Goodman-Kruskal Gamma Measures.

than in the personal interview. Despite this consistency our original characterization of the interrelationships still applies; the differences in general are very small, probably rarely exceeding sampling error.

The final questions we shall examine are spouse's income and total family income. We choose spouse's income because it was the first of a three-question series on income and is subject to the smallest missing data rates for refusals to answer. Total family income, the last question in the series, is asked of everyone in the sample and permits analysis on a larger sample size. The questions utilized an 18-category response card in the personal interview survey; in the telephone survey the respondent was first asked the questions in an open-ended format, the responses of which were collapsed into the 18 categories of the show card for comparison (see Figure 3). Both questions exhibit two differences between modes: (1) larger proportions of telephone respondents give answers from $15,000 to $17,499, and (2) higher proportions of telephone respondents report incomes $20,000 and over. These results omit 13.5 percent of the telephone respondents on the spouse's question and 15.0 percent on the total family income question. Some of those respondents answered the follow-up question with the trichotomous response scheme used for reluctant responders. Except for the category $17,500 to $19,999, all categories above $14,999 have proportionately more telephone respondents than personal interview respondents. In addition to nonresponse differences this result may be influenced by the same phenomenon

Figure 3. Response Distribution for Spouse's Income in 18 Categories Used in Personal Interview Question by Mode of Interview[a]

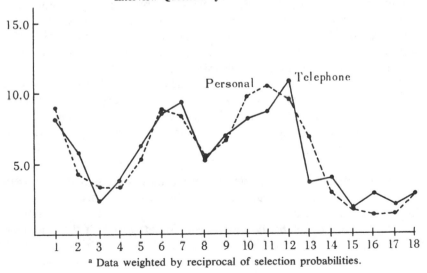

[a] Data weighted by reciprocal of selection probabilities.

discovered with the thermometer items earlier. When the questions are asked in an open-ended format, respondents tend to give answers to the nearest thousand dollars. Category 13 contains those answering $18,000 and $19,000, among others, but its neighboring categories each contain *three* different thousands figures.

Summary and Conclusions

This paper has focused on evidence of differences between two modes of data collection that are not linked to specific substantive topics, but rather to the nature of administration of the modes. Respondent reactions to being contacted for the survey seem to differ in the two surveys. The achieved response rates demonstrated lower cooperation on the telephone than in person, and later national telephone surveys support that finding. Few telephone respondents preferred the telephone as a means of answering the questions, but the vast majority of personal interview respondents preferred face-to-face interviews. In addition, there were greater expressed uneasiness about discussing sensitive topics on the telephone, more refusals to answer questions about their own financial status, and interviewer observations of respondent questions about how much longer the interview would last. This project discovered, in short, that if telephone interviews are to offer higher response rates than similar personal interview surveys, better telephone interview techniques must be investigated. Perhaps the first few moments of interaction should be designed to request no information from the informant but rather attempt to develop trust of the interviewer by the respondent. The techniques could create analogs for the visual stimuli (e.g., physical appearance of the interviewer, credentials, survey materials) that assure face-to-face respondents that the interviewer is a representative of a legitimate research organization.

The second difference between modes discussed was related to questions that typically use response cards in personal interviews. Using two methods of adapting these questions to telephone use, we discovered a sensitivity of the respondents to labeled points on the scales. This was particularly true of scales which were numerically based, that is, the thermometer (0 to 100) scales, and income measures (in dollars). When labels on the cards departed from numbers most commonly offered (those divisible by 5 and 10), large differences between modes were evident. Additionally, it was found that unfolding general responses to the more specific categories of the full scale created larger differences between modes than presenting the entire scale to the telephone respondents and asking them to choose a number representing their feelings. Since scale questions have a long tradition of use in the social sciences, more research on adapting these measures to the telephone is needed. Although differences between modes do exist, we have no clear guidance on which results most precisely represent the true feelings of the respondents. Further, more multivariate analyses of these results and additional experimental variations of question presentation may assist this work.

References

Colombotos, J.
  1965 "The effects of personal vs. telephone interviews on socially acceptable responses." Public Opinion Quarterly 29:457–58.
Groves, R., and R. Kahn
  In   Comparing Telephone and Personal Interview Surveys. New York:
  press Academic Press.
Hochstim, J. R.
  1967 "A critical comparison of three strategies of collecting data from households." Journal of the American Statistical Association 62:976–89.
Kish, L.
  1949 "A procedure for objective respondent selection within the household." Journal of the American Statistical Association 44:380–87.
Locander, W., S. Sudman, and N. M. Bradburn
  1974 "An investigation of interviewing method, threat, and response distortion." Proceedings of the American Statistical Association, Social Statistics Section, 21–27.
Rogers, T. F.
  1976 "Interviews by telephone and in person: quality of responses and field performance." Public Opinion Quarterly 40:51–65.

In Search of House Effects: A Comparison of Responses to Various Questions by Different Survey Organizations

TOM W. SMITH

DISCREPANCIES between Harris and the General Social Survey (GSS) on the confidence in leaders questions have raised the more general question of whether trend analysis can be carried out when the surveys being used were done not only at different times but also by different survey organizations ("houses").[1] If interhouse differences are common in occurrence and large in magnitude, then overtime analysis employing data from different houses becomes highly suspect. It becomes difficult, if not downright impossible, to separate the time effects from the house effects.

To explore this problem, a search was made for instances of different houses asking the identical question at approximately the same point in time. By thus controlling for both question wording and time, the number of factors possibly causing differences between houses is reduced. There remain two main types of factors influencing dif-

Abstract This paper examines the responses to various questions asked by different survey organizations. It considers the question of whether different survey organizations produce similar measurements of public opinion or whether house effects produce dissimilar measurements of the same population.

Tom W. Smith is an Associate Study Director for the National Opinion Research Center.

[1] On a number of confidence items Harris and GSS questions show large differences in marginals and divergent trends. On differences in question wording and form as well as on results, see Ladd (1976–77), Smith (1977), and Turner and Krauss (1978). The GSS is conducting several methodological experiments on its 1978 survey to examine this matter further and Elizabeth Martin, Institute for Research in Social Science, University of North Carolina; Tom W. Smith, NORC; and D. Garth Taylor, NORC, are engaged in an analysis of the GSS-Harris confidence items.

© 1978 by the American Association for Public Opinion Research. This essay originally appeared in *Public Opinion Quarterly*, volume 42, number 4.

ferences: survey-specific response effects, such as question order and position,[2] and general house effects, such as sampling procedures, interview training, and field supervision. The former factor can occur between any surveys which were not exact replications and can occur within houses as well as between houses. The latter factor is not associated with particular surveys, but affects in general all surveys conducted by a house. While it is not possible to separate these factors rigorously with the data at hand, some attention will be devoted to assessing the role of these factors.

The first type of interhouse comparisons examined were split-surveys or cooperative sampling in which two or more houses conducted the field work for a single study. NORC has participated in at least four of these arrangements: the 1954 Stouffer study with AIPO, the 1955 *Academic Mind* study with Roper, the 1960 Steiner television study with Roper, and the 1977 Medical Care Expenditure study with Research Triangle Institute.[3] No interhouse comparisons were made on the *Academic Mind* survey and the 1977 data are not yet available. Cross-house comparisons on the Stouffer and Steiner studies showed very similar results. Generally speaking, there were no apparent house effects on these two studies.

Of course, it can be legitimately argued that these studies represent special cases. With two houses working together on a study, it is usual that special steps are taken to coordinate matters and insure comparability. Thus, while the close correspondence between the houses on these surveys is encouraging, it has limited generalizability. The next type of interhouse comparisons examined comprised those instances when two houses independently asked the same question at the same time. (At the "same time" means that the surveys were either conducted within several months of each other or that a survey by one house was bracketed by prior and subsequent surveys by another house.) Seventeen examples of this type were located before 1950. Since these points had little relevance to the present or to most trend analysis—which can only rarely reach back before the late 1940s—and since marginals were presently available for only 2 of these 17 comparisons, these data were ignored. No examples of this type of comparisons were found in the 1950s or 1960s.[4] Although

---

[2] On these response effects, see Sudman and Bradburn (1974:33–35) and Schuman (1974:10–14).

[3] See Lazarsfeld and Thielens (1958); Stouffer (1963); and Steiner (1963).

[4] A number of examples were, however, found of two houses asking similar, but not identical questions. These included NORC-SRC on job satisfaction, AIPO-Harris on capital punishment, AIPO-Harris on gun regulation, AIPO-Harris on the admission of

Table 1. Marginals[a]

Item/GSS Mnemonic[b]: Response	Time	House	Propor- tion	N	Prob- ability <.05	Differ- ence (T₁-T₂)
Capital punishment	2/72	AIPO	.510	1,507	No	−.020
(CAPPUN):	3/72	GSS	.530	1,609		
Execute	11/72	AIPO	.570	NA[c]	No	−.032
	3/73	GSS	.602	1,492		
	3/74	GSS	.630	1,480		
	3/75	GSS	.601	1,483		
	3/76	GSS	.655	1,496	No	−.010
	4/76	AIPO	.666	1,540		
	3/77	GSS	.672	1,520		
Ideal number of children	3/72	GSS	.246	1,613		
(CHLDIDEL):	1/73	AIPO	.205	1,549		
4 or more	2/74	AIPO	.177	1,562	No	−.014
	3/74	GSS	.191	1,484		
	3/75	GSS	.169	1,488		
Attitudes toward countries	5/72	AIPO	.254	1,540		
BRAZIL:	3/74	GSS	.325	1,474		
+3, +4, or +5	3/75	GSS	.262	1,479		
	6/76	AIPO	.222	1,544		
	3/77	GSS	.250	1,517		
CANADA:	5/72	AIPO	.781	1,540		
+3, +4, or +5	4/73	AIPO	.764	1,528		
	3/74	GSS	.788	1,474		
	3/75	GSS	.774	1,481		
	6/76	AIPO	.788	1,544		
	3/77	GSS	.759	1,517		
CHINA[d]:	5/72(C)	AIPO	.071	1,540		
+3, +4, or +5	5/72(W)	AIPO	.201	1,540		
	4/73	AIPO	.213	1,528		
	3/74	GSS	.142	1,474		
	3/75	GSS	.126	1,480		
	6/76(C)	AIPO	.068	1,544		
	6/76(W)	AIPO	.222	1,544		
	3/77	GSS	.129	1,517		
EGYPT:	4/73	AIPO	.140	1,528		
+3, +4, or +5	3/74	GSS	.188	1,474		
	3/75	GSS	.137	1,481		
	6/76	AIPO	.140	1,544		
	3/77	GSS	.187	1,516		
ENGLAND:	5/72	AIPO	.658	1,540		
+3, +4, or +5	4/73[e]	AIPO	.595	1,528		
	3/74	GSS	.612	1,474		
	3/75	GSS	.575	1,481		
	6/76	AIPO	.633	1,544		
	3/77	GSS	.569	1,516		
ISRAEL:	3/74	GSS	.387	1,474		
+3, +4, or +5	3/75	GSS	.320	1,480		
	6/76	AIPO	.323	1,544		
	3/77	GSS	.353	1,517		

JAPAN:	5/72	AIPO	.362	1,540		
+3, +4, or +5	4/73	AIPO	.396	1,528		
	3/74	GSS	.389	1,474		
	3/75	GSS	.335	1,483		
	6/76	AIPO	.419	1,544		
	3/77	GSS	.323	1,518		
RUSSIA:	5/72	AIPO	.177	1,540		
+3, +4, or +5	4/73[f]	AIPO	.143	1,528		
	7/73	AIPO	.174	1,544		
	3/74	GSS	.182	1,474		
	3/75	GSS	.175	1,481		
	6/76	AIPO	.075	1,544		
	3/77	GSS	.115	1,519		
Judicial punishment	12/72	AIPO	.744	1,504 ⎫	No	.013
(COURTS): Harsher	3/73	GSS	.731	1,494 ⎭		
Afraid to walk alone	3/74	GSS	.448	1,480		
(FEAR):	6/75	AIPO	.443	1,558		
Afraid	3/76	GSS	.439	1,497		
Women for president	7/71	AIPO	.658	1,531		
(FEPRES):	3/72	GSS	.701	1,611		
Vote for	3/74	GSS	.778	1,479		
	3/75	GSS	.778	1,489 ⎫	.049	−.043
	8/75	AIPO	.735	1,515 ⎭		
	3/77	GSS	.771	1,526		
Suitability for politics	3/74	GSS	.436	752		
(FEPOL):	9/74	SRC	.435	1,012		
Agree	3/75	GSS	.477	1,488		
Suitability for politics	3/74	GSS	.326	730 ⎫	No	−.061
(FEPOLY): Men	9/74	SRC	.387	488 ⎭		
Marijuana laws	2/72	AIPO	.152	1,513		
(GRASS):	1/73	AIPO	.157	1,508 ⎫	No	−.026
Legalize	3/73	GSS	.183	1,501 ⎭		
Gun permit	10/71	AIPO	.719	1,502		
(GUNLAW):	3/72	GSS	.702	1,610 ⎫	No	−.014
Opposes	5/72	AIPO	.716	1,540 ⎭		
	3/73	GSS	.735	1,495		
	3/74	GSS	.753	1,477		
	2/75	SRC	.706	452 ⎫	No	−.021
	3/75	GSS	.737	1,488 ⎭		
	2/76	SRC	.726	638 ⎫	No	.011
	3/76	GSS	.715	1,493 ⎭		
	3/77	GSS	.716	1,528		
Misanthropy—evaluation	3/72	GSS	.592	1,611		
of people	11/72	SRC	.589	2,179 ⎫	No	.016
FAIR:	3/73	GSS	.573	1,503 ⎭		
Fair	11/74	SRC	.576	1,543 ⎫	No	−.040
	3/75	GSS	.616	1,488 ⎭		
	3/76	GSS	.592	1,499		
	11/76	SRC	.599	1,873		

227

Table 1.—*Continued*

Item/GSS Mnemonic[b]: Response	Time	House	Proportion	N	Probability <.05	Difference (T_1-T_2)
HELPFUL:	3/72	GSS	.465	1,612		
Helpful	11/72	SRC	.469	2,174	No	.001
	3/73	GSS	.468	1,501		
	11/74	SRC	.507	1,528	.030	−.055
	3/75	GSS	.562	1,488		
	3/76	GSS	.431	1,498		
	11/76	SRC	.519	1,877		
TRUST:	3/72	GSS	.458	1,612		
Trusts people	11/72	SRC	.458	2,179	No	−.001
	3/73	GSS	.459	1,502		
	11/74	SRC	.466	1,551	.004	−.073
	3/75	GSS	.393	1,485		
	3/76	GSS	.444	1,497		
	11/76	SRC	.513	1,882		
Spending for foreign aid	7/71	Roper	.038	1,487		
(NATAID):	3/73	GSS	.042	1,503		
Too little	12/73	Roper	.021	1,766	No	−.009
	3/74	GSS	.030	1,481		
	3/75	GSS	.054	1,489		
	3/76	GSS	.029	1,494		
	3/77	GSS	.034	1,527		
Spending for military	7/71	Roper	.150	1,488		
(NATARMS):	3/73	GSS	.112	1,496		
Too little	12/73	Roper	.150	1,764	No	−.019
	3/74	GSS	.169	1,479		
	3/75	GSS	.166	1,484		
	3/76	GSS	.241	1,492		
	3/77	GSS	.232	1,553		
Spending for cities	7/71	Roper	.415	1,488		
(NATCITY):	3/73	GSS	.482	1,499		
Too little	12/73	Roper	.432	1,757	.007	−.067
	3/74	GSS	.499	1,474		
	3/75	GSS	.471	1,479		
	3/76	GSS	.426	1,492		
	3/77	GSS	.403	1,525		
Spending for crime	7/71	Roper	.611	1,490		
prevention	3/73	GSS	.646	1,497		
(NATCRIME):	12/73	Roper	.640	1,757	No	−.026
Too little	3/74	GSS	.666	1,481		
	3/75	GSS	.656	1,484		
	3/76	GSS	.657	1,489		
	3/77	GSS	.657	1,524		
Spending for drug	7/71	Roper	.618	1,493		
prevention	3/73	GSS	.659	1,483		
(NATDRUG):	12/73	Roper	.579	1,759	No	−.021
Too little	3/74	GSS	.600	1,478		
	3/75	GSS	.551	1,482		
	3/76	GSS	.587	1,493		
	3/77	GSS	.552	1,520		

Spending for education	7/71	Roper	.439	1,488		
(NATEDUC):	3/73	GSS	.490	1,499		
Too little	12/73	Roper	.458	1,752	.047	−.049
	3/74	GSS	.507	1,474		
	3/75	GSS	.490	1,487		
	3/76	GSS	.502	1,495		
	3/77	GSS	.476	1,527		
Spending for environment	7/71	Roper	.559	1,495		
(NATENVIR):	3/73	GSS	.611	1,498		
Too little	12/73	Roper	.459	1,766	<.001	−.131
	3/74	GSS	.590	1,476		
	3/75	GSS	.534	1,490		
	3/76	GSS	.548	1,494		
	3/77	GSS	.475	1,524		
Spending for welfare	7/71	Roper	.178	1,474		
(NATFARE):	3/73	GSS	.198	1,497		
Too little	12/73	Roper	.170	1,762	.010	−.051
	3/74	GSS	.221	1,481		
	3/75	GSS	.234	1,484		
	3/76	GSS	.133	1,493		
	3/77	GSS	.123	1,524		
Spending for medical care	7/71	Roper	.552	1,491		
(NATHEAL):	3/73	GSS	.608	1,497		
Too little	12/73	Roper	.599	1,761	No	−.040
	3/74	GSS	.639	1,477		
	3/75	GSS	.626	1,485		
	3/76	GSS	.605	1,491		
	3/77	GSS	.558	1,526		
Spending for space	7/71	Roper	.063	1,497		
exploration	3/73	GSS	.075	1,503		
(NATSPAC):	12/73	Roper	.035	1,768	<.001	−.042
Too little	3/74	GSS	.077	1,480		
	3/75	GSS	.074	1,490		
	3/76	GSS	.092	1,496		
	3/77	GSS	.101	1,530		
Gun ownership	5/72	AIPO	.435	1,513		
(OWNGUN):	3/73	GSS	.473	1,495		
Owns	3/74	GSS	.462	1,480		
	3/75	AIPO	.464	1,512		
	3/75	AIPO	.453	1,536		
	10/75	AIPO	.474	1,558		
	3/76	GSS	.466	1,493		
Political identification	3/72	GSS	.474	1,607		
(PARTYID):	11/72	SRC	.403	2,702	No	−.018
Democratic	3/73	GSS	.411	1,493		
	3/74	GSS	.423	1,483		
	11/74	SRC	.385	1,570	No	−.019
	3/75	GSS	.404	1,486		
	3/76	GSS	.421	1,497		
	11/76	SRC	.396	2,244	.036	−.049
	3/77	GSS	.444	1,520		

229

Table 1.—*Continued*

Item/GSS Mnemonic[b]: Response	Time	House	Proportion	N	Probability <.05	Difference (T_1-T_2)
Presidential vote, 1968	3/72	GSS	.453	1,056		
(PRES68):	11/72	SRC	.504	1,038 ⎫	.022	.057
Nixon	3/73	GSS	.439	1,005 ⎭		
Presidential vote, 1972	3/76	GSS	.577	943		
(PRES72):	11/76	SRC	.622	1,440 ⎫	No	.025
Nixon	3/77	GSS	.597	919 ⎭		
School integration if a	3/72	GSS	.050	535		
few blacks	7/73	AIPO	.076	449		
(RACFEW):	3/74	GSS	.045	492		
Object	3/75	GSS	.047	473		
	9/75	AIPO	.065	539		
	3/77	GSS	.073	481		
School integration if	3/72	GSS	.232	535		
half black	7/73	AIPO	.305	449		
(RACHAF):	3/74	GSS	.299	492		
Object	3/75	GSS	.262	473		
	9/75	AIPO	.297	539		
	3/77	GSS	.255	481		
School integration if	3/72	GSS	.546	535		
mostly black	7/73	AIPO	.670	449		
(RACMOST):	3/74	GSS	.646	492		
Object	3/75	GSS	.638	473		
	9/75	AIPO	.583	539		
	3/77	GSS	.620	481		
Work if rich	Winter					
(RICHWORK)[g]:	1969/70	SRC	.674	1,523		
Continue working	Winter					
	1972/73	SRC	.658	2,148 ⎫		
	3/73	GSS	.681	831 ⎬	No	−.023
	3/74	GSS	.636	837 ⎭		

[a] Missing values excluded from analysis but "don't knows" retained. All significance tests adjust for multistage sampling by multiplying the standard deviations by 1.414.

[b] Here and elsewhere items are referred to by their standard GSS mnemonic. See Davis et al. (1977).

[c] 1,500 used in calculations.

[d] AIPO (5/72-C) is "Red China"; (5/72-W) is "Nationalist China (Taiwan)." AIPO (6/76-C) is "Communist China"; AIPO (6/76-W) is "Nationalist China (Taiwan)." All others are "China."

[e] "Great Britain" used in AIPO (4/73). "England" used in all others.

[f] "Soviet Union" used in AIPO (4/73); "Russia" used in all others.

[g] Universes differ slightly between houses.

some examples almost certainly exist, none were discovered from available archival sources.

In the 1970s, 38 examples were found. All are cases in which a question selected from Gallup-American Institute of Public Opinion (AIPO). Michigan's Survey Research Center (SRC), or Roper for the GSS was repeated by the original house, thereby overlapping with the GSS series. Table 1 gives the proportions for these questions (see Appendix: Question Wording for the exact usages). Two types of analysis were conducted on these items. For the 33 instances when surveys were fielded within five months a direct comparison was made between the proportions. As Table 1 reveals, the differences were distributed as follows:

Differences in Proportion	*Number of Instances*
.0 to .01	3
.01 to .02	8
.02 to .03	8
.03 to .04	1
.04 to .05	7
.05 to .06	3
.06 to .07	2
.07 to .08	1
.09+	1
	33

There were significant differences in 10 instances and nonsignificant differences in the other 23 cases. The 10 differing cases were not randomly scattered among the cases but came from 2 clusters, 5 national spending items compared between a Roper survey in December 1973 and GSS74, and 2 misanthropy items compared between the 1974 SRC election survey and GSS75, plus 3 other cases—presidential vote in 1968 asked by the 1972 SRC election survey and GSS73, party identification on the 1976 SRC election survey and GSS77, and voting for a woman for president asked by AIPO in August 1975 and GSS75.

Close inspection of the national spending questions indicated a strong likelihood of a house difference in the proportion replying "don't know." Table 2 gives the proportion answering "don't know" on the two Roper surveys and GSS73 and GSS74. On every single item the GSS proportions are lower than Roper. While it is clear that the proportion "don't know" can change over time (Roper73 is lower

China to the UN, AIPO-Harris on votes for eighteen-year-olds, SRC-AIPO on party identification, and NORC-AIPO on abortions. All appear to show the same marginals, similar trends, or both. See Manpower Administration (1974); Erskine (1971a, 1971b); Social Change Archives, GSS; and P. E. Converse (1976:31, 168).

Table 2. Proportion "Don't Know" on National Spending Items, 1971–1974

Item (GSS Mnemonic)	Surveys			
	Roper71	GSS73	Roper73	GSS74
NATCRIME	.163	.061	.089	.051
NATEDUC	.099	.043	.059	.038
NATSPAC	.054	.047	.054	.036
NATFARE	.105	.043	.081	.040
NATAID	.129	.055	.072	.040
NATARMS	.170	.059	.118	.067
NATCITY	.262	.120	.226	.147
NATHEAL	107	.035	.065	.035
NATENVIR	.138	.057	.086	.066
NATDRUG	.129	.063	.096	.055
Mean	.136	.058	.095	.058

than Roper71 in all but one case), it is probable that Roper generates a higher level of "don't knows" than GSS does.[5]

With the "don't knows" excluded from analysis (see Table 3) the differences between Roper73 and GSS74 are reduced in eight instances, unchanged once, and increased once. For 2 of the 5 significant differences (NATEDUC and NATCITY), the reduction was sufficient to make the differences fall within sampling error while three items remained significant (NATSPAC, NATFARE, and NATENVIR.)

Table 3. Change in Difference Between Roper73 and GSS74 on National Spending Items with "Don't Knows" Excluded

Item (GSS Mnemonic)	"Don't Knows" In	"Don't Knows" Out	Change
NATHEAL	−.040	−.021	−.019
NATCITY	−.067	−.027	−.040
NATARMS	−.019	−.011	−.008
NATAID	−.009	−.009	.000
NATFARE	−.051	−.046	−.005
NATSPAC	−.042	−.043	+.001
NATEDUC	−.049	−.040	−.009
NATCRIME	−.026	.000	−.026
NATENVIR	−.131	−.130	−.001
NATDRUG	−.021	+.005	−.026
	−.046	−.032	.013
		(absolute .033)	

[5] In a Roper survey on the United Nations conducted in 1977 for the League of Women Voters Education Fund, questions previously asked by NORC, AIPO, and Potomac Associates all received substantially higher levels of "don't knows" than they had earlier. In these cases, however, there is no temporal overlap between houses to help control for time (League of Women Voters Education Fund, 1977). On other differences between houses, see J.M. Converse (1976–77:515–30).

A second factor of note is that the differences have a definite direction. Even after the "don't knows" have been corrected for, the proportion answering "too little" on Roper73 is lower than on GSS in 8 out of 10 cases (an average difference of −.032). This could represent a house effect but alternative explanations are equally plausible. It could represent a seasonal effect since the lower spending support in Roper was registered in December, the highest month for consumer spending. Having just made or being about to make high personal expenditures, people might be in a fiscally more conservative mood. Or, there could be real shifts because of changing historical events and conditions over the three months between the surveys. Such a likely event was the first energey crisis (the oil embargo crunch). In December 1973, energy was one of the top domestic stories on 15 days out of 31, but in March 1974 it made the headlines only once.[6] While this may have had a general impact on spending, it is clear that it had an impact on the environment question. Support for the environment was much lower in December (−.131) and this was two to three times greater than the other two significant differences (−.043 and −.046). Clearly, many people saw an unfavorable connection between environmental spending and energy (the long delays in the Alaskan pipeline, East Coast offshore drilling, western coal mining, etc.). Whether there is a similar effect on other items is less obvious, but quite possible. Even without accepting a generalized energy crisis effect on other items, we see that it has an impact since the average difference excluding the environment item drops from −.032 to −.021. In brief, the differences on the national spending items seem to indicate that there may be a house effect involving "don't knows." For the three items significantly different once the "don't knows" are removed, one difference is clearly caused by nonhouse effects and the others may be as plausibly explained by seasonal or historical effects as by house effects.

Turning to the next cluster, we see that 2 of the 3 misanthropy items asked on the GSS and the SRC election series differ in 1974–75. What makes these differences so interesting is that two years previously these same items showed virtually no differences at all. From 1972 through 1974 these items appear to be very constant, both within and across houses, but since then they have shown considerable fluctuation. The proportion considering people helpful rose .055 between SRC74 and GSS75 and then fell .131 from GSS75 to GSS76— the largest annual change recorded on any GSS item. The proportion trusting people fell .073 from SRC74 to GSS75, and then rose by .051

[6] Based on top stories listed in *The Official Associated Press Almanac 1975* (1975).

to GSS76. The lack of differences between houses in 1972–73 and the largest fluctuations between GSS75 and GSS76 indicate that the 1974–75 differences may well be due to other reasons besides house effects. Clearly the behavior of the misanthropy items merits closer inspection.

With the national spending and misanthropy clusters examined, there remain three other questions that show significant differences. Voting for a woman for president differs by .043 between GSS75 and AIPO in August 1975, five months later. The five-month interval was the maximum time difference used here for direct survey-to-survey comparisons, and when "don't knows" are excluded, the difference drops to .040 and becomes insignificant. Clearly this is a borderline case. The proportion Democratic differs by −.049 between the 1976 Michigan election survey and GSS77. While no significant differences appear between the 1972 election survey and GSS73 or between the Michigan 1974 election survey and GSS75, the small differences are in the same direction as in 1976–77, a point discussed below. The last case, presidential choice in 1968, has a small but important difference in question wording. On the GSS, Humphrey is the first candidate mentioned, while on SRC, Nixon is named first (there are other differences as well; see the Appendix: Question Wording). This ordering has a known effect on responses, increasing the proportion choosing the first mentioned candidate.[7] As predicted, the GSS point shows .065 less for Nixon than SRC does (GSS72 shows .051 less than SRC).

In brief, it appears that of the nine possible instances of house effects, several can be credited to other causes, the presidential voting differences to an order effect, and the environmental spending difference to a historical effect. Other differences, such as on the remaining national spending items and the misanthropy items, may be due to house effects, but alternative explanations are at least equally persuasive. One fairly substantial example of a house effect appears to be the proportion of "don't knows" on the GSS and Roper national spending questions.

To carry the analysis of house effects further, an analysis was made of the trends shown by 32 of the 38 items, because it was possible to compare trends in these 32 instances. To ascertain the comparability of trends, no-change or constant models were first fitted to the GSS and non-GSS series. If the constant model proved inadequate to explain

---

[7] A candidate ordering effect occurs on both the actual ballot as well as in surveys and is greater when intensity of support for candidates is less. (James Rabjohn, University of Chicago/NORC, personal communication, 9/7/77.) On the presidential voting in 1972 there are signs of a similar but smaller difference between Michigan and GSS.

the series, a linear change model was fitted to the series. Three results could come from this second test. The data could show (1) a linear trend with no significant variation, (2) a significant linear component with a significant amount of unexplained variation, or (3) no significant linear trend.[8]

Next, the house series were compared to see if the GSS and non-GSS series were similar to each other. Often the comparison of interhouse trends was quite difficult. The two series rarely started or ended at the same point in time, so that they only approximately covered the same time span. To match the time spans as closely as possible, it was often necessary to use only part of one series (see Table 4 for the selection of time points). Also, there were often hardly enough points to give a solid measure of time trends. This was especially true for non-GSS series, where only a single point was available in 5 instances, only two points in 18 cases (a minimum of three data points being necessary to detect a nonlinear trend), and three or more points in 10 cases. This created problems when comparing trends, since a one-point "series" is a contradiction and a two-point "series" can only be constant or linear, while a series with three or more points can be constant, linear, linear-component, or nonlinear. In the case of single-point "series," this point was compared to the two points that bracketed it. If it was not bracketed by points from the other house, no trend analysis was done. To handle the two-point cases, it was necessary to consider whether a nonlinear trend on one series was really different from a linear or constant trend produced by a two-point series from the other house.

The house series were judged to be similar if (1) they both tested out as constant and their pooled proportions were not significantly different from each other; (2) a point bracketed by others had a constant fit with these points; (3) both trends tested as linear or linear-component and there was no significant difference between their slopes; or (4) a bracketed point fit in a linear model with the preceding and following points. Trends were judged different when (1) the same type of model applied but the pooled proportions or slopes differed significantly, or (2) different models applied to the separate

---

[8] For the details of the statistical tests applied here, see Taylor (1976). In brief, the first hypothesis tested is that the sample proportions are from a constant universe value, which is estimated to be the pooled average of the proportions. The criterion for the goodness-of-fit is the chi-square statistic that divides the squared deviation of the observed value from the predicted value by the variance of the observed value. This is referred to as the "test for homogeneity." The next hypothesis tested is that the sample proportions are from a linear universe trend. The chi-square goodness-of-fit test is used to compare the actual proportions with their linear estimates. This is referred to as the "test for linearity."

series and this did not appear to be due to the artifact of when or how often the item appeared. Series that fit different models but which showed evidence that this might be due to a shortage of data points and/or differing time spans were classed as "intermediate" (see Table 4).

Inspection of Table 4 indicates that in 21 instances the series were similar; in three instances, intermediate; and in eight instances, different. As in the case of the marginal comparisons, the differences were clustered. Three of the eight disagreements were on country items (EGYPT, ENGLAND, JAPAN), two were from the national spending variables (NATENVIR, NATSPAC), two were misanthropy items (HELPFUL, TRUST), and the last was party identification. The observed differences in these countries could be due to several factors. First, the time series spanned by the two houses were different, with AIPO covering 1972/73–1976 and GSS 1974–1977. To look at this possible effect some more, the subseries for 1975–1977 (GSS-AIPO-GSS) was examined. In each case, significant differences remained. Second, we are not observing items with clear directional trends but, like the national spending items above or the expectation of war question, an item subject to large short-term fluctuations. Current events and/or shifts in foreign policy could well have such an effect on the ranking of countries.[9] A final factor that may contribute to the differences is an order effect, like the one noted in the case of presidential vote above. The Appendix shows that AIPO has asked a different mix of countries in differing orders. While there is no proof of an order effect in this case, such an effect may exist. The national spending and misanthropy variables have been discussed above. The environmental spending difference comes from an episodic effect and the space spending difference may come from this source as well. On party preference, the proportion Democratic is constant for both series. The pooled proportion Democratic estimated from the GSS's (.430) is, however, significantly greater than the Michigan election estimate (.396). Although this −.034 difference is not stable, showing up as significant in only one of the three individual comparisons analyzed earlier, there is a consistent direction to the differences. Part of the difference apparently results from a greater tendency to code respondents "other," "no preference," or some other unread response on the Michigan election surveys than on the GSS's.[10] Among the three mentioned responses (Republican, Democratic, Indepen-

[9] If all these were from one house, this is probably the conclusion most researchers would come to about trends for these countries.

[10] An inspection on GSS and Michigan interview specification, however, revealed no obvious reason for this.

Table 4. Trend Comparisons

GSS Mnemonic	Combined Model	Separate Models GSS	Separate Models Other	Difference in Models Significant	Trends Compared
CAPPUN	Linear	Linear	Linear	No	Similar
CHLDIDEL	Linear	Linear	Linear	No	Similar
COUNTRIES					
BRAZIL	Nonlinear	Nonlinear	Constant	Yes	Intermediate
CANADA	Constant	Constant	Constant	No	Similar
CHINA	NTAPP				NTAPP
EGYPT	Nonlinear	Nonlinear	Constant	Yes	Different
ENGLAND	Linear component	Constant	Constant	Yes	Different
ISRAEL	Nonlinear	Nonlinear	NTAPP	NTAPP	Similar[a]
JAPAN	Linear component	Linear	Constant	Yes	Different
RUSSIA	NTAPP	Linear	Linear	No	Similar[b]
COURTS	Constant				NTAPP
FEAR	Linear component	Constant	NTAPP	No	Similar
FEPRES	Constant	Linear component	Linear	No	Similar
FEPOL	NTAPP	Constant	NTAPP	No	Similar
FEPOLY	NTAPP				NTAPP
GRASS	NTAPP				NTAPP
GUNLAW	Constant	Constant	Constant	No	Similar
MISANTHROPY					
FAIR	Constant	Constant	Constant	No	Similar
HELPFUL	Nonlinear	Nonlinear	Linear	Yes	Different[c]
TRUST	Nonlinear	Nonlinear	Linear	No	Different[d]
NATAID	Nonlinear				Similar[e]
NATARMS	Linear component				Intermediate
NATCITY	Nonlinear				Similar

Table 4.—*Continued*

GSS Mnemonic	Combined Model	Separate Models		Difference in Models Significant	Trends Compared
		GSS	Other		
NATCRIME	Constant				Similar
NATDRUG	Linear component				Similar
NATEDUC	Constant				Similar
NATENVIR	Linear component				Different[f]
NATFARE	Linear component				Similar
NATHEAL	Nonlinear				Similar
NATSPAC	Linear component				Different
OWNGUN	Constant	Constant	Constant	No	Similar
PARTYID	Constant[g]	Constant	Constant	Yes	Different
PRES68	NTAPP				NTAPP
PRES72	NTAPP				NTAPP
RACFEW	Constant	Constant	Constant	No	Similar
RACHAF	Constant	Constant	Constant	No	Similar
RACMOST	Constant	Constant	Linear	No	Intermediate[h]
RICHWORK	Constant	Constant	NTAPP	No	Similar

a 1975–1977 trend constant.

b Excludes AIPO (4/73) "Soviet Union."

c Various subseries were examined 3/72–3/73 and 11/72–11/74 were constant and 3/73–3/75 was linear.

d Constant for early subseries (3/72–3/73; 11/72–11/74) and for all points excluding GSS75.

e Since the GSS series runs from 1973 to 1977 while the AIPO series runs only from 1971 to 1973, it was not appropriate to compare them. Instead the 7/71–12/73 and 3/73–3/74 subseries were checked (3 points in each). Agreement on both lead to a ranking of "similar," disagreement on both a "different" rank, a split decision led to an "intermediate" rank. "Don't knows" were excluded from analysis.

f See discussion of this variable in preceding section.

g Omits GSS72.

h For the two AIPO points the difference is significant at the .042 level making it a "linear" change.

dent), the difference between Michigan and GSS falls to −.022 and becomes insignificant.

Of the three intermediate cases there is one additional item from both the country and national spending questions (BRAZIL and NATARMS) and a school integration item (RACMOST). Possible factors involved in the country and national spending clusters are discussed above. The school integration question is the double-filtered part of the integration question and the two preceding parts show constant and similar trends (see Appendix for filters and wording). On this part, however, the two AIPO data points show a significant difference at the .042 level while the GSS is constant. Obviously, this is a borderline case.

The preceding search for house effects among proportional differences and trends revealed a number of possible candidates. In 10 out of 33 instances response proportions were significantly different. Consideration of nonhouse effects indicated that at least two of the differences (PRES68 and NATENVIR) were due to other factors and the remaining might also be due to temporal or other unisolated factors (e.g., order or context). The analysis also pinpointed the "don't know" response level as a possible example of house effects. The trend analysis showed 8 instances of disagreement, 3 intermediate cases, and 21 nonconflicting series. As with the one-to-one comparison of proportions, nonhouse effects account for at least some of these differences.

It can be argued that because the differing cases are clustered primarily among three questions—national spending, countries, and misanthropy—house effects are not a general or random occurrence but concentrated among particular questions. It might even be argued that since differences are largely restricted to these questions, time, placement, or other factors rather than true house effects are responsible. In sum, while the available data are much less complete than would be desired, what does exist suggests that house effects are not a large and systemic problem. It is clear, however, that both general house effects and survey-specific response effects do occur. To deal with this problem three courses should be followed. First, house and other response effects should be routinely checked for whenever analysis compares two surveys. Second, methodological research is needed in order to (1) document procedural differences between houses and then measure the effect of these differences on results, and (2) assess and calibrate other response effects.[11] Third, in plan-

[11] For a pioneering evaluation of procedural differences between surveys, see Bailar and Lamphier (1977). The literature on response effects is large; see, for example, the following two special issues: Ferber (1977) and Alwin (1977).

ning replication studies, close attention should be given to minimizing such possible effects by duplicating as far as possible, not just question wording but interviewer specifications, question placement, coding rules, and other features.

Appendix: Question Wording

CAPPUN
   (a) AIPO and GSS 1972–73: Are you in favor of the death penalty for persons convicted of murder?
   (b) GSS 1974–76: Do you favor or oppose the death penalty for persons convicted of murder?
CHLDIDEL
   (a) AIPO and GSS: What do you think is the ideal number of children for a family to have?
   (b) AIPO has response "No opinion" while GSS has responses "As many as you want" and "Don't know."
COUNTRIES
   (a) AIPO 5/72: Here is an interesting experiment. You will notice that the boxes on the card go from the HIGHEST POSITION OF PLUS 5, or a country which you like very much, to the LOWEST POSITION OF MINUS 5, or a country you dislike very much. How far up the scale or how far down the scale would you rate the following countries?
   Russia, Brazil, Red China, Japan, England, Nationalist China (Taiwan), Canada
   (b) AIPO 4/73: Has same wording with following list:
   [China, Canada, West Germany, Great Britain, Japan, Italy, France, Chile, Sweden, Soviet Union, Egypt]
   (c) AIPO 7/73: Here is an interesting experiment. You notice that the boxes on this card do [sic] from the HIGHEST POSITION OF PLUS 5—or something you like very much—all the way down to the LOWEST POSITION OF MINUS 5—or something you dislike very much. How far up the scale or how far down the scale would you rate the following organizations:
   CORE (Congress of Racial Equality), FBI (Federal Bureau of Investigation), Ku Klux Klan, AMA (American Medical Association), John Birch Society, NAACP (National Association for Advancement of Colored People), AFL-CIO (labor unions), NAM (National Association of Manufacturers), CIA (Central Intelligence Agency), ACLU (American Civil Liberties Union), your local police department, U.S. Supreme Court, Congress, the press, the United States, Russia
   (d) AIPO 6/76: Here is an interesting experiment. You notice that the ten boxes on this card go from the highest position of plus five—for something you have a very favorable opinion of—all the way down to the lowest position of minus five—or something you have a very *un*favorable opinion of. Please tell me how far up the scale or how far down the scale you rate the following nations.
   England, Communist China, Russia, Sweden, Cuba, France, W. Germany, Italy, Japan, Egypt, Israel, Brazil, Argentina, Australia, Chile, Nationalist

China (Taiwan), Canada, India, Iran, Holland, Switzerland, Poland, Mexico, United States, S. Africa, Philippines

(e) GSS: You will notice that the boxes on this card go from the highest position of "plus 5" for a country which you *like* very much, to the lowest position of "minus 5" for a country you *dislike* very much. How far up the scale or how far down the scale would you rate the following countries? READ EACH ITEM:

Russia, Japan, England, Canada, Brazil, China, Israel, Egypt

COURTS

(a) AIPO and GSS: In general, do you think the courts in this area deal too harshly or not harshly enough with criminals?

FEAR

(a) AIPO and GSS: Is there any area right around here—that is, within a mile—where you would be afraid to walk alone at night?

FEPRES

(a) AIPO omits "were" from GSS question below.

(b) GSS: If you party nominated a woman for President, would you vote for her if she were qualified for the job?

FEPOL

(a) SRC and GSS: Tell me if you agree or disagree with this statement: Most men are better suited emotionally for politics than are most women.

FEPOLY

(a) SRC and GSS: Would you say that most men are better suited for politics than are most women, that men and women are equally suited, or that women are better suited than men in this area.

GRASS

(a) AIPO and GSS: Do you think the use of marijuana should be made legal, or not?

GUNLAW

(a) AIPO and GSS: Would you favor or oppose a law which would require a person to obtain a police permit before he or she could buy a gun?

(b) SRC omits "or she."

MISANTHROPY

(a) SRC and GSS:

(1) FAIR: Do you think most people would try to take advantage of you if they got a chance, or would they try to be fair?

(2) HELPFUL: Would you say that most of the time people try to be helpful, or that they are mostly just looking out for themselves?

(3) TRUST

Generally speaking, would you say that most people can be trusted or that you can't be too careful in dealing with people?

(b) GSS accepts responses of "depends" and "don't know." SRC uses "don't know" only.

NATIONAL PROBLEMS

(a) GSS and Roper: We are faced with many problems in this country, none of which can be solved easily or inexpensively. I'm going to name some of these problems, and for each one I'd like you to tell me whether you think we're spending too much money on it, too little money, or about the right amount. First (READ ITEM A). . . are we spending too much, too little, or about the right amount on (ITEM)?

A. Space exploration program
B. Improving and protecting the environment
C. Improving and protecting the nation's health
D. Solving the problems of the big cities
E. Halting the rising crime rate
F. Dealing with drug addiction
G. Improving the nation's education system
H. Improving the conditions of Blacks
Roper omits "H. Improving the conditions of Blacks."
I. The military, armaments and defense
J. Foreign aid
K. Welfare

OWNGUN
(a) GSS: Do you happen to have in your home (IF HOUSE: or garage) any guns or revolvers?
(b) AIPO 5/72 omits "IF HOUSE: or garage."
(c) AIPO 1975: Do you have any guns in your home?

PARTYID
(a) SRC and GSS: Generally speaking, do you usually think of yourself as a Republican, [a] Democrat, [an] Independent, or what?
(b) GSS had a precoded response of "other" each year and added the response "no preference" in 1975–1977. SRC includes both categories each year.
(c) SRC includes the bracketed articles.

PRES68
(a) SRC—IF RESPONDENT HAS EVER VOTED IN A PRESIDENTIAL ELECTION: Now, in 1968 you remember that Mr. Nixon ran on the Republican ticket against Mr. Humphrey for the Democrats and Mr. Wallace on an independent ticket. Do you remember for sure whether or not you voted in that election?
—IF RESPONDENT VOTED IN 1968 ELECTION: Which one [presidential candidate] did you vote for?
(b) GSS: Now in 1968, you remember that Humphrey ran for President on the Democratic ticket against Nixon for the Republicans, and Wallace as an Independent. Do you remember for sure whether or not you voted in that election?
A. IF VOTED: Did you vote for Humphrey, Nixon or Wallace?

PRES72
(a) SRC—IF RESPONDENT HAS EVER VOTED IN A PRESIDENTIAL ELECTION: Now, in 1972 you remember that Mr. Nixon ran on the Republican ticket against Mr. McGovern for the Democrats. Do you remember for sure whether or not you voted in that election?
—IF RESPONDENT VOTED IN 1972 ELECTION: Which one [presidential candidate] did you vote for?
(b) GSS: In 1972, you remember that McGovern ran for President on the Democratic ticket against Nixon for the Republicans. Do you remember for sure whether or not you voted in that election?
A. IF VOTED: Did you vote for McGovern or Nixon?

RACIAL INTEGRATION OF SCHOOLS

(a) GSS: Would you yourself have any objection to sending your children to a school where a few of the children are (Negroes/Blacks)?

IF NO OR DON'T KNOW TO A: Where half of the children are (Negroes/Blacks)?

IF NO OR DON'T KNOW TO B: Where more than half of the children are (Negroes/Blacks)?

(b) AIPO 7/73: Do you have any children now in grade or high school? IF YES, ASK:

B. Would you, yourself, have any objection to sending your children to a school where a few of the children are black?

IF NO, ASK:

C. Where half are black?

D. Where more than half of the children are black?

(c) AIPO 3/75: As in 1973 except that those answering ''No'' to part C were not asked part D and that last word was ''blacks.''

RICHWORK

(a) GSS: If you were to get enough money to live as comfortably as you would like for the rest of your life, would you continue to work or would you stop working?

(b) SRC uses: ''you'd'' instead of ''you would'' and omits ''or would you stop working.''

References

Alwin, Dwaine (ed.)
   1977   ''Survey design and analysis: current issues.'' Sociological Methods and Research 6 (entire issue).
Bailer, Barbara, and C. Michael Lamphier
   1978   Development of Survey Methods to Assess Survey Practices: A Report of the American Statistical Association Pilot Project on the Assessment of Survey Practices and Data Quality in Surveys of Human Populations. Washington, D.C.: American Statistical Association.
Converse, Jean M.
   1976–   ''Prediciting no opinion in the polls.'' Public Opinion Quarterly
   1977   ''40:515–30.
Converse, Philip E.
   1976   The Dynamics of Party Support: Cohort-Analyzing Party Identification. Sage Library of Social Research, Vol. 35. Beverly Hills: Sage.
Davis, James A., Tom W. Smith, and C. Bruce Stephenson
   1977   Cumulative Codebook for the 1972–1977 General Social Surveys. Chicago: National Opinion Research Center.
Erskine, Hazel
   1971a   ''The polls: Red China and the U.N.'' Public Opinion Quarterly. 35:125–37.
   1971b   ''The polls: the politics of age.'' Public Opinion Quarterly. 35:482–95.

Ferber, Robert (ed.)
  1977 "Recent developments in survey research." Journal of Marketing
        Research 14:(entire issue).
Ladd, Everett Carll, Jr.
  1976– "The polls: the question of confidence." Public Opinion Quarterly.
  1977   40:544–52.
Lazarsfeld, Paul F., and Wagner Thielens, Jr.
  1958 The Academic Mind: Social Scientists in a Time of Crisis. Glencoe,
        Ill.: The Free Press.
League of Women Voters Education Fund
  1977 "Public Opinion on the UN: What Pollsters Forget to Ask."
Manpower Administration,
  1974 Job Satisfaction: Is There a Trend? Manpower Research Monograph
        No. 30. Washington, D.C.: Government Printing Office.
Official Associated Press Almanac, 1975
  1975 Maplewood, N.J.: Hammond Almanac.
Schuman, Howard
  1974 "Old wine in new bottles: some sources of response error in the use
        of attitude surveys to study social change." Paper presented to
        Research Seminar Group in Quantitative Social Science, University
        of Surrey, England.
Smith, Tom W.
  1977 Can We Have any Confidence in Confidence? GSS Technical Report
        No. 1. Chicago: National Opinion Research Center.
Steiner, Gary A.
  1963 The People Look at Television: A Study of Audience Attitudes. New
        York: Knopf.
Stouffer, Samuel
  1953 Communism, Conformity, and Civil Liberties: A Cross-Section of
        the Nation Speaks Its Mind. Gloucester, Mass.: Peter Smith.
Taylor, D. Garth
  1976 "Procedures for evaluating trends in qualitative indicators." In
        James A. Davis (ed.), Studies in Special Change Since 1948. NORC
        Report 127A. Chicago: National Opinion Research Center.
Turner, Charles N., with Elissa Krauss
  1978 "Fallible Indicators of the Subjective State of the Nation." Ameri-
        can Psychologist (forthcoming).

THE INTERVIEWER

Research interest in the interviewer as a source of variable error and bias thrived in the late forties and early fifties (see esp. Hyman et al., 1954). But from then until the late sixties the subject of interviewer effects on survey quality languished.

The resurgence of interest in interviewer effects is probably attributable to two developments, one technological, the other social. The civil rights movement and then the urban riots of the sixties brought with them a spate of studies of racial attitudes among blacks as well as whites (e.g., Marx, 1967; Campbell and Schuman, 1968; Schuman and Hatchett, 1974), and along with them growing concern about the potential influence of interviewers' race on the responses of both groups. The article by Schuman and Converse reprinted in this section reflects these concerns.

The second development, this time a technological one, was the growth of telephone interviewing at the expense of face-to-face research. Although both the early and the more recent research on interviewer effects had indicated that these were likely to be small relative to other sources of error, the fact that telephone interviewing reduced the size of interviewing staffs—and correspondingly, of course, increased interviewing assignments—meant that each interviewer's potential influence on a survey's results was substantially greater than it had been in the past. In addition, the centralized administration that accompanied the shift to phone interviewing made it much easier to randomize case assignments to interviewers, a practice indispensable for this kind of research.

Recent research on interviewer effects has developed along two lines, both reflecting continuity with earlier studies. The first, represented in this collection by Schuman and Converse and by Singer, Frankel, and Glassman, asks to what extent characteristics of the interviewer, either alone or together with characteristics of the respondent, influence responses. The aim of this research is to identify and, if possible, reduce interviewer effects. Such effects have been associated with interviewers' race, age, and experience, but they have generally been small. In the case of attitudes, furthermore, the nature of the effect is typically ambiguous. For example, while Schuman and Converse found black respondents giving more militant replies to black interviewers than to white, these more militant responses are not necessarily more truthful; they, too, may reflect interviewer effects.

The second line of research on interviewer effects attempts to estimate the total amount of response variability which is attributable to the interviewers who are used. Earlier research had estimated this quantity for face-to-face interviews; in the selection reprinted here, Groves and Magilavy cumulated estimates of interviewer effects over nine different centralized telephone surveys by Michigan's Survey Research Center. They found somewhat smaller effects than those previously reported and few differences between open and closed questions or between factual and attitudinal questions.

Still a third line of research on interviewers, associated especially with Charles Cannell, has emphasized the technique of questioning rather than the qualities of interviewers. In the selection included here, Cannell and Miller report on an experiment designed to adapt techniques used in face-to-face interviews to telephone surveys. The experiment was only modestly successful, and they conclude that a good deal of research is still needed on the special requirements for interviewing by telephone.

References

Campbell, Angus, and Howard Schuman (1968)
    "Racial attitudes in fifteen American cities." In Supplemental Studies for the
    National Advisory Commission on Civil Disorders. New York: Praeger.
Hyman, Herbert H., et al. (1954)
    Interviewing in Social Research. Chicago: University of Chicago Press.
Marx, Gary T. (1967)
    Protest and Prejudice. New York: Harper.
Schuman, Howard, and Shirley Hatchett (1974)
    Black Racial Attitudes: Trends and Complexities. Ann Arbor, MI: Institute for
    Social Research.

THE EFFECTS OF BLACK AND WHITE INTERVIEWERS ON BLACK RESPONSES

BY HOWARD SCHUMAN AND
JEAN M. CONVERSE*

This article examines recent evidence on racial effects in interviewing northern urban black respondents on both racial and nonracial topics. It examines such effects by age, education, and several other background variables, and provides some evidence on which responses are distorted: those given to white interviewers, or those to black. Questions dealing with militant protest and hostility to whites showed the greatest sensitivity to interviewer effect. Reports of racial discrimination, poor living conditions, and personal background showed little interviewer influence.

Howard Schuman is Associate Professor of Sociology and Director of the Detroit Area Study at the University of Michigan. Jean Converse is a Research Associate with the Detroit Area Study project, from which the present article is drawn.

ALL RECENT STUDIES of black attitudes with which we are familiar have attempted to match race of interviewer with race of respondent.[1] Such precautions are based on past research showing race to be one interviewer attribute that definitely affects response patterns. The precautions have been heightened by the rise of black consciousness and the obvious mistrust of whites by some prominent black spokesmen. The present report provides recent (1968) evidence on the size, pervasiveness, and nature

* We are indebted to Richard Kulka, who contributed greatly to the early work on this report. This research was supported by funds partly from the University of Michigan and partly from an NIMH Grant (No. 5 R01 MH15537-02). The research was carried out through the Detroit Area Study.

[1] The following recent major studies note that they attempted to use only black interviewers with black respondents: Gary T. Marx, *Protest and Prejudice*, New York, Harper, 1967; Raymond J. Murphy and James M. Watson, *The Structure of Discontent*, Institute of Government and Public Affairs, University of California, Los Angeles, 1967; Nathan S. Caplan and Jeffrey M. Paige, "A Study of Ghetto Rioters," *Scientific American*, Vol. 219, August 1968, pp. 15-21; Angus Campbell and Howard Schuman, "Racial Attitudes in Fifteen American Cities," in *Supplemental Studies for the National Advisory Commission on Civil Disorders*, New York, Frederick A. Praeger, 1968, pp. 1-67. Where complete black assignment was not possible, as in Marx's work, apologies are made and partial measures are taken to avoid "bias" (see Marx, *op. cit.*, p. xxvii).

of racial effects in interviewing urban northern black respondents on both racial and nonracial topics. It examines such effects by age, education, and several other background variables. Finally, it raises questions, although it does not provide definitive answers, about whether effects are always in the direction of more distortion due to white, rather than black, interviewers. Our underlying assumption is that race-of-interviewer effects require continued study as race relations themselves change. Such effects can usefully serve as an indicator of evolving areas of interpersonal tension between blacks and whites, and deserve to be treated as a fact of social life and not merely as an artifact of the survey interview.

The most dramatic example of race-of-interviewer effects is reported by Herbert Hyman in *Interviewing in Social Research*.[2] A 1942 NORC study in Memphis assigned 1,000 interviews with Negro respondents randomly between Negro and white interviewers. The results showed "substantially different results . . . on most of the individual questions." Twenty-one of the twenty-four questions had reliable differences by race of interviewer; the differences were often large, in five cases more than 20 percentage points. Even more impressive than their magnitudes was the innocuous character of several of the questions showing such effects. For example, differences occurred in the self-reporting of education and of car ownership—both underreported to white interviewers. The direction of *all* the results was such as to present a relatively passive view of Negro aspirations and discontents to the eyes of white interviewers.

But Hyman also reports other results from a replication in New York, apparently of about the same date, showing less evidence of interviewer effects: only half the questions produced significant differences (.05 level), and in most cases these were smaller than for Memphis. If Negroes were less intimidated in New York than in the Deep South—or if, as Hyman says, Negro-white relations were less "affectively loaded"—one might also project from the 1940's to the 1970's a decreasing effect of race of interviewer on Negro respondents, since it seems clear that norms supporting Negro subordination have declined in acceptance and enforcement by both races since World War II.

Such effects persisted at least in the South at the beginning of the last decade, however, according to reports by Price and Searles and by Williams.[3] Both reports deal with the same study carried out in

  [2] Herbert Hyman *et al.*, *Interviewing in Social Research*, Chicago, University of Chicago Press, 1954.

  [3] D. O. Price and Ruth Searles, "Some Effects of Interviewer-Respondent Interaction on Responses in a Survey Situation," *Proceedings of the Social Statistics*

1960 in purposively selected urban and rural areas of North Carolina. Price and Searles show that race-of-interviewer effects were greater among rural than urban Negroes, thus in a sense paralleling Hyman's report of differences between the strengths of effects in Memphis and New York. They see this as a reflection of differences in role expectations for blacks in southern rural and urban areas. However, it should be noted that even urban blacks showed more civil rights activism to black interviewers than to white interviewers.

Williams focuses on status rankings and finds that most interviewer effects occurred among respondents of low socioeconomic status. He also introduces a useful refinement by having judges classify questionnaire items in terms of their likely "threat" to Negro respondents when asked by white interviewers. The results generally support the distinction in that only the "high threat" items produced differences. There are some peculiarities, however, in that the most obviously race-relevant threat items (for example, attitudes toward sit-ins) reveal the smallest differences, while larger differences are found for a seemingly milder threat question on reading a newspaper and for a general political question. Williams also appears to provide information on only a selected part of his questionnaire, so that it is not possible to infer the pervasiveness of interviewer effects.

Several other recent studies deal with race of interviewer as a variable, but not in ways that are directly relevant at this point.[4] We shall refer to some of these in later sections.

AIM AND DESIGN OF THE PRESENT STUDY

Our present purpose is to examine race-of-interviewer effects in terms of two general foci: type of question most affected and type of respondent most affected. An entire questionnaire is examined for a representative black sample in a major northern city one year after the urban riots of 1967.

Section, American Statistical Association, 1961, pp. 211-221; J. A. Williams, Jr., "Interviewer-Respondent Interaction: A Study of Bias in the Information Interview," *Sociometry,* Vol. 27, 1964, pp. 338-352. The sampling design is not described in detail, but apparently it was purposive at all major points.

4 Thomas F. Pettigrew, *A Profile of the Negro American,* New York, Van Nostrand, 1964, pp. 50-51 and pp. 116-117; Irwin Katz, "Factors Influencing Negro Performance in the Desegregated Classroom," in Martin Deutsch, Irwin Katz, and Arthur R. Jensen, *Social Class, Race, and Psychological Development,* New York, Holt, Rinehart, and Winston, 1968, pp. 254-289; Barbara Snell Dohrenwend, John Colombotos, and Bruce P. Dohrenwend, "Social Distance and Interviewer Effects," *Public Opinion Quarterly,* Vol. 32, 1968, pp. 410-422; Gerhard E. Lenski and John C. Leggett, "Caste, Class, and Deference in the Research Interview," *The American Journal of Sociology,* Vol. 65, 1960.

A cross-section of Negro dwelling units from the city of Detroit was drawn by area probability methods, and within each dwelling unit the head or wife of head was selected at random, except that persons age 70 and over were considered ineligible.[5] Expected cluster sizes of five were used, and these clusters were assigned (with exceptions noted below) by a systematic random procedure to separate black and white interviewing staffs. The black interviewing staff of 25 individuals consisted mainly of older female professional interviewers employed by the Survey Research Center of the University of Michigan. The white interviewing staff consisted of 17 University of Michigan graduate students in sociology and social work, all of whom were enrolled in or connected with the Detroit Area Study practicum on research methods. These students were young (in their 20's), and about half were men and half women. Both black and white interviewing staffs were rather clearly middle class in economic and social terms.[6]

In addition to the clusters randomly assigned by race of interviewer, a third smaller set of clusters was excluded from the comparative design for practical reasons. The fact that the interviewing began eleven months after a major riot in Detroit and two weeks after the assassination of Dr. Martin Luther King, Jr., had presumably increased racial tensions. We decided against sending white interviewers to certain areas because of the possibility of physical danger.[7] This "noncomparable" subsample was assigned entirely to black interviewers and it is not included in any of the analysis that follows except where explicitly noted. Its omission does not damage the comparison between black and white interviewers, but does exclude a small part of the Detroit black population from that comparison. Several comparisons of the "comparable" and "noncomparable" black samples in their relations to other variables indicate that they behave very similarly; we believe (although we cannot prove) that our findings would not be greatly changed by inclusion of these "noncomparable" respondents.

[5] Additional details about the sampling design and final sample are reported in James House, "Sampling Memorandum on the 1968 Detroit Area Study," hectographed, available from the Detroit Area Study, University of Michigan, Ann Arbor, Michigan.

[6] Although there is a clear age difference between professional Survey Research Center interviewers and Detroit Area Study (DAS) students, analyses of two other DAS surveys (in 1966 and 1969) fail to show any reliable differences on questions when both interviewers and respondents are white. In fact, the only consistent differences between professional and student interviewers is that the former are more apt to indicate in their sketch of the respondent that the interview was enjoyable.

[7] The need for the exclusion seems doubtful in retrospect: interviewers during the field period reported no instances of personal hostility of any type.

A total of 619 interviews was gathered. Table 1 presents the sizes and response rates of all three subsamples, along with information indicating their comparability in terms of important background characteristics. Focusing on the main white and black comparable samples to be analyzed directly for interviewer effects, there is nearly perfect matching in background characteristics. Differences by age,

TABLE 1

MAJOR CHARACTERISTICS OF INTERVIEWER SUBSAMPLES OF 1968 DETROIT AREA STUDY

Characteristic	White Interviewer Sample	Black Interviewer Sample	Noncompar- able Black Sample	Total
Actual N	165	330	124	619
Weighted N[a]	213	426	205	844
Response rate	79.4%	82.6%	88.5%	82.9%
Refusal rate	11.7%	5.7%	2.8%	
Age				
Mean years	42.4	43.0	41.9	
S.D.	12.1	12.5	13.8	
Education				
Mean years	10.3	10.4	10.4	
S.D.	3.2	3.3	2.7	
Total family income per month				
Under $500	42%	44%	65%	
$500–699	30	25	20	
$700 and over	28	31	15	
	100	100	100	
Sex and relation to head[b]				
Male head of house	54%	52%	49%	
Wife	28	27	28	
Female head of house	18	20	23	
	100	100	100	
Income stratum of cluster				
High	55%	55%	21%	
Low	45	45	79	
	100	100	100	

[a] The weighting compensates for the oversampling of high-income addresses, carried out for purposes unrelated to the present analysis. (Sample dwelling units were evaluated from the outside during block listing to provide estimated income level of the occupants. The ratings were averaged for each segment and the segment assigned to a "high" or "low" stratum. Half the low segments were randomly eliminated from the sample. Thus the final raw sample overrepresents higher-income blacks. However, weighting has been used in this analysis to make the sample representative of the Detroit black population. Distributions for the two separate strata are shown at the bottom of the table.)

[b] Sampling *within* household was designed to overselect males slightly to compensate for the usual underrepresentation of black males in surveys. No weighting of sex is used in this analysis.

education, and relation to head of house are very slight and do not approach significance. This has a double implication: first, reports of these variables are presumably not affected by race of interviewer; second, the random assignment procedure to black and white staffs was successful in equating the samples on major background variables.

The slight superiority in response rate of the black comparable sample over the white sample is probably not due to race of interviewer: the student interviewers usually have a lower response rate than the Survey Research Center professionals and the difference here is actually less than for a more recent (1969) Detroit Area Study where all interviewers and all respondents were white. We believe that at least in 1968 equally trained black and white interviewing staffs would have produced quite similar response rates in a metropolitan area such as Detroit. In general, we suspect that any problem regarding response rate today has more to do with white reluctance to enter black areas than to black reluctance to be interviewed by whites.[8]

PERVASIVENESS OF RACE-OF-INTERVIEWER EFFECTS
ACROSS THE QUESTIONNAIRE

Virtually the whole interview schedule has been analyzed for interviewer effects. This includes all questions asked of at least 90 per cent of the respondents, plus all other questions of general importance even though asked of only part of the sample (e.g. service in the armed forces, asked only of males). One hundred and thirty questions have been reviewed following these criteria, out of 173 distinguishable items in the questionnaire.

To facilitate comparisons, we will focus on a single statistic, the correlation ratio (E^2), which allows us to compare variance explained by race of interviewer across all 130 questionnaire items. Such an approach is more useful than emphasis on significance levels because it allows comparison of magnitudes of association between race of interviewer and different types of items.[9] These statistics are

---

[8] The noncomparable respondents live in blocks estimated by listers to be lower in income on the average than the rest of the sample, and this is supported by differences in self-reported income. On the other hand, differences in sex, relation to head of house, and education are slight. The relatively high response rate for the noncomparable black sample may be due in some part to race of interviewer, but data not presented here indicate that lower-income blacks (who predominate in the noncomparable sample) tend to have a higher response rate than higher-income blacks regardless of race of interviewer.

[9] It also reduces somewhat the stress on our particular sample sizes (which partly determine significance levels), although the reliability of the estimates of variance explained continues, of course, to be a function of sample size. We do

only approximations because our dependent variable items do not meet all the assumptions required by analysis of variance. However, we have also tested many of the same associations using nonparametric measures (tau beta especially) and find little difference in any of the conclusions that would be drawn.[10]

Of the 130 questions examined, race of interviewer explains at least 1 per cent of the variance in 34 cases (26 per cent of the items). Of these, variance explained reaches beyond 2 per cent in 11 cases and beyond 3 per cent in 9 more cases. Race of interviewer is thus an explanatory variable that deserves consideration, but it is also clear that it is not so decisive as to pervade all questions in this study. Although our questionnaire included much emotional and explicitly racial material, with other nonracial questions asked as part of a basically racial questionnaire, 74 per cent of the questions do not show reliable differences by race of interviewer. Some additional trends might become reliable with a much larger sample, but it appears that they would be trivial in size by usual standards.

HYPOTHESIZED EXPLANATIONS FOR QUESTION DIFFERENCES

We began with two general hypotheses in attempting to understand why some items show interviewer effects and some do not. Our first hypothesis was that such effects would occur primarily on questions having clear racial content. Although in some sense any topic can have racial connotations, we have drawn an operational distinction between questions that employ racial terms bluntly ("Negro," "white," "race," "discrimination," "Detroit riot") and those that do not. We assumed that the respondent's awareness of his interviewer's race would be particularly heightened with questions that broach racial matters directly.

---

not abandon tests of significance entirely, however, since it turns out that when we explain at least 1 per cent of the variance—the lowest association we regard as useful to interpret—we are always dealing with results significant beyond the .05 level of confidence; when we explain at least 2 per cent of the variance in an item we are always dealing with results significant at the .01 level or beyond. Thus the reader can translate our measures of variance explained into significance if he chooses.

10 We have not attempted to take account systematically of the slight clustering effects inherent in the design. Tests of these and other Detroit Area Study data indicate that for most questions such effects are negligible, rarely involving an increase in variance beyond a factor of 1.1. Some items dealing with factual information related to the neighborhood do show stronger cluster effects, however, and sampling error may account for some apparent bias on several nonracial factual items discussed later. We have also not attempted to adjust our statistics for the use of weighted data, but have tested both weighted and unweighted runs until convinced that the weighting effects are negligible.

Second, we expected interviewer bias to vary with the constraint placed on a respondent by "facts" as he sees them. We reasoned that a respondent would bring more personal certainty to questions he considered factual—his own history and experience—than he would to matters of "opinion."[11] Interviewer influence could thus be expected to operate more strongly, though perhaps largely as an unconscious process, in the realm of opinion where some of the respondent's views might be vaguely formulated or even *un*formulated prior to the interview.

Explicitly racial questions, as defined above, do indeed reveal the expected vulnerability to interviewer effect: 39 per cent of the 54 racial questions reach our minimal level of at least 1 per cent variance explained. For nonracial questions, the comparable figures are 17 per cent of 76 questions. The difference is thus sharp, although by no means complete. The second distinction, between fact and opinion, fails, there being a trend in Table 2 opposite to that predicted

TABLE 2

CATEGORIES OF QUESTIONS AFFECTED BY RACE OF INTERVIEWER

		Variance Explained by Race of Interviewer			
Category	No. of Questions	2% or More	1 — 2%	Less than 1%	Total
Total questions analyzed	130	15%	11%	74%	100%
Racial opinions	40	32%	5%	63%	100%
Racial facts	14	14%	29%	57%	100%
Nonracial opinions	29	3%	11%	86%	100%
Nonracial facts	47	8%	11%	81%	100%

for both racial and nonracial categories. The fact-opinion distinction does illuminate an important difference *within* the racial set of questions: racial opinion effects almost all show up as strong (2 per cent or more variance explained), while racial fact effects more often just reach our minimal level (1 per cent variance explained). Thus, questions that produce the greatest differences by race of interviewer are heavily concentrated in the racial opinion category.

[11] Three judges were asked to classify all 130 items into either "fact" or "opinion." They were unanimous on 75 per cent of the items. The results below use not only unanimous placements but also include majority (two out of three) decisions. However, restriction of the items classified to only those showing unanimity do not change the proportions noticeably.

AN INDUCTIVE ATTEMPT TO DIFFERENTIATE QUESTIONS

Although the simple descriptive hypotheses discussed above proved to be of some value, they neither account for the placement of most questions in Table 2 nor do they provide a satisfactory explanation of the process taking place. Rather than elaborate more *a priori* hypotheses, we decided on an inductive approach to reveal more subtle factors differentiating questions. We present in Tables 3 and 4 those *racial* items showing greatest association (more than 2 per cent variance explained) with race of interviewer, and those showing essentially no association (less than 0.05 per cent variance explained). Inferences based on this approach are largely *post factum* and therefore tentative; since "high" and "low" effect questions are provided in detail, however, readers are free to arrive at explanations other than those we offer. Questions with nonracial content are not presented in detail in tables, but will also be discussed.

In Table 3, almost all the fifteen racial questions showing large race-of-interviewer effects deal with overt hostility toward whites, suspicion of whites, or identification with black militancy. Item 1 requires outright expression of personal distrust, and it shows the largest interviewer effect in the entire study: 12 per cent variance explained and 28 per cent difference between black and white response levels. Similar themes appear in most other items in the table, and also in several other questions showing effects that are reliable but slightly under the lower limit needed for entrance into the table. Moreover, on all these questions, blacks consistently present themselves as less hostile and militant to white interviewers than to black, quite as one would expect from past studies. The only clear exception in Table 3 is item 11, which concerns contact with whites and seems to have nothing to do with militancy, hostility, or suspicion; since possible explanations for this lone item cannot be tested, we must leave it simply as a puzzle.

Our strongest conclusion from Table 3, therefore, is that the degree of anti-white sentiment and militancy measured in a black cross-section sample will differ rather considerably depending upon the racial composition of the interviewing staff. Although the variances accounted for by interviewer in Table 3 are not great in absolute terms, they (and the percentage differences between black and white interviewer marginals) are as large as most associations counted as important in survey results. The interpretation of these interviewer differences is a good deal less certain than the empirical generalization itself. For the moment we will assume that the black respondent suppresses militancy to white interviewers because he senses that

TABLE 3

RACIAL HIGH: QUESTIONS WITH RACIAL CONTENT SHOWING GREATEST DIFFERENCE BY RACE OF INTERVIEWER
(2.0% OR MORE VARIANCE EXPLAINED)

Question	Answer Tested vs. Others	Percent by Race of Interviewer		Difference	Percent Variance Explained (E^2)
		White	Negro		
1. Do you personally feel that you can trust most white people, some white people, or none at all?	Trust most whites	35%	7%	+28%	12.5%
2. Would you say that because of the disturbance in Detroit now feel *more* ready to stand up for their rights, *less* ready to stand up for their rights, or that there hasn't been much change?	More ready	61	84	−23	4.9
3. Some people feel that last summer's disturbance was a *step forward* for the cause of Negro rights. Other people feel that it was a *step backward* for the cause of Negro rights. Which opinion comes closest to the way you feel?	Step forward	30	54	−24	4.7
4. Do you think Negro parents can work better with a Negro teacher than with a white teacher?	Yes, better with Negro teacher	14	29	−15	4.4
5. Suppose there is a white storekeeper in a Negro neighborhood. He hires white clerks but refuses to hire any Negro clerks. Talking with him about the matter does no good. What do you think Negroes in the neighborhood should do to change the situation?	Nothing	26	10	+16	4.1
6. What do you think is the most important thing the city government can do to keep a disturbance like the one last summer from breaking out again in Detroit?	Use of force, police	35	18	+17	3.9

256

Question	Answer				
7. Some leaders want to organize Negroes into groups to protect themselves against any violence by whites. Do you think this is worthwhile or not?	Yes, worthwhile	18%	35%	−17	3.2%
8. In your church, has money ever been collected at Sunday service for the Civil Rights movement?	Yes, money collected	30	46	−16	2.9
9. Do you think city officials in Detroit are *more* willing to listen to Negro demands since the disturbance, *less* willing to listen, or hasn't there been much change?	More willing	59	79	−20	2.7
10. Do you think Negro teachers take more of an interest in teaching Negro students than white teachers do?	Yes, Negro teachers take more interest	26	41	−15	2.5
11. Were there any white students in the schools you attended?	Yes	49	33	+16	2.5
12. Do you think many policemen would use this right [to stop and search on suspicion] unfairly against Negroes?	Yes	70	83	−13	2.4
13. Some people say there should be Negro principals in schools with mostly Negro students because Negroes should have the most say in running inner city schools. Would you agree with that or not?	Yes, agree	26	42	−16	2.4
14. If you were treated impolitely in a downtown store in Detroit, how would you feel. . . very angry, a little angry, or would you not let it bother you?	Very angry	27	42	−15	2.4
15. How do you feel we should refer to last July's disturbance in Detroit: Should it be called a riot, a rebellion, or what?	Rebellion or revolt	50	68	−18	2.0

257

such an attitude threatens himself or appears hostile to the interviewer. Before considering more detailed interpretations, we will
turn to an examination of racial items that do *not* show interviewer
effects, as presented in Table 4.

The only recurrent theme in Table 4 is that of reported discrimination: items 6 through 9 are of this type and none shows an interviewer difference. We may note that such reports are passive rather
than aggressive in connotation (the black respondent describes himself or others as victim, not as potential aggressor). Moreover, discrimination is now so widely acknowledged that the issue may well have
lost the emotional quality it held in earlier days in the rural South.
This point serves to remind us that questions showing interviewer
effects in our own 1968 study may in the future come to seem un-
exciting and therefore not subject to bias.

Our attempt to understand why the remaining racial questions in
Table 4 do not show interviewer effects has suggested two further
points. First, for an item to elicit systematic interviewer bias, the
respondent must be able to see among alternative answers the one
which will especially satisfy the interviewer. For example, the following item seems likely to be disturbing to most respondents, yet shows
little evidence of race-of-interviewer effects:

Suppose someone you knew told you he could "pass" into white society, and was
going to because of the advantages it would give him. How would you feel toward this
person?

Response	To White Interviewers	To Black Interviewers
Approve	17%	19%
Don't care	40	28
Disapprove	40	46
Other	3	7
	100%	100%
	(N = 165)	(N = 330)

Although there is some difference in the percentages for "don't
care," black interviewers receive both slightly more approval of passing and more disapproval of it. We suspect that lack of systematic
effect occurs because even the respondent trying his best to satisfy a
white interviewer lacks an obvious way to do so. He can be reasonably sure that most whites would rather see him less militant on riot
items, but he may wonder whether they would prefer him to endorse passing, oppose it, or simply not care. The same ambiguity may
be at work in items 1-4 of Table 4, in that none provides the respondent with a clear indication of what answer would satisfy his

TABLE 4

RACIAL LOW: QUESTIONS WITH RACIAL CONTENT SHOWING LEAST DIFFERENCE BY RACE OF INTERVIEWER
(0.05% OR LESS VARIANCE EXPLAINED)

Question	Answer Tested vs. Others	Percent by Race of Interviewer		Difference	Percent Variance Explained (E^2)
		White	Negro		
1. Have you ever taken part in any kind of non-violent protest for civil rights?	Yes	25%	25%	0%	0.00%
2. Now that Martin Luther King is gone, who do you think is the single most important Negro leader in the country?	Abernathy	58	58	0	0.00
3. Some people are saying that the assassination of Martin Luther King will drive Negroes and whites further apart. Others think that it will bring them closer together. Which do you think will probably happen? ("No change" is recorded when volunteered.)	Bring together	66	70	−4	0.00
4. Do you and the white families that live around here visit in each other's homes, or do you only see and talk to each other on the street, or do you hardly know each other?	To white interviewers, respondents report less close contact and less no contact.				0.00
5. If using (laws and persuasion, non-violent protest) doesn't work [to gain rights] then do you think Negroes should be ready to use violence?	Yes, use violence	23	23	0	0.00
6. Do you think you were ever refused a job or laid off from a job because of being Negro?	Yes	26	27	−1	0.01
7. Do you think there are many, some, or just a few places in the city of Detroit where a Negro could not rent or buy a house because of racial discrimination?	Many places	36	37	−1	0.00
8. Do you feel that you personally have missed out on getting the kind of job you want and are qualified for because of race?	Yes	26	27	−1	0.03
9. Do you think you have ever been discriminated against when you were trying to buy or rent a particular house or apartment?	Yes	25	27	−2	0.04

interviewer.[12] Such items may, of course, show an increase in random error or in complex interaction effects difficult to identify; but not a systematic difference in item means and percentages between black and white interviewers.

A second qualification concerns the susceptibility of militancy items to interviewer effect. There are three exceptions in the schedule to this effect: two deal with the advocacy of violence (as in item 5, Table 4), and one with feelings of total alienation from the United States. In all three the militant content is far more extreme than in any of the items shown in Table 3 and discussed earlier. Yet for these three items the militant response is given equally to black and white interviewers.[13] Apparently race-of-interviewer affects "militancy" responses only when the items deal with relatively vague sympathies, not when they commit the person to genuinely extreme views or actions.

We interpret this to indicate that the kind of respondent who holds extreme beliefs is so much more intensely committed than the average person, his views so conscious and ideologically crystallized, that he does not mind telling the world about them. The case is similar to that of the radical black spokesman whose role has become one of "telling it like it is," whether to black, white, or mixed audiences. In any case, the practical implication of these results for surveys of black attitudes is that the estimates of *violent* militancy recorded in recent studies are probably not biased up or down because of interviewer effects.[14] Estimates of trends in more vague or generalized black distrust of whites, on the other hand, may be subject to considerable instability depending upon the racial composition of the field interviewing staff.

[12] Item 1 may connote militant action, but on the other hand it suggests the legitimacy of nonviolence and of active participation and concern. Items 2 and 3 deal with events of such recency (as well as political sophistication and abstraction) that a preferred response must be very difficult to guess. Item 4 poses the problem of whether the white interviewer would prefer to see intimate contact between blacks and whites, or almost no contact.

[13] Item 5 in Table 4 is a contingent follow-up to a question asking which is the best way for Negroes to gain their rights—use laws and persuasion, use nonviolent protest, or be ready to use violence. Advocates of violence to the original question are only 6 per cent to black interviewers and 5 per cent to white interviewers, so that although the initial item does not quite qualify for Table 4 (because its explained variance is slightly over 0.05 per cent), there is essentially no difference by race-of-interviewer, just as in the follow-up question. The third item asks whether in the case of "another big world war" the respondent feels "the United States is worth fighting for." Most of the sample (87 per cent) give the conventional patriotic answer, and there is only a one per cent difference by race-of-interviewer. Note that on two of these three items, the extremity of the "angry" response is also indicated by the small percentage of the sample endorsing it.

[14] See Campbell and Schuman, *op. cit.*, pp. 51-57, for such estimates.

WHITE EFFECTS, BLACK EFFECTS, OR BOTH?

With the qualifications just given, we can say that the degree of anti-white sentiment and militancy expressed to survey questions does vary with the race of the interviewing staff.

The classic interpretation of such findings would be that Negroes are afraid to express hostility directly to whites because of possible physical or economic retribution. This seems to us unlikely to be of major importance in private interviews in Detroit in 1968, but certainly cannot be dismissed out of hand. A more contemporary application of this theory emphasizes factors of psychological dominance—specifically, black tension and fear before white judgment and criticism—rather than fear of negative economic or physical sanctions. Finally, an even simpler though related process would be the respondent's wish to avoid offending a polite stranger who has come into his home for a legitimate reason. To accept a guest into your house and then proceed to explain that you neither trust nor feel friendly toward people of his race probably takes more chutzpah than the average respondent possesses.

All of the above interpretations assume that it is the white interviewer who "produces" bias. But one must also consider the possibility that the desire of a black respondent to impress a black interviewer with his militancy is also a factor contributing to bias. This interpretation of a "black effect" runs against the grain of past racial studies, which have focused on dominance-submission theory; but in an era of emphasis on black consciousness and black unity, such a possibility cannot be disregarded, if only as a note for future research. Our findings that interviewer effects are generally limited to items dealing with hostility and militancy is, of course, consistent with either a black or a white effect.

The third possibility of a simultaneous white and black effect is not entirely hypothetical: it is suggested by a supposedly nonracial question which merely asks for the names of the respondent's "favorite actors and entertainers." That respondents clearly supply a racial context, consciously or not, to such a question is revealed systematically when racial categories are used in coding responses:

Respondent Mentions:	White Interviewers	Comparable Black Interviewers	Diff.
Only black entertainers	16%	43%	+27
More black than white entertainers	15	22	+ 7
Equal proportions	18	11	− 7
More white than black entertainers	27	14	−13
Only white entertainers	24	9	−15
	100%	100%	
	(N = 146)	(N = 286)	

The symmetry with which the favorite entertainers' color tends to match the color of the interviewer is hard to explain solely in the traditional terms of fear of whites. The utter neutrality of the question from a political standpoint suggests that we may be dealing with a simple but subtle force for bias rarely considered in the research literature on interviewer effects. The presence of a white or black interviewer may simply serve to stimulate racially "appropriate" images. If this is the case, interviewer effects may at times be more instantaneous and "natural" than we consider them when they are viewed primarily as manifestations of caste or class.[15]

To settle the general issue of validity we would need somehow to obtain independent evidence as to attitudes and facts reported by respondents. For factual information such data are theoretically possible, but there is nothing of a factual nature in the present study that we are able to validate. From past studies there is one piece of evidence implying that more valid information comes from black interviewers. Price and Searles and later Pettigrew report that respondents were more often able to identify political leaders when asked to do so by black interviewers than by whites.[16] Assuming that the interviewers themselves performed in the same way, this result seems interpretable only in terms of suppression or repression of knowledge by black respondents when confronted by white questioners.

From our own study we have been able to devise only one hypothesis that bears directly on the issue. There are three interrelated assumptions: (1) the *attitude* of militancy should be positively associated with *behavior* indicative of militancy; (2) if the behavioral measure of militancy does not vary by race of interviewer, it can be assumed to be equally valid in *both* interviewing situations; (3) the *attitude* of militancy can be interpreted as more valid in situations where its relationship to militant *behavior* is stronger.

Our behavioral question asked whether the respondent had "ever taken part in any kind of nonviolent protest for civil rights." It does not show any difference by race of interviewer. Moreover, this behavioral measure of militancy is indeed positively associated for the

---

[15] Price and Searles, *op. cit.*, suggest a somewhat similar approach to the problem of validity, namely, that it is misleading to assume any single valid response to items such as those in our schedule. Black feelings toward whites are doubtless complex and full of ambivalence, and interviewer effects may best be regarded as indicators of this ambivalence rather than as methodological defects. We are dealing, here, with amorphous concepts like trust, and with questions that the respondent has probably never thought of before in such an abstract way. The exact interpretation of a question and the meaning given to the response alternatives could be situationally defined to a high degree at the moment the question is asked.

[16] Price and Searles, *op. cit.*, p. 219; Pettigrew, *op. cit.*, pp. 116-117.

total sample with an attitudinal measure of militancy.[17] In the total sample those who report participation in civil rights protests show a significantly higher militancy attitude score (a mean of 1.15) than those reporting no participation (a mean of 1.05): $t = 2.65$, 489 $d.f.$, $p < .01$. Finally, when we separate out the two race-of-interviewer situations, we find a higher correlation between protest behavior and militant attitudes among those interviewed by blacks than by those interviewed by whites: the correlation (E) is .15 in the former case and only .04 in the latter. We therefore conclude that militant attitudes are more validly measured in the black interviewer situation than in the white interviewer situation.

Both types of evidence just reviewed suggest that the black interviewing situation is the more valid one. At the same time, we believe it unwise to dismiss completely the idea that there may be ways in which black interviewers introduce bias. First, the entertainer question discussed earlier suggests that many blacks find entertainers of both races attractive, and that the interviewing situation serves primarily to make salient one or the other racial context. Second, although the black interviewers in this study were mostly moderate-appearing middle-aged women, it is possible that future studies in which more obviously militant interviewers are used may stimulate reporting of more militancy than actually exists. Finally, and perhaps most important, there is a type of valid insight that "white effects" in survey interviewing may provide. If white interviewers serve to depress the "natural" level of militancy of black respondents, we must expect something similar to happen in other white-black interaction outside the survey context, for example, in ordinary integrated social situations. Moreover, as caste breaks down in this country, the presence of blacks in social situations no doubt tends to have a similar effect on whites, namely, to decrease open expression of anti-black sentiments. Thus integrated social situations, like "integrated interviewing situations," should inhibit overt hostility on both sides. While this may lead to some underestimation of latent negative feelings, it may also reduce interracial provocations and therefore decrease some of the areas of friction between blacks and whites. W. I. Thomas' well-known proposition becomes relevant here: "If men define situations as real, they are real in their consequences."

[17] A Militancy Scale was constructed from the 12 attitude items in Table 3 dealing most directly with militant protest and anti-white sentiment. Each of the 12 items was first scored on a scale of 0 (low militancy) to 2 (high militancy), with 1 point given to intermediate or neutral responses. The item scores for each respondent were then summed and averaged, yielding a final scale range of 0 to 2. The items in Table 3 excluded from the scale (numbers 8, 11, and 12) were those that seemed to us less clearly indicators of militancy or hostility. The Militancy Scale is discussed further in the section on types of respondents.

NONRACIAL QUESTIONS

Only 5 out of 76 nonracial questions have at least 2 per cent of their variance explained by race of interviewer. Just as implicit racial connotation appears in the largest of these effects already discussed—the entertainer question, with 11.2 per cent variance explained—there is probably racial implication in the fact that respondents report to white interviewers more unqualified approval of Detroit's (then) white Mayor Cavanagh (2.6 per cent variance explained).

The other three nonracial highs relate at least somewhat to social status, though the direction of the bias is not consistent: a larger house and a higher occupational rank for the father are reported to black interviewers (both just over 2 per cent variance explained); but big-city origin is overreported to whites (3 per cent variance explained). If these particular effects on nonracial questions are not indeed "rare chance" events, they would seem to be so idiosyncratic as to be of little use in understanding race-of-interviewer effects; for the great majority of personal background questions, including several direct indicators of status, do *not* show such effects, as summarized below.

When we collect nonracial questions which fall at the same negligible level that we set in examining the racial lows, we acquire a list of 24 questions. The size of the list makes for an unwieldy table but the questions can be discussed in three substantive groupings.[18]

The largest set of questions (13) deals with family background and present demographic factors most of which bear on social status: kinds of income received, amount of income, education of respondent and of spouse, employment status, occupation, contact with the poverty program, as well as length of time in the neighborhood, church attendance, and concern with religion. The low sensitivity of these personal background questions reflects a clear trend across the questionnaire. The subject is *not* completely free of interviewer effect, as we have seen, but the influence is relatively weak: only 6 of the 33 background questions reach 1 per cent of variance explained, and these items present no particular pattern for interpretation.

Six other nonracial questions showing no effect concern the respondent's present satisfaction with his level of education, working conditions, wages, current housing, neighborhood upkeep, and the future economic prospects of his family. This also represents a trend

18 A memorandum has been prepared listing these and all other questions in our study, along with percentage differences and variances explained. A copy may be obtained by writing the authors.

across the questionnaire: complaints about basic life conditions, like complaints about discrimination, can apparently be made as freely to white interviewers as to black.

The five remaining nonracial questions with no interviewer effect are attitudinal items of a rather miscellaneous character.[19] Only one question in this group has great interest: "Do you think the police should have the right to stop and search people they just think look suspicious?" Our population is heavily against such a police right (72 per cent No), with only a 3 per cent difference by race of interviewer. When this question is immediately followed by one with a racial edge ("Would police use the stop and search law unfairly against Negroes?"), as we have seen in Table 3 a sharp interviewer effect emerges. Again we encounter the general trend of our findings, that the ease with which problems and grievances can be aired is not compromised by the interviewer's race until racial mention itself is pointed up or militant sympathies are probed.

TYPES OF RESPONDENTS

Past research and present reasoning suggest that the following background and personality variables may be linked with race-of-interviewer effects: age, region, sex, social class, interest in racial issues, personal confidence, and authoritarianism. Respondents differing on each of these variables (for example, men as against women) are hypothesized to differ also in susceptibility to race-of-interviewer effects.

To reduce repetition in analysis and increase the interpretability of results, we have developed a scale for substantively similar items appearing in Table 3. Of the 15 racial "high effect" items in that table, the 12 were selected that seemed the clearest measures of hostility to whites or support for black militant actions. The resulting index, to be referred to as the Militancy Scale, has an estimated reliability (internal consistency) of .64 over the combined comparable samples.[20] When race-of-interviewer is run against the Militancy Scale, it accounts for 16.6 per cent of the scale's variance, and for 25.9 per cent (16.6 ÷ 64) of the *reliable* variance. Since the scale items were selected on the basis of their known sensitivity to interviewer effects, these relatively high proportions are obviously not

---

[19] One concerns parental authority over children, included as a measure of authoritarianism. A second probes attitudes about a large world war, discussed earlier. Two ask evaluations of Detroit political figures, both of whom proved to be relatively unknown to our sample (from 40% to 64% reporting "don't know enough to say"). The fifth question is discussed in the text.

[20] See footnote 17 above for more details on the construction of the scale.

unexpected. But the 12 items do comprise almost all those in our questionnaire dealing with militancy and hostility, and therefore it is reasonable to expect race of interviewer to account for nearly as large proportions of variance in similar indices in other studies. For this reason, we will interpret this specially constructed scale as a substantive measure of black militancy.

Age. Previous studies (and Table 5) have shown militancy itself to be inversely related to age,[21] and it seems reasonable to expect the more militant younger generation of blacks to be less influenced

TABLE 5

RELATION OF MILITANCY SCALE TO RACE OF INTERVIEWER WITHIN CATEGORIES OF SEVEN BACKGROUND VARIABLES

Variable	N	*Mean Militancy Scores*		*Per cent Variance Explained by Race-of-Interviewer*
		White Interviewers	*Black Interviewers*	
Income				
$500 per month	186	.77	1.22	27.1
$500–699	124	.86	1.22	17.9
$700 and over	159	.95	1.12	4.2
Education				
0–8 years	118	.68	1.12	25.9
9–11 years	145	.88	1.22	16.2
12–17 years	230	.93	1.22	13.1
Age				
18–30 years	94	.96	1.26	12.8
31–40	139	.83	1.23	23.6
41–50	132	.83	1.18	16.4
51–69	123	.80	1.12	16.3
Region of origin				
North	185	.88	1.22	18.4
South	308	.82	1.18	16.2
Sex				
Men	266	.85	1.24	20.3
Women	227	.85	1.13	12.7
Interest in racial issues				
High	198	.91	1.21	11.9
Average + low	287	.82	1.18	20.1
Personal confidence				
High	209	.94	1.22	10.2
Average + low	280	.81	1.16	19.4
Authoritarianism				
Low	228	.88	1.22	14.5
Average + high	264	.82	1.16	18.2
Over-all militancy				
Index	493	.85	1.19	16.6

[21] The studies cited in footnote 1 show inverse relations between age and militancy.

by the race of the interviewer in openly expressing its beliefs. However, we fail to find any clear trend in Table 5 for age to modify race-of-interviewer effects. The effects are least for persons 18 to 30, but greatest for those 31 to 40. The variations by age shown in Table 5 are probably unreliable, and even if reliable would be difficult to interpret. We must conclude that there is little evidence that race-of-interviewer effects are declining among younger blacks.[22]

Region. The findings of Hyman on the Memphis-New York difference and of Price and Searles on rural-urban differences suggest that interviewer effects should be greater for blacks *reared* in the traditional southern segregationist structure than in northern cities. For Detroit residents, the closest parallel to this distinction is region of early socialization. Those respondents reared in the South should show greater interviewer effects than those reared in Detroit or other parts of the North.

Findings bearing on this hypothesis are shown in Table 5. They do not support the prediction. Differences by region of origin are slight, and their direction is the reverse of that predicted.[23] This may mean that regional and urban-rural interviewer effects found in earlier studies have disappeared, but an equally likely interpretation is that adult experience in Detroit eliminates whatever differences based on early socialization may have once existed.[24]

Sex. We expected effects to be greater among black men than among black women. Much writing on traditional racial patterns in America has stressed the unusual problems faced by black males because of the passivity required of them in interactions with whites and the low occupational level open to them.[25] It seemed possible that this would extend to the interviewing situation.

Our measurement problems here are complex because most of our black interviewers and half our white interviewers were female, but we were not able to incorporate sex of interviewer systematically in our sample design. The results in Table 5 reveal a mild trend in the expected direction: males show a greater difference in militancy between the two situations than do females, with the greatest militancy

[22] Results for age with controls for education and income were also obtained from the multiple classification analysis described in footnote 26 below. The adjusted means and the new variance differ only slightly from those in Table 5.

[23] Age and region are associated, but in such a way as to increase the likely relation of both to militancy according to our hypotheses. Hence when neither shows such a relationship, a control for the other is unnecessary.

[24] That region of early socialization is not a particularly powerful variable is further borne out by its small relationship to the Militancy Scale *within* each type of interviewer; there is a trend for blacks of northern origin to be more militant than those of southern origin, but the trend is quite slight.

[25] *Cf.* Pettigrew, *op. cit.*, pp. 15-24.

being shown by black males to black interviewers. If square roots of the correlation ratios are treated as if they are two independent product-moment correlations, the difference between the correlation for males and the correlation for females is *not* significant at the .05 level. We have at most a trend here worth further checking in later research where sex of interviewer can also be controlled.

Social class. As noted earlier, socioeconomic status was found by Williams to be an important conditional variable: interviewer effects occurred most strongly among those low in social status. Where Williams used a complicated seven-indicator measure of social status, however, we have used simply years of schooling and amount of family income, keeping the two separate to aid in interpretation.

Our results, shown in Table 5, support those of Williams: race-of-interviewer effects are greatest among lower-income and lower-educated blacks. The difference between extreme class categories is substantial, especially for income, where 27 per cent of Militancy Scale variance is accounted for among lower-income blacks, as against only 4 per cent among upper-income blacks. The findings for education and for income are essentially the same, suggesting that it is their common meaning in terms of social status that is relevant here, rather than the singular character of either variable (for example, the verbal articulateness that goes with education).[26]

We have not been able to explain adequately why lower-status blacks are more affected by race of interviewer than higher-status blacks. Williams suggests that blacks of low status are economically more dependent on whites and therefore feel more intimidated,

---

[26] Since both income and education are related to age, it is necessary to control for the latter in order to show that the relationships of militancy to the two social class indicators are not spurious. Employing multiple classification analysis (MCA), we used age and education to predict militancy scores within each race-of-interviewer sample. The adjusted means within the white sample for each education category (from low to high) become .68, .88, and .92; within the comparable black sample they become 1.15, 1.22, 1.20. A comparison of these figures with those in Table 5 shows essentially no change from the gross means. When this analysis is carried out with age and income as predictors, the following adjusted militancy means are obtained: white sample—.76, .88, .94; comparable black sample—1.24, 1.21, 1.12. Again there is little change from the gross means for income categories in Table 5. There is a slight accentuation of a trend in the black comparable sample for income to be *inversely* related to militancy. The trend is small and is not supported by a similar one for education, hence we regard it as probably unreliable. If it should hold up in later studies, it would indicate that among black respondents interviewed by black interviewers, militancy is greatest for those with least education. Further analysis of the relations among education, income, and militancy scores shows that when cross-tabulation is used to allow for interaction, militancy scores are particularly *low* among those in the comparable black sample who combine relatively low education and relatively high income.

but while this may have been true in rural North Carolina, it does not seem very plausible in the anonymity of a metropolis like Detroit.[27] Williams also suggests that higher-status blacks are better able to understand the genuine neutrality of the interviewing situation, that is, to separate it from "real life." This seems to us a plausible interpretation, but neither Williams nor we are able to offer any direct evidence for it, and our failure to find education a more powerful conditional variable than income seems to contradict such a cognitive emphasis. We also investigated several other hypotheses without notable success. For example, there is the possibility that attitudes of lower-status blacks are generally less stable and thus more subject to interviewer bias of all types, but this does not seem to be true for attitude areas outside of militancy in our study. Another possibility is that status groups differ in relevant psychological factors, such as "authoritarianism," but controls for such variables (several of which are treated in succeeding sections) do not show them to function as intervening variables in this way. In sum, a satisfactory explanation for the specification of race-of-interviewer effects by social status remains to be found.

If we turn from the causes of status differences to their implications, it is useful to consider the conclusions one would draw from a study of Table 5 if only *one* race of interviewer were used. An analyst examining the data collected only by *white interviewers* would find militancy scores positively related to social status, and would conclude that as blacks become better educated and attain higher incomes they are likely to become more militant.[28] With *black interviewers*, however, there is no clear systematic variation in mean militancy scores by respondent's status. Hence an analyst examining such data would conclude that militancy is spread fairly evenly over the black social class structure and is not a function of such factors as low economic status at the one extreme or high educa-

[27] There is some inconsistency between this explanation and Williams' emphasis on the concept "social distance" to characterize the gap between interviewer status and respondent status. His actual explanation focuses on the educational and economic status of the Negro respondents, not on the "distance" between their status and that of the white interviewers. Neither Williams' main assumptions about white interviewer expectations, nor any evidence in the North Carolina study, suggests that low-status white interviewers would have produced less "bias" from low-status Negroes. On the contrary, low-status whites might well have been perceived as having even less liberal expectations than middle-status whites, and thus have produced more bias despite the reduction in social distance.

[28] This conclusion, incidentally, is the one drawn by Daniel Patrick Moynihan in a 1969 memorandum to the President, where he argues that black militancy is largely a matter of elite ideology and that it lacks roots in the black lower class. Moynihan's memorandum, originally dated January 3, 1969, was published in *The New York Times*, March 11, 1970.

tion at the other. The evidence we have summarized about validity supports the latter interpretation.

Furthermore, if we assume that lower-class blacks tend to suppress their militancy in "real-life" contact with whites, then the conditions affecting the "*expression* of militancy" are themselves important to study, as we noted earlier in another context. To the extent that participation in "black only" movements provides personal insulation from white influence, it is lower-class members particularly whose militancy should be stabilized by racial solidarity. Black social organization may thus increase the ranks of the militant not so much by new conversions as by providing psychological protection for those more vulnerable to whites.

Authoritarianism. Our questionnaire included three *F*-scale type items designed to measure authoritarian personality traits.[29] We expected those with higher scores to be more submissive to white interviewers and therefore more open to interviewer effects. Table 5 shows a trend in the direction predicted, but it is so slight that it must be regarded as failing to confirm the hypothesis.

Interest in racial issues and personal confidence. Previous research on political attitudes suggests that opinions are most stable when they concern matters of considerable interest and salience to the respondent.[30] Persons who have little intrinsic involvement in a topic would seem more apt to be influenced by external cues. We asked interviewers to rate each respondent after the interview in terms of his "interest in talking about racial matters" ("very interested," "average interest," "reluctant"). A second interviewer rating dealt with the respondent's general social confidence and poise in the interview situation. Our expectation was that less confident individuals would be more apt to respond to the interviewer than to the questions. Table 5 exhibits trends in the predicted direction for both ratings, with less involved and less confident respondents showing greater race-of-interviewer effects. The trends are not significant at the .05 level, however, and hence cannot be taken as established on the basis of the present data.

[29] The following three items were used:
1. "A child should never be allowed to talk back to his parents or else he will lose respect for them. Would you mostly agree or disagree?"
2. "If a child is unusual in any way, his parents should try to get him to be more like other people. Would you mostly agree or disagree?"
3. "What do you think is the most important thing a child should learn: some say it is obedience and respect for authority; others say it is to be independent and decide things for himself. What do you think?"

[30] *Cf.* Philip E. Converse, "The Nature of Belief Systems in Mass Publics," in *Ideology and Discontent,* edited by David E. Apter, New York, Free Press, 1964.

CONCLUSIONS

This study of race-of-interviewer effects has shown that such effects continued to occur in 1968 in a major northern city. They are limited primarily to questions dealing with militant protest and hostility toward whites. Within this sphere, however, differences by race of interviewer tend to be as large as most associations treated as important by survey analysts. Indeed, when a 12-item scale is created from militancy items showing large interviewer effects, race of interviewer accounts for a quarter of its reliable variance. Questions dealing with reports of discrimination and basic living conditions, on the other hand, show very little interviewer effect. Matters of personal and family background, including direct indicators of social status, also show little influence from race of interviewer.

We were only partly successful in locating segments of the black population especially susceptible to interviewer effects. The clearest finding is that effects are a good deal stronger at the lowest status levels than at the upper levels; when our black sample is divided into three income categories, the association of race of interviewer to militancy is six times greater at the bottom than at the top. On the other hand, contrary to expectations, interviewer effects do not lessen noticeably among younger blacks or those born in the North.

So far as we can tell from indirect evidence, race-of-interviewer effects involve primarily black suppression or repression of existing attitudes when interviews are carried out by whites, rather than the arousal of more militant sentiments when the interviewers are black. However, one of the largest effects discovered in this study occurs not on a militancy question but rather on one calling simply for the names of the respondent's favorite entertainers. Black entertainers are mentioned much more to black interviewers, white entertainers to white interviewers. The nonthreatening nature of the question and the symmetrical distribution of the responses suggest that interviewer effects may be partly a frame-of-reference phenomenon. Given the amorphous and shifting nature of human attitudes and beliefs, the race of the interviewer (and of the Other more generally) may crystallize attitudes in a direction not previously known for certain even to the respondent. Whatever the truth of such speculations, future race-of-interviewer studies need to address themselves squarely to issues of validity in all their complexity.[31]

[31] We noted earlier that attitudes toward a white candidate for mayor in Detroit showed interviewer effects. A way of exploring validation in this case would be to obtain post-election reports of actual voting behavior to compare with pre-election sentiments toward the candidates.

The Effect of
Interviewer Characteristics and
Expectations on Response

ELEANOR SINGER, MARTIN R. FRANKEL,
AND MARC B. GLASSMAN

AFTER a period of relative neglect, interviewer effects in social surveys are beginning to receive increasing attention.[1] This paper presents the results of an investigation of such effects in telephone interviews, in a study which replicates many of the questions asked earlier both by Singer and Kohnke-Aguirre (1979) and by Sudman and his colleagues (1977) in personal interviews.

Although the effects so far documented in personal interviews have been modest,[2] the potential for bias is much more serious in telephone

[1] For a review of earlier research, see Sudman and Bradburn (1974) or Weiss (1975). For another recent study see Tucker (1983).

[2] Sudman and his colleagues (1977), for example, found that interviewers generally accounted for about 7 percent of the variance when the proportion explained was measured by the ratio of the sum of squares between interviewers to the total sum of squares, and about 2 percent when measured by w^2, which corrects for the number of interviewers. In the present study, the variance explained by the uncorrected measure ranged from .03 to .09.

Abstract This study reports on two sets of findings related to interviewer effects, derived from a national RDD sample of the adult population. The first of these concerns the effect of interviewer characteristics and expectations on overall cooperation rates; the second, the effect of interviewer characteristics and expectations on item nonresponse and response quality. We found that interviewers' age, the size of the interviewing assignment, and interviewers' expectations all had a strong effect on overall cooperation rates; the relation of experience to response rate was curvilinear in this sample. Age and education have consistent but statistically insignificant effects on item nonresponse. The effect of interviewers' expectations on responses within the interview resembles that in earlier studies, but is less pronounced and less consistent.

Eleanor Singer is a Senior Research Associate at the Center for the Social Sciences. Martin R. Frankel is Professor of Statistics at Baruch College, CUNY. Marc B. Glassman is an independent statistical consultant in New York City. The authors wish to thank Ed Blair, Charles F. Cannell, Howard Schuman, and Seymour Sudman for reading and commenting on an earlier draft of the paper. The research was made possible by grant SES-78-19797 to the senior author.

interviews, where typically fewer interviewers take a much larger number of interviews. Consequently, the effect of each interviewer's performance on response rate and response quality is magnified many times. At the same time, the fact that each interviewer on a telephone survey can be assigned to a random sample of respondents makes such effects easier to investigate and avoids the methodological weaknesses plaguing the studies by Singer and Kohnke-Aguirre and by Sudman et al., namely, the confounding of area and interviewer effects.

The study reported here replicates important features of both studies mentioned above. It was done by the same survey organization—NORC, used a virtually identical survey instrument, and used identical questions for measuring interviewer expectations, plus some additional questions.

There were also several important differences. The present study was carried out by telephone, rather than in person, and with a largely inexperienced interviewing staff. Whereas only experienced interviewers had been used in both earlier studies, and 27 of the 59 who had worked on the Sudman study participated in the Singer study as well, 80 percent of the staff on the phone survey had had less than a year's interviewing experience, or none at all.[3] Furthermore, although women were used in all three studies, the staffs for the personal interview surveys were largely white, whereas the staff for the phone survey was 80 percent black. Finally, whereas 70 interviewers had worked on the earlier Singer study, only 35 interviewers were used in the present one.

The primary purpose of the phone survey, like the earlier study by Singer, was to assess the effect of informed consent procedures on response rates and response quality in social surveys, or, more generally, to investigate the effect of variations in the introduction to the interview on response. (For a detailed description of the research design, see Singer and Frankel, 1981.) The study utilized an RDD sample of telephone numbers, stratified by area and exchange, each

---

[3] Hindsight suggests a number of reasons for this. To begin with, having each interviewer work on a small replicate national sample meant that she had to be able to work both daytime and evening hours in order to screen the relatively large number of nonworking, nonhousehold numbers included in her assignment. In addition, in order to complete the field work in a reasonable time, interviewers had to commit themselves to working about 30 hours a week, including at least one weekend day, for a period of about six weeks. Finally, in order to permit data entry and updating of assignments, interviewers could work only every other day. These constraints, together with (1) location of NORC's telephone facility on Chicago's South Side, (2) restriction of the interviewing staff to women, in order to parallel the staffing on the earlier study, and (3) hiring during August and September, when few students were available, made recruitment of interviewers very difficult.

number being linked from the time of its generation with one of the four experimental treatments (introductions). Interviewers were required to list (by age) all household members and to select the appropriate respondent according to a sampling table.

Two strategies were developed in order to balance interviewer effects in the study and to permit their analysis. First, separate national RDD replicate samples were generated for each interviewer, each consisting of four "pools" of numbers, one for each of the four experimental treatments. Second, only a small subset of the telephone numbers from each of the four pools was assigned to an interviewer at one time, the assignment of new numbers being based on how many interviews of each experimental treatment an interviewer had already attempted—an attempt being defined as completion of the screening interview and identification of the respondent.[4] Ideally, this method would have equalized the number of attempts of each of the four treatments by each interviewer; in practice, because we did not use an on-line system and because of the need to consolidate interviewing assignments for economic reasons, we approximated but did not achieve equality.[5]

The interview schedule was substantially the same as that used in the earlier study of informed consent in personal interviews (Singer, 1978). Following some questions about conventional leisure activities were sections dealing with emotional well-being and mental health, drinking, marijuana use, and sexual behavior. A number of demographic items, among them income, were also included. Also measured were respondents' opinions about a number of ethical issues in survey research, as well as their reactions to the interview.

Prior to the start of field work, each interviewer completed a short questionnaire designed to measure her attitude toward the survey instrument, the informed consent variables, and the expected difficulty of screening households, persuading respondents to be interviewed, and asking the questions. We also obtained information about such background variables as age, education, and prior interviewing experience. In the following section, we explore the effect of these demographic characteristics and attitudinal variables on response

---

[4] In order to achieve a completed sample of about 1,100 interviews with a staff of 35 interviewers, we began with 40 interviewing assignments consisting of four samples of 750 numbers each, the numbers from all four samples being presented to interviewers in one randomized sequence. Each interviewer's assignment was to complete 12 attempts for each treatment, or 48 attempts altogether.

[5] Variations by interviewer in the number of attempts per treatment were relatively small, but variations among interviewers in the total number of interviews they attempted were sizable, ranging from less than 10 to 187.

rates to the survey as a whole. We then investigate the effect of these variables on item nonresponse and response quality.

Effect of Interviewers' Characteristics and Expectations on Response Rates to the Survey

The overall completion rate for the study was 52.4 percent. This figure is significantly lower than that in Singer's previous study of informed consent in personal interviews, which achieved an average completion rate of 67 percent, and those in other national RDD telephone surveys (e.g., those reported by Groves and Kahn, 1979), which have generally achieved an average completion rate of about 70 percent.

The low completion rate is *not* primarily a consequence of difficulties in screening households; some 86.1 percent of the telephone households were screened, compared with 87 percent of those in the personal interview sample.[6] Instead, the difficulty apparently lies in persuading respondents to participate in the interview, once they have been selected by probability methods. Only 60.9 percent of the selected respondents in the telephone survey ultimately agreed to be interviewed, compared to 77 percent of those in the personal interview informed consent sample.

Nor is this low response rate a function of the experimental variables themselves; differences among the four conditions were not large and were not statistically significant. By contrast, screening rates among interviewers ranged from 67.4 percent to 100 percent, and response rates from 42.9 percent to 95.7 percent.[7] Completion rates ranged from 35.7 percent to 91.7 percent.[8]

In an effort to understand the reasons for these variations, we investigated the effect of all the interviewers' demographic characteristics on which we had information, as well as all the attitudinal variables with a zero-order correlation of .20 or higher with either the screening rate or the response rate. (Distributions of responses to the expectation questions are shown in Table 1.) Those with correlations

---

[6] Three measures of cooperation are distinguished in this study. The *screening rate* is defined as the number of respondents selected divided by the number of household numbers minus ineligible informants and non-English-speaking informants. The *response rate* is defined as the number of interviews completed divided by the number of respondents selected minus non-English-speaking respondents. The *completion rate* is the product of the screening rate and the response rate.

[7] Although the response rate is defined independently of the screening rate, the two are modestly intercorrelated: $r = .23$; $p = .106$.

[8] In the personal interview study by Singer (1978), response rates varied from 27.2 to 93.3, and screening rates from 33.3 to 1.00.

Table 1. Interviewers' Expectations of Difficulty in Screening Households, Administering Questionnaires, and Asking Questions on Specified Topics (N = 35)

Expectation About:	Very Easy (%)	Moderately Easy (%)	About Average[a] (%)	Moderately Difficult (%)	Very Difficult (%)
Screening households	6	34	43	17	0
Persuading respondents to take part	3	29	35	29	3
Asking questions (on this survey)	37	40	11	11	0
Asking questions about:					
Sports	80	17	3	0	0
Happiness and well-being	69	23	9	0	0
Evaluations of this interview	60	29	6	3	3
Attitudes toward surveys	60	26	9	6	0
Religion	57	20	17	3	3
Drinking beer, wine or liquor	46	40	11	3	0
Race	43	29	14	11	3
Mental health	40	17	23	9	11
Using marijuana	32	18	24	18	9
Getting drunk	29	26	26	15	3
Income	26	26	29	14	6
Petting and kissing	21	21	32	21	6
Intercourse	11	14	34	20	20

[a] For the first three questions in Table 1, the heading for this response was "neither easy nor difficult"; for the remainder, it was "about average."

above .20 with the *screening* rate included interviewers' expectations concerning the ease of asking questions on this survey; their expectations concerning the ease of asking questions about marijuana and mental health; their expectations about the effect of giving respondents information about the content of the study ahead of time; and their belief that the benefits of surveys outweigh their burden on respondents. Attitudinal variables that were correlated at .20 or better with the *response* rate included interviewers' expectations about the ease of asking questions about marijuana, drinking, and mental health, and expectations about the ease of persuading respondents to agree to an interview.

The demographic variables (age, education, race, and prior interviewing experience) were entered into the regression equation first, as a block, in order to let them explain as much of the variation in cooperation rates as possible. Also included in the first block of variables was the number of cases assigned to each interviewer, which had a substantial negative zero-order correlation with cooperation rates. The attitudinal variables were entered as a second block.

Because we were especially interested in the effect of interviewers' expectations concerning cooperation rates, these variables were included in the equations regardless of their correlation with the dependent variables.

For ease of presentation, the results of these analyses are displayed in the form of a multiple classification analysis in Table 2. Variables which had no significant effect on the dependent variables in the exploratory regressions were dropped from the final equations shown.[9]

As can be seen from Table 2, age, experience, and the number of cases assigned to an interviewer all had a sizable effect on both the

Table 2. Screening and Response Rates, by Interviewers' Demographic Characteristics[a]

	N	Screening Rate	N	Response Rate
Age				
18–21	9	81.5 (79.3)	9	63.4 (61.2)
22–34	11	90.8 (89.7)	10	69.1 (65.9)
35+	11	89.1* (92.0)	11	72.1 (76.8)
Experience				
None	13	83.2 (82.3)	12	70.0 (68.5)
Less than one year	12	91.0 (90.7)	12	73.1 (71.4)
One or more years	6	89.1* (92.3)	6	56.3* (62.7)
Number of cases				
07–30	13	91.3 (91.2)	13	77.8 (79.4)
46–79	11	85.1 (84.1)	10	62.4 (62.8)
88–224	7	84.2* (86.0)	7	60.0* (56.3)
Expectations about response rate				
Moderately easy	11	—	11	77.37 (78.9)
Neither easy nor difficult	10	—	10	65.48 (65.9)
Moderately difficult	9	—	9	60.94*(58.6)
		$R^2 = .593$		$R^2 = .800$

* $p\ (F) < .05$.

[a] Cell entries are mean scores, adjusted by MCA for the other variables in the equation, which has been reestimated to include only those variables identified as significant in earlier models. Unadjusted scores are shown in parentheses.

[9] We experimented with other forms of these equations, substituting phone interviewing experience for interviewing experience in general, a logarithmic transformation of an ungrouped age variable, a squared term to represent the curvilinear relationship of experience to both the screening and the response rate, and a logarithmic transformation of the ungrouped variable representing caseload.

The best-fitting alternative equation for response rate included categorical versions of age, cases, and experience; a squared term for experience; and the expectations variable. All of these had statistically significant effects on the response rate, together explaining 71 percent of the variance.

For the screening rate, the best-fitting alternative equation includes the categorical versions of age, experience, and cases, and a squared term to represent the bend in the regression line for experience. Together, these account for 43.5 percent of the variance, considerably less than in the case of the response rate. The expectations variable is not significant.

screening rate and the response rate. (Education was positively, but not significantly, related to both screening and response rates; race had no significant effect on either rate.) Older interviewers had a greater likelihood of screening households and persuading respondents to be interviewed, although, so far as screening rates are concerned, it might be more nearly correct to describe extreme youth as a penalty rather than age as an advantage: Interviewers who were between the ages of 18 and 21 had an adjusted screening rate of 81.5; those between 22 and 34, 90.8; and those who were 35 or older, 89.1.

The number of cases assigned to an interviewer had a powerful negative effect on both screening and response rates, especially on the latter, where the difference between interviewers assigned 7 to 30 cases and those assigned 88 to 224 cases was almost 18 percentage points. We do not know the reasons for this effect. Heavy caseloads were largely the result of consolidation of assignments toward the end of the interviewing period, and a number of factors may have contributed to the observed association: (1) Cases remaining at the end of the interviewing period may have been the more difficult cases; (2) there was less time to follow up these cases; (3) interviewers may have become discouraged or fatigued by the heavy assignments, especially when combined with the other two factors.

Experience is the only variable we examined whose effect was counter-intuitive, especially in the case of response rates. In screening households, interviewers with some experience achieved more success than those with none; but beyond a year, the benefit of experience levels off and may even decline. In the case of response rates, the gain with initial experience is more modest, and the drop beyond one year is precipitous. We have been unable either to analyze away this result (e.g., by transforming variables) or to account for it (e.g., although the experience variable measures face-to-face experience, all but one of those who had done face-to-face interviewing also had telephone experience). This result, however, is based on only six interviewers.

When the attitudinal variables were examined with demographic characteristics controlled, none of them had a significant effect on the screening rate. Expectations about the ease of persuading respondents to be interviewed, however, had a strong and significant effect on response rate. Interviewers who expected that it would be easy to achieve cooperation had a response rate of 77.8; those who expected it to be neither easy nor difficult, 62.4; and those who expected it to be moderately difficult, 60.0.[10]

---

[10] Only one interviewer expected it to be "very" easy and one "very" difficult; these were grouped with the moderates.

Such an effect of expectations on response rate—which persists in the face of a variety of controls—was not found by either Sudman and his colleagues or by Singer and Kohnke-Aguirre,[11] but the expectations question in both of these studies differed somewhat from that in the present one.

Intrigued by the unexpectedly robust effect of interviewers' expectations, we looked at the demographic and attitudinal characteristics available to us to see whether any of them would predict such expectations. Two of the variables we examined were significantly related to expectations concerning the ease of screening households: prior phone experience, and expectations about how easy or difficult it would be to ask the questions on this survey. Similarly, two variables were significantly related to interviewers' expectations concerning the ease of persuading respondents to be interviewed: Older interviewers were more sanguine; and those who had a more optimistic view of the effect of giving respondents information about content also expected to have an easier time persuading them to agree to be interviewed.

Given the very small number of interviewers,[12] we do not want to overclaim these findings. Nevertheless, they do suggest that interviewers' attitudes toward what they are asked to do may be more important than the task itself. In this study, variations in the introduction to the interview had no discernible effect on response; but interviewers' attitudes toward the introduction were related to their expectations of response rates, and such expectations, in turn, influenced the response rates they achieved. It is possible, of course, that attitudes toward the introduction and expectations of response both reflect more general attitudes of optimism or pessimism on the part of interviewers, and such measures should be included in future research.

Effect of Interviewers' Characteristics and Expectations on Item Nonresponse and Response Quality

In addition to looking at the effects of interviewers' characteristics and expectations on their achieved response rates to the survey, we

---

[11] The latter did, however, find an effect of general expectations on item nonresponse and response quality. See Singer and Kohnke-Aguirre, 1979: 251–52.

[12] The four interviewers whose cooperation rates were based on fewer than seven households were excluded from the analyses, which are based on an N of 31. The group is not only small, but also skewed with respect to most of the variables of interest to us: 25 of the 31 interviewers were black; 9 were between the ages of 18 and 21, and only 11 were over 35; 13 had never interviewed before, and 12 others had had less than a year's experience. The group of most experienced interviewers contains only six cases.

also examined the effect of these variables on response rates to individual items and on response quality.[13]

EFFECT OF EXPECTATIONS OF GENERAL DIFFICULTY IN ASKING QUESTIONS

All interviewers were asked, "How easy or difficult do you expect it will be to ask the questions on this study?" Distributions of responses are shown in Table 1.

Unlike the Singer and Kohnke-Aguirre study, the present study found no indication that interviewers who expected questions to be "very easy" to ask had lower item nonresponse rates than those whose expectations were less optimistic. Table 3 includes all questions to which the nonresponse rate totaled 3 percent or more; on only 6 of the 23 do interviewers who expected the questions to be "very easy" have lower nonresponse rates than interviewers who expected them to be moderately easy. Even if the comparison is limited to questions on sensitive topics identical to those analyzed in the in-person survey (the first 11 questions in Table 3), only 4 of the 11 show this particular pattern. If anything, the findings appear to be the reverse of those hypothesized: Interviewers who expect questions to be "very easy" to ask tend to have *higher* nonresponse rates than those with lower expectations.

Nor is there any indication that expectations of general difficulty affected the *quality* of response obtained by interviewers. Table 4 shows data for the same items as those analyzed in the earlier study, with the exception of questions about masturbation, which were not included in the telephone survey. Differences among groups of interviewers with differing expectations are not statistically significant, nor is there any consistent tendency for those with the most optimistic expectations to obtain the greatest acknowledgment of sensitive behavior.

EFFECT OF EXPECTATIONS OF SECTION DIFFICULTY

Besides being asked how easy or difficult they expected the questions in general to be, interviewers were asked about their expectations concerning each section; the distributions of responses to these questions are also shown in Table 1. Table 5, which is identical to Table 3 except for the omission of the four items on informed consent

---

[13] Although in this analysis interviewer expectations are treated as a characteristic of respondents, computations of statistical significance are based on an N of 35 interviewers. While this is an approximation of the results that would be obtained if averages were calculated for each interviewer, it yields a more conservative estimate than would be obtained if an N of 1,016 were used.

Table 3. Item[a] Nonresponse,[b] by Interviewers' Expectations Concerning Ease of Asking Questions

| | Item Nonresponse | | |
| | Very Easy (%) | Moderately Easy (%) | Neither Easy Nor Difficult/ Moderately Difficult (%) |
Item			
No. of friends who smoke pot	10.7	8.4	8.7
No. of joints smoked	5.2	0.9	6.6
No. of friends drunk	9.0	8.4	5.2
No. of beers per time[c]	2.7	4.3	3.8
No. of wines per time[c]	3.1	4.1	3.7
No. of drinks per time[c]	6.9	4.6	4.7
No. of times drunk[c]	1.3	3.9	0.5
Petting during last month	4.1	2.0	0.9
Sex during past month	5.3	3.7	1.7
No. of times sex[c]	4.4	8.5	5.8
Earned income	11.9	7.4	7.0
Attitude toward surveys[c]	3.0	4.0	1.9
Organization doing survey	27.3	31.5	28.8
Information about purpose	5.1	2.7	0.4
More info about purpose	6.2	3.0	2.6
Income from Social Security	4.7	2.0	1.7
Income from pensions	5.3	1.3	2.2
Income from interest	5.3	1.3	2.6
Income from dividends	5.5	1.3	3.1
Income from welfare	5.3	1.3	3.5
Income from unemployment	5.3	1.3	3.9
Income from friends	5.3	1.3	4.4
Income from other sources	5.5	3.4	5.7
N Interviewers/N Respondents[d]	13/487	14/298	22/229

[a] All items with a nonresponse rate of more than 3 percent are included in this table.

[b] "Nonresponse" includes refused, don't know, and not asked.

[c] Subquestions asked of part of sample only.

[d] The number of respondents varies from item to item, depending on whether a question was asked of the total sample or a subsample. Numbers shown here are for the total sample. As noted in the text, the number of respondents interviewed also varied considerably from one interviewer to another. None of the comparisons are significant when evaluated on the basis of interviewer, rather than respondent, N's.

issues, shows the nonresponse rates obtained by interviewers with varying expectations about the difficulty of each of the corresponding sections.

Here, for the first time, there is some suggestion of an interviewer expectation effect. On 11 of the 13 items asked of the total sample, interviewers who expected a section to be "very easy" obtained lower nonresponse rates than those who expected that section to be moderately or very difficult, though none of the differences are statistically significant and the increases over the four categories of the expecta-

Table 4. Responses[a] to Selected Items,[b] by Interviewers' Expectations Concerning Ease of Asking Questions

Item	Very Easy	Moderately Easy	Neither Easy Nor Difficult/ Moderately Difficult
Petting during past month	.76	.79	.77
Sex during past month	.65	.70	.68
Ever drank liquor	.83	.81	.82
No. of friends drunk	1.27	1.17	1.13
Ever smoked pot	.37	.40	.38
No. of friends who smoke	1.06	.95	1.07
Earned income	16,300	16,500	17,600
Langner score	3.25	3.30	3.22
N Interviewers/N Respondents[c]	13/487	14/298	22/229

[a] Mean scores (income, Langner score, no. of friends drunk, no. of friends who smoke pot) or proportion saying yes. Scores are adjusted by means of MCA for interviewers' education, age, and prior phone experience.

[b] The items were selected to match those in Singer and Kohnke-Aguirre (1979). No question about masturbation was asked on the phone survey, however.

[c] The number of respondents varies from item to item, depending on whether a question was asked of the total sample or a subsample. Numbers shown here are for the total sample. As noted in the text, the number of respondents interviewed also varied considerably from one interviewer to another.

tion variable are not monotonic. Parallel findings were obtained among interviewers varying in experience, though it is the group without *any* experience in which the effect is most pronounced, with all 13 comparisons showing the pattern described above.

Table 6, which shows mean responses (either the proportion saying yes, or mean scores) to eight items asked of the total sample, likewise contains modest evidence for the operation of interviewer expectation effects. On six of the eight, interviewers who expected a section to be moderately or very difficult obtained lower estimates from respondents than interviewers who expected it to be very easy. But again, differences are neither monotonic nor significant.

The evidence for the effect of interviewer expectations on item nonresponse and response quality is, thus, considerably more tenuous in this study than in the preceding one. Some possible reasons for this are discussed in the concluding section.

EFFECTS OF INTERVIEWERS' DEMOGRAPHIC
CHARACTERISTICS

In addition to interviewers' expectations, we examined the effect of three demographic characteristics on item nonresponse and response quality: previous phone experience, education, and age. Previous experience with telephone interviews had no apparent effect on item

Table 5. Item Nonresponse, by Expected Section Difficulty

| | Item Nonresponse | | | |
| | Very Easy (%) | Moderately Easy (%) | Neither Easy Nor Difficult (%) | Moderately/ Very Difficult (%) |
Item				
No. of friends who smoke pot	12.2 (303)[a]	13.5 (126)	7.4 (324)	7.3 (260)
No. of joints smoked	3.6 (110)	4.9 (41)	3.4 (116)	5.8 (104)
No. of beers per time	4.2 (283)	3.2 (379)	2.5 (120)	
No. of wines per time	4.5 (287)	3.1 (390)	2.7 (146)	
No. of drinks per time	7.5 (292)	3.4 (383)	8.2 (146)	
No. of times drunk	3.3 (209)	0.5 (188)	1.4 (289)	2.4 (124)
No. of friends drunk	8.4 (273)	12.9 (233)	4.0 (351)	9.0 (156)
Petting during past month	1.8 (226)	1.8 (114)	1.5 (270)	4.5 (403)
Sex during past month	2.3 (128)	3.3 (151)	1.6 (246)	7.1 (351)/ 2.9 (138)[b]
No. of times sex	7.1 (85)	8.9 (90)	7.1 (183)	4.2 (216)/ 4.0 (99)[b]
Earned income	12.5 (263)	10.1 (358)	6.1 (257)	8.1 (136)
Income from Social Security	0.8 (263)	5.3 (358)	3.1 (257)	2.9 (136)
Income from pensions	1.9 (263)	5.3 (358)	2.7 (257)	2.9 (136)
Income from interest	2.3 (263)	5.3 (358)	2.7 (257)	2.9 (136)
Income from dividends	2.7 (263)	5.3 (358)	2.7 (257)	3.7 (136)
Income from welfare	2.3 (263)	5.3 (358)	2.7 (257)	4.4 (136)
Income from unemployment	2.7 (263)	5.0 (358)	2.7 (257)	5.1 (136)
Income from friends	2.3 (263)	5.0 (358)	3.1 (257)	5.9 (136)
Income from other sources	3.0 (263)	5.9 (358)	3.9 (257)	8.1 (136)

[a] Numbers shown are for respondents. For the number of interviewers who consider each section "very easy," "moderately easy," etc., see Table 1. None of the differences are significant when evaluated on the basis of interviewer, rather than respondent, N's.

[b] The second set of figures refers to interviewers who expected these questions to be "very difficult" to ask.

nonresponse. Interviewers with prior phone experience did tend to elicit "better" responses (i.e., more acknowledgment) to most of the drinking questions, though few of the differences were significant. On the more sensitive items, prior phone experience made no difference in response quality.

The effects of education on item nonresponse, while not significant, are nevertheless consistent: Interviewers with a college or graduate degree tend to have the lowest nonresponse rate; those without any college education, the highest. However, education does not appear to be consistently related to response quality.

The effect of age on item nonresponse parallels its effect on overall response rates. The youngest interviewers tend to have the highest item nonresponse rates, especially on questions pertaining to income; but, because of the small numbers involved, these effects are not statistically significant. There is no discernible effect of interviewer age on response quality.

Table 6. Responses[a] to Selected Items,[b] by Expected Section Difficulty

Item	Very Easy	Moderately Easy	Neither Easy Nor Difficult	Moderately/ Very Difficult
Ever smoked pot	.40 (293)[c]	.34 (125)	.38 (311)	.38 (255)
No. of friends who smoke pot	1.10 (262)	.90 (108)	1.00 (290)	1.05 (237)
Petting during last month	.77 (219)	.73 (111)	.84 (259)	.73 (395)
Sex during past month	.75 (125)	.60 (145)	.74 (239)	.61 (342)/ .71 (134)[d]
Langner score	3.40 (381)	3.41 (155)	3.03 (209)	3.13 (232)
Earned income	16,700 (224)	15,700 (315)	17,500 (234)	17,600 (124)
Ever drank liquor	.84 (354)	.82 (457)	.78 (174)	
No. of friends drunk	1.28 (243)	1.14 (197)	1.17 (332)	1.30 (139)

[a] Mean scores (income, Langner score, no. of friends drunk, no. of friends who smoke pot) or proportion saying yes. Scores are adjusted by means of MCA for interviewers' education, age, and prior phone experience.

[b] The items were selected to match those in Singer and Kohnke-Aguirre (1979). No question about masturbation was asked on the phone survey, however.

[c] Numbers shown are for respondents. For the number of interviewers who consider each section "very easy," "moderately easy," etc., see Table 1. None of the differences are significant when evaluated on the basis of interviewer, rather than respondent, N's.

[d] The second set of figures refers to interviewers who expected these questions to be "very difficult" to ask. On other questions too few interviewers selected this category to permit a separate analysis.

Summary and Conclusions

This article has reported two sets of findings related to interviewer effects: the effect of interviewer characteristics and expectations on overall cooperation rates, and the effect of interviewer characteristics and expectations on item nonresponse rates and response quality.

With respect to overall cooperation rates, we found that age was significantly related both to screening and to response rates: Older interviewers obtained better cooperation. This effect was independent of their interviewing experience, suggesting that some quality associated with age—perhaps self-confidence, perhaps a tone of voice that respondents find reassuring—is responsible for the effect.

Some experience is better than none, with respect to both screening and response rates. But with longer experience, the screening rate levels off and the response rate actually declines. We have not been able to account for this paradoxical finding. However, because of the small number of interviewers involved and the disproportionate number of young and inexperienced interviewers among them, these findings await replication with larger and more representative samples.

The size of the interviewing assignment had a negative effect on both screening and response rates, but we do not know whether this is because interviewers' motivation declines with large assignments or because these assignments include an unusually large number of difficult cases.

None of the attitudinal variables we examined had a significant effect on the screening rate. Interviewers' expectations about the ease of persuading respondents to be interviewed did, however, have a strong and significant effect on the response rate. Interviewers whose attitudes were more optimistic achieved significantly higher response rates than those with less sanguine expectations.

Although in the present study we have been able to demonstrate the effect of interviewers' expectations on response rates, we have so far been unable to account for much of the variation in such expectations. Of the admittedly few characteristics on which we have information, only two were significantly related to expectations concerning response: age, and beliefs about the effect of disclosing more information about content ahead of time. Although these variables do not predict much of the variation in expectations, they do suggest that interviewers' attitudes toward a questionnaire are potentially more important than the questionnaire itself in influencing the response rate to the survey.

The second set of findings we have reported pertains to the effect of interviewers' expectations and characteristics on item nonresponse and response quality. Prior phone experience had no effect on item nonresponse and very little on response quality, but such differences as existed favored interviewers with experience. Interviewers with more education tended to obtain lower item nonresponse rates, although education had no consistent effect on response quality. Finally, the effect of age on item nonresponse paralleled its effect on overall response rate to the survey, although because of the small number of interviewers differences were not statistically significant. There were no consistent or significant effects of age on response quality.

Results from the present study provide only partial replication of the effects of interviewers' expectations previously reported by Sudman and his colleagues and by Singer and Kohnke-Aguirre. Interviewers' expectations about the ease of asking questions "on this survey" have no discernible effect on response quality; the effect on item nonresponse tends, if anything, in a direction opposite to that anticipated. The effect of expectations concerning the difficulty of individual sections resembles that found in earlier studies but is less pronounced and less consistent.

There are several possible reasons for these differences between studies. First, the present study, unlike either of the two earlier ones, was done by phone rather than in person; and it is possible that interviewer expectations achieve their effect on responses to individual items more readily in personal than in telephone interviews.

Second, the response rate to the present survey was much lower than that to the personal interview study, and it is possible that interviewer expectations have effects on responses to individual questions only "at the margin": if "marginal" respondents refuse to be interviewed altogether, interviewer expectations may exert little or no further effects.

Finally, the failure to find strong or consistent interviewer expectation effects on individual questions may be attributable to the relatively small variation among interviewers in their expectations of how difficult it would be to ask the questions on this survey. Both of the earlier studies providing a baseline for comparison exhibited a greater spread in the responses to these questions.

Unfortunately, the findings reported in this paper raise more questions than they answer. The possibility afforded by telephone interviews, of assigning cases to interviewers at random, means that interviewer effects can be investigated systematically. We have found—as, indeed, other investigators have—that such effects are much more powerful, at least so far as overall cooperation to the survey is concerned, than the introduction to the interview itself. But because of the small group of interviewers and the skewed distribution of interviewer characteristics such as age and experience, we are much less certain of the variables that produce these effects, or of the reasons why they do so. Even the finding in the present study that interviewer characteristics, including expectations, have little discernible effect on responses to individual questions is subject to the suspicion that had the overall response rate to the survey been higher, these effects might have been larger.

Such sources of total survey error as question order and question wording are receiving a great deal of scrutiny. The findings reported here suggest that research on interviewer effects, relatively neglected of late, deserves much more attention than it has yet received.

References

Groves, Robert M., and Robert L. Kahn
   1979   Surveys by Telephone: A National Comparison with Personal Interviews. New York: Academic Press.
Hyman, H. H., et al.
   1954   Interviewing in Social Research. Chicago: University of Chicago Press.

Singer, Eleanor
   1978 "Informed consent: effects on response rate and response quality in social
         surveys." American Sociological Review 43:144–62.
Singer, Eleanor, and Luane Kohnke-Aguirre
   1979 "Interviewer expectation effects: a replication and extension." Public Opinion
         Quarterly 43:245–60.
Singer, Eleanor, and Martin R. Frankel
   1982 "Informed consent procedures in telephone interviews." American Sociologi-
         cal Review 47:416–26.
Sudman, Seymour, and Norman M. Bradburn
   1974 "Response effects in surveys." Chicago: Aldine.
Sudman, Seymour, Norman M. Bradburn, Ed Blair, and Carol Stocking
   1977 "Modest expectations: the effects of interviewers' prior expectations on re-
         sponse." Sociological Methods and Research 6:177–82.
Tucker, Clyde
   1983 "Interviewer effects in telephone surveys." Public Opinion Quarterly
         47:84–95.
Weiss, Carol H.
   1975 "Interviewing in evaluation research." Pp. 355–96 in Elmer L. Struening and
         Marcia Guttentag (eds.), Handbook of Evaluation Research, Vol. 1. Beverly
         Hills, Calif.: Sage.

Measuring and Explaining Interviewer Effects in Centralized Telephone Surveys

ROBERT M. GROVES AND LOU J. MAGILAVY

INTERVIEWER variance or interviewer effects reflect the tendency for answers provided by the respondent and recorded in a questionnaire to vary depending on which interviewer is assigned to the respondent. In order to obtain estimates of these effects, "interpenetrated" designs are typically introduced, which randomly assign sample cases to interviewers. Although several researchers have touted the possibility of cheap interpenetration in centralized telephone surveys (see Groves and Kahn, 1979; Tucker, 1983), routine measurement has been found to be a greater challenge than previously assumed. This article sum-

Abstract Estimates of interviewer effects on survey statistics are examined from nine surveys conducted over a six-year period at the Survey Research Center. Estimates of intraclass correlations associated with interviewers are found to be unstable, given the number of interviewers (30–40) used on most surveys. This finding calls into question inference from earlier studies of interviewer effects. To obtain more reliable information about magnitudes of interviewer effects, generalized effects are constructed by cumulating estimates over statistics and surveys. These generalized correlations are found to be somewhat smaller than those reported in the past literature. Few differences in generalized interviewer effect measures are found between open and closed questions or between factual and attitudinal questions. Small reductions in effects *were* obtained when a Computer Assisted Telephone Interviewing (CATI) system was used; there was some evidence of elderly respondents being more susceptible to interviewer effects; the number and type of second responses to open questions were affected by interviewer behavior; and changes in interviewing techniques reduced interviewer effects.

Robert M. Groves is an Associate Research Scientist in the Survey Research Center and an Associate Professor in the Department of Sociology at The University of Michigan. Lou J. Magilavy is a Ph.D. candidate in the Department of Biostatistics at The University of Michigan. Data in this article were collected in projects supported by the National Science Foundation and the National Center for Health Statistics. The views in this article do not necessarily represent those of either organization. An earlier version of this article was presented at the meetings of the International Statistical Institute, 1983. The authors appreciate the comments of Leslie Kish, Stanley Presser, and Howard Schuman on earlier versions, and extend their gratitude to Richard Curtin for access to the data from the Surveys of Consumer Attitudes.

marizes six years of research in the measurement of interviewer effects in centralized telephone surveys, on topics ranging from health experiences to political attitudes. We attempt to address two weaknesses in past research—problems of estimation (obtaining precise and accurate estimates of interviewer effects) and problems of explanation (learning what design features affect the magnitude of interviewer effects).

Study Designs

Eight of the nine surveys examined used a two-stage stratified national sample of randomly generated telephone numbers, following the design of Waksberg (1978). The ninth survey, the 1980 Post Election Study, was a telephone reinterview with respondents chosen earlier in an area probability sample. In all surveys one adult was randomly selected in each sample household. As shown in Table 1, response rates ranged from 59 percent to 87 percent, with unanswered numbers included in the denominators of these rates.[1] Row 4 lists the number of interviews obtained from the random assignment of telephone numbers to interviewers. Interviews resulting from nonrandom assignments (e.g., refusal conversions, select appointments) were excluded from both those numbers and the following analyses. Also presented is the number of interviewers employed for each study and the average workload (i.e., number of interviews) per interviewer. Not only does average workload vary across studies, from 12 for the November 1981 Survey of Consumer Attitudes to 58 for the Health in America Survey, but workloads within studies exhibit a similar degree of variation. All the studies collected standard demographic data in addition to data on the specific topics listed in Table 1. The 30 variables analyzed for the Survey of Consumer Attitudes are identical in each of the five months. The number of statistics analyzed for each study ranges from 25 to 55.

Estimation of Interviewer Effects

THE INTERVIEWER EFFECTS ESTIMATOR

To compare interviewer effects across statistics and to maximize comparability to past interviewer variance research we utilize an intraclass correlation, based on a one-way analysis of variance, using interviewers as the factor, $\rho_{int}^* = S_a^2/(S_a^2 + S_b^2)$, where S_a^2 is the between interviewer variance and S_b^2 is the within interviewer variance, with

---

[1] The lowest response rate, 59 percent, reported for the Study of Telephone Methodology reflects an exceptionally large proportion of unanswered numbers. In later studies, improved methods of identifying nonworking numbers have caused a decrease in this proportion and consequently a more accurate response rate.

Table 1. Study Descriptions and Summary of Overall Findings

Study Description and Summary Statistics	Study of Telephone Methodology	Health and Television Viewing	Health in America	1980 Post Election Study	Monthly Survey of Consumer Attitudes				
					Nov '81	Dec '81	Jan '82	Feb '82	Mar '82
Field period	Apr– May 1976	Mar– Apr 1979	Oct– Dec 1979	Nov– Dec 1980	Nov '81	Dec '81	Jan '82	Feb '82	Mar '82
Response rate	59%	67%	80%	87.3%	73.5%	72.8%	73.3%	76.9%	73.8%
No. interviewers	37	30	33	22	31	28	21	25	26
No. interviews	1529	954	1918	697	370	350	386	379	366
Average workload	41.3	31.8	58.1	31.7	11.9	12.5	18.4	15.2	14.1
Major topics	Political economic & social issues	Health and TV viewing	Health	Political issues	Economic issues	Economic issues	Economic issues	Economic issues	Economic issues
No. variables analyzed	25	55	23	42	30	30	30	30	30
Range of ρ^*_{int}	−.0080 .0560	−.0150 .1650	−.0070 .0097	−.0154 .1710	−.0217 .0895	−.0373 .0546	−.0221 .0916	−.0419 .0657	−.0356 .0729
Mean values									
ρ^*_{int}	.0089	.0074	.0018	.0086	.0184	.0057	.0163	.0090	.0067
$deff_{int}$	1.36	1.23	1.10	1.26	1.20	1.07	1.28	1.13	1.09

large positive values of ρ^*_{int} reflecting large interviewer effects. This is the measure described more fully by Kish (1962) and used frequently in this literature. His studies of factory workers' job attitudes produced ρ^*_{int}'s of −.03 to .09 (mean = .02). O'Muircheartaigh and Marckwardt (1980) presented fertility statistics most susceptible to interviewers, with ρ^*_{int}'s between .00 and .19 (mean = .07). Feather (1973) in a health survey found a range of ρ^*_{int}'s of −.01 to .03 (mean = .006). Freeman and Butler (1976), in a study of attitudes toward mental retardation, displayed unusually high values of ρ^*_{int} (mean = .04), that might be attributable to the use of nonprofessional interviewers. The overall average for all these statistics from personal interview surveys is .018. Tucker (1983) presented mean ρ^*_{int}'s from 11 telephone surveys ranging from −.003 to .008 (overall mean = .004) for political and social attitudes.[2]

For this research we estimated ρ^*_{int} after interpenetrating the sample within shifts of a centralized telephone interviewing facility. This randomization of assignment within shift is an added constraint on the model, the effect of which was judged to be negligible in these studies.[3]

It is important to realize that the effect of the interviewer on the overall variance of survey statistics is a function of ρ^*_{int} *and* the size of

[2] In citing previously published values of ρ^*_{int}, we note that most of these accounts provide poor descriptions of the survey design features that might affect interviewer errors—the question format and wording, interviewer training procedures, nonresponse and recording error differences across interviewers, and any other effects of the survey organization. Often only a small number of survey statistics are presented, sometimes only to illustrate the *largest* interviewer effects observed.

[3] A separate appendix describing interpenetration problems in a centralized facility is available from the authors.

the interviewer workload, m. The variance of a survey statistic is inflated by the factor $deff_{int} = [1 + \rho^*_{int}(m - 1)]$. Thus, if interviewers complete large numbers of cases, say 50, even ρ^*_{int}'s as small as .01 can inflate the variance by a factor of 1.5 over that expected without interviewer effects.[4]

Perhaps the most important weakness of the past research is the lack of attention to the stability of the ρ^*_{int} estimates. None of the studies above give guidance about whether similar effects might be expected in replications of the surveys. Given the model of interviewer effects, the precision of the ρ^*_{int} is a function of the number of interviewers used and the number of cases completed by each. Many of these studies used only a few interviewers, but the reader is not cautioned about the likelihood of different levels of interviewer effects being observed in replications of the survey.[5]

MAGNITUDES AND PRECISION OF ESTIMATED INTERVIEWER EFFECTS

In the space allowed it is impossible to describe the results of each study in detail, but Table 1 presents the range of ρ^*_{int} estimates obtained in each study, along with their mean values.[6] The average values of the ρ^*_{int}'s seem to lie below .01 over the nine surveys and to exhibit large variability over the different statistics examined. The highest average ρ^*_{int} (.0184) is found for one of the Consumer Attitude Surveys, but comparison over the other months for the same statistics shows means as low as .0057. The lowest average ρ^*_{int} (.0018) is found for a mainly factual survey on health conditions, Health in America. This survey also had the largest interviewer workload.[7]

Table 2 illustrates the importance of past studies' failure to measure the stability of ρ^*_{int} by presenting standard errors for 30 ρ^*_{int} statistics, 10 from each of three studies.[8] These standard errors are estimates of the

[4] This also implies that the inflation of variance is smaller for subclass statistics in the same survey, where m is smaller.

[5] Some authors base their conclusion that serious interviewer effects are present on the results of a standard F-test. This test is subject to several assumptions which may be violated. For example, the interviewer workloads often exhibit a great deal of variation and the variances within interviewer assignments may not be constant across interviewers.

[6] Some of the statistics are means computed on continuous variables. For discrete variables, ρ^*_{int} for the proportion choosing the modal response category is presented.

[7] This fact, together with other observations, has made us begin to consider enhancing the response error model underlying ρ^*_{int} to reflect larger interviewer variability during the initial cases completed by interviewers.

[8] In order to estimate the sampling variance of the ρ^*_{int}'s a jackknife estimator was used by dividing the sample into subsamples associated with each interviewer. Although the properties of the jackknife estimator are known in the case of a linear statistic, it has also performed well empirically for a variety of nonlinear estimators including regression and correlation coefficients (Kish and Frankel, 1972). These empirical results suggested its use in this case.

dispersion of the distribution of ρ^*_{int}'s over replications of the surveys, with variation due to the selection of different interviewers from the population of all interviewers and from sampling variability of the respondents. This table illustrates well the range and magnitude of ρ^*_{int} values estimated throughout the nine surveys. *The standard errors for the measures of interviewer effects are often larger in size than the estimates themselves,* leading one to conclude that the values of ρ^*_{int} presented here could have been much larger *or much smaller* had different sets of interviewers been chosen to work on the surveys.

In order to relate our results to past research, these standard error estimates can be used to illustrate the largest ρ^*_{int}'s likely to be encountered with these designs. If we assume that the ρ^*_{int}'s are distributed roughly according to a t-distribution, we can estimate the value beyond which only 10 percent of the ρ^*_{int} values lie. These are called the "maximum" values of ρ^*_{int} in Table 2. The values of ρ^*_{int} presented in Table 1 are lower than the averages from past personal interview surveys; the *maximum values* of ρ^*_{int}'s, however, are in the general range of those estimates.

It has been assumed for some time that the measurement of interviewer effects would be enhanced by centralized telephone interviewing facilities. The ability to incorporate an interpenetrated design at a relatively small cost makes this an attractive setting for the evaluation of interviewers. However, it remains difficult to draw conclusions from the results presented here because of the imprecision of these estimates. The instability of the estimates is mainly due to the small number of interviewers employed for telephone surveys. Since the past literature in the area has generally failed to address the problem of imprecision, it is possible that many of the effects judged to be important in those studies would not be found in replications.

Remedies for Instability of Interviewer Effect Estimates

The researcher faced with unstable estimates of interviewer effects has the alternatives of ceasing their measurement, altering the survey design to improve their precision (chiefly by increasing the number of interviewers used), or increasing their precision through replication of surveys. Ceasing attempts to measure this source of survey error seems premature; the other two options deserve thorough comment.

Increasing the number of interviewers is not recommended in this case, because the hiring and training of larger numbers of interviewers may force a change in essential survey conditions that help to determine the magnitudes of interviewer effects in the survey data. If, for example, the number of interviewers were increased greatly, the quality of training or amount of supervisory attention given to each inter-

Estimated Proportions or Means	ρ^*_{int}	S.E.	"Maximum" ρ^*_{int}
HEALTH AND TELEVISION VIEWING			
Having had arthritis or rheumatism	.0227	.0132	.0400
Having had diabetes	−.0059	.0053	.0010
Not drinking beer in month	.0040	.0091	.0159
Not drinking hard liquor in month	.0152	.0117	.0305
Not visited doctor in 6 months	.0266	.0144	.0455
Reporting week of last doctor's visit	.0310	.0152	.0509
Number of ameliorative health behaviors reported	.0285	.0141	.0470
Number of ways mentioned that TV is good or bad for children	.0157	.0129	.0326
Number of "bad reactions" to medicine	.0076	.0133	.0250
Number of health symptoms reported	−.0032	.0062	.0049
HEALTH IN AMERICA			
Number of doctor visits past 2 weeks	.0092	.0076	.0192
Number of hospitalizations during the past year	.0040	.0041	.0094
Reporting excellent health status	.0085	.0077	.0186
Reporting 2–4 doctor visits past year	.0002	.0035	.0048
Mean number of chronic conditions	.0096	.0063	.0179
No bed days during the past year	−.0070	.0029	−.0032
No operations past year	−.0031	.0030	.0008
No bed days past 2 weeks	−.0057	.0025	−.0024
2 wks–6 months since doctor visit	.0003	.0042	.0058
2 wks–6 months since dental visit	.0017	.0048	.0080
SURVEY OF CONSUMER ATTITUDES, DEC '82			
Better off financially than last year	−.0232	.0171	−.0008
Saw increase in prices during the last 12 months	.0101	.0181	.0338
Percent change in prices during the last 12 months	−.0325	.0178	−.0092
Feel now a bad time to buy house	.0112	.0239	.0425
Feel now a good time to buy major household items	.0242	.0258	.0580
Expect decrease in interest rates next 12 months	.0089	.0271	.0444

Table 2. (Continued)

Estimated Proportions or Means	ρ^*_{int}	S.E.	"Maximum" ρ^*_{int}
Expect increase in unemployment next 12 months	−.0210	.0151	−.0012
Expect no change in their financial situation next 12 months	.0308	.0269	.0660
Expect family income to increase 15% or less next 12 months	.0546	.0385	.1050
Believe government's economic policy fair	.0508	.0361	.0981

viewer might be altered (ignoring the higher costs incurred with such a design). With departures from training guidelines interviewer variance might increase. Thus, we face the Heisenberg-like result that to measure a particular survey error well *in a single survey,* we may change its value.

Another way to obtain useful knowledge about the average levels of interviewer variability is to repeat measurement of interviewer effects over surveys. By cumulating results over surveys we hope to take advantage of the fact that averages of the same survey statistic over replications have greater stability than a single measure of it. Ideally, averages would be constructed from identical measures of the same population, using the same interviewer selection and staffing rules, and the same statistics. For example, four replications of a survey might reduce the standard errors of average ρ^*_{int}'s by half, relative to those from a single survey.[9] Rarely, however, are exactly equivalent measures obtained in several repeated studies. Lacking that, cumulation of ρ^*_{int} estimates over statistics and across surveys might be attempted within the same survey organization. This is similar to the construction of generalized sampling variance estimates in complex samples. Given the weaknesses of the other approaches, generalized interviewer effect estimates obtained by averaging over surveys are attractive.

In Figure 1 the cumulative distribution of ρ^*_{int} values is plotted for each study over all statistics for which ρ^*_{int} was calculated. It may be observed that in general the *shapes* of the distributions are related to sample size and numbers of interviewers, with the range of values of ρ^*_{int} decreasing as these increase in number. This mirrors the estimates of standard errors of ρ^*_{int}. We see that while each study yielded some

[9] This assumes independence in the selection of interviewers across the replications and no change in true values of interviewer effects over replications.

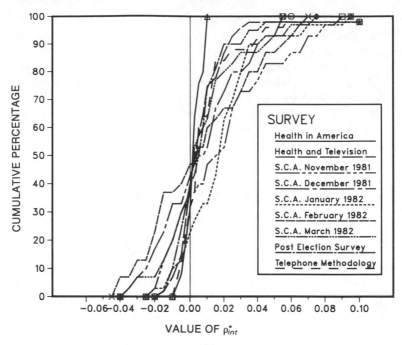

Figure 1. Cumulative Distributions of Interviewer Effect Measures (ρ^*_{int}) for Nine SRC Surveys

examples of high values of ρ^*_{int}, the majority of values cluster below 0.01. The mean values of ρ^*_{int} and the ranges are given in Table 1.

Cumulation of estimates of interviewer effects in figures such as Figure 1, together with other summary values of ρ^*_{int} over surveys and statistics, can demonstrate likely magnitudes of ρ^*_{int} to be expected, given a set of interviewer procedures. Further, as estimates of individual statistics are replicated, similar figures can be constructed for subsets of statistics (e.g., figures for questions on particular domains of attitudes; open questions versus closed questions).

The overall mean ρ^*_{int} is .009 for the nine surveys and approximately 300 statistics examined. Viewing this mean as an average of 300 independent statistics would imply a standard error about it of *approximately* .001, using the guidance of Table 2.[10] Such an average implies an increase in variance of estimates by roughly 10 percent for each 10

---

[10] This is based on a weighted average sampling variance of .0004575 on individual ρ^*_{int}'s and an assumption of independence among the ρ^*_{int}'s. The lack of independence of the various ρ^*_{int}'s stems from the use of the same interviewers and respondent pairs on multiple statistics of the same survey. It is expected that the correlation among such ρ^*_{int}'s would act to increase the standard error of the mean ρ^*_{int}.

interviews added to the interviewers' workloads (relative to the hiring of other interviewers to complete the study). Such results might guide design decisions (following Kish, 1962) to minimize variance of statistics, given fixed resources. The optimal workload is approximately $\sqrt{Ca(1 - \rho^*_{int})/c\rho^*_{int}}$, where Ca is the cost of hiring and training an interviewer and c is the cost of completing one interview. For SRC RDD surveys with 20–30-minute questionnaires, Ca is about \$309 and c, about \$18; thus, a ρ^*_{int} of .01 implies an optimal workload of 41 or 42 interviews.

Explaining the Magnitude of Interviewer Effects

In addition to lack of concern about stability of estimates, another weakness in the interviewer effects literature is the failure to seek *explanations* for interviewer effects. The explanations for effects might lie within the nature of interviewer training guidelines, of the interviewer task (e.g., probing instructions, mode of interviewing), or of the survey instrument (e.g., question type). We were able to examine three design features—the form of the question, the type of interviewer behavior used, and the use of computer assistance in the data collection. In addition to these design features we also monitored certain aspects of interviewer behavior and examined characteristics of both the interviewers and the respondents as correlates of interviewer effects.

THE INFLUENCE OF QUESTION FORM ON INTERVIEWER EFFECTS

Previous personal interview surveys have examined question type in an effort to identify the correlates of interviewer variability. Different question types may present to the interviewer communication tasks that vary in complexity. For example, factual questions (those for which there is a knowable, verifiable answer) might be thought to be less subject to effects of different wording or inflection in their delivery than would be attitudinal questions (e.g., "How many times in the last two weeks did you visit a physician's office?" versus "How well do you like TV game shows?"). The results from past studies are mixed, some of them finding attitudinal questions subject to higher interviewer variance. Kish (1962), for example, found no important differences in interviewer effects by question type. However, several studies (Hansen et al., 1961; Fellegi, 1964; O'Muircheartaigh, 1976; Feather, 1973; Collins and Butcher, 1982) have concluded that factual items are less susceptible to interviewer effects. Larger effects have been observed for attitudinal questions, especially those with open-ended responses (O'Muircheartaigh, 1976), for emotionally charged questions (Fellegi,

1964), for difficult items such as income and occupation (Hansen et al., 1961), and for questions which lacked specification regarding the acceptable interviewing procedure (Feather, 1973).

All 297 statistics from the nine different surveys were classified as factual or attitudinal (155 factual questions and 142 attitudinal questions), and since some questions were used in several surveys, there was an opportunity for replicated comparisons. When we examine these results, there appears to be no evidence that factual items as a class are subject to any different interviewer effects than are attitudinal questions. Over all surveys, the average value of ρ^*_{int} was .0098 for factual items compared to .0085 for attitudinal items.

Another variation in question form concerns whether the respondent is supplied answer categories for his choice or is free to formulate his own answer—closed questions versus open questions. Again using data from eight of the nine different surveys, we separated open and closed questions and compared ρ^*_{int}'s. Despite suggestions that open questions might be subject to larger interviewer effects, there was no tendency for this to be the case over 63 open and 192 closed questions examined from the eight surveys. In fact, five of the eight surveys produced higher estimates of ρ^*_{int} for closed questions. Over all surveys, the average value of ρ^*_{int} for closed questions was .0082 compared to .0124 for open-ended responses.

There were, however, aspects of interviewer behavior in using open questions that did vary. For example, some open questions ask the respondent to mention several entities that belong to a certain set (e.g., "What do you think are the most important problems facing the country at this time?"); one statistic of interest is the number of different entities that are mentioned. This count is a function both of the respondent's ability to articulate problems and the interviewer's behavior in probing for more mentions. The number of responses to a question appears to be subject to greater interviewer differences than the substantive response category into which the answers are coded. For example, for six questions asked in the Surveys of Consumer Attitudes, the ρ^*_{int}'s for the percentage giving two mentions are higher each month than the ρ^*_{int} values for the modal response category of the first mention. Over all months, the average value of ρ^*_{int} for the percentage giving two mentions was .0162 compared to an average value of .0007 for the modal category of the first mention. The ρ^*_{int} for the substantive category of the second mention was .0120, close to the .0162 for the proportion with second mentions. This suggests the differential behaviors that determine whether a second mention is given also might influence substantive responses on the second mention.

EFFECTS OF INTERVIEWER BEHAVIOR GUIDELINES ON INTERVIEWER VARIABILITY

In a series of experimental surveys (of which Health in America and the study of Health and Television Viewing are two), interviewers were trained to limit their verbal interaction with the respondent to a specified set of probes or feedback, in addition to the survey questions (following Cannell et al., forthcoming). Most of these statements were entered into the questionnaire itself and were varied to fit the response behavior of the respondent. Interviewers were not permitted to engage in any other conversation with the respondent. Two groups were used: one (experimental) which limited interviewers only to feedback written in a special version of the questionnaire, and another (control) which permitted them to use at their discretion only a small number of statements in response to answers given by respondents (e.g., "I see."). Although both restricted interviewer behavior to a set of specified actions, the first technique was hypothesized to improve reporting (i.e., reduce response bias) over the second.

In both surveys the differences between the ρ^*_{int} values for the cases with specified feedback and those using feedback at the discretion of the interviewer were small relative to the standard errors of the estimates. Since one of these studies (Health in America) has unusually low ρ^*_{int}'s overall, one might speculate that both procedures reduce interviewer effects relative to typical SRC training procedures. A tendency was observed for estimates from the half-sample with specified feedback to be smaller. Combining 57 of the variables from both surveys, 58 percent of the estimates obtained from the experimental group were smaller (mean value of $-.0024$) than those calculated for the control group (mean value of .0142). Such a finding merits attempts at replication over different substantive topics.

EFFECT OF COMPUTER ASSISTED TELEPHONE INTERVIEWING (CATI)

Another experimental study used terminals to display the survey questions, route the interviewer through the questionnaire, accept, and check on the values of answers recorded by the interviewer. A CATI system thus eliminates certain types of interviewer errors. One study, Health in America, randomly assigned cases to the use of a CATI system or to the use of a paper questionnaire (Groves and Mathiowetz, 1984). Each interviewer used both systems at different times throughout the study. The same questionnaire was used on both systems. Out of the 25 variables compared, the CATI cases have lower ρ^*_{int} values on 18 of the variables, with an average value of $-.0031$ compared to an average value of .0048 for the paper questionnaire. The differences, however, were small relative to the standard errors of the ρ^*_{int}'s. Attempts to replicate these results are needed.

INTERVIEWER CHARACTERISTICS AND INTERVIEWER EFFECTS

Failure to read a question exactly as printed, inability to follow skip patterns correctly, and reading a question too fast, all are believed to contribute to errors in recorded data (Marquis and Cannell, 1969; Lansing et al., 1971). The Health in America survey monitored interviewers during the survey in order to measure these aspects of interviewer behavior. Two types of behavior, question reading and clarity and pace of question delivery, were analyzed in detail. Even with the special emphasis given to training interviewers for this study, interviewers showed significant variation in the proportion of questions read correctly for many of the variables. For 80 percent of the variables there was a significant difference between interviewers in the proportion of questions read well (i.e., correct pace, clear speech). We found, however, that these differences in interviewer delivery were not correlated with the magnitude of interviewer effects for statistics computed on these variables (e.g., the proportion choosing a particular category).

To search further for this relationship, we created scatterplots of the squared deviation of the individual interviewer's means from the overall study mean by scores from the monitoring data. We expected a positive relationship between an interviewer's squared deviations and the proportion of "incorrect" behavior. No such relationship was apparent. In both the Health in America and the Health and Television Viewing Surveys, we also examined other measures of interviewer performance such as their response rate, productivity, and supervisor evaluations. Again, we found no relationship between any one of these variables and interviewer deviations from survey averages. The so-called "better" interviewers on these characteristics did not deviate any more or any less from the overall mean than did the other interviewers.[11]

---

[11] Most telephone data yield distributions of interviewer means that contain few outliers and have relatively smooth patterns about the overall survey mean. The Health in America survey, however, had many measures where one or two interviewers were extreme outliers to the distribution. Over different statistics the identity of the outliers varied. To evaluate the impact of these extreme values we again performed the interviewer variability analysis for five statistics with high values of ρ^*_{int} (mean value of .0075), eliminating one or two outliers in each case. For each variable the new estimate of ρ^*_{int} was much smaller, with a mean value of $-.0004$ over the five variables. In other words, in that study one or two interviewers were responsible for most of the measured variability.

RESPONDENT CHARACTERISTICS AND INTERVIEWER EFFECTS

For the Health and Television Viewing Survey we examined levels of interviewer variability by sex, education, and age of respondents. The predominance of female telephone interviewers and potential differences in their interaction with female and male respondents suggested the possibility of differences in interviewer effects by sex of respondent. We found little evidence that the gender of the respondent is related to interviewer effects. Although the mean value of ρ^*_{int} over all questions was slightly higher for female respondents, further investigation by question type found mixed results. For some question types the estimates of ρ^*_{int} were larger for males; for other question types the estimates were larger for females. In all cases the differences in the estimates were small.

Although past empirical results vary (Cannell et al., 1977; Schuman and Presser, 1977), it is reasonable to argue that poorly educated respondents might be more easily affected by the behavior and status of the interviewer than more highly educated respondents. Lower education groups may seek greater help from the interviewer in answering the questions or may use the inflection of the interviewer's voice as a cue for responses to questions they find difficult. Values of ρ^*_{int}, however, do not appear to be larger for respondents with less than 12 years of education. Even when estimates of ρ^*_{int} are calculated by question type, differences by respondent education are not apparent.

Respondents were also categorized into five groups according to age. We expected larger values of ρ^*_{int} for the oldest age group. There is some evidence that telephone surveys suffer greater nonresponse among older persons (Groves and Kahn, 1979), and we sought evidence that those who do respond might be more subject to influence by the interviewer because of their own suspicion about the nature of the survey, or greater tendency to fatigue during the 30-minute interview on the telephone. Sudman and Bradburn (1973) have noted that older respondents exhibit greater response errors on questions requiring recall of factual material. In fact, the oldest age group tends to have larger ρ^*_{int} values than other age groups. Over all question types, the oldest age group had an average value of ρ^*_{int} equal to .0274 compared to an average value of .0012 for others.[12] As we noted earlier, ρ^*_{int} measures both variation in nonresponse and response errors over interviewers. These higher ρ^*_{int}'s for the elderly may relate to variation across interviewers in nonresponse rates among the elderly.

[12] There is also evidence that the 35–49-year-old group experiences higher ρ^*_{int}'s (mean .0099) but there is no theoretical justification for such a finding.

Summary and Speculations

The instability of estimates from any single survey is the major impediment to measuring interviewer variability. Through cumulating results over many surveys, we obtained generalized estimates of interviewer effects. The analysis showed that for SRC telephone surveys, typical ρ^*_{int} values cluster below .01, an average somewhat smaller than those reported from personal interview surveys, which average closer to .02. We argued that such average ρ^*_{int}'s are useful for guiding decisions regarding how many interviewers to use in order to minimize the variance of estimates, given fixed available resources. In addition, the cumulation of estimates over surveys within the organization could be used to provide more specific information regarding what topics or measurement types might be subject to larger or smaller ρ^*_{int}'s and thus require smaller or larger optimal workloads.

We also attempted to study correlates of interviewer effects. Our results supported others in finding that attitudinal questions are themselves not subject to greater interviewer effects than "factual" items. Open questions are not inherently subject to greater interviewer variability, but the number of distinct answers obtained to an open question appears to be sensitive to interviewer differences. These effects do not apparently influence the substance of the *first* mentioned answer, but appear to be the result of variable probing behavior, that affects both the likelihood of the respondent giving a second mention *and* the substance of that response.

Behavior may be able to be altered to reduce interviewer effects, through use of both controlled feedback and probing and of CATI systems that control the flow and questioning sequences of the interview. These are promising results that deserve further research because they offer the designer real hope of reducing this source of survey error.

In contrast, there was an unfortunate lack of success in using common indicators of performance to predict interviewer effects. Data obtained from monitoring interviewers and the traditional indicators of interviewer quality (response rate, productivity, and supervisory evaluations) seemed to be unrelated to the errors measured by between-interviewer variability. This result casts doubt on the relevance of these indicators for survey quality versus their value for measurement of cost efficiency of surveys.

Finally, we pursued a search for respondent level attributes that were related to interviewer effects. Gender and education of respondent were essentially uncorrelated to the effect, but age of the respondent was related. Older respondents were found to exhibit larger susceptibility to interviewer effects than younger respondents. Given past low response rates among the elderly in telephone surveys, this result might reflect more differential nonresponse bias across interviewers than differential response errors.

Readers of this article need to be cautious in their inference from these results. The studies examined are chiefly health and economic attitude surveys; they use interviewers hired and trained using SRC procedures; supervision, survey administration, and response rates are those achieved by SRC. Since ρ_{int}^*'s can be affected by all these attributes of survey design and practice, these results are applicable to other centralized telephone surveys to the extent their features resemble those of our nine surveys.

References

Cannell, C., L. Oksenberg, and J. Converse
   1977   Experiments in Interviewing Techniques: Field Experiments in Health Reporting 1971-1977. National Center for Health Services Research.
Cannell, C.F., R.M. Groves, L.J. Magilavy, N.A. Mathiowetz, and P.V. Miller
   Forthcoming "An experimental comparison of telephone and personal health surveys." Vital and Health Statistics, Series 2 Reports.
Collins, M., and B. Butcher
   1982   "Interviewer and clustering effects in an attitude survey." Journal of the Market Research Society 25(1):39–58.
Feather, J.
   1973   A Study of Interviewer Variance. Department of Social and Preventive Medicine, University of Saskatchewan.
Fellegi, Ivan P.
   1964   "Response variance and its estimation." Journal of the American Statistical Association 59:1016– 41.
Freeman J., and E.W. Butler
   1976   "Some sources of interviewer variance in surveys." Public Opinion Quarterly 40:79–91.
Groves, R.M., and R.L. Kahn
   1979   Surveys by Telephone. New York: Academic Press.
Groves, R.M., and N. Mathiowetz
   1984   "Computer assisted telephone interviewing: effects on interviewers and respondents." Public Opinion Quarterly 48:356–69.
Hansen, M.H., W.N. Hurwitz, and M.A. Bershad
   1961   "Measurement errors in censuses and surveys." Bulletin of the ISI 38(2):351– 74.
Kish, L.
   1962   "Studies of interviewer variance for attitudinal variables." Journal of the American Statistical Association 57:91–115.
Kish, L., and M.R. Frankel
   1972   "Inferences from complex samples." Journal of the Royal Statistical Society (B) 36:1–37.
Lansing, J.B., S.B. Withey, and A.C. Wolfe
   1971   Pages 219–318 in Working Papers on Survey Research in Poverty Areas. Survey Research Center, The University of Michigan.
Marquis, K.H., and C.F. Cannell
   1969   A Study of Interviewer–Respondent Interaction in the Urban Employment Surveys. Survey Research Center, The University of Michigan.

O'Muircheartaigh, C.A.
  1976 "Response errors in an attitudinal sample survey." Quality and Quantity 10:97–115.
O'Muircheartaigh, C.A., and A.M. Marckwardt
  1980 "An assessment of the reliability of WFS data." World Fertility Survey Conference, Methodology Session No. 6.
Schuman, H., and S. Presser
  1977 "Question wording as an independent variable in survey analysis." Sociological Methods and Research 6(2):151–70.
Sudman, S., and N. Bradburn
  1973 "Effects of time and memory factors on response in surveys." Journal of the American Statistical Association 68:805–15.
Tucker, Clyde
  1983 "Interviewer effects in telephone surveys." Public Opinion Quarterly 47:84–95.
Waksberg, J.
  1978 "Sampling methods for random digit dialing." Journal of the American Statistical Association 73(361):40–46.

A Study of Experimental Techniques for Telephone Interviewing

PETER V. MILLER AND CHARLES F. CANNELL

TELEPHONE surveys are not a new phenomenon, but academic and governmental organizations have only recently made serious investments in the method. As of this writing, for example, the Bureau of the Census has conducted only one study involving "cold" telephone interviews—a random-digit dialing sample of Michigan residents.

Reducing the cost of surveys is the primary motivation for developments in telephone interviewing. Many researchers still see the telephone interview as the somewhat disreputable "poor relation" of the personal contact. If it were not for financial exigencies, these people would probably not view the telephone as a preferable (or even a viable) means of collecting survey data.

This attitude may be one reason why we know little about what constitutes effective telephone interviewing techniques. The telephone survey has been treated as a necessity, rather than as an

Abstract This investigation focused on the effects of experimental interviewing procedures, which were developed in face-to-face interviews, on reporting in telephone contacts. Respondents in a national RDD sample ($N = 1,054$) were randomly assigned to be interviewed with one of two experimental procedures, or a control technique. The experimental procedures involved two different combinations of three interviewing techniques which had been found to be effective in personal interviewing studies—commitment, instructions, and feedback. The techniques are designed to better inform respondents about reporting tasks and to motivate them to perform the tasks well. The findings suggest that the experimental procedures can improve reporting in telephone interview, although the effects in this study were not as strong as we expected. This research may be seen as a beginning step in the development of optimal telephone interviewing procedures.

Peter V. Miller and Charles F. Cannell are members of the Survey Research Center, Institute for Social Research and Department of Communication, The University of Michigan. Others having major responsibility for this research include Marianne Berry, James Lepkowski, M. Lou Magilavy, and Nancy Mathiowetz. This paper is based on work supported by the National Science Foundation, Grant No. SOC-07287. The findings and conclusions are those of the authors and do not necessarily reflect the views of the foundation.

opportunity. The goal seems to have been to make the telephone interview as good as the face-to-face contact (even though the quality of data from personal interviews is sometimes not very good). Also, since survey research has been rooted largely in the personal interview context, researchers have had little choice but to treat that type of contact as "normal" and to employ widely varying personal interview procedures on the telephone. Therefore, the unique limitations and advantages of the audio-only medium for interview communication have not been systematically investigated.

We come to research on telephone interviews with some years of experience investigating personal interview techniques. This work has taught us that careful manipulation of the communication from interviewer to respondent can pay off in improved survey reporting. The general objectives of these manipulations—to better inform survey respondents about the nature of the reporting tasks, and to motivate them to take on the tasks with effort and care—seem to be ones which are relevant to the telephone interview context. Therefore, while the techniques were developed and tested in personal interviews, we felt that the messages they are intended to convey might also be beneficial in the telephone interview. Moreover, it was clear to us that systematic investigation into interviewing techniques for telephone interviews should be begun. This article summarizes our first attempt at such a study and discusses its clear implications and its puzzles.

Communication Issues in Telephone Interviews

Some factors which differentiate the style of communication in telephone and face-to-face interviews are obvious. Use of visual cues such as "show cards" is impossible in telephone contacts (unless the materials have been mailed to respondents before the interview and they agree to use them). As a result, investigators have been concerned about the comprehensibility to respondents of some response tasks when they are presented over the phone. The "channel capacity" of the telephone is limited.

Other differences in communication between telephone and face-to-face modes are more subtle and involve not only perceptual mechanisms but also social custom. Communication by telephone may be less intimate than in-person dialogue. The inability to see conversational partners (their facial expressions, gestures, and so forth) may lead to heightened uncertainty about the affective meaning behind their words and whether they understand what we are trying to convey. In addition, the place of dialogue, which often is regulated by nonverbal cues in face-to-face interaction, has to be maintained by verbal or paralinguistic utterances in telephone conversations. Further, since the household telephone is normally used for speaking with friends and family and for self-initiated business communication, any call from a stranger is likely to be treated with suspicion. In other words, custom dictates what sorts of telephone contacts are "appropriate," and some people may view any call which does not fall in these categories as an unwarranted intrusion.

In research on mediated communication, investigators have found support for hypotheses that the visual channel is important to conveying affect and evaluation of others (Ekman, 1965; Mehrabian, 1968) and for regulating conversational flow (Kendon, 1967; Duncan, 1972). Tasks involving transmission of factual information and cooperative problem-solving appear relatively unaffected by whether the participants can see each other or not (see Williams, 1977). But there is a consistent tendency for subjects to be less confident of their judgments in no-vision conditions, and to express a preference for face-to-face contact (Williams, 1977; National Research Council, 1979).

The implications of these findings for telephone interviewing are several. In personal interviews, the elements of visual communication plus the preinterview acquaintance period allow interviewers easily and naturally to establish both the legitimacy of the interview and the image of themselves as pleasant, understanding, and safe persons with whom to interact. The interviewer's physical presence permits the communication of attention to, interest in, and acceptance of what the respondent has to say, through nonverbal as well as verbal indicators. By contrast, telephone interviews, which may surprise and disturb respondents, lack the sense of legitimacy of the personal contact. In addition, the phone interview may seem somewhat more mechanical. The pace of interaction—unregulated by nonverbal cues—may be faster on the telephone, leading to hurried and perhaps less thoughtful responses (see Groves and Kahn, 1979).

These comparisons imply that the telephone may produce data of lower quality than those collected in person. But it is also possible that the limited channel capacity of the telephone may eliminate distracting or biasing cues from the interviewer, and that phone communication's affective distance may be a boon when the questions in the interview concern very sensitive matters. Several studies comparing telephone and face-to-face interviews have involved such hypotheses (Colombotos, 1969; Hochstim, 1967; Sudman, Bradburn, et al., 1979).

To summarize these ideas, it appears that interviewing by telephone may be advantageous in some ways and disadvantageous in others. In any case, the nature of communication in the interview will be affected by the medium through which it takes place. To minimize the potential drawbacks of telephone communication and to maximize its potential advantages, interviewing procedures should be devised which are attuned to the special constraints of the medium. Our investigation began by considering whether interviewing techniques found useful in face-to-face interviews might be relevant for telephone contacts.

Interviewing Procedures

In personal interviewing studies (see Cannell et al., 1981), we have sought to impress upon respondents the seriousness of the survey and to motivate them to undertake good reporting behavior through a *commitment* procedure, in which they agree to be conscientious and hard-working in answering questions. We have also developed techniques which are designed to *instruct* respondents on what is expected of them in performing question-answering tasks well. Finally, we have attempted to tailor verbal *feedback* to particular respondent behaviors, so that interviewees are both informed and "rewarded" when response tasks are properly performed.

COMMITMENT

Since a telephone interview is likely to be an unusual situation (and perhaps one which arouses suspicion), there seems to be a particular need for orienting the respondent to the requirements of the experience. He or she should understand that the interview is a serious undertaking and that some effort will need to be expended in order to perform response tasks adequately. The technique we have used in personal interviews to help motivate respondents is *commitment*.

The concept of commitment has received considerable attention within social psychology and sociology. Within sociology, commitment has been used to account for the fact that people can persist in consistent goal-related activity even in the face of adverse experiences that could be expected to discourage them from further effort (Becker, 1960; Goffman, 1961; Johnson, 1973). Within social psychology, commitment has become a key concept in theoretical positions growing out of cognitive dissonance theory (Brehm and Cohen, 1962; Gerard, 1968; Gerard et al., 1974; Kiesler, 1971). In personal interviews we operationalized commitment by having the respondent sign a statement. On the telephone a commitment statement is read. The statement used in this research was:

In this research, it's important for The University of Michigan to get accurate information—that is, to get exact details on every item, even on those which may seem unimportant to you. It may take extra effort for you to report accurately. Are you willing to think carefully about each question in order to give accurate information?

If the respondent agreed, the following statement was read:

For our part, we will keep all information you give very confidential. Of course, the interview is voluntary. Should we come to any question you do not want to answer, just let me know and we'll move on to the next one.

INSTRUCTIONS

Besides attempting to motivate respondents in this way, we also have tried in personal interviews to orient them to the interview by the use of *instructions* on the purpose and goal of questions and on how to go about performing tasks. Respondents typically pick up cues on what is expected of them incidentally through interaction with the interviewer. These "lessons" are indirect, and may not serve to improve reporting. Rather than this haphazard procedure, we write instructions in the questionnaire at various points for the interviewer to read. By using instructions that are more detailed and frequent than in most surveys, we apply the distinction clarified in learning theory between intentional and incidental learning (Postman, 1964; McLaughlin, 1965), and expect instructions to function directively.

Two types of information incorporated in the instructions procedure parallel two main functions of instructions identified by researchers concerned with task performance: to clarify the goal of the performance, and to clarify the specific tasks involved in achieving the goal (Gagne, 1964; Hackman, 1969). The first type clarifies the goals of the interview by informing the respondent what is expected of him or her in general, i.e., accurate and complete answers define good performance.

In the telephone study described here these general goals were articulated in the commitment statement, reproduced above, and in statements read at various junctures in the questionnaire, such as the following:

In this interview we want to get as much information as we can.
This includes things which may seem small and unimportant as well as important things.

Instructions were also reiterated in the form of questions:

We said earlier that for some of these questions you would need to search your memory thoroughly. How difficult has it been to remember the things we have asked you so far . . . has it been very difficult, somewhat difficult, or not at all difficult?

The second type of information details more specifically how the respondent should go about producing accurate answers. Examples of specific question instructions include:

For this question you will need to think back and remember whether you have *ever* had any of them (health conditions) even if it might be a long time ago.

In answering the next few questions it may help you to be accurate if you check a program listing or TV guide.

We're interested in all television watching, even short times. We find that if people think hard, they can sometimes remember other times when they saw or heard the television, even though they weren't paying much attention.

In addition to these two directive functions, instructions also can serve to motivate performance (Bandura, 1969; Marlatt, 1972). Cues to perform in the prescribed manner generated from the informational content can motivate the individual to carry out the described activities.

FEEDBACK

Instructions, however, are not complete without *feedback* to respondents on how well they have carried out the response task. The idea of programming feedback in interviews occurred to us after an analysis of personal interview interactions. This research demonstrated that much of the interaction that takes place in a face-to-face survey interview is not prescribed by the strict asking and answering of questions (Cannell and Robison, 1971; Cannell et al., 1975). The findings led us to focus on the two-way process, or chaining of behaviors, between the interviewer and the respondent, rather than the separate activity of each.

In this view of the communication, the reactions that respondents receive from the interviewer in response to their earlier answers are important determinants of their behavior later in the course of the interview. The reactions of interviewers to respondents' answers constitute a feedback to respondents that can influence their behavior in general and the accuracy and completeness of the reported information in particular. As we noted earlier, much of this "secondary communication" is likely to be nonverbal in face-to-face interaction.

Feedback reactions most likely serve two functions: (1) they may inform the respondents of what is expected of them (i.e., how to answer the question, what constitutes a complete, satisfactory answer), and (2) they may communicate approval of the way the question was answered. It is therefore useful to conceptualize the various interviewer reactions in terms of both informational value and motivational effect, as reinforcers capable of shaping the respondents's behavior.

Following our practice, feedback statements were designed into the questionnaire of the telephone study reported here, standardizing and controlling this important process. In general, feedback statements were made contingent on "good" performance, and both negative and positive statements were used. For example, interviewers measured the length of time that the respondents took to think over answers to some of the questions which required the respondents to search their memories. Respondents who took less than three seconds before replying negatively were read the following:

> As I mentioned, sometimes it's hard for people to remember everything. Perhaps if you think about it a little more, you will remember something you missed. Was there anything at all?

Positive feedbacks, on the other hand, were used to indicate to the respondent that the answer given fulfilled the goals of the question. For example,

> Thanks. This is the sort of information we're looking for in this research. It's important to us to get this information.
> These details are helpful.

Commitment, instructions, and feedback, in summary, are three procedures which we have used in personal interviews in an effort to improve reporting. The techniques became part of a "script" for the interview, which interviewers are trained to use in a standardized manner. In this way, we seek to reduce between-interviewer variability in the use of techniques, as well as to communicate more productively with respondents. Because the telephone presents some special problems of communication which may be reduced by the procedures, we thought that testing the techniques in phone interviews would be a good place to start in developing interviewing procedures specifically for that medium,

What Is Improved Reporting?

In order to test the value of the interviewing techniques we have just described, one must have an idea of what "good" reporting is. To formulate this concept, we need to look beyond the subject matter of a survey to the basic response tendencies at work in the question-answering process. In reporting experiences and events, for example, we must be concerned with under- or overreporting likelihoods. For attitudinal items, the respondent's position may be based on little or no information, or the response may reflect "socially accepted" ideas. Generally speaking, we are interested in increasing response validity by combating these potential errors through better interview communication.

In studies where validity information (records of events) on the issues of interest was available, several reporting tasks with predictable response errors have been identified. As one might expect, the longer the period of *time* between the event to be reported and the interview, the more likely the event is to be underreported (see Cannell and Fowler, 1963; Neter and Waksberg, 1965). The likely *salience* of the event for the respondent also has an impact on response validity. For example, if hospital stays involve serious illnesses, the hospitalizations are more accurately reported (Cannell et al. 1965). When housing repairs are costly, they are better remembered (Neter and Waksberg, 1965).

Social desirability is likely to influence reporting of an event as well. If the experience is embarrassing or threatening to the respondent, it is likely to go unmentioned in the interview. Similarly, events which put the respondent in a good light may be overreported (Sudman, Bradburn, et al. 1979).

In sum, research has identified systematic errors associated with certain common response tasks which are presented to survey respondents. On the basis of these record-check studies, we can make reasoned assumptions about the likely direction of error in questions which make similar demands, but for which no external validating information exists. The effectiveness of the experimental techniques is determined by testing their ability to reduce the bias which we assume exists in these measures. In previous research with personal interviews, we have found that the interviewing techniques described above do help to reduce the bias assumed in a variety of measures.[1] In the present telephone study, we again selected questions which are likely to have systematic error tendencies by virtue of the tasks presented to respondents—requiring them to expend considerable effort or to disclose potentially embarrassing information. We test the ability of the interviewing procedures to reduce bias by comparing the results obtained for these questions for respondents who were interviewed with the special techniques to the findings for respondents who were interviewed with a "control" procedure.

[1] See Cannell et al., 1981, for a summary of these findings.

Study Design

EXPERIMENTAL TREATMENTS

Our experience with research on the experimental interviewing techniques suggested that the effects of the techniques were additive. In the one study comparing all procedures, more reduction in bias appeared to be achieved when commitment, instructions, and feedback were combined in the questionnaire than when any one or two of the techniques were used. The pattern across nine dependent variables was quite consistent: the experimental group which was interviewed with all three techniques always had a higher mean score on items which we expected to be underreported, although the increment in reporting over and above the commitment and instructions group was not large (see Cannell et al., 1977). Therefore, it seemed reasonable to expect that the three techniques together would improve reporting in the telephone study, when compared to a control interviewing procedure.

At the same time, it was clear that operating in a new communication medium mandated replication and an examination of the individual effects of techniques which might be particularly important in a nonvisual environment. *Feedback* seemed to fit well in that category. We reasoned that respondents might be particularly sensitive to verbal feedback when the interviewer can give no other kind of indication that responses have been understood and that they meet the criteria set out by instructions and questions.

This hypothesis was tested with a design with two experimental groups—one with commitment and instructions built into the questionnaire and one with commitment, instructions, and feedback included. We anticipated a linear improvement in reporting on various measures from the control group to the commitment and instructions treatment to the group with all three procedures. This design allows the assessment of the effect of commitment and instructions alone, and of the incremental effect of feedback when added to those techniques.

CONTROL GROUP

The nature of the appropriate control is a complex question. The ideal is to create an "average" group of interviewers using "average" techniques. But neither of these averages exists. Interviewers vary in their use of techniques, both within and across survey organizations. This freedom of action makes constructing the ideal control difficult. We have the choice of one group of interviewers who do interviews using all techniques (thus serving as their own controls), or several groups of interviewers, each of which uses only one set of techniques. The disadvantage to the single-group solution is that the interviewers must be tightly constrained in their use of techniques in the control and experimental groups, so that the integrity of the experimental manipulation is preserved. We don't want interviewers applying experimental procedures in the control condition.

The problem with the multiple-group option is that, even with random assignment, the chances are good that interviewers assigned to one condition will be systematically different from those in other experimental groups. The total number of interviewers we use for a study is so small (in this case, 30) that the inference that differences in findings between treatments is due to the effect of the techniques is always threatened by the possibility of interviewer differences between the treatments.

These problems force a compromise in formulating the control interviewing procedure. Because we want to be able to see the effects of the different procedures clearly—uncluttered by interviewer differences between treatments or by interviewer's application of experimental techniques in the control group—we chose to train one group of interviewers to execute all the experimental procedures and we used a *strict* control group. The strict control procedure offers a spare background for viewing experimental effects since it required interviewers simply to read questions and record answers without extraneous communication of any kind. While not representative of "standard" interviewing practice, which gives interviewers much more freedom in ad-libbing communication with respondents, the strict control provides the clearest perspective on the experimental effects, and its use was important in this developmental study of telephone interviewing.

DEPENDENT MEASURES

To determine the effects of the interviewing treatments, we incorporated in the questionnaire measures which varied on a dimension of task difficulty due to their demands on memory and organizational ability, or due to their demands for self-disclosure. The topics of the study—health and media use—presented a fertile ground for questions which we could use to assess interview procedure differences. In health, we asked questions about current and past experience with illness (including some potentially embarrassing or threatening conditions), as well as health practices, alcohol consumption, and the dates of physician visits. We hypothesized that the experimental interviewing procedures would produce higher reporting levels for a set of open questions asking about *current illness* and *symptoms,* and well as for queries about *bad reactions to medicine* and *health practices*. We also expected more reporting of *health conditions* and *mental health symptoms* in a set of closed questions. In addition, we hypothesized that respondents in the experimental treatments would report more *consumption of alcoholic beverages* and would be more precise in reporting *dates of physician visits*.

The media questions asked respondents to report *attitudes toward types of television programs* and to indicate their level of agreement with various *reasons for watching TV*. For these items, we expected commitment, instructions, and feedback to lead to more disclosure of socially undesirable viewpoints. We also asked respondents to express their *opinions about television's effect on children* in two open questions. Since giving opinions in that format requires more memory and organizational effort than is true in closed questions, we expected respondents in the experimental groups to give more mentions than those in the control group.

We performed some additional tests of the interviewing techniques by asking respondents about their *donations to charity* and by noting the extent to which they *checked records* in order to answer health questions. We also wanted to know if the techniques would reduce the *level of nonresponse in income reporting,* sometimes a considerable problem in telephone interviews. All in all, we tested the effects of commitment, instructions, and feedback on a set of measures for which we expected an under- or overreporting bias due to the kinds of demands we think they place on respondents. Our assumptions about measurement error are supported by data in some cases for the health items (health conditions, for example, have been found to be underreported in record-check studies).

THE SAMPLE

In previous studies testing the interviewing procedures, we have restricted the sample of respondents to get a homogeneous group for experimentation. We wanted to control respondent variability in experience which might confound or attenuate experimental differences, and so we did the original research with samples of white women aged 18–65, mainly in the Detroit area. This telephone study departs from that pattern in that we had a national sample of men and women from various social and ethnic backgrounds. The sample ($N = 1,054$) was drawn through random-digit-dialing. Following Waksberg (1978), the design was a two-stage stratified sample. A double sampling scheme was used after the fifth week of the study in an attempt to reduce nonresponse bias. The overall response rate was approximately 67 percent, including unanswered numbers in the denominator of the response rate. Each telephone number in the sample was assigned randomly to one of the three experimental groups. The data were collected in early spring, 1979, by Survey Research Center interviewers using a computer-assisted telephone interviewing (CATI) system.

Analysis and Findings

MEDIA VARIABLES

Table 1 displays the mean differences among the experimental treatments on several dependent variables described above. For the questions dealing with mass media use, we find significant differences between the control group and the experimental treatments in two of the three cases. The *attitudes-toward-television-shows* index measures respondents' liking for five types of programs which range from socially desirable ("news" and "educational and cultural" programs) to socially undesirable offerings ("sexy" shows, e.g.). The lower the score, the more the respondent admits disliking the "highbrow" or

Table 1. Differences in Reporting Among Experimental Interviewing Treatments (Means)

	Control (N = 364)	Commitment + Instructions (N = 347)	Commitment + Instructions + Feedback (N = 343)
Media			
Attitudes toward TV shows (index)	19.4	18.8*	18.8*
Reasons for watching TV (index)	18.1	16.9*	17.2*
Opinions about children and TV	3.7	3.9	3.9
Health			
Number of responses to four open questions	5.7	6.8*	6.9*
Number of conditions reported in closed questions	2.4	2.8*	2.8*
Mental health symptoms (index)	7.9	8.2	8.3*
Amount of wine consumed in previous month (glasses)	3.3	4.6	3.2
Amount of beer consumed in previous months (glasses)	7.5	8.3	7.6
Amount of liquor consumed in previous month (ounces)	4.7	6.3	6.1
Number of charities contributed to in past year	1.5	1.4	1.6

NOTE: Ns vary slightly across dependent variables due to missing data.
* Differences between control and experimental groups significant at .05.

liking the "lowbrow" programs. The commitment and instructions group and the group with all three treatments have significantly lower mean values on the index compared to the control. This finding is mostly due to the fact that respondents in the experimental groups report that they like to watch "sexy" and "police and crime" shows more than respondents in the control. We view this tendency to disclose more socially undesirable attitudes as an indication of more valid reporting in the experimental groups.

The *reasons-for-watching-TV* index consists of five items which measure the tendency for respondents to watch TV unselectively. The lower the score on this measure, the more respondents say that they watch television "for company," or "because there is nothing else to do at the time," for example. Since watching television may be seen as a somewhat uncultured activity in and of itself, watching without a specific program to motivate the activity may be viewed as particularly socially undesirable. The items for this scale were taken from Steiner's (1963) study of the use of television. The significantly lower scores for the two experimental groups, compared to the control, suggest that the interviewing procedures produced more reporting of potentially threatening information. Finally, and unlike the two attitude indices, the experimental interviewing procedures did not produce more mentions in questions concerning *television's effects on children*. We had hypothesized that respondents would have a tendency to truncate their answers on this and other open questions because of the effort involved to recall, organize, and give a response. Following this reasoning, the experimental procedures should have produced more mentions by encouraging respondents to expend more effort in answering.

HEALTH VARIABLES

For the health variables in the survey, we found significant differences between mean reporting levels for three of six tests. Similar to our findings in previous studies, the experimental procedures produced more *mentions in open questions* concerning health symptoms and conditions and health practices. Again we assume an underreporting bias in these questions, since they require respondents sometimes to report sensitive information, and sometimes to recall and organize nonsalient details for reporting.

The two experimental groups also show more *health conditions* reported in a set of *closed questions* which covered experiences in the year prior to the interview, and also whole-life events. Some of the conditions in the list presented to respondents were potentially threatening to report (e.g., hemorrhoids), while others were somewhat ambiguous and especially required respondents to define categories and decide whether their individual circumstances fit the situation. We hypothesized that the experimental interviewing procedures would aid respondents in this task both by motivating them to expend the effort and by communicating a broadly inclusive general definition of the health conditions. The findings support these expectations.

A *mental-health-symptom* index (using items similar to ones designed by Langner[2]) also shows a significant difference between the control and the instructions-commitment-feedback group. The five questions in this index ask respondents to report the frequency with which they experience physiological and psychological symptoms which are markers of mental illness. A higher score indicates more frequent experience with such symptoms, and we assume that this is more valid reporting.

The other items in Table 1, concerning *alcohol consumption* and *donations to charity,* do not show significant differences in reporting between interviewing treatments. These results were surprising to us, since we had anticipated more reports of drinking in the experimental groups and less reporting of charity donations.[3]

A second puzzling aspect of Table 1 is the general finding of no difference between reporting levels in the two experimental groups. The addition of feedback to commitment and instructions in the questionnaire did not produce differential reporting on any of the dependent variables. This runs counter to our experience in a personal interview study (Cannell et al., 1979), and is all the more surprising since we had expected the effects of feedback to be, if anything, *more* pronounced in telephone interviews. The absence of nonverbal cues in telephone communication seemed to us to make verbal feedback important in giving respondents information on their performance and in motivating them. The absence of any incremental effect of feedback over instructions and commitment belies this point of view. We will return to this issue later to speculate on the reasons for the finding.

INTERACTION TESTS

In addition to these analyses, we also tested for interactions of the interviewing techniques with sex, since our previous studies had

---

[2] The five items we selected were based on those which asked about psychiatric symptoms which respondents rated as most socially undesirable to disclose, in a methodological examination of the Langner scale by Dohrenwend and Dohrenwend, 1969.

[3] We also did not discover significant differences between the experimental treatments for nonresponse to the income question, or for interviewers' perceptions of respondents' record-checking frequency.

involved only female respondents and we wanted to see whether the effective use of the procedures was dependent on the sex of the respondent. While it appeared that for some variables, female respondents showed more effects of the techniques, none of the sex-by-treatment interactions were statistically significant. The same analysis for education also found no differential effect of the techniques for respondents with more or fewer years of schooling.

PRECISION OF REPORTING

Table 2 displays the precision-of-physician-visits reporting by experimental treatment. Respondents' answers are classified by whether they indicated that their last doctor's visit occurred within a given week, within a particular month, or within a broader period. One can see looking down the table that as the time lag between the last reported doctor's visit and the interview increases, respondents in the experimental conditions become relatively more precise in their answers. The differences between the groups are not large, but the tendency is for more precise reporting of this (probably) nonsalient event by respondents who were interviewed with the experimental procedures.

Discussion

Overall, the findings in this study suggest that the interviewing procedures which were developed in personal interviews with a homogeneous group of respondents can have some impact on response validity in telephone interviews involving a heterogeneous sample. The limited empirical support indicates that the experimental interviewing techniques can address positively some of the problematic issues of communication in a telephone interview.

At the same time, the support is clearly limited. There is also no evidence at all that the feedback technique has an incremental effect on reporting over and above commitment and instructions. On the whole, we find that the interviewing techniques had weaker effects in this telephone study than in our personal interview research, but the comparison is confounded by differences in the measures, samples, and the particular application of the techniques in the different studies. In other words, we are not sure whether the interviewing procedures actually work less well on the telephone or whether other factors peculiar to this initial telephone effort may be responsible for the findings. But, to illustrate the difference in effectiveness of the interviewing techniques in the face-to-face and tele-

Table 2. Precision of Reporting of Most Recent Doctor's Visit by Experimental Interviewing Treatment

	Control		Commitment + Instructions		Commitment + Instructions + Feedback		Totals	
	N	%	N	%	N	%	N	%
Visit occurred within last 6 months[a]								
Precise within a week	148	84.1	146	87.4	125	79.1	419	83.6
Precise within a month	24	13.6	16	9.6	26	16.5	66	13.2
Less precise than within a month	4	2.3	5	3.0	7	4.4	16	3.2
Totals	176	100.0	167	100.0	158	100.0	501	100.0
Visit occurred 7–19 months prior to interview[b]								
Precise within a week	48	42.8	62	50.8	66	53.2	176	49.2
Precise within a month	45	40.2	43	35.3	41	33.1	129	36.0
Less precise than within a month	19	17.0	17	13.9	17	13.7	53	14.8
Totals	112	100.0	122	100.0	124	100.0	358	100.0
Visit occurred more than 19 months prior to interview[c]								
Precise within a week	6	9.8	6	12.4	9	17.3	21	13.0
Precise within a month	23	37.7	21	43.8	22	42.3	66	41.0
Less precise than within a month	32	52.5	21	43.8	21	40.4	74	46.0
Totals	61	100.0	48	100.0	52	100.0	161	100.0

[a] 15 cases deleted due to missing data or 0 visits.
[b] 10 cases deleted due to missing data or 0 visits.
[c] 9 cases deleted due to missing data or 0 visits.

phone contexts, a personal interview study (Cannell et al., 1977) found that the mean number of mentions to 16 open questions about health was 63 for the control group, 72 for instructions plus commitment, and 75 for instructions plus commitment plus feedback. Comparatively, Table 1 shows that the responses to four open questions on health in the telephone study described here differed by an average of only one mention between the control and experimental groups. And, while the group with all three techniques evidenced higher reporting on all nine dependent variables in the personal interview study (but not always significantly so), the similar treatment in this study did not follow that linear pattern.

In the case of feedback, we have speculated upon and tested a variety of explanations for why the technique did not contribute a unique effect over and above commitment and instructions. One possibility that we cannot test is that feedback is interchangeable with one or both of the other procedures. This idea does not square with our notion of what feedback does in the interview, or its particular role in telephone communication, but it is certainly a possibility for exploration in future research.

We did test to see whether feedback utterances might be aversive to respondents, by cross-tabulating the number of feedback remarks received with responses to subsequent questions at different points in the interview. We also looked at whether any interviewers might have pulled down the averages on measures obtained from respondents in the feedback group due to possibly inept or half-hearted feedback practice. We looked at the demographic composition of the treatment groups to see if they differed significantly, despite random assignment. Finally, we examined the effects of feedback in this study for white women respondents only, so as to compare the results with personal interviews in earlier research. As mentioned before, this comparison is complicated by the fact that the measures in the different studies are not strictly parallel, and the implementation of the feedback technique was different in different studies.[4] Unfortunately, none of these analyses identified the reason for the lack of incremental effect of feedback.

It may be that we did not operationalize the feedback procedure in the most effective way. In these telephone interviews, we programmed a good deal of "backchannel" feedback for respondents because we felt that these utterances might be important to maintain

---

[4] For example, on the telephone we had many noncontingent short utterances to serve as messages to respondents that the interviewer was still on the phone and listening.

contact between interviewer and respondent. The backchannel feedback essentially told respondents that interviewers were still on the line and listening to their answers. It may be, however, that this sort of feedback reduced the power of our usual reinforcement techniques which are contingent upon the type of response elicited, since interviewees may have learned implicitly from the backchannel remarks that any response behavior was appropriate.

It is also possible that the special affective quality of telephone communication may have had an effect on respondents' perceptions of the feedback statements. If respondents treated the interview like other unexpected telephone contacts (e.g., sales pitches), they may have viewed the feedback statements as "phony" or insincere. Since there was no visual feedback accompanying the statements, respondents had no way to check the sincerity of the interviewers' remarks. It may be that the greater effectiveness of feedback in personal interviews is attributable, at least partially, to the fact that feedback statements in that setting were supplemented by visual feedback cues. The greater effectiveness of the commitment and instructions procedures in the personal interview may also be due partially to the additional nonverbal cues in that interaction.

Conclusion

In planning this study, we reasoned that the special character of telephone communication must be taken into account when devising interviewing techniques to maximize response validity in the telephone interview. We have tested some interviewing procedures which were developed in personal interviews as a beginning step in the development of special telephone procedures. The techniques do appear to have some effects, but they are fewer and of a different nature than we anticipated. The major conclusion is that telephone interviewing is not simply the transfer of face-to-face techniques to the telephone. Different communication patterns and respondent motives and the lack of visual cues appear to require considerable developmental research before identifying optimal telephone interviewing techniques.

References

Bandura, Albert
   1969   Principles of Behavior Modification. New York: Holt, Rinehart, and Winston.
Becker, H. S.
   1960   "Notes on the concept of commitment." American Journal of Sociology 66:32–40.

Blankenship, A.
1977 Professional Telephone Surveys. New York: McGraw Hill.
Brehm, J. W., and A. R. Cohen
1962 Explorations in Cognitive Dissonance. New York: Wiley.
Cannell, Charles, Gordon Fisher, and Thomas Bakker
1965 Reporting of Hospitalization in the Health Interview Survey. Washington, D.C.: PHS Vital and Health Statistics, Series 3, No. 6.
Cannell, Charles F., and Floyd J. Fowler
1963 A Study of the Reporting of Visits to Doctors in the National Health Survey. Research Report. Ann Arbor, Michigan: Survey Research Center.
Cannell, Charles F., Sally A. Lawson, and Doris L. Hausser
1975 A Technique for Evaluating Interviewer Performance. Ann Arbor, Michigan: Survey Research Center.
Cannell, Charles F., Peter V. Miller, and Lois Uksenberg
1981 "Research on interviewing techniques." In Samuel Leinhardt (ed.), Sociological Methodology 1981. San Francisco: Jossey-Bass.
Cannell, Charles F., Lois Oksenberg, and Jean M. Converse
1977 "Striving for response accuracy: experiments in new interviewing techniques." Journal of Marketing Research 14:306–15.
1979 Experiments in Interviewing Techniques: Field experiments in health reporting, 1971–1977. Ann Arbor, Michigan: Survey Research Center.
Cannell, Charles F., and Sally Robison
1971 "Analysis of individual questions." In Lansing, et al., Working Papers on Survey Research in Poverty Areas. Ann Arbor, Michigan: Survey Research Center.
Colombotos, John
1969 "Personal versus telephone interviews: effect on responses." Public Health Reports 84 9:773–82.
Dohrenwend, B. P., and B. S. Dohrenwend
1969 Social Status and Psychological Disorder: A Causal Inquiry. New York: Wiley.
Duncan, S.
1972 "Some signals and rules for taking speaking turns in conversation." Journal of Personality and Social Psychology 23:283–92.
Ekman, P.
1965 "Differential communication of affect by head and body cues." Journal of Personality and Social Psychology 2:726–35.
Gagne, R.
1964 "Problem solving." In Arthur W. Melton (ed.), Categories of Human Learning. New York: Academic Press.
Gerard, H. B.
1968 "Basic features of commitment." In R. P. Abelson et al. (eds.), Theories of Cognitive Consistency: A Source Book. Chicago; Rand McNally.
Gerard, H. B., E. S. Conolley, and R. A. Wilhelmy
1974 "Compliance, justification, and cognitive change." In Berkowitz (ed.), Advances in Experimental Social Psychology (Vol. 6). New York: Academic Press.
Goffman, E.
1961 Encounters. Indianapolis, Ind.: Bobbs-Merrill.
Groves, R. M., and R. L. Kahn
1979 Surveys by Telephone: A National Comparison with Personal Interviews. New York: Academic Press.
Hackman, J. R.
1969 "Toward understanding the role of tasks in behavioral research." Acta Psychologica 31:97–128.

Hochstim, Joseph R.
1967 "A critical comparison of three strategies of collecting data from households." Journal of the American Statistical Association 62:976–82.
Johnson, M. P.
1973 "Commitment: a conceptual structure and empirical application." The Sociological Quarterly 14:395–406.
Kendon, A.
1967 "Some functions of gaze direction in social interaction." Acta Psychologica 26:2–63.
Kiesler, C. A.
1971 The Psychology of Commitment. New York: Academic Press.
Langner, T. S.
1962 "A twenty-two item screening score of psychiatric symptoms indicating impairment." Journal of Health and Human Behavior 3:269–76.
McLaughlin, B.
1965 "Intentional and incidental learning in human subjects: the role of instructions to learn and motivation." Psychological Bulletin 63:359–76.
Marlatt, G. Alan
1972 "Task structure and the experimental modification of verbal behavior." Psychological Bulletin 78, 5:335–50.
Mehrabian, A.
1968 "Inference of attitudes from the posture, orientation, and distance of a communicator." Journal of Consulting and Clinical Psychology 23:283–92.
National Research Council
1979 Privacy and Confidentiality as Factors in Survey Response. Washington, D.C.: National Academy of Sciences.
Neter, John, and Joseph Waksberg
1965 Response Errors in Collection of Expenditures Data by Household Interviews: An Experimental Study. Bureau of the Census, Technical Paper No. 11.
Postman, L.
1964 "Short-term memory and incidental learning." In A. W. Melton (ed.), Categories of Human Learning. New York: Academic Press.
Steiner, Gary A.
1963 The People Look at Television: A Study of Audience Attitudes. New York: Knopf.
Sudman, S., N. Bradburn, and associates
1979 Improving Interview Method and Questionnaire Design. San Francisco: Jossey-Bass.
Waksberg, Joseph
1979 "Sampling methods for random digit dialing." Journal of the American Statistical Association 73:361–40–46.
Williams, E.
1977 "Experimental comparison of face-to-face and mediated communication: a review." Psychological Bulletin 84:963–76.

VALIDATION

There is no more fundamental issue in survey research than whether the answers given by respondents are correct. Do individuals accurately report their attitudes, behaviors, and personal situations? Although the fact–attitude divide is a fuzzy one, research on measurement error has taken very different approaches in the two domains. Validating the answers to factual items has involved the comparison of survey responses with observations from nonsurvey sources, typically administrative records. This can be done at the aggregate level (e.g., comparing the proportion of Reagan voters from a sample survey with the proportion of Reagan votes recorded at the polls), but the results of such comparisons may be due to sample composition (coverage or response rate problems), not respondent accuracy. Thus most research on measurement error has been carried out at the individual level.

One of the earliest and most comprehensive validation investigations was the Denver Validity Study of 1949 (Parry and Crossley, 1950). Inaccurate reports were found to range from 37% on contributions to charity to 14% on possession of a library card to 2%–3% on home and automobile ownership.

The causes of misreporting include both forgetting and social desirability biases. A study on the reporting of hospitalizations by Cannell, Fisher, and Bakker (1965) demonstrates both forces at work. The longer ago the hospitalization occurred, the shorter it was, and the more embarrassing the diagnosis, the less apt it was to be reported in the interview.

What are the consequences of inaccuracy for multivariate analysis? In some cases they are limited. In the selection that opens this section, for example, Katosh and Traugott found that the tendency of some respondents to falsely claim they voted did not lead to major changes in inferences about a series of characteristics that distinguish voters from nonvoters. In the next selection, however, Presser presents a case where overreporting substantially affected conclusions about the strength of the relationship between voting and political interest.

Both these studies, as is common in validation research, depended on matching survey respondents to entries in official records. In the reprinted article by Miller and Groves the matching procedure is itself shown to be a source of error. The discrepancies between survey and records (and therefore inferences about inaccuracy) were dramatically affected by the rules used to match cases. Consequently much of our knowledge about measurement error remains tentative.

The next two articles illustrate research designed to reduce the misreporting problem. Each demonstrates that changes in survey procedures can affect the extent of inaccuracy. The study by Bradburn, Sudman, Blair, and Stocking shows that long items are better than short ones and open questions better than closed questions in eliciting reports of sexual behavior and alcohol consumption. Similarly, the article by Zdep, Rhodes, Schwarz, and Kilkenny shows that a technique known as "Randomized Response" improves the reporting of drug use.

Studies of measurement error in attitudes, represented by the last two selections, have necessarily taken a very different tack. Andrews used a multimethod–multitrait design to assess the measurement properties of a large set of survey items, most of which are subjective. Measuring each construct in several ways allows him to partition the variation in an item into a valid or true component and a component due to the way the measurement is made. On that basis, he identifies formal features of questions associated with greater accuracy.

Bishop, Oldendick, Tuchfarber, and Bennett's analysis of answers to a fictitious item provides another way of examining measurement error in the attitudinal realm. Because their item was fictitious, the proportion who expressed an opinion on it may represent a minimum estimate of response error. However, Bishop et al. suggest that the resulting "nonattitudes" may not represent random error, but rather general attitudinal dispositions.

References

Cannell, Charles F., Gordon Fisher, and Thomas Bakker (1965)
    "Reporting of hospitalization in the health interview survey." Vital and Health
    Statistics, ser. 2, no. 6, i–71.
Parry, Hugh J., and Helen M. Crossley (1950)
    "Validity of responses to survey questions." Public Opinion Quarterly 14:61–80.

The Consequences of Validated
and Self-Reported Voting Measures

JOHN P. KATOSH AND MICHAEL W. TRAUGOTT

FOR some time, political scientists have been developing and testing models of electoral behavior based upon measurements containing a relatively large amount of error. Even when the underlying concepts implied very simple and straightforward measures of recall or reports of political participation, such as registration status or voting behavior, a variety of social psychological pressures were known to result in systematic overreports of eligibility and participation (Dinerman, 1948; Miller, 1952; Parry and Crosley, 1950; Cahalan, 1968). And the magnitude of the reporting errors has been substantial, in the range of 15 to 25 percent greater self-reported participation rates than validated ones (Clausen, 1968; Traugott and Katosh, 1979).

In this paper, our interest is to report on recent validation efforts, comparing data collected in the "on-year" election of 1976 with the

Abstract This paper reports on the results of validation of the self-reported registration status and voting behavior of respondents in the 1976 and 1978 American National Election Studies. The results indicate about one in seven of the respondents misreported their registration status or voting behavior. Comparative analyses are conducted using simple regression models to see if differences in their explanatory power arise using validated and self-reported dependent variables. The results show that there are no major changes in the fundamental nature of basic relationships that have been observed since the first surveys were conducted. Analysis of the effects of overreported participation on estimates of the partisan division of the vote in three sets of subnational contests reveals a likely "bandwagon" effect.

John P. Katosh is a doctoral student in the Department of Political Science and Michael W. Traugott is Senior Study Director in the Center for Political Studies at the University of Michigan. Portions of the data utilized in this article were made available by the Inter-university Consortium for Political and Social Research. The data for the 1976 and 1978 American National Election Studies were originally collected by the Center for Political Studies of the Institute for Social Research, The University of Michigan, under a grant from the National Science Foundation. Neither the original collectors of the data nor the Consortium bear any responsibility for the analyses or interpretations presented here. The comments of an anonymous reviewer, which resulted in a fruitful extension of the analysis, are gratefully acknowledged.

"off-year" election in 1978, in order to ascertain whether misreporting varies with the electoral context. Furthermore, we are interested in submitting certain basic models of electoral participation to comparative tests in which the dependent variable is alternatively measured on the basis of self-report and then through a check of administrative records. Our purpose is not the fundamental revision of the models themselves, but an estimation of the consequences of using error-laden or relatively error-free measures of registration status and voting behavior. In attempting to determine the boundaries of the magnitude and direction of the relationship between a variety of predictors and self-reported and validated behavior, we will gain a better understanding of the confidence we place in what we think we know about the roots of electoral participation.

The 1978 Vote Validation Study

Immediately following the completion of interviewing for the Center for Political Studies 1978 National Election Study, members of the field staff were directed to visit the local administrative office which was responsible for the maintenance of individual registration and voting records. The staff was instructed to obtain from the official records the registration status and 1978 voting behavior for each respondent to the election study.

Rather than assuming respondents who reported being registered to vote were registered at their current address (where the interview was conducted), the 1978 election study included, for the first time, a question on the interview schedule which asked respondents who reported being registered, "Are you registered to vote at your current address?" Respondents who answered negatively—and about one in nine did—were then asked to provide the address at which they were registered. In most cases this produced an address in another part of the town or county in which they resided, but in some instances an address in another part of the country was given. In either event, for these respondents an official records check was made for both the address at which the interview was conducted and the reported registration address. When a reported registration address was in a "non-sample" county, the records check was done by telephone by a member of the study staff.

The first set of research findings reported here presents the results of a comparison of the respondents' self-reports of registration status and voting behavior with the information obtained from the official records. The presentation includes a discussion of the magnitude of the misreporting of electoral participation and the characteristics of those who misreported their registration or voting in 1978, as well as a comparison with the results obtained from a similar study following the 1976 election. The second set of findings concern the effects of using self-reported and validated measures as variables in a variety of models of electoral behavior. The third set examines the effects of misreporting on the partisan division of the vote.

Vote Validation Results

The results from the 1978 Vote Validation Study indicate that only 62 percent of the election study respondents were found to be actually registered, compared to the 73 percent who reported during their interviews that they were registered to vote. And while 55 percent of the respondents claimed to have voted in the 1978 general election, the results of the validation study yielded a turnout figure 12 percentage points lower (43%). As was the case for 1976, both of these "validated" figures are much closer to the Census Bureau's reported estimates and to aggregate election returns than were the original self-reported figures. In fact, the 1978 validated participation rates were about one to three percentage points lower than the Census Bureau estimates.

The primary source of these differences between the estimates generated from the Michigan surveys and those conducted by the Census Bureau are methodological (Clausen, 1968; Census Bureau, 1979; Traugott and Katosh, 1979). The greater reliability of the bureau estimates comes primarily from larger sample sizes, a higher response rate, and conceivably, the fact that all interviews are conducted within a two-week period shortly after the election. The bureau interview is a supplement to the November Current Population Survey and is extremely brief (usually from eight to ten questions). The Michigan interviews start the day after election and continue till late December, a period at about eight weeks. The specific questions on registration and voting are virtually identical in the two surveys,[1] but the Michigan

---

[1] In the 1978 November Voting Supplement Questionnaire used by the Bureau of the Census, the question wordings and sequence used to obtain information about each household member were as follows:

This month we have some questions concerning registration and voting.
41. Is . . . a citizen of the United States?
42. In any election some people are not able to vote because they are sick or busy, or have some other reason, and others do not want to vote. Did . . . vote in the election on November 7th?
44. (If NO, to Q. 42) Was . . . registered to vote in the November 7th election?
In the 1978 American National Election Study conducted by the Center for Political Studies, the question wordings and sequence were as follows:

interview takes over one hour and is filled with political content that has supported analysis by a generation of social scientists. It is the validity of this research which is being addressed by the data presented here.

The discrepancies between the self-reported and validated participation rates reported in Table 1 are irrefutable documentation that a substantial amount of misreporting of registration status and voting behavior occurs in the CPS National Election Studies, as it undoubtedly does in other national political surveys. And the net effect is to consistently overstate the levels of participation in a socially desirable direction—being registered and having voted. The differences in the CPS self-reported and validated registration rates for 1976 and 1978 were 8 and 11 percentage points, respectively. And, while both of the 1978 voting rates reflect the drop-off effects of "surge and decline" (Campbell, 1960), the differences between the self-reported and validated rates are of the same magnitude for the two election years— about 12 percentage points.

We define "misreporters" as those respondents whose self-report of registration status or voting behavior in the election survey could not be verified when the official record check was made. Some are people who reported that they were registered or that they voted, but for whom no official record of that behavior was found. Others reported that they were not registered or did not vote, but according to the

Table 1. Comparison of National Election Study, Validation, and Census Bureau Participation Rate Estimates, 1976 and 1978

	Registration Rates		Voting Rates	
	1976	1978	1976	1978
Election Study self-report	77%	73%	72%	55%
	(2,865)	(2,268)	(2,415)	(2,292)
Validation	69	62	61	43
	(2,344)	(2,262)	(2,329)	(2,230)
Census Bureau[a]	67	63	59	46

NOTE: All rate entries are percentages of respondents registered or voting, either by self-report or validated.

[a] The sample N's for the Census Bureau's Current Population Survey are not published. Rather, the data are weighted to estimate the entire U.S. eligible voting population.

Q.H1. In talking to people about elections, we often find that a lot of people were not able to vote because (they weren't old enough), they weren't registered, they were sick, or they just don't have time. How about you—did you vote in the elections this November?

Q.H8. (If NO or Don't Know in Q.H1) Were you registered to vote in this election?

Citizenship of each household member was ascertained during enumeration of its composition. Only persons 18 or older and citizens, as of November 7, 1978, were eligible respondents in the survey, and they were only asked about their own behavior.

official records they actually were registered or had voted. Those survey respondents whose names were not obtained in the survey, and hence could not be checked, are excluded from classification, as are those respondents whose reports of registration or voting status were not obtained during the survey. Those respondents who resided in places where the voting records could not be checked are also excluded from a vote classification.

The extent of registration and vote misreporting can be determined from Table 2, which categorizes the 1976 and 1978 Election Studies respondents' reports of their registration status and voting behavior by information obtained in the two Vote Validation Studies. It can be ascertained from these data that approximately 14 percent of the sample respondents were misreporters. Among these people, 2.1 percent "underreported" their registration status and 12.3 percent "overreported" it, while 1.3 percent "underreported" their voting behavior and 12.8 percent "overreported" it. All these results are virtually identical to the percentages obtained from the 1976 study (Traugott and Katosh, 1979). The comparable figures were 3.2 percent "underreporters" and 12.3 percent "overreporters" of registration, 1.1 percent "underreporters" and 12.2 percent "overreporters" of voting.

Data in Table 3 characterize the misreporters from the 1976 and 1978 studies according to a selected list of variables and, in some instances, selected categories within those variables. Among the demographic variables, race and, to a lesser extent, age and income appear related to whether or not a respondent was a misreporter. In 1978 the relationships between those latter variables and registration misreporting are weaker than in 1976 and virtually nonexistent for vote misreporting. Neither sex nor education seem to be related to misreporting. Among the attitudinal variables there appear to be some differences for registration misreporters on all three indices—efficacy, trust, and duty. For those who misreported voting, however, no clear pattern emerges. Likewise, neither of the two partisanship components—direction or strength—seem related to misreporting.

Effect of Misreporting on Models of Electoral Participation

While a variety of social scientists are interested in methodological problems of response validity and the overreport of registration status and voting behavior, the major substantive concern for those who study elections is the effects of misreport on standard models of electoral participation. In particular, do the well-established and commonly observed relationships between a variety of independent measures and self-reported registration and voting behavior hold

Table 2. Vote Validation Respondent Classification by Election Study Self-Reports of Registration and Voting, 1976 and 1978

Vote Validation Respondent Classification	1976 Election Study Self-Report[a]						1978 Election Study Self-Report					
	Registered			Voted			Registered			Voted		
	Yes	No	NA	Yes	No	NA	Yes	No	NA	Yes	No	NA
1. Registration recorded Vote recorded	1,358	55	4	1,390	27	0	949	10	1	931	29	0
2. Registration recorded No voting information	28	1	0	23	6	0	29	3	0	18	14	0
3. Registration recorded No record of voting	157	18	1	70	106	0	373	34	13	123	294	3
4. No record of registration No record of voting	288	439	9	217	519	0	274	558	18	162	683	5
5. Missing data[b]	36	21	0	32	25	0	28	10	4	16	22	4
	1,867	534	14	1,732	683	0	1,653	615	36	1,250	1,042	12

NOTE: The boxed figures represent those individuals who are considered to be "misreporters."

[a] These data were adopted from Table 2 of Traugott and Katosh, 1979.

[b] This category includes cases in which the name of respondent was not obtained, an incomplete address for registration was available, or, in 1976, the respondent resided outside the P.S.U. and record check was attempted.

Table 3. Selected Characteristics of Respondents Who Misrepresented Their Registration
or Voting, 1976 and 1978

	% Misreporting Registration		% Misreporting Voting	
	1976	1978	1976	1978
Total Sample[a]	15%	14%	14%	14%
Sex				
Male	17	14	15	15
Female	15	15	12	14
Education				
Grade school	14	13	15	13
High school	16	14	12	13
College	15	16	14	16
Age				
18–24	22	17	18	14
45 or older	12	12	12	13
Race				
Nonwhite	24	26	20	21
White	14	13	12	13
Income				
Less than $6,000	22	17	19	16
$20,000 or more	12	14	10	15
Political efficacy				
Very low	17	15	15	15
Very high	13	11	12	11
Political trust				
Very low	16	17	13	16
Very high	16	9	12	13
Citizen duty				
Very low	22	20	15	12
Very high	15	15	14	16
Party identification				
Democrat	16	16	16	15
Independent	16	15	13	14
Republican	13	11	11	14
Partisan strength				
Strong	16	14	14	15
Weak	15	15	14	15
Independent & Independent-leaner	13	15	16	14

[a] Excluding those respondents whose names were not obtained (category 5 in Table 2)
and, for voting only, respondents who resided in places where the voting records could
not be checked (category 2 in Table 2).

up—or perhaps even increase in strength—when the dependent variable is validated registration and voting behavior?

For the purposes of testing the effects of measurement of the dependent variable, three representative regression models were used to predict registration status and voter participation (Campbell et al., 1960; Milbrath and Goel, 1977; Verba and Nie, 1972). The first was a simple socioeconomic status (SES) model using the usual trichotomous measure of education—grade school, high school, college—and a four-level collapsing of family income—less than $8,000, $8,000 to $14,999, $15,000 to $22,999, and more than $23,000—as predictors. The second test consisted of a social psychological model employing three five-level attitudinal measures—citizen duty, political efficacy, and trust in government—as independent variables. Third, a party identification model was tested in which strength of preference— strong, weak, leaner, independent—and direction of preference— Democrat, Independent, Republican—were the predictors. Finally, a model combining all of these elements was used. The dependent variable in each regression was a dichotomous variable for which a 1 designated the existence of the trait in question (registration or voting—self-reported or validated) and a 0 its absence. (See Appendix for a description of the coding for each of these variables).

In order to facilitate pairwise evaluations of the models, three simple tests were employed. The first was based upon the total variance explained in each of the two dependent variables. The second and third tests were based upon examination of the standardized regression coefficients in order to ascertain whether the relative importance of any of the variables in the regression changed and whether the direction of any of the relationships was reversed.

Data in Table 4 summarize the consequences of using self-reported and validated dependent variables in regression models of registration for 1976 and 1978. The proportion of variance explained is virtually identical in each of the pairwise tests, yet in all but one instance greater for the self-reported measure. Furthermore, there are no changes of signs associated with the betas, and none of the statistically significant coefficients shift in their relative importance. All of the models consistently explain more variance in registration status in the "on-year" of 1976 than in the "off-year" of 1978, although the results from the party identification model are less distinct than the others.

Of the simple models, the one based upon the three political attitudes explains the most variance in registration status, ranging from 6 to 11 percent. Only two of the measures—citizen duty and political efficacy—are consistently significant, and duty is clearly the more important of the two. The other two models have equivalent, limited explanatory powers. In the socioeconomic status model, education and income have about equal explanatory power. In the party identification model, the strength dimension is substantially more important than the directional one.

In the combined model, at least the most significant predictor from each of the three simple models remains important. Citizen duty and strength of party identification are by far the two best predictors of

Table 4. The Consequences of Using Validated and Self-Reported Dependent Variables in Regression Models of Registration, 1976 and 1978

	1976				1978			
	Self-Reported		Validated		Self-Reported		Validated	
Simple SES model	R = .189 (R² = .036) (N = 2,644)		R = .194 (R² = .038) (N = 2,656)		R = .152 (R² = .023) (N = 1,972)		R = .151 (R² = .023) (N = 1,972)	
	b	beta	b	beta	b	beta	b	beta
Education	.05 *	.12	.06 *	.13	.06 *	.09	.04 *	.06
Income	.07 *	.11	.08 *	.11	.04 *	.09	.05 *	.12
Attitudinal model	R = .332 (R² = .110) (N = 2,302)		R = .290 (R² = .084) (N = 2,310)		R = .282 (R² = .080) (N = 2,181)		R = .243 (R² = .059) (N = 2,176)	
	b	beta	b	beta	b	beta	b	beta
Citizen duty	.13 *	.30	.11 *	.22	.12 *	.27	.11 *	.23
Political efficacy	.03 *	.11	.05 *	.15	.02 **	.05	.02 **	.05
Trust in government	-.01	-.03	-.01	-.02	-.02 **	-.05	-.01	-.02
Party identification model	R = .190 (R² = .036) (N = 2,823)		R = .156 (R² = .024) (N = 2,836)		R = .189 (R² = .036) (N = 2,198)		R = .167 (R² = .028) (N = 2,186)	
	b	beta	b	beta	b	beta	b	beta
Strength of identification	.08 *	.19	.07 *	.14	.09 *	.19	.08 *	.17
Direction of identification	.02	.03	.06 *	.09	.03 **	.05	.04 *	.07
Combined model	R = .371 (R² = .138) (N = 2,132)		R = .341 (R² = .116) (N = 2,138)		R = .328 (R² = .108) (N = 1,873)		R = .284 (R² = .081) (N = 1,867)	
	b	beta	b	beta	b	beta	b	beta
Education	.03 *	.09	.04 *	.11	.04 **	.06	.02	.03
Income	.03 **	.05	.03	.05	.02 *	.06	.04 *	.10
Citizen duty	.11 *	.26	.10 *	.19	.11 *	.23	.10 *	.19
Political efficacy	.02 **	.06	.03 *	.10	.01	.04	.01	.02
Trust in government	-.01	-.04	-.02	-.04	-.03 *	-.06	-.01	-.03
Strength of party ID	.07 *	.16	.07 *	.14	.07 *	.16	.07 *	.14
Direction of party ID	.01	.01	.01	.02	-.00	-.01	.01	.02

* Coefficient significant at .01 level.   ** Coefficient significant at .05 level.

registration status. Although this model has the greatest proportion of explained variance associated with it, the amount is only marginally greater than for the attitudinal model alone.

Data in Table 5 summarize the consequences of using validated and self-reported dependent variables in regressions of voter participation in 1976 and 1978. The statistical results are essentially the same as for the registration models, although the levels of variance explained are substantially higher. More variance is explained using the self-reported rather than the validated measure of voting. The major difference from the registration models is that the party identification equation explains more of the variance in voting behavior in 1978 than in 1976, clearly a function of the "surge and decline" phenomenon in the off-year electorate.

The best of the simple models of voting behavior is again the social psychological one, which explains 7 to 14 percent of the variance. The SES model is the next best in these terms, and the party identification model is last. In 1978, using the validated measure, the importance of education and family income is reversed; and only income remains significant in the 1978 combined model regression.

In summary, there are no substantial differences in the fundamental nature of relationships between predictors or in the explanatory power of models of registration and voting behavior regardless of whether self-reported or validated measures of the dependent variables are used. Slightly more variation can be explained in the self-reported measures which contain error than in the validated measures.

Effects of Misreporting on the Division of the Vote

When the effects of validated and self-reported measures of political behavior on the direction of the vote are considered, a much different analytical situation arises. First of all, interest is focused upon voting to the virtual exclusion of registration. And secondly, many researchers would be as interested in final preelection survey estimates of the expected partisan division of the vote as they would in the accuracy of postelection analysis of what happened (Traugott, 1980).

Overreporting of turnout in presidential contests seems to have clear and well-understood consequences for survey estimates of the partisan division of the results (Traugott and Katosh, 1980). Since 1952, the effect in postelection surveys has appeared as a type of "bandwagon" effect in support for the winning candidate, taking into account the short-term forces of the campaign. That is, the reported

Table 5. The Consequences of Using Validated and Self-Reported Dependent Variables in Regression Models of Voter Participation, 1976 and 1978

	1976				1978			
	Self-Reported		Validated		Self-Reported		Validated	
	b	beta	b	beta	b	beta	b	beta
Simple SES model	R = .258 (R² = .066) (N = 2,250)		R = .246 (R² = .061) (N = 2,224)		R = .174 (R² = .030) (N = 1,988)		R = .167 (R² = .028) (N = 1,943)	
Education	.07 *	.16	.09 *	.19	.08 *	.11	.06 *	.08
Income	.10 *	.15	.07 *	.10	.05 *	.10	.05 *	.12
Attitudinal model	R = .374 (R² = .140) (N = 2,310)		R = .309 (R² = .096) (N = 2,280)		R = .281 (R² = .079) (N = 2,204)		R = .261 (R² = .068) (N = 2,147)	
Citizen duty	.14 *	.30	.12 *	.23	.13 *	.27	.12 *	.23
Political efficacy	.06 *	.19	.06 *	.16	.02 **	.05	.03 *	.09
Trust in government	−.01	−.02	−.00	−.00	−.02	−.04	−.02	−.03
Party identification model	R = .187 (R² = .035) (N = 2,375)		R = .179 (R² = .032) (N = 2,346)		R = .211 (R² = .044) (N = 2,220)		R = .194 (R² = .038) (N = 2,155)	
Strength of identification	.08 *	.18	.08 *	.16	.10 *	.20	.09 *	.18
Direction of identification	.04 *	.07	.07 *	.10	.07 *	.11	.07 *	.11
Combined model	R = .419 (R² = .176) (N = 2,138)		R = .373 (R² = .139) (N = 2,112)		R = .338 (R² = .114) (N = 1,887)		R = .307 (R² = .094) (N = 1,842)	
Education	.05 *	.12	.07 *	.15	.06 *	.08	.03	.04
Income	.05 *	.07	.03	.04	.03 *	.07	.04 *	.10
Citizen duty	.12 *	.25	.11 *	.20	.11 *	.22	.10 *	.19
Political efficacy	.04 *	.12	.03 *	.09	.01	.02	.02	.05
Trust in government	−.01	−.03	−.01	−.02	−.02	−.04	−.02	−.03
Strength of party ID	.07 *	.15	.07 *	.14	.09 *	.18	.08 *	.15
Direction of party ID	.01	.02	.04 **	.06	.03 **	.05	.04 **	.05

* Coefficient significant at .01 level.   ** Coefficient significant at .05 level.

vote division favored the winner in proportion to his winning margin, compared to his expected vote (Converse, 1966), and the overreport of his vote was due primarily to a disproportionate amount of support from persons who said they voted for him but whose participation could not be confirmed.

However, the comparison of the effects of alternative measures of voting behavior on the distribution of voter preferences in nonpresidential elections is complicated by a number of issues. In off-year elections, there are no national candidates running for office whose names appear on every ballot. Therefore, analysis of the direction of the vote should ideally be restricted to the partisan division of votes within subnational constituencies; failing that, it might be based upon the votes cast for different candidates running for the same type of office aggregated across a number of subnational constituencies. These include contests held in congressional districts across the entire country or in the subset of states in which senatorial or gubernatorial seats are at stake. Data of the latter type, appropriate for a tentative test of these effects upon contests for U.S. representative and senator, as well as governor, are available from the 1978 American National Election Study survey and provide the basis for the comparison of the consequences of validated and self-reported measures of voting on the resulting distributions of party (but only indirectly candidate) preference.[2]

There are two competing though not necessarily mutually exclusive hypotheses which might be tested in the context of estimating the vote division for these three offices. In one case, knowing that there is a tendency for Democrats to overreport their turnout compared to Republicans, we might expect the distributions of the direction of

[2] The analysis which follows is based upon selected survey responses according to the office, from only those self-reported voters who lived in states in which there were gubernatorial and senatorial elections in 1978, as well as contests for the U.S. House. Furthermore, the hypotheses suggest that the analysis be limited to those races involving incumbents, so no data from states or congressional districts involving "open" races were included. The responses were then aggregated to the national level for all those who met the above residency criteria. The general form of the voting questions was:

Q.H10.(Interviewer: show Respondent ballot card) Here is a list of candidates for the major races in this district. How about the election for House of Representatives in Washington. Did you prefer one of the candidates for the U.S. House of Representatives?
Q.H10a.Which candidate was that?
Q.H12.How about the election for the United States Senate? Did you prefer one of the candidates for the U.S. Senate?
Q.H12a.Which candidate was that?
Q.H14.How about the election for Governor—did you prefer one of the candidates for Governor?
Q.H14aWhich candidate was that?

self-reported vote for these lower-level offices to be more Democratic than the analogous distributions obtained from validated voters. In this case, there is no expectation of an office- or campaign-specific effect below the national level, only a party-specific one.

The second hypothesis—based upon what we have learned in the presidential case—suggests that the disparity between self-reported and validated estimates will be a function of the disparity between the winners' actual performance and the expected normal vote outcome of the election, tempered by candidate visibility. Campaigns for statewide office are now quite extensive, resulting in the expenditure of millions of dollars and engendering considerable media coverage in the form of news and advertising, particularly on television. As a result, both the senatorial and gubernatorial candidates in a race are quite visible by the end of the campaign. In these contests, defection rates—votes cast by self-described partisans for candidates of the other party—have generally been increasing over time and seem to be a function of a candidate's campaign resources and effectiveness. The direction of the defections might favor either the incumbent or the challenger, as they do in the presidential case. In House races, however, constituencies are more compact. The campaigns are much smaller in scope and involve much less media coverage because of the poor fit between media markets and congressional districts (Goldenberg and Traugott, 1980). Here the defection rates have also been increasing, but almost uniformly in the direction of the incumbent. Being the incumbent is synonymous with being advantaged by the short-term forces of the campaign and a virtual guarantee of reelection.

The ideal test of these competing hypotheses would involve a detailed state and district-level comparison of election returns, the normal vote estimate for the relevant constituency, and the two survey-based estimates of the vote division. Then the hypothesized bandwagon effect for misreporters relative to valid voters could be analyzed for a number of individual races. Unfortunately, the Michigan surveys are not designed to support such detailed analysis at the subregional level. Instead, national-level estimates of the partisan vote division for each of these three races were produced from the survey so that defection rates could be compared for validated and misreported voters in contests involving incumbent candidates seeking reelection.

The competing hypotheses about the effects of misreporting participation on estimates of the partisan division of the vote lead quite straightforwardly to expectations of two different patterns of defection which might be found. If it is simply a respondent's party identification which is providing the internal cue for misreporting vote direction in contests below the presidency—and short-term campaign forces do not have a role—then the defection rates should always be greater for validated voters than for misreporters. If we take incumbency as an indicator of campaign advantage, however, then defection rates should always be greater in that candidate's direction than toward the party of the respondent. Furthermore, the defection rates should be relatively greater in the incumbents' favor in House races, where that candidate status is synonymous with the campaign advantage, than in either the statewide gubernatorial or senatorial contests. Data designed to test these hypotheses are presented in Table 6.

The distribution of defection rates, controlling on the party and status of candidates for these three races, seem to support the bandwagon hypothesis at the expense of the notion that the respondents' party identification is the basis for their misreporting candidate support. The defection rates among misreporters are clearly in the direction favoring incumbents, and they are rarely less than equivalent rates for validated voters. More important, the data suggest that the direction of misreporting seems to favor the winning candidate.

In the House races, where being the incumbent virtually assures victory and by a comfortable margin, defections to the challenger range from only 3 to 6 percent. For the statewide contests where both

Table 6. Defection Rates Among Validated and Misreported Voters in Contests for Governor, U.S. Senator, and Representative Involving Incumbents, 1978

Contests	Democratic Incumbents		Republican Incumbents	
	Defections to Democrats	Defections to Republicans	Defections to Democrats	Defections to Republicans
House races				
Validated voters	54%	6%	3%	54%
	(108)	(194)	(124)	(113)
Misreported voters	46	3	4	67
	(24)	(59)	(22)	(24)
Senate races				
Validated voters	23	11	6	32
	(26)	(54)	(72)	(106)
Misreported voters	60	25	17	24
	(5)	(20)	(30)	(25)
Gubernatorial races				
Validated voters	28	13	9	40
	(109)	(119)	(64)	(83)
Misreported voters	53	20	11	41
	(17)	(40)	(18)	(17)

NOTE: All rate entries are percentages of respondents registered or voting, either by self-report or validated.

candidates are visible by the end of the campaign and defection is generally more rampant in the electorate, the defection rates of the misreporters to the challengers are greater than in the House races, ranging from 6 to 25 percent. They are also greater than for validated voters in the same type of races, presumably a reflection of the greater number of successful challenges in these races compared to the House. However, only an intensive extension of this analysis at the constituency level could ascertain with reasonable certainty that these misreported defections were in fact in the direction which favored "upset" winners. This clearly constitutes a potentially fruitful avenue for future research.

Summary and Conclusions

The analysis presented above provides information about the validity and reliability of two important measures commonly used in studies of electoral behavior. The first part of the presentation discussed the nature and extent of misreports of the registration status and voting behavior of respondents in national surveys conducted in conjunction with the two recent general elections. In the second part, the effects of such errors on the strength and direction of basic relationships between these measures and the respondents' socioeconomic status and political attitudes were tested.

The analysis of the magnitude of errors showed a consistent misreporting of approximately 14 percentage points and a consistent overreporting of approximately 12 percentage points for both registration status and voting behavior in both 1976 and 1978. Because turnout was characteristically much lower in the off-year general election of 1978, this level of overreport is proportionately much greater. Given the unidirectional nature and the patterns of misreporting associated with various socioeconomic and attitudinal groups in the population, we are left with a strong suspicion that some respondents feel compelled to give socially acceptable responses in the interview situation. As for the effects of misreported turnout on postelection estimates of the division of the vote, there is strong evidence of a bandwagon effect in support of the winner, tempered by the candidate's relative electoral performance.

Of more immediate concern to political scientists who have been analyzing almost 30 years of data in the SRC/CPS election survey time series, what are the potential effects of these misreporting errors which we must assume are present in all the studies? Fortunately, we do not find any major changes in the fundamental nature of the basic relationships that have been observed since the data were first collected. Of much less concern is the consistent observation that slightly stronger relationships appear when the self-reported measures are used instead of the validated ones, although the differences are very small.

In this regard, the Vote Validation Studies conducted in conjunction with the 1976 and 1978 National Election Studies must be labeled a collective success for political scientists. While we have been able to increase our understanding of the methodological problems associated with the conduct of interviews about political behavior, we have not as a result suffered a catastrophic loss of any of the substantial body of knowledge about electoral behavior that we have been assembling for the past three decades.

Appendix
Variables Used in the Regression Runs Reported in Tables 4 and 5

Education
  1 grade school
  2 high school
  3 college

Income
  1 less than $8,000
  2 $8,000–$14,999
  3 $15,000–$22,999
  4 $23,000 or more

Trust in government, political efficacy, citizen duty
  1 very low
  2 low
  3 medium
  4 high
  5 very high

Party identification—direction
  1 Democrat
  2 Independent
  3 Republican

Party identification—strength
  1 Independent
  2 Independent-leaner
  3 weak
  4 strong

Registration—self-report & validated
  0 not registered
  1 registered

Voting—Self-report & validated
  0 did not vote
  1 voted

References

Campbell, Angus, Gerald Gurin, and Warren Miller
  1954   The Voter Decides. Evanston: Row and Peterson.
Clausen, Aage
  1968   "Response validity: vote report." Public Opinion Quarterly 41:56–64.
Converse, Philip E.
  1966   "The concept of a normal vote." In A. Campbell, P. Converse, W. Miller, and D. Stokes, Elections and the Political Order. New York: Wiley.
Dinerman, Helen
  1948   "1948 votes in the making—a preview." Public Opinion Quarterly 12:585–98.

Goldenberg, Edie N., and Michael W. Traugott
  1980   "Congressional campaign effects on candidate recognition and evaluation." Political Behavior 2:61–90.
Milbrath, Lester W., and M. L. Goel
  1977   Political Participation. Chicago: Rand McNally.
Miller, Mungo
  1952   "The Waukegan study of voter turnout prediction." Public Opinion Quarterly 16:381–98.
Parry, Hugh J., and Helen M. Crossley
  1950   "Validity of responses to survey questions." Public Opinion Quarterly 14:61–80.
Traugott, Michael W.
  1980   "Estimating election outcomes from surveys of the electorate." Paper presented at the Special National Workshop on Research Methodology and Criminal Justice Program Evaluation, Baltimore.
Traugott, Michael W., and John P. Katosh
  1979   "Response validity in surveys of voting behavior." Public Opinion Quarterly 43:359–77.
U.S. Bureau of the Census
  1979   "Voting and registration in the election of November 1978." Current Population Reports, Series P-20, No. 344, U.S. Printing Office, Washington, D.C., 1979.
Verba, Sidney, and Norman Nie
  1972   Participation in America. New York: Harper and Row.

Is Inaccuracy on Factual Survey Items Item-Specific or Respondent-Specific?

STANLEY PRESSER

PERHAPS the most fundamental question in survey research is that posed in the title of Herbert Hyman's 1944 paper, "Do They Tell the Truth?" Implicit in Hyman's question are issues that should concern every survey analyst. These include the level of inaccuracy in survey data, the characteristics of inaccurate reporters, and the extent to which inaccuracy is respondent-specific as opposed to item-specific.

The earliest large-scale effort to address these issues, the 1949 Denver Community Study, still ranks among the most extensive investigations into the validity of survey data. At the end of the study's field period, record checks were conducted for 14 items asked during the interview. On the first issue, concerning levels of inconsistency between respondent claims and official records, Parry and Crossley (1950) reported that the discrepancies ranged from 2 percent (for an item on home ownership) to 38 percent (for an item on Community

Abstract The assumption that reporting errors are uncorrelated across survey items was tested using data from the 1949 Denver Community Survey. Respondent reports to 14 questions in that study were later validated with official records. Inaccuracy was found to be item-specific for questions about seven generally unrelated subjects. By contrast, for seven questions on electoral behavior, all of which were significantly associated, the assumption of uncorrelated errors was clearly violated: respondents inaccurate on one of the seven were disproportionately inaccurate on each of the other six. This held for groups defined by sex, age, education, and political interest. The correlated error term, combined with a tendency for levels of inaccuracy to be greater for those who expressed higher political interest, substantially increased the size of the relationship between voting and political interest. The implications of these results for survey research are discussed.

The author is Director of the Detroit Area Study in the Sociology Department, at the University of Michigan. This paper was begun while he was at the University of North Carolina's Institute for Research in Social Science. Patricia Rector rendered excellent assistance in setting up the computer work, and George Rabinowitz provided valuable help with part of the analysis. Duane Alwin, Frank Andrews, James House, and Howard Schuman offered good criticisms of an earlier draft.

Chest contribution), and were almost entirely in one direction—that of respondent overreport. Many years later, Cahalan (1968) took up the second issue by analyzing the relation between inaccuracy in the Denver data and respondent age, sex, and socioeconomic status (as estimated by the interviewer). He argued that his results showed a tendency for younger and lower SES respondents to be less accurate, particularly about voting.

The discovery that invalidity on different items is associated with a constant set of characteristics does not necessarily resolve the third issue about whether invalidity is respondent-specific or item-specific, for the two issues need not be related. Younger respondents, for example, may be more likely than older ones to misreport across a number of items, but it may be different young people who misreport on the different items. The issue of respondent- versus item-specific inaccuracy has never been examined with the Denver data. This is surprising since the issue bears on an assumption common in survey analysis. Many analysts who examine bivariate or multivariate relationships do not assume perfect measurement of individual variables, but most analysts do assume that the inaccuracy in different variables is unrelated. In statistical parlance, this is the assumption of uncorrelated error terms.

Unlike the questions about levels of invalidity and characteristics of inaccurate respondents, the issue of uncorrelated errors has rarely been examined in a record-check study. Such investigations typically involve only a single variable (e.g., Hyman, 1944; Lansing, et al., 1961; and Wyner, 1980), not the multiple validations needed to determine if errors are independent. Even some studies that examine more than one variable ignore the question. Traugott and Katosh (1979), for example, carried out validations of claims about both registration and voting, but treated them separately, providing no indication of whether the two sets of errors were associated. Similarly, Cannell, et al. (1965) analysed respondent inaccuracy about various aspects of hospitalization experience (length of stay, nature of illness, etc.), but were silent on the extent to which inaccuracy was related across items.

I have been able to locate only two record-check studies that address the error correlation issue.[1] In a survey of University of New Hampshire students, Hamilton (1981) discovered that errors in reports of Verbal SAT score were related to errors in reports of both Mathe-

---

[1] There are also a handful of studies that draw inferences about error correlations from data on reliability (e.g., Siegel and Hodge, 1968, and Bielby and Hauser, 1977). Error is assessed in a different manner in these analyses than in record check studies.

matical SAT score and grade point average. In a survey of black mothers receiving public assistance, Weiss (1968) validated answers to four different items and found that, "Except for the questions on registration and voting . . . respondents inaccurate on one question were not more likely to be inaccurate on others [p. 623]." The purpose of the present paper is to explore this issue further with data from a general population. I test the assumption of uncorrelated errors in the Denver study and examine the consequences of departures from it.

Description of the Data

The Denver Community Survey was conducted in the second quarter of 1949 by the University of Denver's Opinion Research Center. A systematic random sample of 1,350 names was drawn from the 1948 Denver City Directory. The addresses corresponding to the selected names were then divided equally into five geographical areas constructed to be as similar as possible according to Census measures of socioeconomic status. Field work in each area was carried out by nine interviewers who received randomized assignments of equal size. Of the designated respondents, 278 turned out to be ineligible (had moved from the city, were under 21, did not speak English, etc.), and 920 provided usable interviews, for a response rate of 86 percent.[2]

Answers to 14 of the survey items were later checked against appropriate official documents. The validated items asked about ownership of a home and automobile; possession of a public library card, driver's license, and telephone; voter registration status and participation in six different elections; contribution to the Community Chest; and respondent's age. (See the Appendix for exact question wordings.) As earlier authors have noted, the records used to validate respondent reports doubtless contain errors. In addition, the checking process itself was a potential source of error. Although the error introduced by these sources is apt to be both small and randomly distributed, the possibility that these factors affected the pattern of results presented below cannot be ruled out. As a convenient

---

[2] Assignments to interviewers were randomized to permit the study of interviewer effects. See Smith and Hyman (1950) and Feldman, et al. (1950–51), or Hyman (1954). For further description of the sampling and field operations see Crossley and Fink (1951) and Parry and Crossley (1950). This is an appropriate place to credit the original investigators—Don Cahalan, Helen Crossley, and their associates—for the unusually complete documentation (prepared in 1949) that accompanies the data at the Roper Center, where the study is archived. Many contemporary surveys are not nearly as carefully documented.

shorthand, however, estimates based on the record data will be referred to as actual or true values.

Results

In order to determine whether respondents who were inaccurate on one item were disproportionately inaccurate on other items, a measure of validity was constructed for each of the 14 questions. Respondents who reported correctly on an item were assigned a score of 0 for that item, those who reported incorrectly were given a score of 1. These measures were then interrelated. Of the resulting 91 relationships, 23 attain statistical significance ($p < .05$ as assessed by chi-squared) and 21 of the 23 are between electoral items. As may be seen in Table 1, inaccuracy is related across all the voting and registration questions. On every one of the seven electoral items, having given an invalid response is associated with having provided an invalid answer on each of the other six.[3] The two other significant relationships ($r = +.07$ and $+.09$) are between the driver's license item and both Community Chest contribution and vote for president in 1948. Almost without exception, the remaining 68 nonsignificant associations are of trivial size.[4] In sum, the assumption of independent errors fits the

Table 1. Relationships between Errors on Seven Electoral Items[a]

	Primary	*Charter*	*Mayor*	*Congress*	*Pres 44*	*Register*	*% Invalid*[b]
Pres 48	.31	.19	.38	.30	.26	.58	13.9
Primary		.24	.31	.25	.24	.16	25.7
Charter			.39	.37	.21	.07	33.6
Mayor				.41	.33	.23	29.9
Congress					.39	.21	23.9
Pres 44						.30	25.6
Register							14.1

[a] The relationships are represented by Pearson r's for the 2×2 cross-tabulation of accurate-report versus inaccurate-report on one item and accurate-report versus inaccurate-report on the other. All the correlations (based on between 765 and 916 cases) are significant beyond the .0001 level, except for the .07, which is $p < .05$. (The N's vary because of the differing number of respondents who said "don't know" or "can't remember" to each question.)

[b] Between 86 and 97 percent of the errors are overreports.

[3] Because a very high proportion of the errors are in one direction, the correlations reflect covariance in the direction of error, not simply covariance in the tendency to err. This was confirmed by recomputing the entries in Table 1 using a trichotomous error measure ($-1,0,1$) instead of the dichotomous one. The correlations were quite similar to those reported in the table (the mean of the 21 recomputed correlations was .32 compared to .29 in Table 1).

[4] There are five positive correlations (four of .06, and one of .09) that attain borderline significance ($p < .10$). Although it is worth noting that three of them involve the

results for the nonelectoral questions, but is violated by the results for the electoral items.

The two sets of findings parallel the extent to which the characteristics themselves are actually related. Based on the record data, the true mean intercorrelation among the electoral items is .50; for the 70 remaining pairs it is .09. The true correlation between having voted for president in 1944 and having voted for mayor in 1947, for instance, is .46, whereas the true correlation between owning an automobile and having voted in the mayoral election, to take an example from the second set, is .10. The larger the true correlation between two items, the greater the association of their measurement errors. This can be seen for the electoral questions by comparing the actual inter-item correlations (Table 2) with the inter-error correlations for the same variables (Table 1). The Pearson r between the two sets of results is .93. Overall, then, the assumption of uncorrelated errors is justified for the variables that bear no relationship to each other, but unjustified for the variables that are interrelated.[5]

Table 2. Relationships between Seven Electoral Items Based on Official Records[a]

	Primary	Charter	Mayor	Congress	Pres 44	Register[b]
Pres 48	.54	.43	.60	.55	.41	.75
Primary		.46	.48	.48	.36	.41
Charter			.56	.54	.41	.33
Mayor				.64	.46	.46
Congress					.61	.44
Pres 44						.49

[a] The correlations in this table are based on the same cases that were used in Table 1 (those with nonmissing data in the survey).

[b] It is worth noting that the Register item measures whether a respondent was registered to vote at *any* time between 1943 and 1949.

---

driver's license item (with voter registration, vote for mayor, and vote for president in 1944), this is exactly the number to be expected by chance when added to the two significant nonelectoral correlations mentioned in the text. (Excluding the 21 electoral item pairs, there are 70 correlations, and .10 of 70 is 7.) In addition, however, there are four negative correlations of .06, which reach borderline significance. In each case, people who gave an inaccurate reply to the library card item were *less* likely to have given an inaccurate answer to another item (those on home ownership, Community Chest contribution, voter registration, and vote for president in 1948). The only clue I have to this puzzling finding is that invalid responses on the library card item differ from those on most of the other 13 items in two important respects: "yes" answers were coded as inaccurate if the respondent's card had expired or if there was a card on record for another member of the respondent's family but not for the respondent. Thus there are two forces that could have produced inaccuracy on this item that were unlikely to apply to the other items.

[5] All the departures from this rule involve the home, phone, and automobile items. These questions are related among themselves and to many of the other questions, but the errors of measurement for the various pairs tend not to be associated. This is

I next examined whether the error correlations across the various electoral items were produced by respondents with distinctive background characteristics. This possibility was assessed with variables known to play a role in electoral involvement: sex, age, education, and interest in political affairs (Campbell et al., 1960). (The interviewer ratings of socioeconomic status were not analyzed because such measures tend to be unreliable and have fallen into disuse. See Mosteller, 1944 and Feldman, et al., 1950–51.) Table 3 presents information on the relationship between these variables and the extent of intercorrelation among the errors of the seven electoral questions. The analysis involved recalculating the error correlations in Table 1

Table 3. The Mean Correlation Between Errors on Seven Electoral Items by Sex, Education, Age, and Political Interest[a]

	Sex	
Men		Women
.28		.30
(366–422)		(397–494)

		Years of Schooling			
0–7	8	9–11	12	13–15	16+
.42	.32	.28	.23	.28	.28
(80–101)	(104–132)	(137–174)	(209–238)	(136–161)	(91–102)

			Age[b]			
21–25	26–29	30–39	40–49	50–59	60–69	70+
.26	.15	.26	.29	.32	.39	.28
(84–93)	(64–76)	(170–206)	(152–177)	(148–176)	(94–119)	(45–62)

		Political Interest[c]		
Least Interested	—	to	—	Most interested
(1)	(2)	(3)	(4)	(5)
.28	.25	.29	.30	.31
(78–95)	(121–158)	(247–300)	(224–261)	(81–89)

[a] The N's are given as ranges because of the varying amounts of missing data on the seven items.

[b] This is self-reported age. Age from the record check is not available, only the approximate size and direction of the difference between the two.

[c] This is a summative index based on the question, "We are finding out how much interest people take in various problems. For example, which of these degrees of interest [A great deal, some, practically none, don't know] would you say you take on The Marshall Plan. . . . Activities of the city administration. . . . Labor relatons. . . . The Denver Public Schools. . . . U.S. policy toward Spain. . . . City planning in Denver. . . . City elections for Mayor. . . . Unemployment in the U.S. . . . The situation of Denver Negroes. . . . Presidential elections?"

probably due to the very small amount of inaccuracy on the three variables—between 2 percent and 3 percent. (The levels of invalidity for the remaining questions not presented in Table 1 are: Community Chest, 37 percent; library card, 14 percent; driver's license, 12 percent; and age, 8 percent. The library card and Community Chest figures differ slightly from those in Parry and Crossley, 1950.)

for each subgroup. To save space, only the mean of the 21 associations is shown. (For the total sample in Table 1, the mean is .29.) The results reveal an almost uniform level of correlated error. Although there are some very slight trends, the striking feature of the table is the similarity among groups. The tendency to be inaccurate across different questions is clearly present in each of the subgroups.[6]

These findings raise an important question about the inferences drawn from surveys: How are bivariate or multivariate analyses affected when measurement errors are correlated? In the Denver data it seemed possible that the correlated errors might distort conclusions about the determinants of voting. To test this, the effect of sex, age, education, and political interest on total number of votes (a summative index of the six vote items) was estimated separately using respondent reports and official records (Table 4). The two data sources yield fairly similar regressions with sex, age, and education. With political interest, however, they produce quite dissimilar regressions. Interest explains over twice as much variation in voting in the survey data as it does in the official data. An analyst who had access only to the survey data would draw a misleading inference about the importance of political interest as a determinant of voting.[7]

Table 4. Regressions Predicting Total Number of Votes[a]

| Dependent Variable from: | Coefficients for | | | | R^2 | F (Prob) |
	Sex	Age	Education	Political Interest		
Respondent reports	.34				.005	n.s.
Official records	.11				.001	n.s.
Respondent reports		.63			.188	.0001
Official records		.50			.155	.0001
Respondent reports			.12		.005	.05
Official records			.14		.009	.01
Respondent reports				.72	.114	.0001
Official records				.42	.050	.0001
Respondent reports	.02[b]	.66*	.19*	.59*	.300	.0001
Official records	.15[b]	.55*	.24*	.29*	.222	.0001

* $p < .001$.
[a] N's vary from 698 to 718.
[b] n.s.

[6] The same results are obtained with unstandardized regression coefficients as with correlation coefficients.
[7] Regressions using the individual vote items show differences between the survey data and the official data that are very similar to those obtained with the total-vote index.

In part, the survey results are distorted by subgroup differences in the propensity to be inaccurate. Table 5 presents the average amount of inaccuracy over the seven electoral questions by age, sex, education, and political interest. The most notable effect involves political interest, which shows a systematic relation to inaccuracy. Although respondents at all levels of interest contributed invalidity, the greater the interest claimed, the more frequent was the inaccuracy—a finding that holds when education (which is moderately related to interest) is controlled. Expressing interest in political matters and giving inaccurate replies apparently share something in common. This contributes to the inflated survey estimate of the effect of interest on voting that was observed in Table 4.[8]

Table 5. The Mean Error Rate on Seven Electoral Items by Sex, Education, Age, and Political Interest[a]

		Sex			
	Men		Women		
	.27		.24		
	(423)		(497)		
		$R^2 = .002$, $F = 2.00$, n.s.			

		Years of Schooling			
0–7	8	9–11	12	13–15	16+
.33	.25	.27	.21	.27	.23
(102)	(132)	(176)	(239)	(161)	(102)
		$R^2 = .004$, $F - 4.17$, $p < .05$			

			Age			
21–25	26–29	30–39	40–49	50–59	60–69	70+
.12	.19	.28	.30	.27	.26	.26
(93)	(76)	(207)	(177)	(179)	(119)	(62)
			$R^2 = .01$, $F = 11.25$, $p < .001$			

		Political Interest			
(1) Least Interested	(2)	(3)	(4)	(5) Most Interested
.20	.21	.24	.29	.34
(96)	(159)	(302)	(261)	(89)
		$R^2 = .02$, $F = 18.26$, $p < .0001$		

[a] This table includes all respondents. Essentially the same results are obtained if only respondents with nonmissing values on all seven electoral items are included.

[8] Table 5 also shows that compared to other respondents those in their twenties gave fewer inaccurate answers and those with less than eight years of schooling gave more such answers. This contributes to the somewhat exaggerated survey-based estimate of the effect of age on voting and to the slightly diminished survey estimate of the effect of education on voting (Table 4). The Table 5 finding that the very young were more accurate reporters differs from Cahalan's conclusion that younger people were *less* accurate reporters because different measures are involved. Cahalan relied not on total inaccuracy, but on the proportion who actually voted among those claiming to have voted. This disregards respondents who accurately said they had not voted as well as those who inaccurately said they had not done so.

Although the distortions in the Table 4 survey regressions are caused in part by subgroup differences in level of error, they are also due to the fact that errors are correlated across the electoral items. This may be illustrated with the case of political interest. In the survey data, the correlation between interest and total vote is a function of (a) the correlation between interest and actual total vote multiplied by the standard deviation of the actual total vote, plus (b) the correlation between interest and total error multiplied by the standard deviation of the total error. The standard deviation of the total error is in turn composed of two terms: the sum of the variances of the six errors (which equals 1.23) plus two times all the covariances (which equals 1.89). Thus both the correlated errors (the covariance term) and the interest differences in level of error (the correlation between interest and total error) work to inflate the association of total vote with interest.[9]

Discussion

The assumption of uncorrelated errors is ubiquitous in data analysis. The results presented here suggest that this assumption may frequently, though not always, be appropriate. Measurement errors for unrelated pairs of variables were found to be independent, but errors across a set of related electoral items showed clear associations. Thus when measures shared nothing in common (e.g., having a library card and owning a telephone), the forces that led to inaccurate reports on the items were also unrelated. For interrelated questions, however, the causes of inaccuracy were apparently similar. Whatever led a respondent to answer incorrectly on one electoral question was connected to the factors leading to inaccuracy on the other electoral items. Whether this connection was due to the similarity in content of the electoral questions (in the sense that they tap a single phenomenon), or to the fact that answers to the questions reflected characteristics that were different but related (in the sense that disparate phenomena such as race and income are related), can-

---

[9] The correlation of interest with respondent reported total vote (.34) is equal to:

$$\frac{(r_{12})(S_2) + (r_{14})(S_4)}{S_3}$$

where $r_{12} = .22$, $S_2 = 2.13$, $r_{14} = .19$, $S_4 = 1.76$ (or $\sqrt{1.23 + 1.89}$), and $S_3 = 2.42$, and variable 1 is political interest, 2 is actual total vote, 3 is respondent reported total vote, and 4 is total error.

not be determined with the Denver data, but is an important issue for future research.

Taking all the items together, the evidence indicates that inaccuracy is largely item-specific in the Denver data. Even on the vote items where inaccuracy has a respondent-specific component, there is only a partial overlap among the errors. The respondents responsible for this effect may have been consciously aware of overreporting their votes. But the process may also have been a more subtle one, affecting respondents' memories. This seems especially likely for an action like voting, which is neither central to the lives of most people nor performed frequently.[10]

The consequences of correlated errors can be serious, at least for cases in which errors are correlated with both true values and other respondent characteristics. (In the Denver data, the correlation between errors and true values is very high because the errors are mainly in one direction.) The present analysis illustrates how correlated errors can distort associations. The frequency with which this occurs is a matter in need of much more research (for some reassuring evidence see Katosh and Traugott, 1981).

The present results also have a special implication for studies of political interest. Numerous investigations have found interest in politics to be related to political participation (Milbrath and Goel, 1977:46). Yet most, if not all, of the evidence depends on self-reported measures of participation. The findings presented here suggest that the error in such measures is due disproportionately to individuals who express interest in politics. People who claimed to be interested in politics were particularly likely to have misreported that they voted in the Denver survey. This suggests either that reports of interest were exaggerated (possibly due to the same social desirability bias that may have contributed to the voting overreports), or that the size of the association between interest and participation has been overestimated in past work.

---

[10] One factor that might affect reporting accuracy is question context. (In this connection, it is worth noting that the interest questions preceded the vote items in the Denver survey by about half a dozen questions. In between were questions about past residences, age, marital status, and number of children.) Response accuracy might also be affected by interviewer experience. Feldman, et al., (1950–51) analyzed three of the items from the Denver study and showed that inaccurate reports on two of them were significantly more frequent among less experienced interviewers. However, of the remaining 11 items, just one yields even a borderline significant difference and it is in the opposite direction, greater inaccuracy among interviewers with more experience. Thus, at least for this survey, interviewer experience appears to play a minor role in response validity.

Appendix
Wordings for the 14 Validated Items

---

10. May I ask your age?

14. Here are some questions about registration and voting in Denver. Have you been *registered* to vote *in Denver* at any time since 1943?

14A. (IF "YES" OR "DON'T KNOW") Have you voted in any election in Denver? since 1943, either in person or by mailing an absentee ballot back to Denver? (IF "NO" TO 14 OR 14A, SKIP TO QUESTION 16.)

15. We know a lot of people aren't able to vote in every election. Do you remember *for certain* whether or not you voted in any of these elections: First—

The presidential election last November when Dewey ran against Truman? (IF "YES") Did you vote in Denver or somewhere else?

The primary election last September? (IF "YES") Did you vote in Denver or somewhere else?

The city charter election a year ago last November—that was 1947?

The city election two years ago, when Stapleton ran against Newton for Mayor?

The congressional election during the big blizzard of 1946? (IF "YES") Did you vote in Denver or somewhere else?

The presidential election in 1944, when Dewey ran against Roosevelt? (IF "YES") Did you vote in Denver or somewhere else?

21. Do you have a library card for the Denver public library in your own name?

22. Do you have a Colorado driver's license that is still good?

23. Do you happen to own an automobile at the present time? (IF "YES") Does the car have Colorado plates or plates from some other state?

25. Did you yourself happen to contribute or pledge any money to the Community Chest during its campaign last fall?

30. Do you or your family rent, or own, the place where you live?

33. Is there a telephone in your home in your family's name?

NOTES: In two cases, Community Chest contribution and automobile ownership, negative answers were not verified and simply coded as accurate. (The four respondents who said their automobile was registered in another state were coded as inaccurate, though no attempt was made to verify the claims.) Age was checked against driver's license records, a somewhat less ideal standard than those used for the other variables (though in many cases a birth certificate was probably required on application for a license). Only age differences of more than one year were coded as errors.

References

Bielby, William T. and Robert H. Hauser
  1977 "Response error in earnings functions for nonblack males." Sociological Methods & Research 6:241–80.
Cahalan, Don
  1968 "Correlates of respondent inaccuracy in the Denver validity survey." Public Opinion Quarterly 32:607–21.
Campbell, Angus, Philip E. Converse, Warren E. Miller, and Donald E. Stokes
  1960 The American Voter. New York: Wiley.
Cannell, Charles F., Gordon Fisher, and Thomas Bakker
  1965 Reporting of Hospitalization in the Health Interview Survey. Washington, D.C.: National Center for Health Statistics, Series 2, Number 6.
Crossley, Helen M., and Raymond Fink
  1951 "Response and non-response in a probability sample." International Journal of Opinion and Attitude Research 5:1–19.

Feldman, J. J., Herbert Hyman, and C. W. Hart
1950– "A field study of interviewer effects on the quality of survey data." Public
51 Opinion Quarterly 15:734–61.
Hamilton, Lawrence
1981 "Self-Reports of academic performance." Sociological Methods & Research
10:165–85.
Hyman, Herbert
1944 "Do they tell the truth?" Public Opinion Quarterly 8:557–59.
Hyman, Herbert, and associates
1954 Interviewing in Social Research. Chicago: University of Chicago Press.
Katosh, John P., and Michael W. Traugott
1981 "The consequences of validated and self-reported voting measures." Public
Opinion Quarterly 45:519–35.
Lansing, John B., Gerald P. Ginsburg, and Kaisa Braaten
1961 An Investigation of Response Error. Urbana: University of Illinois.
Milbrath, Lester, and M. L. Goel
1977 Political Participation, 2nd ed. Chicago: Rand McNally.
Mosteller, Frederick
1944 "The reliability of interviewers' ratings." Pp. 98–106 in Hadley Cantril (ed.),
Gauging Public Opinion. Princeton: Princeton University Press.
Parry, Hugh J., and Helen M. Crossley
1950 "Validity of responses to survey questions." Public Opinion Quarterly
14:61–80.
Siegel, Paul M., and Robert W. Hodge
1968 "A causal approach to the study of measurement error." Pp. 28–59 in Hubert
M. Blalock and Ann B. Blalock (eds.), Methodology in Social Research. New
York: McGraw Hill.
Smith, Harry L., and Herbert Hyman
1950 "The biasing effect of interviewer expectations on survey results." Public
Opinion Quarterly. 14:490–506.
Traugott, Michael W., and John P. Katosh
1979 "Response validity in surveys of voting behavior." Public Opinion Quarterly
43:359–77.
Weiss, Carol H.
1968 "Validity of welfare mothers' interview responses." Public Opinion Quarterly
32:622–33.
Wyner, Gordon A.
1980 "Response errors in self-reported number of arrests." Sociological Methods &
Research 9:161–77.

Matching Survey Responses to Official Records: An Exploration of Validity in Victimization Reporting

PETER V. MILLER AND ROBERT M. GROVES

THE RECORD CHECK study has a prominent place in the literature on survey methodology. In seeking to validate self-reports of "matters of fact" and to test the efficacy of different data collection techniques, researchers in a variety of fields have sought to ascertain the degree of match between survey reports and external record evidence for events of interest. The results of these investigations have shaped not only data collection procedures, but also widely held beliefs about the mechanisms underlying error in self-reports. In this article, we scrutinize the procedures of the record check study itself in an analysis of results from recent research on victimization reporting. Our findings offer a different focus for interpretation of record check results. We call for a more complete, standardized procedure for reporting record check findings and for a more critical view of their results.

Abstract Record check studies—involving the comparison of survey responses with external record evidence—are a familiar tool in survey methodology. The findings of a recently conducted reverse record check study are reported here. The analyses examine match rates between survey reports and police records, employing more or less restrictive match criteria—e.g., using various computer algorithms versus human judgments. The analyses reveal marked differences in the level of survey–record correspondence. Since the level of match rate appears highly variable depending on the definition of a "match," we advocate reexamination of the "lessons" of previous record check studies which employed only vaguely specified match criteria. We argue, further, that record evidence may best be employed in constructing alternative indicators of phenomena to be measured, rather than as the arbiter of survey response quality.

Peter V. Miller is Associate Professor of Communication Studies and Research Faculty, Center for Urban Affairs and Policy Research, Northwestern University. Robert M. Groves is Associate Research Scientist, Survey Research Center, Institute for Social Research, University of Michigan. Research for this article was partially supprted by a contract from the Bureau of Justice Statistics, U.S. Department of Justice. The article does not necessarily represent the views of the Department of Justice. The authors are indebted to Allen H. Andrews, Superintendent of Police, Peoria, Illinois, for making the study possible and to Dr. Charles Cannell, Dr. Charles Cowan, and Dr. Wesley Skogan for insightful comments on an earlier draft. The authors are responsible for any errors which remain.

Background

The use of record evidence to check self-reports has formed the basis for a number of discussions of survey error. For example, Parry and Crossley (1950), in an often cited article, used records of voter registration, voting, library card holding, and contributions to a charitable fund to check reports of those activities from a survey. Similarly, Bradburn et al. (1979) attempted to match survey reports of voter registration, voting, library card holding, bankruptcy, and drunk driving to records of those activities. The findings of these studies suggested that socially desirable activities (e.g., voting) tend to be overreported—more reports of such events were found in surveys than could be located in records— and that undesirable activities or states (bankruptcy) tended to be underreported. Bradburn et al. interpret the findings of their matching analysis as the effects of "question threat" on self-reports.

"Administrative" record check research in other fields has led both to alterations in data collection techniques and to a further buttressing of the conclusions from the studies already cited. Methodological research which preceded the inception of the National Crime Survey (NCS), for example, included three record check studies using police records (Yost and Dodge, 1970; Dodge, 1970; and Turner, 1972) which examined various survey procedures for gathering reports of victimization. During the course of these investigations, the NCS questionnaire was modified substantially, and beliefs were formed about the amount and type of error in victimization reporting. Like the previously reviewed research, these studies noted that crimes tended to be underreported when compared with police record evidence and that certain events, such as assaults, were more likely to be underreported than were less serious episodes, such as larcenies.

Study Questions

Police records, like hospital, doctor, or voting records have had the surface appeal of a tangible criterion against which to compare survey reports.[1] A contributing factor to this impression has been the unproblematic way in which the act of matching a survey report and a record of the event has been described in the record check literature. In the "typical" investigation, matching is done by human comparison of the

---

[1] In this article, we set aside serious questions which may be raised concerning the standard treatment of record evidence as "truth" in record check studies. A number of writers—e.g., Marquis (1978), Skogan (1976, 1981)—have critiqued the assumption that record evidence is free of error and that mismatches between survey reports and records are always proof of error in the self-reports.

survey protocol and the record. Once matching is complete, matched and unmatched cases are compared analytically on characteristics such as date, type of event, etc. The results of such analyses are the basis for claims such as, "nonsalient events are underreported." These analyses rest on the ability of judges unambiguously to assign "match" or "non-match" designations to every survey case. The match exercise, however, is not without complexity: the coder must determine whether the person interviewed is the same person named by the record and then test the correspondence between event details expressed in each source. In both tasks, there are a variety of more or less restrictive criteria which can be employed to assess the degree of fit. Thus, the matching step represents a set of decisions about relevant criteria for comparison and allowable values on each criterion.

It is rather surprising, therefore, to see virtually no space in reports of record check studies devoted to this crucial step. The nature of a match is left undefined in most reports. While some degree of intercoder agreement is sometimes required, the procedures which led to consensus are not specified. No mention is made of the study rules which may subject coders to implicit pressures to find matches or to disagree at the slightest provocation. No comparisons are made of match rates derived from human decisions and ones derived from other means, such as computer algorithms. Finally, matches are considered "dichotomous" propositions: one match rate using one set of (unspecified) criteria is presented, rather than a *range* of match rates based on various definitions of correspondence. Producing a single match rate based on a set of ill-specified human decisions gives the illusion that match decisions are unproblematic observations and shifts the focus of inquiry to a consideration of the flaws in survey reports.[2]

In the analyses to follow, we present the findings of a reverse record check of victimization reporting as a range of match ratios derived from machine and human matching processes, and using more or less restrictive, reasonable match criteria. We illustrate the highly variable nature of match ratios depending on the considerations which go into constructing them. Our analysis compares the ratios produced via various machine algorithms with the one produced through human judgments. Our findings lead us to question the nature of match ratios reported in previous record check studies.

---

[2] We do not mean to imply that the matching procedures in all previous record check studies have been haphazard. Rather, matching procedures in such studies have not been a focus of inquiry, and consequently there has been little attention paid to reporting details of the procedures. In victimization research, see, for example, Turner (1972), Sparks, et al. (1977) and Schneider (1977) for a comparison of the varying levels of specificity with which matching procedures are reported.

Study Design

Approximately 1300 police records for January–September 1981 were sampled from the Peoria, Illinois, Police Department files. During October and November, 1981, interviews were sought from all persons at least 12 years old in the households attached to the telephone numbers listed for the victims of the crimes. In addition, some 570 telephone numbers in the Peoria area were generated by RDD (Random Digit Dial) methods and called to obtain interviews. These cases were added to the sample in order to conceal from the interviewers the fact that known crime victims were being called.[3] In the following analysis, we consider only the police record households.

Approximately 370 of the sample police records had nonworking or nonresidential telephone numbers; other records reflected multiple victimizations of the same person or of several persons simultaneously. When all these facts were accounted for, about 900 distinct working household numbers were linked to sample police records.

An interview was completed with at least one person in approximately 765 of these households, resulting in a household level response rate of 85 percent. A total of 1577 persons were interviewed in the police record households, and we estimate that this represents about 75 percent of all persons at least 12 years old in those households.

PROCEDURES FOR MATCHING RESPONDENTS WITH POLICE RECORD VICTIMS

The first type of matching problem we want to consider is the overlap between the people listed on the police records and the people we interviewed by calling the phone numbers listed for them on the records. Our intent in the matching process was to reflect levels of uncertainty in determining whether the victim listed by the police matched an interviewed person. To this end, on each variable listed as a match criterion, levels of certainty of the match were recorded. This permits the categorization of people as definite matches, definite nonmatches, or as one of several intermediate categories. Matching people in records and survey reports is the most basic sort of match undertaken in record check studies; it may seem straightforward at first blush, but it can be complex indeed, as seen in the following match rules.

Using the information collected during the interview, three variables were chosen for use in person-level matching: (a) first name, (b) age, and

---

[3] This procedure attempts to reduce the likelihood that interviewers might obtain more victimization reports merely because they know that each sample case reported a crime. Not all record check studies have used this design. In some, namely Dodge (1970), the interviewers knew that all sample cases were listed as victims on police records. In other studies, e.g., Sparks, et al. (1977), extensive "salting" with nonrecord cases was done.

(c) gender. The age match used year of birth as reported in the police record and the interview record. The gender match used the recorded data on the police record and the interviewer observation in the interview case.

The name match produced the largest difficulties. A sampling of various kinds of cases indicates the problems faced by the matching process:

Misspellings (e.g., "Wilbur" vs. "Wilber")
Possible second names (e.g., interview "Harold," record "Z. H. Smith")
Possible initials (e.g., interview "Harold," record "H. Z. Smith")
Name not listed on the interview (e.g., interview "Husband," record "Thomas Ziegler")
Possible different names for same person (e.g., interview "Maude," record "Mrs. John Terpes")
Qualifications to names (e.g., interview "Jerome, Jr." vs. record "Jerome Johnson").

To deal with these classes of person identification comparisons, we implemented the following four-category code for name matches:

1) Definite match: includes exact first name matches, and misspellings judged to be misspellings, e.g., "Dorathy" and "Dorothy"; nicknames, e.g., "Mike" and "Michael"; qualifications to names, e.g., "Frank, Jr." and "Frank, Sr." Both are coded as "1."
2) Potential matches: includes initials, e.g., "D. J." vs "Donald"; no first names, e.g., "Mr. Thompson" vs. "Norman Thompson"; possible second names, e.g., "Paul" vs. "Irvin P. Barr."
3) No name listed in interview, e.g., "Sister," "Household informant," "No Name."
4) Definite nonmatches: includes cases with names on both records that are clearly different, e.g., "Donna" vs. "Robert."[4]

Three variables, age, gender, and name, were combined to determine a match status group that consisted of 13 different categories. For each police-listed victim, assignment to one of the 13 match categories was performed with reference to the respondents associated with the victim's

---

[4] We must note that person matching in this study was somewhat more difficult than is probably the case in other record check investigations because of the amount of name information we had to work with. Because of the need to conceal from the interviewers the fact that we were using a victim sample, we followed standard SRC procedures for household listing, which do not permit collecting information on respondents' last names. Previous record check studies which had full name information undoubtedly did not encounter the same level of complexity in matching persons. On the other hand, some of these investigations have been criticized for using name/address samples of victims, possibly cuing the interviewers that the listed person should have something to report.

telephone number. As shown in Table 1 categories 1−12 are devoted to those cases for which listed victims and at least one respondent at the listed phone number are of the same sex *and* have the same reported age within nine years *and* are not definite name mismatches. Others are classified into group 13; thus, group 13 consists of all cases where police record victims and respondents do not match on gender *or* are definite name mismatches *or* have reported age differences of 10 or more years.

In households with multiple respondents, there were only six cases in which more than one household member could have been coded as a "possible match" (codes 1−12) with the victim. In all other such households, all but one household member were easily assigned to code 13.

Table 1. Match Categories for Police Report Victims with Interviewed Households

| Group Number | Match Category | | Number of Victims[a] | % of Victims |
	Name Match	Age Difference		
1	Definite match	0−1	361	47.0%
2	Potential match	0−1	13	1.7
3	Probable nonmatch	0−1	91	11.9
4	Definite match	2	2	.3
5	Potential match	2	0	0.0
6	Probable nonmatch	2	0	0.0
7	Definite match	3	2	0.3
8	Potential match	3	0	0.0
9	Probable nonmatch	3	2	0.3
10	Definite match	4−9	2	0.3
11	Potential match	4−9	0	0.0
12	Probable nonmatch	4−9	6	0.8
13	Definite nonmatch or different gender	10 or more or different gender	287	37.4
Total			766	100.0

[a] There were 765 different telephone numbers sampled from police records, where at least one person provided an interview. One of these households contained two sample victims, and therefore there are 766 victims who could have been a respondent.

Table 1 shows that the most restrictive definition of victim match would result in 47 percent of the police-reported victims from interviewed households having a match with a respondent in that household (definite name match, gender match, age within one year). If we ignore name as a criterion and emphasize sex and age, over 60 percent of the reported victims match with a police record.

Comparing these match rates with previous victimization reverse record checks, we note that our most conservative estimate of person match is roughly the same as the "interview completion rate" (43 percent) reported by Sparks et al. (1977). Our most liberal estimate is slightly less than the "completion rates" of the three NCS pretest record checks, which ranged from 63 percent to 69 percent. All of these previous studies began with *name* samples from police records, and interviewers were instructed to locate the named persons. We gave interviewers a *telephone number* sample and directed them to take interviews with all eligible respondents (12+ years of age) at eligible (noncommercial working) numbers. The person-matching process in our study, therefore, was more difficult than that of previous investigations. The point here, however, is that in addition to sampling frame, the nature and stringency of the match criteria can markedly affect person match estimates. Additionally, it is interesting to note that, across studies, attempts to locate victims listed on police records result in finding about one-half to two-thirds of them (assuming that "matched" cases constitute found victims).[5] The relatively low level of success in finding victims listed on police records provides another sobering context for record check study interpretation.

Incident Level Matching Procedures

Another way to compare our work to past record check studies is to examine the variability in *incident* match ratios across a wide range of match criteria. That is, to what extent do police reports of particular events match survey reports of incidents which matched respondents say they have suffered? How is the match level affected by various match rules? Considering only definitely matched persons (Group 1 of Table 1), two general types of *incident* match procedures were used; the first were completely computer-based rules based on recorded characteristics of the incidents; the second were human judgments based on the written summaries of incidents in police records and interview schedules.

COMPUTER-BASED MATCHING RULES

Three variables recorded both on the police record and on the interview incident form were used for the computer matching procedures: type of crime code assigned to the incident, date of the incident, and location of the incident. Type of crime codes were assigned to interview incidents using the same procedures used in National Crime Survey data pro-

---

[5] Even in the case of the Chicago Police Department's (1983) investigation of its own records of "unfounded" crime, 40 percent of the investigated records yielded no determination as to whether the crime report had been appropriately listed as baseless or not, since the "victims" in these cases could not be located. The problem of finding victims is intimately related to the very definition of crime, as the Chicago investigation reveals, since without a located victim no crime can be said to have occurred.

cessing. The type of crime code used in the Peoria police record system was a four-digit code which was generally compatible with the coding used in NCS. Exceptions to this compatibility existed in the record coding system's lack of distinction between crimes with and without injury to the victim. A collapsing of the two coding systems to create a single compatible code of 23 categories was performed (see Miller et al. 1982).

For matching on the date of the incident, the month of occurrence of the incident was asked of each respondent who reported a victimization. Similarly a date was recorded by the responding officer in the police records.

Matching on location of the incident is somewhat more complicated. The NCS incident report form (which we employed in this study) employs a field-coded question to determine the location of the crime. The answer categories are:

1. In own home
2. In detached structure near home
3. Vacation home
4. Near home
5. Public transportation
6. Friend's, neighbor's home
7. On street, in motor vehicle
8. Restaurant, bar
9. Office, factory
10. Other commercial building
11. Apartment parking lot
12. Other parking lot
13. School building
14. School property
15. Park, playground
16. Other
17. Don't know

Police record information on location of the crime was not coded numerically in the record, unlike type of crime and date information. SRC coders were assigned the task of coding the location of the crime described by police verbally in the records using the code employed in the interview schedule. Although the records were generally fully detailed on the crime location, there were some difficulties involving the categories "in own home," 'near own home," and "on the street." Where no reasonable solution could be found, missing data values were assigned.

With coding complete, an automated count was performed of the incidents that had the same values on the three variables—type of crime, date, and location. To measure the sensitivity of the results to variation in complexity of the coding, different aggregations of the codes in the three variables were introduced. For the type of crime coding, for example, some match ratios are based on a 23-category code; others on a 4-category code. Similarly, a 17-, 4-, and 2-category code were compared for location of the incident. For the date variable, contrasts are made between reports in the same month, within one month of one another, and within three months of one another.[6]

What results from the various collapsing rules are 24 different criteria for determining if there is a match between the incident report and the police report. The most stringent match rule requires the two reports to have the same month of occurrence, the same location on the full 17-category coding, and the same crime type on the 23-category code. The figures presented in Table 2 are match ratios: the number of incidents mentioned in the interview with the same values on the match variables as the police record. If more than one interview incident matches in a single person's interview, the interview would contribute two units to the numerator. Thus, it is possible that the ratio can exceed 1.0.

Using the most stringent rule the match ratio is .136; only a few of the crimes sampled are matched by reports by persons interviewed in the survey. That ratio can be almost doubled by relaxing the rule to include those interview reports dated a month before and a month after the police record date (analysis number 2, with a .236 match ratio). In summary, analyses 1−19 in Table 2 use different numbers of categories on the location and type of crime variables and different dating requirements. Using the three variables in all of their forms produces a range in match ratios from .136 to .736. The latter match ratio uses a two-category location code ("in or near own home" vs. "somewhere else"), a four-category type of crime code ("physical assaults," "larceny," "burglary," and "other"), and the most liberal date code (three months before or after the police report). The use of the three match variables alone thus can produce a wide range of match ratios; full understanding of a match ratio requires knowledge of the details of the coding of the match variables.

Past record check studies may not have used all three variables simultaneously; indeed, the most frequent strategy appears to be one in which reports are matched on incident characteristics exclusive of the date of the victimization. (The "matched" reports then are analyzed for dating accuracy). Analyses 20 through 24 present match data using the "no date" rule. If, for example, no date criterion is used but the most stringent location and type of crime code criteria are used, the match ratio is .36. If, however, the two-category location and four-category crime type coding are used (the loosest match coding), we find a .90 match ratio.

When the machine match criteria are further limited to only a single variable, type of crime, the most disaggregated crime type coding (with

---

[6] While we clearly advocate full reporting of match procedures, editorial considerations rule out a complete description of these codes. See Miller, et al. (1982) for details.

23 categories) yields a .77 ratio of matched crimes to police reports. The most liberal match criterion, using only a four-category type of crime match, yields a ratio over 1.0. The ratio greater than 1 results from the fact that some victims reported more than one incident with the same type of crime code as the police reported crime.

To summarize the computer-based matching analyses, we have seen that match rates can be constructed using only three criteria, with different values on each, which range from about .14 to a nearly perfect fit. These efforts to create empirical rules for matches between interview reports and police records yield less than satisfactory results to a researcher seeking to evaluate the nature of reporting error. This dissatisfaction stems from the ease with which the match ratio can be manipulated by changes in explicit criteria for matching. With the lack of documentation on matching procedures that is common in the literature on record check studies it is difficult to interpret the findings of past studies. Inference from these studies is a function of the reported match ratios; match ratios are a function of matching criteria. Without analysis of the sensitivity of the reported ratios to the criteria, any inference is subject to challenge.

USING HUMAN JUDGMENT FOR MATCH DECISIONS

A problem with computer match procedures concerns the limited set of variables on which matches can be made. Incident reports, both in the police record and in the interview, have theoretically thousands of different characteristics. Few of these are coded on both data sets in such a way that comparisons can be made. At the end of any such exercise with computer matching, questions still remain unanswered about the nature of the correspondence between the interview report and the police report. Two reports can match on two, four, or ten characteristics and still be reports about *different* incidents. Machine matching procedures in some cases appear poor substitutes for human review that can simultaneously consider many variables *and* utilize any other information for matching that may be available on only a subset of the police records or interview reports. This selective supplementation of match criteria so easily performed by human review has no doubt led many past researchers to use human judgment to produce match decisions.

To provide some comparison to past studies, a "manual match" procedure was performed in this study. The procedure had research assistants compare the written summaries of the incident. On the police record there was a written summary that was entered by the reporting officer and was sometimes updated after the initial report with new information about the incident. At the end of the incident report in the interview, the

Table 2. Incident Match Results for Various Incident
Match Criteria Among Matched Victims[a]

| Analysis No. | Incident Match Criteria | | | Victim Interview Reports Matching the Sampled Police Report | |
| | Difference Between Months | Number of Categories in Match Variable | | | |
		Location of Incident	Type of Crime	No.	Ratio Matching Interview Reports/ Police Reports
1	0	17	23	33	.136
2	1	17	23	57	.236
3	0	4	23	50	.207
4	0	17	11	43	.178
5	1	4	23	86	.355
6	1	17	11	71	.293
7	0	4	11	60	.248
8	1	4	11	102	.421
9	3	17	23	71	.293
10	3	4	23	113	.467
11	3	17	11	87	.360
12	3	4	11	135	.558
13	0	17	4	49	.202
14	1	17	4	79	.326
15	0	4	4	73	.302
16	1	4	4	123	.508
17	3	17	4	96	.397
18	3	4	4	167	.690
19	3	2	4	178	.736
20		17	23	87	.360
21		4	4	207	.855
22		2	4	218	.901
23			23	186	.768
24			4	278	1.149
25	0	manual	match	87	.360
26	≤1	manual	match	134	.554
27	≤3	manual	match	144	.595
28	match on	manual	code	173	.715

[a] The case base for Table 2 ($N=242$) is definitely matched victims (Group 1 from Table 1), *excluding* those cases where the information on sampled police records did not permit adequate comparison of survey reported incidents and police recorded incidents. The excluded cases are ones, for example, where the person recorded on the police record was found and interviewed, but the police record contained too little information to judge whether or not the incident in question matched the survey report. Also excluded were cases where the incidents on the police record were commercial crimes since such incidents were not covered by the survey questionnaire. Thus, Table 2 only includes definitely matched victims whose survey reports were "matchable" to police recorded incidents. Incidents are weighted to remove the few duplicate reports of the same incident by a respondent.

interviewer typed in a summary of the events in the incident. These summaries often described the relationship between victim and offender, gave a short sketch of the events of the crime, and described effects for the victim (e.g., what property was stolen, what injuries were suffered). The location of the crime was often listed, but no dates of the events were recorded. In the vast majority of cases these summaries were the only information used by the research assistants to judge whether the two reports described the same event. In a small number of cases where there were two or more interview incident reports that were very similar, the dates of the police record incident and the interview incident were compared to inform the decision. Also in such situations and in cases where the police record did not list all of the salient details of an incident, supplementary police files were checked to see whether a match existed. For example, if an interview recorded that certain items were stolen, but the police record did not name the items specifically, the "property record" files were reviewed for the victim in question to distinguish between similar incidents or to determine if a single interview incident matched the police report.

The rule used in determining whether two reports described the same event could be termed one of omission versus exclusion. Two descriptions were judged to describe different events if there were some contradictions (e.g., a tape deck stolen from a parked vehicle without any damage to the car versus a tape deck stolen by first breaking out the side window) Two descriptions were judged to describe the same event if there appeared to be omissions in one of the reports that would not lead to a logical contradiction (e.g., a tape deck *and* some cassettes stolen from a car by first breaking a window versus a tape deck stolen from a car by first breaking a window). The judges worked together discussing each case. They were instructed to be absolutely sure about a match decision when it was made. Problem cases were turned over to a supervisor for resolution.

Table 2 presents match ratios based on the manual match procedures. The match procedure itself (without concern for a date match criterion) produces a match ratio of .715 (Analysis 28). This is quite comparable to the match ratio achieved by the 23-category type of crime code alone (with no constraint on date or location). The ratio is almost double that achieved by the combination of a 17-category location and a 23-category type of crime code.

If consideration of the reported date of the incident is added to the analysis of the manual match (Analysis 25), then the match ratio declines, to .36 for reports in the same month. It increases to .554 for those within one month, and to .595 to those within three months (Analyses 26 and

27). One can note that this pattern of increase in match ratio by relaxing the date criterion is similar to the findings of Sparks and others (1977: Table III.4) that when all "telescoped" incidents and accurately dated ones are combined, the match rate is some 40 points higher than if only accurately dated incidents are counted in the numerator.

Discussion and Conclusion

The foregoing analyses have illustrated the malleability of "matches" in record check studies. We have seen that, depending on the criteria employed, the values allowed on them, and the procedures for matching (machine vs. human), we can produce match ratios which range from .14 to around 1.00. These findings lead us to question the common practice of measuring and reporting a single match rate in record check studies. For the sake of replicability alone, it is clear that such investigations should produce a carefully defined *range* of match statistics. Such a practice would more fully inform other investigators about the ways in which self-reports depart from record evidence.

Further, our match approach raises some conceptual issues about the nature of matches in record checks. For example, is a misdated event merely "telescoped," or is it possibly not the same event as the one in the record file? Standard procedure in previous studies has been to match incidents irrespective of date, and then to analyze the amount of "telescoping" that occurred in reporting. While in many cases respondents only have one event of a given type to report within a reference period, some crime victims suffer multiple, similar incidents. For these people, code named "series victims" in the National Crime Survey, we cannot be sure that a "telescoped" report is not, in actuality, a report of a *different* crime of the same type. This problem is particularly acute in victimization record checks, since it is believed that series victims account for a large portion of all victimization events, but it may also arise in other substantive areas (e.g., doctor visit record checks).

It may be argued that the variability in match results is not so great in areas such as health, voting, or financial reporting, and that we have emphasized the disparity in match rates in our selection of criteria and code collapsing rules. We suspect that victimization record checks may evidence higher levels of match variability than, say, hospitalization studies. However, this is an empirical question and we hope that data can be brought to bear on it. As for the design of our machine match analyses, which do show widely different match ratios, it appears that the most stringent match criteria we employ are more restrictive than those used in past studies, while the most liberal standard is probably more liberal than ordinarily would be employed in a match analysis. We must emphasize, however, that it is not clear what criteria have been used in most past studies. Further, it is interesting to place the "human" match results in the context of the machine match findings and to note its closer fit to the more liberal rules we devised.

While record check studies typically do not specify match criteria carefully, this is not to say that the problem of matching itself has escaped the attention of survey statisticians. Considerable work has been done by government statisticians in Canada and the United States in response to the need for the merging of large data files involving, for example, Census and Social Security information. The matching research has focused on issues ranging from theoretical models for matching (e.g., Fellegi and Sunter, 1969) to pragmatic discussions of matching assumptions and procedures in federal studies (e.g., Office of Statistical Policy and Standards, 1980). This work is directly relevant to the problem of matching in record check studies since it addresses the nature of error in matching and desiderata in selecting match characteristics.

But the problematic nature of match analysis has been ignored in previous record check studies in favor of a focus on the "bottom line"— the extent to which survey data depart from "truth," as measured by the record evidence. Reporting the variability in match rates—by expressing uncertainty about the fit between the two kinds of evidence— reinforces the view that record evidence does not represent unassailable truth. Records of events may have more value in providing alternative indicators of the object of survey report, rather than as means for validating the reports. Record samples, in addition, offer substantial practical advantages for methodological research on rare events such as crime. Thus, while we do not believe that record check studies offer a panacea for assessing error in survey data, we feel that such designs can provide important insights about the product of different data collection schemes. Our call for a different focus on match results is not an attack on the method itself.

References

Bradburn, N., S. Sudman, and Associates
    1979 Improving Interview Method and Questionnaire Design. San Francisco: Jossey
        Bass.
Chicago Police Department, Bureau of Administrative Services, Auditing and Internal
    Control Division
    1983 "Detective division reporting practices." Internal report.
Dodge, R.
    1970 "Victim recall pretest—Washington, D.C." Washington: U.S. Bureau of the
        Census, memorandum.

Fellegi, I., and A. Sunter
   1969   "A theory for record linkage." Journal of the American Statistical Association 64:1183–1210.
Marquis, K.
   1978   "Record check validity of survey responses: a reassessment of bias in reports of hospitalizations." The Rand Corporation.
Miller, P., R. Groves, and V. Handlin
   1982   "Peoria reverse record check study: initial data analysis." Research report, U.S. Bureau of Justice Statistics.
Office of Federal Statistical Policy and Standards
   1980   "Report on exact and statistical matching techniques." Statistical Policy Working Paper 5. U.S. Department of Commerce.
Parry H., and H. Crossley
   1950   "Validity of responses to survey questions." Public Opinion Quarterly 14:61–80.
Schneider, A.
   1977   The Portland Forward Records Check of Crime Victims. Eugene: Oregon Research Institute.
Skogan, W.
   1976   "Crime and crime rates." In W. Skogan (ed.), Sample Surveys of the Victims of Crime. Cambridge, MA: Ballinger.
   1981   Issues in the Measurement of Victimization. Research report. Washington: U.S. Bureau of Justice Statistics.
Sparks, R., H. Genn, and D. Dodd
   1977   Surveying Victims. New York: John Wiley and Sons.
Turner, A.
   1972   The San Jose Methods Test of Known Crime Victims. Washington: National Criminal Justice Information and Statistical Service.
Yost, L., and R. Dodge
   1970   "Household survey of victims of crime: second pretest—Baltimore, Maryland." Washington: U.S. Bureau of the Census, memorandum.

Question Threat
and Response Bias

NORMAN M. BRADBURN, SEYMOUR SUDMAN, ED BLAIR
AND CAROL STOCKING

O NE CRITICISM of using self-reports to estimate the frequency of different activities is that there may be systematic bias in such reports. The bias is believed to be toward overreporting for socially desirable behaviors (e.g., voting), and toward underreporting for socially undesirable behaviors (e.g., intoxication) and for those of a personal nature about which respondents may feel uneasy talking with others, particularly strangers (e.g., sexual behavior). Because investigators often have no practical alternative to reliance on self-reports, it is important to understand as fully as possible the sources of these reporting biases, and, where possible, to use question formats and control variables that will enable the investigator to minimize or adjust for the reporting biases. This article presents the results of a study designed to investigate factors related to behavioral reports typified by underreporting.

We can distinguish two kinds of questions which might lead respondents to distort their responses: (1) anxiety-arousing questions about, for example, behaviors that are illegal or contra-normative or about

Abstract Perceived normative threat influences responses to questions in surveys. Respondents who report that questions about an activity would make most people very uneasy are less likely to report ever engaging in that activity than are persons who report less uneasiness. If respondents do not admit to participating in an activity, perceived threat appears to have acted as a gatekeeper to prevent further questions. Since perceived threat is associated with underreporting, some simple adjustment methods may be used to improve behavioral estimates.

Norman M. Bradburn is Chairman, Department of Behavioral Sciences, and Senior Study Director, National Opinion Research Center, University of Chicago; Seymour Sudman is Professor of Business Administration, Sociology and the Survey Research Laboratory, University of Illinois at Urbana-Champaign; Ed Blair is Assistant Professor of Marketing, University of Houston; Carol Stocking is Senior Survey Director, National Opinion Research Center, University of Chicago. Research for this study was supported by funds from NSF Grants GS-43203 and GS-43245.

© 1978 by the American Association for Public Opinion Research. This essay originally appeared in *Public Opinion Quarterly*, volume 42, number 2.

behaviors that, though not socially deviant, are not usually discussed in public without some tension, and (2) questions about highly desirable or socially condoned behavior, like voting. The two kinds of questions are closely related, since they both involve social definitions of "desirable" behavior, but they differ in one important respect—with the first kind of question it is the report of committing acts that is contra-normative; with the second, it is the report of *not* doing something that is contra-normative. One might characterize the difference as that between questions about sins of commission and those about sins of omission. One might speculate that answers to questions about sins of commission will be biased toward underreporting and that questions about sins of omission will be biased toward overreporting.

The conflict between the role demands of the "good respondent" and the tendency to present oneself positively is resolved in the respondents' answers, but, unfortunately, the investigator does not know in any individual case, unless he has independent validation data, which way the conflict was resolved. One can, however, investigate covariation between the perceived social sensitivity of a topic and the responses to questions on that topic to determine the relative magnitude of response variance produced by tendencies toward anxiety reduction and positive self-presentation.

In this article we shall investigate threatening questions (i.e., those that tend to arouse anxiety in respondents). We assume that the effect of threat is in only one direction—toward underreporting. In the absence of any independent validation data, we assume that greater reports of contra-normative behavior indicate less response bias, recognizing, of course, that such an assumption might not be true for all respondents. What is contra-normative behavior in the society as a whole may be socially valued by some subcultures and therefore over-reported by its members. For surveys of the total population, we assume that such subcultural differences will have minimal effects on total estimates and that underreporting is, for practical purposes, all that is going on.

There is considerable empirical evidence that the reporting of certain behaviors in surveys decreases as questions increase in their degree of threat. Sudman and Bradburn (1974) summarize the literature prior to 1970 on this topic, including studies by Cannell and Fowler (1963); Clark and Wallin (1964); Clark and Tifft (1966); David (1962); Ellis (1947); Kahn (1952); Kinsey et al. (1948); Knudsen et al. (1967); Levinger (1966); Mudd et al. (1961); Poti et al. (1962); Sarason (1956, 1957, 1959); Thorndike et al. (1952); U.S. National Center for Health Statistics (1971); Wallin and Clark (1958); Yaukey et al. (1965); and Young (1969). Locander et al. (1976), Johnson and DeLamater (1976), and DeLamater and MacCorquodale (1975) report more recent experiments.

Methods and Results

The results reported below come from a nationwide U.S. sample survey of 1,172 adults conducted by the National Opinion Research Center during the summer of 1975. The survey was conducted as an experiment in which the relationships between question structure, question length, wording familiarity, and response effects were examined. The experiment was a 2^3 factorial design in which two levels of question structure (open- and closed-ended), two levels of question length (questions with introductions exceeding 30 words and question with shorter introductions or none at all), and two levels of wording familiarity (a standard question form and a familiar form in which the respondent supplied his own words for the question topic) were employed. Thus, eight different forms of the questionnaire were used.

Segments of households were selected by probability methods from NORC's sampling frame. Within each segment, eight respondents were selected with quotas for sex, age, and working women so that one of each questionnaire form was used in each segment. The order of the forms was systematically rotated across segments. The substantial form effects that emerged are reported elsewhere (Blair et al. 1977). Forms and perceived threat did not interact. In this paper the data are combined across forms.

The threatening questions were placed within the framework of a leisure activity study. After opening questions about such general recreational activities as going to a movie, dining at a restaurant for pleasure, going bowling, playing golf, listening to the radio, and watching television, respondents were asked a series of questions on satisfaction and happiness with life. These items were followed by questions concerning gambling, drinking and getting drunk, smoking marijuana, using stimulant or depressant drugs, and sexual behavior. This order was selected by a priori judgment so that the questions became more threatening as the interview progressed.

The respondent's perceptions of normative threat were obtained at the end of the interview through the following question:

Questions sometimes have different kinds of effects on people. We'd like your opinions about some of the questions in this interview. As I mention groups of questions, please tell me whether you think those questions would make *most people* very uneasy, moderately uneasy, slightly uneasy, or not at all uneasy. How about the questions on:

There followed a list of topics that had been treated in the interview.

This type of question, which indirectly taps uneasiness, had previously been found (Locander, 1974) to be related to underreporting of arrests for drunken driving and declared bankruptcies in a study where independent validation data were available. The indirect form of the question, asking about the respondent's perception of the way most people would feel, appears to be a better indicator of uneasiness than direct questions about whether the respondent felt uneasy about the question. The "indirect" question is, in fact, a direct question about the respondent's perception of social norms. We interpret the responses as perceptions of the strength of the norms against discussing these topics openly with strangers—for example, reporting accurately on behavior. As the perceived strength of the norms increases, we would expect that there would be more inclination to present oneself favorably and thus to distort responses in the direction of underreporting. In addition, we directly asked respondents which of the questions they felt were too personal, and we asked the interviewers to rate the questions for difficulty in the interview. We also have a behavioral measure in the proportion of respondents who declined to answer the questions with differing levels of threat.

Table 1 presents the ratings for the different question topics. They are ordered by increasing frequency of uneasiness, or the perceived strength of the norms against discussing the topics freely. The second and third columns of the table give the interviewer reports of the percentage of respondents for whom the question topic caused difficulty in the interview and the proportion of the respondents who reported (on an open-ended question) that the indicated question topic was too personal. In the final column are the behavioral data—that is, the proportion of the respondents who refused to give any answer to the questions in that topic area. For those areas in which there were multiple questions about activities (e.g., social activities) the figure is the average "no answer" for the battery of questions. If the questions were filtered (e.g., "Did you do X in the past year; if yes, in the last month? . . . ") the "no answer" proportion is for the first question in the series.

The question topics were selected a priori to cover a range of normative strength. The ratings by the respondents indicate that we succeeded in selecting questions which practically no one believed would make people very uneasy. While the interviewer reports of difficulty with questions are generally lower than respondents' ratings of their threat, the rank order of difficulty and uneasiness is very close (rho=.89). The respondents' reports about which questions were too personal *for them* show little variance. Only the sexual behavior questions were reported to be too personal by a substantial proportion. The

Table 1. Ratings of Question Topics (Percent of 1,172 Respondents[a])

Question Topics	Make Most People Very Uneasy (R's Rating)	Caused Difficulty in Interview (Interviewer Rating)	Question Too Personal (R's Rating)	No Answer on Actual Question
Sports activities	1%	0%	0%	0.1%
Leisure time and general leisure activities	2	0	0	0.2
Social activities	2	4	0	0.8
Occupation	3	3	2	0.1
Education	3	2	1	0.3
Happiness and well-being	4	6	2	0.3
Drinking beer, wine, or liquor	10	10	3	0.1
Gambling with friends	10	3	2	0.2
Income	12	9	6	4.8
Petting or kissing	20	19	0	0.3
Getting drunk	29	9	2	2.3
Using stimulants or depressants	31	12	3	0.1
Using marijuana or hashish	42	10		0.4
Sexual intercourse	42	27	34	6.0
Masturbation	56	29		6.7

[a] Actual N varies slightly from question to question because of no answers.

behavioral measure of threat—refusal to answer a question—also reveals very little variance among the question topics. Only sexual behavior and income show any substantial number of "no answers," and these are far below both the uneasiness ratings and the interviewers' reports of difficulty. Such data suggest that the proportion of "no answers" is not a very good indicator of the potential threat of a question.

The income question appears to be special in that it departs furthest in its ranking by the other measures from the general normative ratings given by the respondents. It is about in the middle in respondents' ratings of uneasiness and in the interviewers' ratings of difficulty, but it is the second highest in respondents' perceptions of "too personal" questions (although way behind sex) and has the second highest "no answer" rate. If "don't knows" are combined with "no answers," income is the most troublesome of the standard social characteristics questions typically used in surveys.

There are several ways to react to a question that causes uneasiness about answering truthfully. Respondents can refuse to answer the question at all, indicating that they feel that the question is inappropriate in the context of the interview, or respondents can distort answers in the direction of the more socially desirable or least ego-threatening response. For the questions used in this study, we assume the direction of distortion to be denial of engagement in activities when the respondent has in fact done so. In order to make it easier for respondents to refuse individual questions, we told them at the beginning of the interview that some of the questions we were going to ask might make them feel uneasy and that they need not answer any particular question if they did not want to. In spite of this introduction, as we have seen in Table 1, very few respondents refused to answer even the most threatening questions.

It seems likely that instead of refusing outright many respondents simply reported that they did not engage in some particular activity when they in fact did, thereby resolving the dilemma of being a good respondent by answering the question, but still presenting a positive self-picture to the interviewer. We suspect that such a tendency would be particularly marked among those who feel that there are strong norms against discussing such topics in an interview situation. We can test this hypothesis by looking separately at the distribution of responses to the behavior items for those who rated each of the topics as making most people "very uneasy." If the respondents resolved their dilemma in the way that we have suggested, we should find that those who rated the question topic as making more people "very uneasy" also reported less behavior in that category.

For the most part, the data support this expectation (Table 2). Those who reported that most people would feel "very uneasy" about answering questions on a particular topic were less likely to report having engaged in that behavior than were people who said that most people would feel only "moderately" or "slightly uneasy" about the question. For example, of the 120 respondents who reported that most people would be made "very uneasy" by questions on gambling, 11 percent reported that they had played cards for money during the past year, as compared with 32 percent of the 419 respondents who reported that most people would be made "slightly uneasy" by questioning about gambling. Combining across all gambling activities, those respondents saying "very uneasy" reported an average of .49 gambling activities in the past year, as compared with an average of 1.13 gambling activities reported by respondents who said questions on gambling would make most people "slightly uneasy." Those who felt that most people would be "not at all uneasy" about answering the question showed an inconsistent pattern, a finding to which we shall return later.

For the question about satisfaction with life as a whole, on which we would expect overreporting, we did find that those few who felt that such questions would make people feel "very uneasy" were more

Table 2. Reported Behavior by Level of Uneasiness about Question

	Percent of Those Who Felt . . . Who Reported			
Topics	Very Uneasy	Moderately Uneasy	Slightly Uneasy	Not at All Uneasy
Av. no. sports activities[a]	$.60_{(15)}$[b]	$1.00_{(26)}$	$1.36_{(74)}$	$2.09_{(1,042)}$
Av. no. leisure activities	$4.42_{(28)}$	$5.04_{(79)}$	$5.36_{(121)}$	$5.80_{(932)}$
Happiness and well-being (very satisfied with life)	$29.00_{(41)}$	$18.00_{(117)}$	$21.00_{(432)}$	$33.00_{(558)}$
Gambling				
Played cards for money	$11.00_{(120)}$	$30.00_{(155)}$	$32.00_{(419)}$	$34.00_{(456)}$
Bet on sports	8.00	16.00	21.00	20.00
Bet on elections	3.00	12.00	10.00	11.00
Betting pool	5.00	18.00	19.00	18.00
Played dice	3.00	6.00	7.00	8.00
Bought lottery ticket	18.00	20.00	24.00	27.00
Av. no. gambling activities	.49	1.01	1.13	1.18
Drinking				
Ever drunk beer or ale	$67.00_{(119)}$	$82.00_{(166)}$	$82.00_{(432)}$	$80.00_{(438)}$
Ever drunk wine or champagne	60.00	82.00	89.00	80.00
Ever drunk hard liquor	63.00	84.00	85.00	84.00
Intoxication				
Intoxicated during past year	$24.00_{(327)}$	$36.00_{(233)}$	$38.00_{(332)}$	$27.00_{(230)}$
Marijuana				
Ever smoked marijuana	$18.00_{(480)}$	$33.00_{(217)}$	$26.00_{(220)}$	$15.00_{(250)}$
Drugs				
Ever used depressants	$14.00_{(359)}$	$15.00_{(279)}$	$10.00_{(276)}$	$5.00_{(231)}$
Sex				
Petting and kissing in last month	$63.00_{(224)}$	$81.00_{(281)}$	$78.00_{(340)}$	$71.00_{(301)}$
No answer	7.00	3.00	2.00	1.00
Intercourse in past month	$59.00_{(474)}$	$75.00_{(296)}$	$75.00_{(209)}$	$53.00_{(167)}$
No answer	9.00	4.00	1.00	2.00
Masturbation in past month	$10.00_{(630)}$	$11.00_{(208)}$	$7.00_{(148)}$	$8.00_{(132)}$
No answer	6.00	4.00	4.00	2.00

[a] Statistical tests of significance are not reported on these data because we are not testing hypotheses in the strict sense and are using hypotheses suggested by the data. See Kruskal (1968: 245–47).

[b] Figures in parentheses are the case bases on which the percentages or averages are calculated.

likely to report being "very satisfied" than those in the "moderately" or "slightly" category, but not than those in the "not at all" category.

This pattern of reporting does not vary much for respondents with different socioeconomic and demographic backgrounds. Sex, race, income, occupation, region, and city size have no significant effect. Education and age have statistically significant effects, but the differences in reporting across education and age groups do not form an interpretable pattern.

One important point must be made about the findings. The effect of rating a topic as having high normative threat tends to show up only in the first question about the topic, which is typically: "Have you ever used/done . . .?" If the respondent replies "yes," then a series of questions follow about frequency or quantity of behavior. Normative threat appears to act as a screen so that those who report uneasiness about the topic select themselves out of the entire battery of questions by simply saying that they have never done or used the subject of the questions. If, however, they admit having used or done the thing asked about, level of uneasiness does not appear to influence reports of frequency or quantity of behavior. In a separate paper (Blair et al., 1977), question structure (open or closed) and length (of introductions) have been shown to have an important effect on reports of frequency and amount of behavior, if the respondent admits having engaged in the behavior at all. The question wording variables, however, were not related to the initial reports of ever having engaged in the behavior.

Thus, it appears that there is a two-step process which affects answers to questions about threatening behaviors. In the first step, respondents who may have engaged in the behaviors but find it contranormative to discuss this in the interview resolve the conflict between reporting accurately and presenting a positive self-image by denying that they have ever engaged in the behavior. In the second step, the question wording encourages or discourages efforts to report accurately the extent of the behavior.

The differences in reporting are mainly between those who report that most people would be "very uneasy" in talking about a particular topic and all others. In some cases, however, particularly concerning those questions about topics rated as more threatening, those reporting that most people would be "not at all uneasy" in discussing the topic should also have lower levels of reporting actual behavior. It is to this finding that we now turn.

The Nonthreatened Respondent

In hypothesizing a relationship between normative threat and behavioral underreporting, we assumed that there was no relationship between perceived normative threat and a person's behavior; that is, we assumed that respondents' perceptions of the norms about talking about certain kinds of behavior were independent of whether they had actually engaged in such behavior. This assumption implied that the norms are "social facts" that are more or less accurately and uniformly known. We expect that the probability of a particular type of behavior actually occurring would be equal across all categories of response about the normative threat of that type of behavior. Thus, when we observe that the proportion of people who report engaging in some particular behavior is lower in one response category, we interpret this as evidence of underreporting rather than as evidence of a real difference.

This assumption of independence of the perception of social norms and actual behavior is, however, somewhat tenuous when applied to behavior that is more seriously contra-normative. People who have not engaged in the behavior may have a "clear conscience" and estimate other people's willingness to talk about the topic differently from those who have engaged in the behavior and have a "guilty conscience." In this case there would be an interaction between the perceived normative threat and the respondents' own behavior such that their own behavior becomes part of the determinant of the perceived norms.

If there were such an interaction between the respondent's actual behavior and their perception of norms about discussing the topic with strangers, we would expect that the occurrence of a contra-normative behavior would really be higher for respondents with higher perceptions of general uneasiness. That is, among respondents who report that most people would be "not at all uneasy" about discussing a topic, a smaller proportion would actually engage in the behavior than would be the case among respondents who report that most people would feel "slightly uneasy," "moderately uneasy," or "very uneasy." Underreporting by respondents who report "very uneasy" would cause a non-monotonic relationship between reported behavior and perceived uneasiness, with reported behavior rising and then falling across uneasiness categories.

Such a non-monotonic relationship is what we find for topics that 20 percent or more of the respondents rated as making most people "very uneasy." In response to these topics, we find the proportions of respondents reporting the behavior to be lower for both of the two extreme groups—"very uneasy" and "not at all uneasy"—than for the intermediate categories. If our interaction hypothesis is true, the lower behavioral reports among those who say "very uneasy" are primarily due to underreporting, and the lower reports among the "not at all uneasy" are primarily due to real differences in behavior. While such an interpretation is plausible, we do not have any external validation data to test out this hypothesis.

Revised Estimates of Threatening Events

Assuming that respondents who report that a question would make most people "very uneasy" are underreporting their behavior in that area provides a simple method for improving estimates of threatening behaviors. Revised estimates may be obtained either by assuming that "very uneasy" respondents behave like all other respondents, or by assuming that "very uneasy" respondents behave like the "moderately" uneasy respondents.

For the gambling, drinking, and petting and kissing questions, the revised estimates are 2 to 8 percent higher than the initial estimates. For the more threatening intoxication, marijuana, and sexual intercourse questions, revised estimates exceed original estimates by larger amounts, from 8 percent for the sexual intercourse question to 27 percent for the marijuana questions. These larger differences occur because a larger fraction of the sample reports being "very uneasy" about these questions so that the impact on the overall estimate is greater.

Common sense suggests that revised estimates which incorporate supplementary information about uneasiness are improved estimates. Obviously, one would like direct proof that revision is improvement, but in this study we could not get validating evidence. Locander's (1974) earlier study did have such validation information available from record checks. Respondents who reported that questions about traffic violations and declaration of bankruptcy would make most people very uneasy reported only 27 percent of validated events, compared to about 75 percent for respondents who perceived these questions as less threatening. Even respondents who reported that these extremely threatening questions would make most people somewhat uneasy or not at all uneasy underreported behavior. Use of a supplementary question on perceived threat will provide an improved estimate, but not an unbiased estimate.

It may be interesting to compare this estimation technique with randomized response procedures used for estimating threatening behavior (see Reinmuth and Geurts, 1975). Randomized response procedures assume that respondents will tell the truth if their anonymity is guaranteed by use of the randomized response mechanism. While some evidence shows that randomized response procedures do improve estimates, other evidence shows that response effects do remain. In the Locander et al. (1976) study, for example, 35 percent of those respondents who had been arrested for drunken driving did not report this arrest when using a randomized response procedure. Randomized response methods and the use of supplementary information on perceived threat both yield improved, but not perfect, estimates, and both methods make assumptions about respondent behavior that are partially, but not completely, true.

Comparison of These Results with Other Data

Table 3 compares both the unadjusted and adjusted estimates from the previous section to some comparative data from other sources. Since the different experimental forms did have effects on the number of times behaviors were reported, once the respondent had admitted them (Blair et al., 1977), the estimates for some of the items are given separately by form.

In general, the unadjusted data are very similar to results from other surveys. As examples, a national study conducted by Temple University's Institute of Social Research (Wilson, 1975) estimated that 68.8 percent of adults had engaged in intercourse in the past month, and the unadjusted estimate from this study is 68.6 percent. It was estimated that 19 percent of respondents had ever smoked marijuana in a national study conducted by the Response Analysis Corporation (Abelson and Atkinson, 1975), compared to 21.7 percent in this study.

Adjusted estimates are larger than comparative surveys, indicating that current estimates are somewhat low. That current estimates are low can be seen in the estimates for beer, wine, and liquor consumed, where even the adjusted estimates using the best forms understate sales by at least one-fourth. Our study did not ask how many ounces of beer, wine, and liquor were consumed, but how many glasses. The conversion to ounces was made by assuming that the average wine glass contained three ounces. Similarly, it was assumed that a glass or can of beer contained twelve ounces, and that a drink of liquor contained one ounce.

Summary

It is evident from the results of this study that the perceived normative threat of a topic influences responses to questions. Respondents who report that questions about an activity would make most people very uneasy are less likely to report ever engaging in that activity than are persons who are only moderately uneasy. Perceived threat thus acts as a gatekeeper to prevent further questions.

If respondents admit to participating in an activity, perceived threat appears to have no effect on the level of activity reported. While the

Table 3. Unadjusted Data, Adjusted Data,[a] and Comparison Data

Items	Unadjusted	Adjusted	Comparison Data
Engaged in intercourse past month	68.6%	74.0%	68.8%
Mean annual frequency of intercourse (all adults)			
Long, open forms	90	101	
Short, closed forms	72	79	76[b]
Ever smoked marijuana	21.7%	27.6%	19%[c]
Number of times drunk beer in past year (for adults who drank beer in past month)			
Long, open form	124	126	
Short, closed form	73	74	82.41[d]
Number of times drunk wine in past year (for adults who drank wine in past month)			
Long, open form	77	76	
Short, closed form	47	49	42.95[d]
Number of times drunk liquor in past year (for adults who drank liquor in past month)			
Long, open forms	68	65	
Short, closed forms	48	49	56.21[d]
Ounces of beer consumed per capita in past year (all adults)			
Long, open form	2,046	2,099	
Short, closed form	1,163	1,173	3,982[e]
Ounces of wine consumed per capita in past year (all adults)			
Long, open form	206	225	
Short, closed form	104	106	304[e]
Ounces of liquor consumed per capita in past year (all adults)			
Long, open forms	86	87	
Short, closed forms	65	67	234[e]

[a] The "very uneasy" group has been given the mean of the "moderately uneasy" group as an adjustment.
[b] Wilson (1975).
[c] Abelson and Atkinson (1975).
[d] Harris (1974).
[e] United States Brewers Association, Inc. (1975).

effects of perceived threat on response are important, they are smaller than the effects of question structure, which do change levels of reported activity.

Since perceived threat causes underreporting, some simple adjustment methods may be used to improve estimates of threatening behavior. These assume that respondents who report being very uneasy are at least as likely to participate in an activity as those who report being moderately uneasy or all other respondents.

References

Abelson, Herbert I., and Ronald B. Atkinson
  1975   Public Experience with Psychoactive Substances. Prepared for the National Institute on Drug Abuse. Princeton, N.J.: Response Analysis Corporation.
Blair, Ed, Seymour Sudman, Norman Bradburn, and Carol Stocking
  1977   "How to ask questions about drinking and sex: response effects in measuring consumer behavior." Journal of Marketing Research 14:316–21.
Cannell, Charles F., and Floyd J. Fowler
  1963   "A comparison of a self-enumerative procedure and a personal interview: a validity study." Public Opinion Quarterly 27:250–64.
Clark, Alexander L., and Paul Wallin
  1964   "The accuracy of husbands' and wives' reports of frequency of marital coitus." Population Studies 18:165–73.
Clark, John P., and Larry L. Tifft
  1966   "Polygraph and interview validation of self-reported deviant behavior." American Sociological Review 31:516–23.
David, Martin
  1962   "The validity of income reported by a sample of families who received welfare assistance during 1959." Journal of the American Statistical Association 57:690–85.
DeLamater, John, and Patricia MacCorquodale
  1975   "The effects of interview schedule variations of reported sexual behavior." Sociological Methods and Research 4:215–36.
Ellis, Albert
  1947   "Questionnaire *versus* interview methods in the study of human love relationships." American Sociological Review 12:541–53.
Harris, Louis, and Associates, Inc.
  1974   Public Awareness of the NIAAA Advertising Campaign and Public Attitudes toward Drinking and Alcohol Abuse. Prepared for the National Institute on Alcohol Abuse and Alcoholism. New York: Louis Harris.
Johnson, Weldon T., and John D. DeLamater
  1976   "Response effects in sex surveys." Public Opinion Quarterly 40:165–81.
Kahn, Robert L.
  1952   "A comparison of two methods of collecting data for social research: the fixed-alternative questionnaire and the open-ended interview." Ph.D. dissertation, University of Michigan.
Kinsey, Alfred C., Wardell B. Pomeroy, and Clyde E. Martin
  1948   Sexual Behavior in the Human Male. Philadelphia: Saunders.
Knudsen, Dean D., Hallowell Pope, and Donald P. Irish
  1967   "Response differences to questions on sexual standards: an interview-questionnaire comparison." Public Opinion Quarterly 31:290–97.
Kruskal, W. H.
  1968   "Tests of significance." Pp. 238–50 in David Sills (ed.), International Encyclopedia of the Social Sciences, Vol. 14. New York: Macmillan and the Free Press.
Levinger, George
  1966   "Systematic Distortion in spouses' reports of preferred and actual sexual behavior." Sociometry 29:291–99.

Locander, William B.
   1974   "An investigation of interview method, threat, and response distortion." Ph.D. dissertation, University of Illinois.
Locander, William B., Seymour Sudman, and Norman Bradburn
   1976   "An investigation of interview method, threat and response distortion." Journal of the American Statistical Association 71:269–75.
Mudd, Emily H., Marvin Stein, and Howard E. Mitchell
   1961   "Paired reports of sexual behavior of husbands and wives in conflicted marriages." Comprehensive Psychiatry 2:149–56.
Poti, S. J., B. Chakraborti, and C. R. Malaker
   1962   "Reliability of data relating to contraceptive practices." Pp. 51–65 in C. V. Kiser (ed.), Research in Family Planning. Princeton, N.J.: Princeton University Press.
Reinmuth, James E., and Michael D. Geurts
   1975   "The collection of sensitive information using a two-stage, randomized response model." Journal of Marketing Research 12:402–07.
Sarason, Irwin G.
   1956   "Effect of anxiety, motivational instructions, and failure on serial learning." Journal of Experimental Psychology 51:253–60.
   1957   "Effect of anxiety and two kinds of motivating instructions on verbal learning." Journal of Abnormal and Social Psychology 54:166–71.
   1959   "Relationships of measures of anxiety and experimental instructions to word association test performance." Journal of Abnormal and Social Psychology 59:37–42.
Sudman, Seymour, and Norman M. Bradburn
   1974   Response Effects in Surveys: A Review and Synthesis. Chicago: Aldine.
Thorndike, Robert L., Elizabeth Hagen, and Raymond A. Kemper
   1952   "Normative data obtained in the house-to-house administration of a psychosomatic inventory." Journal of Consulting Psychology 16:257–60.
United States Brewers Association, Inc.
   1975   The Brewing Industry in the United States: Brewers Almanac 1975. Washington, D.C.: USBA.
U.S. National Center for Health Statistics
   1971   Effect of Some Experimental Interviewing Techniques on Reporting in the Health Interview Survey. Vital and Health Statistics, Series 2, No. 41. Washington, D.C.: U.S. Government Printing Office.
Wallin, Paul, and Alexander Clark
   1958   "Cultural norms and husbands' and wives' reports of their marital partners; preferred frequency of coitus relative to their own." Sociometry 21:247–54.
Wilson, W. Cody
   1975   "The distribution of selected sexual attitudes and behavior among the adult population of the United States." Journal of Sex Research 11:46–64.
Yaukey, David, Beryl J. Roberts, and William Griffiths
   1965   "Husbands' vs. wives' responses to a fertility survey." Population Studies 19:29–43.
Young, Barbara A.
   1969   "The effects of sex, assigned therapist or peer role, topic intimacy, and expectations of partner compatability on dyadic communication patterns." Ph.D. dissertation, University of Southern California.

The Validity of the
Randomized Response Technique

S. M. ZDEP, ISABELLE N. RHODES, R. M. SCHWARZ, AND
MARY J. KILKENNY

IN the considerable literature that has appeared on the randomized response technique (RRT), only one study (Lamb and Stem, 1978) has addressed its validity. However, this study utilized a convenience sample of rather small size, thereby limiting generalizability of results.

Originally proposed by Warner (1965), RRT is a method designed to obtain reliable information when dealing with sensitive issues on surveys. In instances where the technique was used, it has been assumed that "reliable information" meant valid information. In the technical sense, this, of course, is not necessarily so. Therefore, it is the purpose of this research to investigate the validity of the technique, using a nationwide probability sample of adults.

The split-sample version of the RRT developed by Moors (1971) was used in the present study. Parameters for maximizing the effectiveness of this technique in a field situation were established by Zdep and Rhodes (1976).

Determining the validity of a method such as RRT is not easy, precisely because RRT offers an alternative to direct questioning in situations where direct questioning is likely to result in obtaining socially desirable responses rather than truthful responses. Validation, then, requires that RRT results be compared with some other estimate of the sensitive characteristic in the population. To be sure, if this estimate were available, there would be no need for using RRT, which is costly and inefficient to administer.

S. M. Zdep is senior vice president, Isabelle N. Rhodes and Mary J. Kilkenny are vice presidents, and R. M. Schwarz is a survey director at Opinion Research Corporation, Princeton, New Jersey. The authors would like to express their appreciation to the ORC General Public Caravan, under whose auspices these data were gathered.

This seemingly vicious circle, however, is not totally closed. It is possible to conduct a validation using a sensitive issue that is rapidly approaching acceptability of sorts among vast segments of our society. Marijuana usage seems to qualify, and therefore we decided to use as our sensitive question, "Have you at any time used marijuana?" By comparing the results obtained for this question in a randomizing device to results obtained independently using direct questioning at approximately the same time, it is possible to demonstrate criterion-related validity as defined by the American Psychological Association (1966). This was certainly important, but in addition, we wanted to demonstrate empirically just how effective RRT could be in yielding patterns of results on the basis of preestablished hypotheses.

In view of the massive amounts of unconflicting data already gathered regarding marijuana usage among various subgroups in the population, it was suggested (1) that RRT should reestablish these differential usage rates, and (2) that the magnitude of the discrepancy between RRT and direct questioning techniques should be predictable, at least in an ordinal sense, on psychological and/or sociological bases. The following hypotheses were advanced:

1. For the total population and for each subgroup within the population, RRT estimates of usage should be *larger* than estimates obtained through direct questioning techniques. This differential would be attributable to false-negative reporting during direct questioning (Zdep and Rhodes, 1976). Although marijuana usage is becoming more and more accepted (Thorpe, 1975; Thomas et al., 1977; *The New York Times*, 1977), some individuals feel that there is a stigma attached to admitting to personal usage in an interview situation, and this was likely to account for much of the anticipated false-negative reporting.

2. Prevalence of marijuana usage ought to be inversely related to age, since it has been found almost universally that younger age groups are most likely to experiment with it (Gallup, 1977; *The New York Times*, 1977; *Chicago Tribune*, 1977).

3. The *discrepancy* between RRT and direct questioning techniques should vary by age group. For the youngest individuals (aged eighteen to twenty-five) the methods should yield almost identical results. For older age groups (twenty-six to thirty-four, and thirty-five to forty-nine), RRT results should be *larger* than those obtained by direct questioning, simply because members of these age groups are more likely to feel the need to conceal the use of marijuana (Gallup, 1977; *The New York Times*, 1977; *Washington Post*, 1978). This is especially true among the middle age group (thirty-five to forty-nine), who

have established roles in family, work, and community, and for whom admitting to the use of marijuana creates some dissonance in terms of these roles. For those aged fifty and over, the usage prevalence data obtained by way of either method was hypothesized to be quite low, and this was assumed to be in accordance with actual behavior.

4. As far as sex-related differences were concerned, it was hypothesized that underestimates of usage obtained by direct questioning would be greater for females. This is because in our society females tend to be less aggressive and take fewer risks than their male counterparts (for example, see Bennett and Cohen, 1959; Edwards, 1954; Jackson, 1967). They would therefore be less likely than males to admit under direct questioning that they had used marijuana.

5. Finally, in terms of race, it was suggested that actual usage patterns for whites and nonwhites ought to be similar. Sociological theories would indicate that higher frustration levels for blacks (Bourne, 1974) are associated with higher substance abuse. However, generally higher economic and educational levels for whites would tend to place them in situations (universities, parties, jobs, etc.) where substances such as marijuana are more readily available. Moreover, evidence which seems to indicate minimal physiological consequences to marijuana use (Domino et al., 1974), also leads us to anticipate reasonably high usage levels among whites as well as blacks.

Method

The marijuana usage question was included in a randomizing device technique utilizing a national probability sample of 2,084 adults on Opinion Research Corporation's General Public Caravan. Split-samples of 1,043 and 1,041 were utilized in which the marijuana usage question and one of two nonsensitive questions were used. The nonsensitive questions were:

Sample A—Have you attended church or synagogue within the past week?
Sample B—Have you ever given blood, either to a blood bank or directly to another person?

A coin toss determined whether the sensitive or nonsensitive question would be answered. Only the respondent (not the interviewer) was aware of the results of the coin toss. (See Zdep and Rhodes, 1976, for details on the methodology.)

Criterion data for comparison purposes were obtained from the Sixth Annual Report from the Secretary of HEW to the U.S. Congress on *Marijuana and Health*. Results in this report were based on a survey conducted between January and April, 1976. Our survey was conducted during May 1976.

Results

The results of the construct validation are presented in Table 1. The first hypothesis was supported in that, for the total sample, RRT estimates of usage were slightly greater than estimates obtained by direct questioning (24 percent versus 21 percent). RRT results were also greater for all subgroups studied, with the exception of the very youngest age group. RRT reports of usage were inversely related to age—the greatest usage was found among the youngest group.

The pattern of results by age was as hypothesized. Minimal discrepancy between methods was found among the youngest age group, and in fact, the direct questioning technique yielded a higher usage estimate (53 percent versus 48 percent). This difference exceeds sampling tolerances at the .95 confidence level, and it is suggested that, because marijuana usage may be fashionable among this age group, false-positive reporting to the direct questioning may have contributed to the discrepancy.

However, for each of the three older age groups, we obtained the predicted pattern of differences between RRT and direct questioning techniques. Among the group aged thirty-five to forty-nine, direct questioning seemed to underestimate usage by a factor of more than three (6 percent versus 19 percent).

In terms of sex, although the underestimate in marijuana usage under direct questioning for females was greater than that obtained for males, the difference is not statistically significant (one-tailed test at the 95 percent confidence level).

Table 1. Reported Marijuana Usage by Demographic Categories

	Percent Using	
	Direct Questioning[a]	Randomized Response Technique
Age		
18–25	53	48
26–34	36	45
35–49	6	19
50 and older	—	3
Male	29	31
Female	14	17
White	21	24
Nonwhite	25	24
Total sample	21	24

[a]SOURCE: *Marijuana and Health.* Sixth Annual Report to the U.S. Congress, 1976.

In the last comparison, based on race, it was hypothesized that usage patterns for whites and nonwhites (almost exclusively blacks) ought to be similar. Surprisingly, the RRT usage rates were identical (24 percent). Direct questioning techniques had indicated significantly higher usage rates among nonwhites (25 percent versus 21 percent). The RRT results, while showing prevalence of usage for black and white groups to be more similar than direct questioning, are not significantly different from direct questioning techniques for the sample sizes used herein.

Discussion

Not only were favorable results obtained when RRT data were compared to a direct questioning criterion on a sensitive issue with minimal stigma, but the construct validation data were even more enlightening. In terms of marijuana usage, it appears that the RRT technique is demonstrably superior to direct questioning when dealing with population subgroups where a differential sensitivity to the question can be assumed. Apparently, the only reason why direct questioning results for marijuana usage do not more seriously underestimate overall RRT approximations is that for direct questioning, false-negative reporting among older groups is compensated for by false-positive reporting among the young.

These results suggest that RRT tends to become increasingly appropriate as the perceived sensitivity of the question increases. Marijuana usage is a comparatively benign topic, yet there seem to be serious underestimates of its usage among certain population groups. Consider, on the other hand, an issue such as heroin usage, which is not at all accepted by society in general. Given this heightened sensitivity toward the issue, it would therefore not seem surprising if current direct questioning yielded usage prevalence estimates far smaller than those actually existing among the U.S. population.

References

American Psychological Association
  1966 Standards for Educational and Psychological Tests and Manuals. Washington, D.C.: APA.
Bennett, E. M., and L. R. Cohen
  1959 "Men and women: personality patterns and contrasts." Genetic Psychology Monographs 59:101–55.
Bourne, P. J.
  1974 Issues in Addiction. New York: Academic Press.

Chicago Tribune
  1977 "Teens would rather 'make war, not love, survey indicates." January 14: p. 5, col. 5.
Domino, E. F., P. Rennick, and J. Pearl
  1974 "Dose-effect relations of marijuana smoking on various physiological parameters in experienced male users." Clinical Pharmacology and Therapeutics 15:514–20.
Edwards, A. E.
  1954 Manual for the Edwards Personal Preference Schedule. New York: Psychological Corporation.
Gallup Poll
  1977 "Teen age use of marijuana growing." Washington Post, May 15: p. 5, col. 5.
Jackson, D. N.
  1967 Personality Research Form Manual. Goshen, New York: Research Psychologists Press.
Lamb, C. W., Jr., and D. E. Stem, Jr.
  1978 "An empirical validation of the randomized response technique." Journal of Marketing Research 15:616–21.
Moors, J. J. A.
  1971 "Optimization of the unrelated question randomized response model." Journal of the American Statistical Association 66:627–29.
The New York Times
  1977 "Marijuana smoking in public increases as penalties drop." November 28: p. 18, col. 1.
Thomas, R. B., S. A. Luber, and J. A. Smith
  1977 "A survey of alcohol and drug use in medical students." Diseases of the Nervous System 38:41–43.
Thorpe, Clairburne B.
  1975 "Marijuana smoking and value change among college students." College Student Journal 9:9–16.
U. S. Government, Secretary of Health, Education, and Welfare
  1976 "Marijuana and health." Sixth Annual Report to the U.S. Congress.
Warner, Stanley L.
  1965 "Randomized response: a survey technique for eliminating evasive answer bias." Journal of the American Statistical Association 60:63–69.
Washington Post
  1978 "Marijuana use by teenagers grows sharply, survey shows." May 9: p. 1, col. 4.
Zdep, S. M., and Isabelle N. Rhodes
  1976 "Making the randomized response technique work." Public Opinion Quarterly 40:531–37.

Construct Validity and
Error Components of Survey Measures:
A Structural Modeling Approach

FRANK M. ANDREWS

THERE is growing recognition that measurement errors in any kind of data—including survey research data—can have profound effects on statistical relationships. Some kinds of measurement errors make bivariate relationships appear stronger than they really are; others make bivariate relationships appear too weak. The effects of measurement errors on multivariate relationships can be great, and also

Abstract Measurement errors can have profound effects on statistical relationships, and better information on the quality of measures seems needed. This study uses a new technology—structural modeling of data from special supplements to regular surveys—to generate estimates of construct validity, method effects (a major source of correlated error), and residual error (mainly random error) for a broad set of measures obtained from five national surveys and an organizational survey (total respondents = 7,706). Analysis of these estimates suggested that a typical survey item, when administered by a respected survey organization to a general population sample, can be expected to yield 50–83 percent valid variance, 0–7 percent method effects variance, and 14–48 percent residual variance. Multivariate analysis showed that over two-thirds of the variation in measurement quality could be explained by 13 survey design characteristics; characteristics of respondents explained a small additional portion. Results provide: (a) information on design conditions associated with better (or worse) measurement quality, (b) empirically based suggestions for improving measurement quality in future surveys, and (c) a set of coefficients for predicting the quality of measures not studied here.

Frank M. Andrews is Program Director in the Survey Research Center and Professor of Psychology and of Population Planning at the University of Michigan. Gerald A. Cole and Mary Grace Moore made numerous and substantial contributions to the work reported here. The author is grateful to David Bowers, Angus Campbell, Charles Cannell, Philip Converse, Richard Curtin, Daniel Denison, and Robert Groves for allowing us to include methodological supplements in some of their surveys. Earlier versions of this paper were presented at the 1980 Annual Meeting of the American Psychological Association, at the 1982 Annual Meeting of the American Association for Public Opinion Research, and at the 1982 Conference on Health Survey Research Methods. This research was supported by grant #SOC78–07676 from the National Science Foundation.

complex. Under certain combinations of error, an observed relationship can be "wrong" in both direction and magnitude. However, if one has information about the validity and error composition of the measures being analyzed, more informed judgments can be made about the underlying relationships that are of primary interest.

Insightful survey researchers have always been interested in the quality of their data, and new information about data quality has been a major contributor to the development of survey technology. Much attention has been devoted to *sampling errors,* and there now exist good ways to estimate their magnitudes and much knowledge about how to reduce them. One kind of *measurement error,* bias (a consistent tendency for a measure to be higher or lower than it "should be") has also received considerable attention (Sudman and Bradburn, 1974). However, while bias can produce serious distortions in percentages, means, and other measures of central tendency, and hence is a threat that must always be considered, a bias that is constant for all respondents does not affect linear relationships at either the bivariate or multivariate level. It is other kinds of measurement errors that intrude on relationships—*random* and *correlated measurement errors.*[1] (Key terms are defined below.) These are the kinds of measurement errors investigated in this study.

For each of the measures included in any particular analysis, one would like, ideally, to be able to apportion the total variance into three components: valid variance, correlated error variance, and random error variance. From this, one could know the extent to which the true bivariate relationships (i.e., the relationships among the concepts being investigated) were being attenuated (because of random measurement error) and/or inflated (because of correlated measurement error). In addition, one could sort out the complex effects that random and correlated measurement errors have on multivariate statistics such as regression coefficients, multiple and partial correlation coefficients, and path coefficients.[2]

A pair of examples, taken from the data of this study, will illustrate how misleading even a simple bivariate relationship between observed measures can be when allowance is not made for the effects of measurement errors. In Survey 2, the observed product-moment correlation between items having to do with perceptions about changes in

[1] The conceptualization of measurement quality used here is similar to that discussed by Heise and Bohrnstedt (1970) and by Zeller and Carmines (1980).
[2] The important impact that measurement errors have on statistics of relationships has received some attention in recent years (e.g., in sociology by Bohrnstedt and Carter, 1971; in psychology by Linn and Werts, 1973; in political science by Asher, 1974; in statistics by Cochran, 1970), but it still goes unrecognized by many data analysts.

business conditions over the past year and in the coming year averaged .41.[3] After allowing for measurement error, however, the true relationship between respondents' perceptions was estimated to be .70. Thus in terms of overlapped variance, the observed relationship was only about *one-third* of what it should have been (17 percent versus 49 percent). In this case, random errors led to a gross deflation of the relationship. However, this does not always occur. Survey 5 produced a relationship of .44 between evaluations of own health and of work that had to be done around the house; but after allowing for measurement error, the true relationship was estimated to be .30. Here, correlated error overwhelmed random error, and the observed percentage of overlapped variance was more than *double* what it should have been (19 percent versus 9 percent).

This study has four major goals, none of which has been pursued previously in a large-scale and systematic way: (1) Test the feasibility of incorporating a particular kind of methodological supplement in regular ongoing national and organizational surveys and of using structural model estimation techniques to generate estimates of measurement quality. (2) Provide descriptive information about estimated construct validity, method effects, and residual error for a broad range of survey measures as implemented by the standard data collection procedures of a respected survey organization. (3) Account for why some survey measures have higher (or lower) measurement quality than others. (4) Provide a means for predicting the construct validity and error components of other survey measures not actually examined in this study. These goals lead to a more general outcome of considerable importance to survey researchers and other users of survey data: more knowledge about how to produce better data.

1. Basic Notions About Validity and Measurement Error

DEFINITIONS

Validity refers explicitly to *construct validity*—the extent to which an observed measure reflects the underlying theoretical construct that the investigator has intended to measure (Cronbach and Meehl, 1955; American Psychological Association, 1974).[4] As noted by Zeller and

---

[3] This is an average of nine different correlations (ranging from .24 to .55) that assessed this relationship.

[4] As is common (but not universal) practice, in this study a measure's validity is expressed as the correlation between the measure and the underlying construct; hence the square of this figure will indicate the proportion of valid variance in the measure. (For example, a measure having a validity of .8 would consist of 64 percent valid variance.)

Carmines, construct validity is different from several other types of validity—content, concurrent, predictive—and involves different notions from those of reliability, but "is the most appropriate and generally applicable type of validity used to assess measures in the social sciences" (1980:83).

The difficulty in estimating construct validity arises from its explicit linkage to an unmeasured theoretical construct, and many discussions of construct validity stress the importance of a theoretical model in the construct validation process. Recently developed structural modeling techniques allow theoretical models to enter the analysis in much more explicit and powerful ways than could be achieved before and, as will be described in Part 3, such models play a fundamental role in the present study.

Random measurement error refers to deviations (from the true or valid scores) on one measure that are statistically unrelated to deviations in any other measure being analyzed concurrently. Conversely, *correlated measurement error* refers to deviations from true scores on one measure that *do* relate to deviations in another measure being concurrently analyzed. Note that whether an error gets classified as correlated or random depends on what other measures happen to be included in a given analysis.[5]

METHOD EFFECTS AND CORRELATED ERRORS

A major reason that correlated errors appear in survey research is because analysts examine multiple measures derived by the same method. When the method by which a measure was obtained affects scores on that measure (a form of measurement error that is very likely to be present to some degree), and when measures reflecting the same method effects are analyzed together, these similar method effects produce correlated errors. A brief example will illustrate the phenomenon.

Imagine a survey item that asks respondents to evaluate their own

---

[5] The deviations that constitute random or correlated errors each average to zero across the respondents being examined. If deviations do not average to zero, it is possible to apportion these deviations into two components: a constant, which is the "bias" discussed previously—an important source of error in its own right, but which does not affect relationships and is not addressed in this investigation—and the remaining part, in which deviations do average to zero across respondents.

This use of the term *correlated error* emphasizes an important general aspect of these errors. Other phrases sometimes used to refer to the same phenomenon include *systematic error* and *halo effects*. However, our use of *correlated error* is different from the way the term has sometimes been employed in investigations of interviewer effects—i.e., the extent to which all respondents interviewed by a single person systematically score too high or too low on a single measure (Bailar, 1976; Fellegi, 1974; Hansen, et al., 1961; Krotki, 1978; Krotki and MacLeod, 1979).

health by picking one of several answer categories ranging from "very good" to "very bad." The answers will vary—partly because people differ in the way they perceive their own health (valid variance). In addition, the answers may vary because people interpret the answer categories differently (e.g., "very good" may mean something more positive to some respondents than to others). This is measurement error attributable to the method (methods variance).

Now, if a second survey item using the same response scale is included in an analysis with this item on health, and if each respondent is consistent in the way he or she interprets the meaning of these categories (as could be expected), the measurement errors attributable to the method would be the same in both items. Respondents who tended to be "too high" on the first item—because of the way they interpreted the answer categories—would also tend to be "too high" on the second item—because it used the same categories. This overlap in method effects generates covariation between the items, and this covariation is added to any covariation that may exist between the concepts tapped by the items. The covariation attributable to common method effects—which is correlated error—strengthens the observed correlation if a positive relation exists among the concepts, or weakens the observed correlation if a negative relation exists among them.

Method effects can occur for any type of survey item if there can be variation in the interpretation of (or reaction to) the introduction, the question, and/or the response scale. This applies to nearly all survey items.

Method effects are not the only source of correlated errors. Correlated errors will appear whenever respondents differ, these differences affect the way respondents answer two or more items, and these differences are not linked to the concept(s) the items were intended to tap. However, method effects are probably the major source of correlated error in survey data. In our own empirical investigations—described in Part '3 of this paper—we have not found substantial and systematic correlations among the measurement errors that could be attributed to anything other than method effects. Nor have other studies produced compelling evidence of substantial correlated errors arising from other sources—at least up to now.[6] Nevertheless, correlated error in survey data is a topic that merits further investigation.

---

[6] This is not to deny, however, that discussions of social desirability effects, yea-saying effects, and the like have suggested that these *might* be sources of correlated error.

2. Sources of Data

SURVEYS AND METHODOLOGICAL SUPPLEMENTS

The data used in this study come from six different surveys. Five of these contacted probability samples of American adults who lived in households; the sixth was a survey of workers in a large Canadian corporation. Table 1 lists these surveys, the population each represents, the number of respondents, the method of data collection, and the substantive content of the measures used in the present investigation. The total number of respondents was 7,706 (the median number per survey was about 900; range: 376 to 3,767). Four surveys used telephone interviews to collect the data, one used face-to-face interviews, and one used a group-administered questionnaire. All were conducted as part of the regular ongoing research activity of the University of Michigan's Survey Research Center.

The basic strategy for the present investigation was to select several important concepts from the regular content of each survey, and then to add a few (6–20) additional items tapping these concepts in such a way that a multimethod-multitrait data design would be

Table 1. Data Sources

No.	Survey Date and Method	Population Represented	Number of Respondents	Number of Measures	Concepts Assessed in Multimethod-Multitrait Design
1.	August 1978 personal interview	A	3,767	19	Quality of life: assessments of housing, standard of living, self, family life, community, health, life-as-a-whole
2.	January 1979 telephone interview	A	884	24	Reports about past and anticipated changes in business conditions, personal finances, health, keeping up with the news
3.	March 1979 telephone interview	A	560	9	Behavioral reports on eating too much, drinking beer, watching television
4.	July 1979 telephone interview	A	1,173	18	Reports about past and anticipated changes in business conditions, personal finances, health, keeping up with the news
5.	September 1979 telephone interview	A	946	12	Quality of life: assessments of financial security, housework, health, life-as-a-whole
6.	Fall 1979 group-administered questionnaire	B	376	24	Ratings of organization of work, firm's interest in workers' welfare, improvement of working conditions, group members' knowledge about jobs, quality of groups' response, group decision making, behavioral reports of eating too much, drinking beer, watching television
	Totals		7,706	106	

NOTE: A = American adults living in households. B = Employees of Canadian business firm.

achieved (Campbell and Fiske, 1959). In other words, each of the selected concepts (traits) was to be assessed by several different methods—i.e., by several distinctively different response scales. Careful attention was devoted to ensuring that the several items intended to tap a single concept all assessed exactly the *same* concept despite their using different response scales. The supplementary items were incorporated into the questionnaire in such a way that they constituted an integral part of the interview.[7]

MEASURES FOR WHICH QUALITY ESTIMATES WERE OBTAINED

To provide a broad base for our methodological findings, the survey measures used in this study—the primary measures—are a large and intentionally heterogeneous set. In all, there are 106 primary measures that tap the 26 different concepts listed in Table 1. Many of the concepts were included in two different surveys to reduce the chance that measurement conditions in any one survey would be confounded with characteristics of the concept itself.

In a further effort to broaden the base for our findings (and, at the same time, to make the measurement model estimable), a large number of different but commonly used response scales were included. In each survey, at least three different response scales were used. Across all six surveys, there was a total of 14 different scales. Table 2 provides the details. To minimize confounding the effects of

Table 2. Measurement Methods (Response Scale Formats)

No.	Short Name	Nature of Scale	Survey[a]
1.	Yes/No	Two categories labeled "yes," "no"	3,4
2.	Better/worse-3	Three categories labeled "better," "same," "worse," plus—for some but not all measures—a "don't know" category	2,4
3.	Better/worse-unfold	A two-stage sequence in which respondent indicates a general response (e.g., "better," "in between," or "worse") and then answers a second question to refine the position (e.g., "a lot better" or "somewhat better") or to indicate he/she hadn't "thought much about it"	2,4
4.	Goodness	Five categories labeled "very good," "fairly good," "neither good nor bad," "not very good," "not at all good"	1

[7] We expected respondents would recognize topics they had discussed previously, so explanations such as the following were sometimes included: "This next section asks about some of the same things we have already talked about, but the questions are different. We are doing research to find the best way to ask these questions. Just tell me which answer seems to fit your situation."

Table 2. (Continued)

No.	Short Name	Nature of Scale	Survey[a]
5.	Satisfaction	Seven categories ranging from "completely satisfied" through "neutral" to "completely dissatisfied" with unlabeled intermediate categories	1,5
6.	Delighted/terrible-7	Seven categories labeled "delighted," "pleased," "mostly satisfied," "mixed," "mostly dissatisfied," "unhappy," "terrible," plus an off-scale "no feelings at all" category	1
7.	Delightful/terrible-unfold	A two-stage sequence in which respondent first indicates a general response ("good," "bad," or "mixed") and then answers a second question to refine the position (e.g., "delighted," "pleased," "just mostly satisfied")	5
8.	Ladder	Description of a ladder with 10 steps ranging from "worst feelings" to "best feelings;" respondent indicates his/her position	5
9.	Graphical assessment	Line ranging from 100 (labeled "perfect") to 0 (labeled "terrible") with each decile marked	1
10.	Agree/disagree	Five categories labeled "agree strongly," "agree moderately," "in the middle," "disagree moderately," "disagree strongly;" alternatively: "agree a great deal," "agree somewhat," "mixed feelings—not sure," "disagree somewhat," "disagree a great deal"	2,6
11.	Extent	Five categories labeled "to a very little extent," "to a little extent," "to some extent," "to a great extent," "to a very great extent"	6
12.	Frequency-4	Four categories labeled "almost every day," "every few days," "once or twice," "not at all"	3
13.	Frequency-9	Nine categories labeled "never," "hardly ever," "some of the time," "somewhat less than half," "about half the time," "somewhat more than half," "most of the time," "nearly all of the time," "all of the time," plus an off-scale "don't know" category	6
14.	Frequency-days	Respondent reports actual number of days per month	3

[a] The numbers in this column refer to the surveys listed in Table 1.

response scale and survey, or response scale and concept, many of the response scales were used in more than a single survey, and all were used with several (3–8) different concepts.

EXAMPLE ITEMS AND TERMINOLOGY

Although it is not feasible to present the exact wording and format for all 106 primary measures (these are available from the author), Table 3 presents all nine primary measures from Survey 3. These nine measures tap the three concepts listed for Survey 3 in Table 1, using the three response scales listed for Survey 3 in Table 2. (These nine items constituted less than 20 percent of the total interview for Survey 3 and were interspersed with other material.)

In considering characteristics of items, it is useful to distinguish three distinct parts, and these can easily be seen in the example items in Table 3. There may be an *introduction,* which is followed by one or more *questions,* and each question has a *response scale,* i.e., a set of answer categories. Together, the introduction (if any), the question, and the response scale constitute the *survey item.* The survey item, when answered by a set of respondents, provides a *survey measure,* i.e., data for analysis.

OTHER VARIABLES

In addition to the variables whose quality was to be assessed (the primary measures), this investigation makes use of a substantial number of other variables to account for variation in the quality

Table 3. The Nine Primary Measures from Survey 3

1. Now turning to things you eat and drink. Some people feel they eat too much. During the past month, how often do you feel you ate too much? Almost every day, every few days, once or twice, or not at all?
2. During the past month were there more than ten days when you drank some beer? (YES/NO)
3. During the past month were there more than four days when you watched TV just to get away from the ordinary cares and problems of the day? (YES/NO)
4. As you know we're trying to get the most accurate information we can so I'd like to ask you about a few thing we have already talked about. These may sound like the same questions, but they give you different answers to choose from. Please tell me how often each has been true for you over the past *month.*
   4A. During the past month *how often did you drink beer?*
   Almost every day, every few days, once or twice, or not at all?
   4B. During the past month were there more than two days when you *ate too much?* (YES/NO)
   4C. How often during the past month did you watch TV just to *get away from the ordinary cares and problems of the day?*
   Almost every day, every few days, once or twice, or not at all?
5. Here are the last questions about things we asked earlier.
   5A. On about how many days during the past month did you drink at least one glass of beer?
   5B. On about how many days during the past month did you eat too much?
   5C. On about how many days during the past month did you watch TV just to get away from the ordinary cares and problems of the day?

assessments. These include reports by respondents about some of their own personal characteristics, ratings by respondents about the survey in which they participated, ratings by interviewers about the respondents, judgments by study staff about characteristics of the primary measures, and objective information about the respondents, the primary measures, and the design of the survey in which each primary measure was included. In all, 46 such other variables were examined. These are described in Part 4 of this report.

3. Estimating the Quality Components of Survey Measures

GENERAL STRATEGY

The measurement quality estimates were derived from a structural model of the measurement process. This model is based on a set of causal assumptions which are grounded in classic measurement theory and involve the basic notions about data quality discussed in Part 1 of this report.

In accord with classic measurement theory (and with what seems intuitively reasonable), a respondent's recorded answer to a survey item is assumed to reflect three types of influences: (1) the way that particular respondent feels about the concept the survey researcher intended the item to tap (e.g., the respondent's perception about changes in his or her health); (2) the way that respondent reacts to the method used for obtaining the data (particularly, in our case, the response scale); and (3) everything else that might affect a recorded answer (e.g., lapses of memory by the respondent, misunderstanding by the interviewer, etc.).

A graphic portrayal of the measurement model used for Survey 3 appears in Figure 1. (Each of the other surveys used functionally identical models, but modified to accommodate varying numbers of concepts, response scales, and items.) As is common practice (e.g., Joreskog and Sorbom, 1978), the exhibit shows measured variables (the primary measures) as rectangles. Unmeasured variables are shown as ovals or circles; the ovals represent the underlying concepts tapped by the items and the circles the response-scale-based sources of measurement error. One-way arrows indicate direct causal influences; two-headed arrows indicate relationships between concepts where no assumption about causality is made. (The shortest one-way arrows in Figure 1 allow for residual variance to influence the observed measures.) Technically, this is a confirmatory factor analysis model and could be expressed as nine simultaneous equations.[8]

---

[8] Texts and manuals on structural modeling (e.g., Joreskog and Sorbom, 1978) describe procedures for writing such sets of equations.

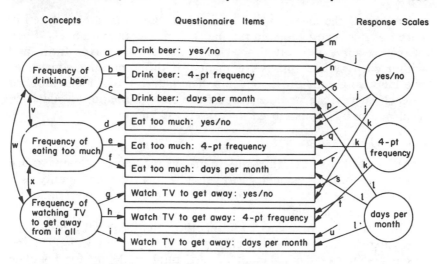

Concepts   Questionnaire Items   Response Scales

Figure 1. Schematic Form of Structural Model

If one has confidence in such a model (a topic addressed below), some of the parameters can be interpreted as measurement quality assessments because they indicate the extent to which variation in a given measure reflects (1) differences among respondents with regard to the underlying concept, an estimate of construct validity (parameters a–i in Figure 1), (2) differences among respondents in the way they interpret and use the response scale, a major source of correlated error (parameters j–l), and (3) the extent to which the measure reflects other influences, primarily random measurement error (parameters m–u). Other parameters can be interpreted as estimates of the true relationships among the concepts (parameters v–x).

The process of estimating the structural model involves finding a unique set of strengths for the causal linkages (parameters a–l), imputed correlations among latent concepts (parameters v–x), and variances for the residual error sources (parameters m–u) that will produce a set of *predicted* relationships among the observed measures that come as close as possible to the *observed* relationships among these measures. In this study these parameter values were obtained by the maximum-likelihood estimation technique incorporated in the LISREL computer program (Joreskog, 1978; Joreskog and Sorbom, 1978).[9]

---

[9] As indicated in Figure 1, an equality constraint was imposed on each set of method effect parameters (the sets of j, k, and l parameters), and each method effect was

Generating the measurement quality estimates that are analyzed in Part 4 of this report required running 125 measurement models. Each of the six surveys involved a series of models of a given form, and within each series, runs were made for different (and sometimes overlapping) groups of respondents. The nature of the model applied to each survey can be determined from the information available in Tables 1 and 2, as has been illustrated for Survey 3.[10]

RELEVANT PRECEDENTS

Although this study represents the first broad scale attempt to use structural modeling technology to generate measurement quality estimates for data from regular on-going surveys, this investigation is grounded on prior work.

The basic idea of using a multimethod-multitrait data design for assessing validity and method effects was proposed by Campbell and Fiske (1959). As the potential of structural modeling for handling multimethod-multitrait data become recognized, many investigators advocated its use (e.g., Alwin, 1974; Boruch, et al., 1970; Schmitt, et al., 1977). The general usefulness of structural models for illuminating the nature and quality of social data now seems well established, and measurement models receive extensive attention in a number of recent texts on social measurement and analysis (e.g., Zeller and Carmines, 1980; Bohrnstedt and Borgatta, 1981; Sullivan and Feldman, 1979; Namboodiri, et al., 1975).

Although theoretical and methodological discussions about the use of measurement models are no longer rare, only recently have investigations that actually use the new modeling technology to estimate data quality begun to appear (Andrews, 1979; Andrews and Crandall, 1976; Mason, et al., 1976; Kluegel, et al., 1977; Robins and West, 1977; Bielby and Hauser, 1977; Bielby, et al., 1977a, 1977b; Mare and Mason, 1980; and Corcoran, 1980.)

---

constrained to be independent of all other latent variables. These constraints ensured that the model's estimates of method effects reflected the assumptions that each method effect was a statistically unique phenomenon and that it had an equal impact on all measures based on that method. These constraints also helped to identify the other parameters in the model. (The fact that the models estimated for this study fit as well as they did suggests that it was not unreasonable to assume that the response scale factors were statistically independent of one another and of the substantive concepts being measured. This result is consistent with those from a previous study (Andrews and Crandall, 1976), where relationships among response scale factors were left unconstrained and empirical estimates showed them to be very weak.)

[10] This same approach can be applied straightforwardly to Surveys 2, 5, and 6, which involve complete 3×8, 3×4, and 3×8 method-by-trait designs, respectively. Surveys 1 and 4 are complicated by the fact that the multimethod-multitrait data design was not complete—i.e., some concepts were not assessed by all methods.

REASONS FOR CONFIDENCE IN THE ESTIMATES

Beyond the fact that other investigators are using and advocating the same general approach as has been used in this study, what empirical evidence is there that suggests that the results from our modeling analyses provide reasonable estimates of data quality?

Appropriateness of the data for the measurement model. The measurement model assumes the data can be adequately explained within the confines of an additive linear system. Furthermore, given that product-moment correlations were input to the LISREL computer program, they are assumed to appropriately represent the actual relationships in the data.[11] To see whether these assumptions were met, the data from each survey were scanned for instances of marked skews, nonlinearities, and nonadditives. In most cases we concluded that the data in their original form were appropriate for analysis; in a few instances a transformation was effected to reduce skew and/or curvilinearity before the correlations were computed.

Adequacy of the measurement model. Models that work well (1) are theoretically reasonable, (2) manage to closely account for the observed relationships in the data, and (3) do so with parameters that are themselves of reasonable magnitude. How well did the models used in this study rate on these criteria?

1. The theoretical relevance of the model has already been discussed. The model represents a direct implementation of classic measurement theory, and the primary measures (those represented in the multimethod-multitrait matrices) were designed specifically for use with this model.

2. Models of the form displayed in Figure 1 proved to fit the data well, i.e., they did a good job in accounting for the actual relationships among the measures. In over a hundred runs involving the application of this model to different sets of variables and/or different sets of respondents, this model consistently produced predicted relationships that tended to be close to the observed relationships. The mean absolute deviation between predicted and observed correlations was always less than .10, and in most runs it was less than .05.[12]

---

[11] Readers who are sophisticated with regard to structural modeling may wonder how the use of correlations as input to the model interacted with the equality constraint imposed on each set of method effect parameters (the *only* reason that it would make any difference whether input was correlations or covariances). A check showed that all measures obtained using any one method tended to have similar variances, and hence it made no difference whether correlations or covariances were used as input to the models.

[12] This examination of the congruence between observed and predicted relationships, as well as our general approach to the topic of model fit, is in accord with perspectives

3. Although a very wide range of parameter values was obtained, in nearly all cases these values were reasonable in the light of theoretical expectation. Specifically, validities, methods effects, and residual errors should all be within 0 to 1. Although there was no constraint on the estimation of parameters to prevent the occurrence of unreasonable values, they very rarely occurred. Out of 2,115 validity estimates that were generated, none was less than 0 and only 19 (0.9 percent) exceeded 1.00 (the highest was 1.13). Of 2,115 method effect coefficients, none was less than 0 and none exceeded 1.00. Of 2,115 residual error coefficients, 32 (1.5 percent) were less than 0 and none was greater than 1. In short, out of more than 6,000 measurement quality estimates, 99.2 percent had reasonable values, and the few that fell outside the reasonable range were not far outside.[13]

Thus, on the criteria of theoretical reasonableness, adequacy of fit, and reasonableness of estimates, the model seems good. Of course, this is not to say that this model always produced the best possible fit. In many cases, minor modifications could be made that would modestly improve the fit. However, despite considerable searching, we have been unable to find any way to change the model that would produce consistent and substantial improvements in fit.[14]

---

advocated by Bentler and Bonett (1980) in an article on assessing how well models fit data. Their article was not published until after all computing for this study had been completed, but had we been able to compute the fit indices they propose for each of the 125 models we ran, there is little doubt that the indices would show that our models account for most of what is going on in the data.

One general indicator of model fit is the ratio of chi square to the degree of freedom. The median value of this ratio over the 125 models was 1.87 (mean value = 2.24). These low values are another indication of the satisfactory fits obtained.

[13] One might ask why *any* unreasonable estimates were generated. Our guess is that they result from minor inconsistencies in the input correlations arising from some respondents being omitted from the calculation of one correlation (because their data were missing on one or both of those particular variables) while different respondents were omitted from other correlations. Although the use of pairwise missing data deletion from correlation matrices has this drawback, it generally leads to less serious problems than what can occur with casewise deletion, in which a great many respondents can be lost from the entire matrix.

[14] One exploration took advantage of the fact that all of the respondents to the July survey had also participated six months earlier in the January survey—i.e., this pair of surveys constitutes a two-wave panel. The data were collected in this way specifically to allow investigation of whether the residual variance really looks like random error, or whether there is some part of it which, while independent from that of any other measure assessed in any one survey, might be a reliable aspect of that particular item. Results of this panel analysis were clear: There was little, if any, reliable unique variance for any of the 12 measures that had been repeated. (The estimates of the reliable unique variance components ranged from 0 percent to 11 percent with a mean of 2 percent). This is further important evidence that it seems appropriate to use the residual parameters in our measurement models as estimates of random error.

4. Analysis of the Measurement Quality Estimates

ANALYSIS STRATEGY

The preceding stages of this research resulted in the generation of a large number of measurement quality estimates. Specifically, there were 2,115 sets of estimates, where each set consists of a validity estimate, a method effect estimate, and a residual error estimate for a particular survey item as it was answered by a particular group of respondents on a particular occasion. The next step in the research was to analyze these quality estimates to determine under what conditions they tended to be higher and under what conditions lower.

This was done in three steps. First, simple descriptive statistics showing the level and variation of these measurement quality estimates were examined. Second, the effects of survey design characteristics were examined. A series of multivariate analyses explored how aspects of survey design—characteristics of response scales, item wordings, the topic investigated, and questionnaire design—related to each of the three measurement quality estimates. Third, after the effects of survey design characteristics had been removed, the effect of respondent characteristics—age, education, sex, and many others—were examined.

This strategy provides a direct way of addressing some of the key questions in survey research—how to achieve more valid measures. The approach, however, is unusual. Few previous studies have had a sufficient number of measurement quality estimates, together with information about the survey and respondent characteristics associated with each estimate, to make a direct multivariate analysis of those estimates feasible.

It is important to note that this analysis strategy involves a shift in data bases. When the measurement quality estimates were being *generated,* the "cases" were individual respondents—as is conventional for most survey analysis. When the quality estimates were being *analyzed,* the "cases" were survey-items-as-administered-to-a-particular-set-of-respondents.[15] For example, one of the "cases" in this data set is a survey item about satisfaction with own health that was answered on a 7-point scale of satisfaction in August 1978 by a representative sample of Americans 71 to 90 years old. This is just one among more than 2,000 such cases.

---

[15] Creation of this new data set required transcription of a large number of LISREL-produced measurement quality estimates and assembly of many descriptive characteristics for each survey item. These data were then punched, verified, and built into a computer data file. The reliability of this coding process was checked for a sample of the cases. The coding accuracy rate was found to be 99.4%, a level that was judged to be highly satisfactory.

DATA QUALITY—LEVEL AND VARIATION

Table 4 presents basic descriptive information about the measurement quality levels, and the variation in those levels, observed in this research. Presented there are the univariate statistics for all 2,115 estimates of each of the three measurement quality components that will be "dependent variables" in this analysis.[16] These results are of considerable interest in their own right.

The first row in Table 4 presents the means for the estimates of validity, method effect, and residual error. Note that the average validity is .81, the average method effect is .16, and the average residual error effect is .53. These figures, when squared, indicate that the "typical" survey measure examined in this research consisted of 66 percent valid variance, 3 percent method variance, and 28 percent residual variance. (These sum to 97 percent. The discrepancy from 100 percent presumably reflects minor imperfections in the way the measurement model used to generate the quality estimates fit some of the data.) Although no claim is made that the set of survey items examined here is representative of all items used in current surveys, this set of items is broader and more heterogeneous than any other we know of whose quality has been estimated, and hence these estimates for the quality of our "typical" item probably provide the best available information about these aspects of measurement quality for single-item survey measures tapping rather specific attitudes and behaviors.[17]

Table 4. Measurement Quality Estimates—Average Level and Variation

	Validity	Meth. Eff.	Res. Error
Mean	.81	.16	.53
Median	.81	.16	.55
Standard deviation	.10	.11	.16
Number of estimates	2,115	2,115	2,115

NOTE: The estimates of validity and method effects are based on lambda parameters from LISREL; the estimates of residual error are based on the *square roots* of the theta parameters from LISREL.

[16] The measurement quality estimates are taken directly from the structural modeling analyses described in Part 3. The validity and method effect estimates are the LISREL-produced lambda parameters, and the residual error estimate is the *square root* of the LISREL-produced theta parameter. The square root transformation of the theta parameter was used so all three measurement quality estimates would be on the same scale—i.e., the *square* of each of them indicates the percentage of variance of the indicated kind in the survey measure.

[17] The median quality estimates presented in the second row of Table 4, and the following skew and kurtosis coefficients for these quality estimates, confirm that their distributions are approximately normal. The skew coefficients for the estimates of validity, method effects, and residual error are, respectively: −.48, .21, and −.77; kurtosis coefficients are: .42, −.46, and 1.14.

Table 4 also presents the standard deviations of the quality estimates. These range from .10 to .16. For the validity estimates, which
have a standard deviation of .10, one can infer that about two-thirds
of all validity estimates fell in the range .71 to .91. Hence, about
two-thirds of the survey measures examined here contained between
50 percent and 83 percent valid variance; roughly one-sixth contained
more than 83 percent valid variance, and about one-sixth had less
than 50 percent valid variance. Comparable calculations for method
effects suggest that two-thirds of the measures had between 0 percent
and 7 percent method variance. Similarly, two-thirds of the measures
had between 14 percent and 48 percent residual variance.

SURVEY DESIGN CHARACTERISTICS AND DATA QUALITY

The next step of the analysis was to perform a series of multivariate analyses to attempt to explain the observed variation in the
quality estimates. Given the nature of the available predictor variables
and the lack of previous exploration in this area, it was important that
the multivariate analyses be able to incorporate nominal-scale predictors, nonlinear relationships, and interactive (i.e., nonadditive) effects. Accordingly, multiple classification analysis using pattern variables (Andrews, et al., 1973) and SEARCH (formerly known as AID—
Sonquist, et al., 1974; Survey Research Center Computer Support
Group, 1981) were selected as the primary multivariate analysis
methods.

Predictive power of survey characteristics. After considerable exploration using various combinations of the available independent
variables, a final multivariate analysis was selected that used 13
predictors.[18] (One of these predictors was a pattern variable based on
two more basic variables). These 13 predictors are listed in Table 5,
together with an indication of the explanatory power of each, both

---

[18] Key questions addressed in these preliminary analyses had to do with (1) an
appropriate and feasible set of predictors for the MCA, (2) whether important interactions were present that, without special treatment, would be unrepresented in the
additive MCA model, and (3) whether the predictors were defined in a sufficiently
general way that they could be used in future studies of measurement quality. In
addition to the survey characteristic variables that finally entered the analysis, 11
others were also examined. (There were—as expected—certain combinations of survey
design characteristics that were perfectly or nearly perfectly confounded with others.
These had to be identified and handled in some way—by eliminating one of the
potential predictors from the analysis or by combining appropriate categories). In
addition, a series of SEARCH runs was helpful in selecting the more useful predictors
when some had to be omitted and in assuring that no major interactions were being
missed. Given that the proportions of variance explained in the final SEARCH runs were
extremely close to the R^2s achieved by the multiple classification analyses (presented in
Table 5), we can be confident that the MCA model is appropriate for these data.

Table 5. Summary Results from Multiple Classification Analysis Using 13 Aspects of Survey Design to Predict Validity, Method Effects, and Residual Error

| | Quality Component Being Predicted | | | | | | |
| | Validity | | Meth. Eff. | | Res. Error | | |
	Adj. eta²	MCA beta²	Adj. eta²	MCA beta²	Adj. eta²	MCA beta²	Mean beta²
Characteristics of response scale							
Number of scale categories	.19	.56	.20	.68	.25	.74	.66
Explicit "Don't know" option	.06	.31	.09	.45	.02	.30	.35
Category labeling	.00	.27	.04	.28	.00	.15	.23
Explicit midpoint	.01	.01	.03	.06	.01	.00	.02
Characteristics of the item							
Absolute vs. comparative	.00	.28	.15	.15	.02	.33	.25
Length of intro. & question	.12	.13	.27	.35	.12	.10	.19
Questionnaire design, data collection							
Battery length	.10	.17	.09	.19	.13	.44	.27
Position of item in questionnaire	.24	.13	.22	.18	.24	.16	.16
Data collection procedure	.02	.03	.18	.24	.01	.02	.10
Characteristics of the topic							
Sensitivity to social desirability	.09	.07	.04	.00	.11	.08	.05
Content specificity	.06	.06	.04	.00	.07	.04	.03
Experience versus prediction	.04	.01	.04	.00	.05	.01	.01
Content salience	.08	.01	.09	.00	.08	.00	.00
Joint explanatory power of 13 predictors (R^2 adj.)	.66		.72		.67		
N (number of quality estimates)	2,115		2,115		2,115		

NOTES: Eta², the squared correlation ratio, shows the proportion of variance in a dependent variable explained by one predictor variable considered alone. The coefficients shown here include an adjustment for shrinkage likely to occur upon replication.

MCA beta² is a measure of the strength of relationship between a dependent variable and a predictor while holding constant the effects of all other predictors included in this analysis.

R^2, the squared multiple correlation coefficient, shows the proportion of variance in a dependent variable explained by all predictors jointly. An adjustment for likely shrinkage upon replication has been incorporated.

singly and in combination with all others, and with an indication of the total explanatory power achieved by the entire set. Table 6 presents more detailed results from this analysis and shows the effect on each of the three measurement quality estimates of each category of each predictor variable, both before and after holding constant the other predictors.

One of the first things to note in Table 5 is that the characteristics of survey design represented in this analysis account for a large part of the variation in the estimates of validity, method effects, and

Table 6. Effects of Survey Design Characteristics on Data Quality[a]

	No. Estimates	Validity Biv.	Validity Mult.	Meth. Eff. Biv.	Meth. Eff. Mult.	Res. Error Biv.	Res. Error Mult.
Characteristics of the response scale (4 variables)							
Number of scale categories							
2	120	−.00	−.06	.04	.11	.02	.04
3	364	−.09	−.13	−.07	−.05	.14	.22
4–5	542	.01	.04	.00	.01	−.00	−.06
7	650	.02	.00	−.03	−.02	−.01	.04
9–19	208	.04	.01	.09	.21	−.09	−.07
20+ or actual frequency	231	.05	.14	.07	−.13	−.14	−.28
Explicit "Don't know" option							
No	1,516	−.02	−.04	.02	.04	.01	.06
Yes	599	.04	.09	−.05	−.11	−.03	−.14
Category labeling							
All categories labeled	1,502	−.00	−.04	−.01	.04	.00	.03
Some categories unlabeled	613	.00	.08	.03	−.09	−.01	−.10
Explicit midpoint							
No	532	.02	.02	−.03	.05	−.03	.01
Yes	1,583	−.01	−.01	.01	−.02	.01	−.01
Characteristics of the item (2 variables)							
Absolute versus comparative							
Absolute	1,275	.00	−.04	.03	.01	−.02	.07
Comparative	840	−.01	.07	−.05	−.02	.03	−.11
Length of intro. and question							
Short intro., short question	56	−.02	−.05	−.04	−.01	−.09	−.02
Short intro., medium question	231	−.03	−.05	−.03	.03	.06	.08
Short intro., long question	259	−.06	−.01	−.04	−.03	.09	.05
Medium intro., short question	249	−.03	.03	−.01	−.08	.05	−.04
Medium intro., medium question	365	−.02	.06	−.00	−.08	−.01	−.07
Medium intro., long question	44	.12	.06	−.02	−.09	−.16	−.05
Long intro., short question	351	.00	−.00	.11	.05	−.04	−.00
Long intro., medium question	219	.03	.00	.02	.07	−.05	−.00
Long intro., long question	341	.03	−.03	−.06	.07	−.19	.06
Questionnaire design (3 variables)							
Battery length							
1 item (i.e., not in battery)	537	−.05	.03	−.03	−.04	.08	−.10
2–4 items	519	.03	.05	.03	.02	−.08	−.11
5–9 items	736	.02	−.03	−.03	−.03	−.02	.09
10 or more items	323	−.00	−.07	.04	.10	.02	.14
Position of item in questionnaire							
1–5 (i.e., among first five items)	148	−.09	−.01	−.06	.03	.15	.03
6–25	280	−.09	−.02	−.03	−.02	.13	.05
26–35	336	.01	.04	.00	−.01	−.01	−.07
36–39	276	.04	.02	−.07	−.03	−.04	−.03
40–100	493	.05	.04	.00	−.05	−.10	−.06
101–200	309	.02	−.04	−.00	.07	−.01	.08
201–348	273	−.02	−.06	.11	.06	.01	.08

Table 6. *(Continued)*

	No. Estimates	Validity Biv.	Mult.	Meth. Eff. Biv.	Mult.	Res. Error Biv.	Mult.
Data collection procedure							
Telephone interview	1,332	.01	−.01	−.03	−.02	−.02	.01
Face-to-face interview	399	−.02	.00	.09	.10	.03	−.01
Group administered							
questionnaire	384	.01	.04	−.01	−.05	.02	−.04
Characteristics of the							
topic (4 variables)							
Sensitivity to							
social desirability							
Low or medium	1,587	−.02	−.02	.01	.00	.03	.03
High	528	.05	.05	−.04	−.00	−.09	−.08
Content specificity							
Low	700	−.02	−.03	−.01	.01	.04	.04
Medium	401	−.02	−.01	.04	−.00	.04	.02
High	1,014	.03	.02	−.01	−.01	−.04	−.03
Experience versus prediction							
Actual experience	1,753	.01	.00	.01	−.00	−.02	−.01
Predictions	362	−.04	−.02	−.05	−.00	.08	.04
Content salience							
Low	445	−.05	.01	−.02	−.01	.08	−.01
Medium	1,056	.03	.01	−.02	−.00	−.03	.00
High	614	−.01	−.01	.05	.01	.00	.01

NOTE: The estimates of validity and method effects are based on lambda parameters from LISREL; the estimates of residual error are based on the *square roots* of the theta parameters from LISREL.

STATISTICAL SIGNIFICANCE: By conventional tests of significance, a difference between most pairs of multivariate coefficients of .02 or more is significant at the $p = .05$ level. Standard errors for the multivariate coefficients (Hill, 1979) range from about .002 when N is 800 to about .01 when N is 50.

[a] Bivariate coefficients show deviations from the mean that are associated with membership in the designated category; multivariate coefficients are similar except effects of other predictors have been held constant by multiple classification analysis.

residual error. As shown by the adjusted R^2s, the survey design characteristics account for 66 percent to 72 percent of the variance in the dependent variables. This is an important finding, for it shows that much of the variation in measurement quality can be explained, and hence measurement quality is subject to prediction in other surveys and perhaps to improvement.

As indicated in Table 5, the characteristics of survey design have been grouped into four conceptually distinct sets. The first includes four aspects of the response scale used with the survey item. Next comes a set of variables that tap several characteristics of the survey item itself. The third set has to do with the design of the questionnaire or interview schedule and the data collection mode. The final set of survey characteristics includes four variables tapping various aspects of the topical content of the survey item.[19]

The beta^{2}s in Table 5 indicate the relative importance of the various survey characteristics in accounting for validity, method effects, and residual error. (The eta^{2}s, which reflect the simple bivariate relationships, are also interesting, but the multivariate results—reflected in the beta^{2}s—are the more useful.) The most important aspects of survey design, as indicated by average beta^{2}s of .25 or more, are the number of answer categories in the response scale, whether these answer alternatives include a "Don't know" category, battery length, and whether the item uses an absolute or comparative perspective. Making appropriate choices with respect to these design characteristics can, apparently, have an important impact on the measurement quality in a survey. Survey characteristics with a more moderate and/or less general effect (average beta^{2}s in the range .15 to .24) include whether answer categories are all labeled, the length of the question and its introduction, and the position of an item in the questionnaire. Choices with respect to these matters can also have important effects on measurement quality. Equally interesting are the design characteristics that did *not* have substantial effects on data quality. These include all four aspects of the topic being asked about, whether the answer scale includes an explicit midpoint, and the data collection procedure. The effects of some of these design matters have been the subject of considerable debate among survey researchers, and it is of interest to find that—at least in this study—they have relatively little impact on measurement quality.

Specific effects of survey design. In Table 6 one can see the way each of these characteristics of survey design relates to validity, method effects, and residual error. Presented there are the effects of each category of each predictor variable on each component of measurement quality, both before and after controlling for the effects of the other predictors. The coefficients in the *Biv.* columns are results from the simple bivariate analysis (the relationships that are summarized by the eta^{2}s in Table 5), and the coefficients in *Mult.* columns come from the multiple classification analyses (and are summarized by the beta^{2}s in Table 5). As noted earlier, the multivariate analysis results probably are the more useful.

The multivariate coefficients in Table 6 show the amount by which the quality component would go up or down from the mean (presented in Table 4) if a measure had the characteristic indicated and there were no effects from any of the other predictor variables. For

[19] These four variables were based on ratings made by project staff members.

example, the $-.06$ effect on validity of using an item with a 2-point answer scale means that, holding everything else constant, validities of such items can be expected to be 6 "points" lower than that of the average item—i.e., $.75$ ($=.81 - .06$). Although the coefficients presented in Table 6 may appear small to the uninitiated reader, in many cases they show sharp and important effects.

Number of scale categories. The number of answer scale categories is shown in Table 5 to have the biggest effects on data quality, and the multivariate coefficients in Table 6 show that, in general, as the number of answer categories goes up, data quality goes up—i.e., validity tends to increase and residual error tends to decrease. (The trend for method effects is less clear, though at its extremes it follows the general trend.) The validity and residual error results show an interesting and possibly important curvilinearity at the low end of the scale: Both 2-point and 3-point scales give less good measurement quality than scales with four or more categories, but 2-point scales are not as bad as 3-point scales.

These results are consistent with a wide-ranging and uncoordinated literature showing that use of more categories (at least up to 5–7) produces a more accurate reflection of the underlying variation. See, for example, Bollen and Barb (1981), Cochran (1968), Conner (1972), Cox (1980), Lissitz and Greene (1975), Martin (1978), Pearson (1913), and Ramsey (1973). This previous body of literature, however, would not have predicted the marked superiority of our "20+" category, and it is possible that this aspect of our results is an artifact (for the reasons in footnote 21).

Explicit "Don't know" option. According to Table 5, the second most important survey characteristic is whether the answer categories include an explicit "Don't know" option. The effect of this design matter is clear and consistent: Inclusion of an explicit "Don't know" category was associated with better data—higher validity, lower method effects, and lower residual error. The reasonable idea that one should let respondents "opt out" if they lack the requisite information or opinions receives strong endorsement.

Battery length. The third most important predictor denotes whether the item is included in a battery with other items, and if so, how long that battery is. The primary effect here is with respect to residual error, but the results for validity and for method effects, though weaker, tend to follow the same trend. The results show that the longer the battery, the lower the data quality.

Including items in batteries where all share a common introduction and/or identical answer scale offers obvious advantages with regard to efficiency and speed, but these results suggest that such gains come at the cost of reduced measurement quality if the battery consists of more than just a few items. It is possible that respondents and/or interviewers recognize the "production line" character of this survey strategy and that it promotes carelessness in the way questions are asked and answered.

One might have guessed that what mattered would not be the total length of the battery in which an item is included but rather how far into a battery the item is located. Both characteristics of items were examined, and, to our surprise, battery length showed stronger relationships to each of the measurement quality components than did position in battery. By logical necessity, the two variables were highly correlated, and it was not feasible to retain both in the multivariate analysis.

Absolute versus comparative. The fourth most important predictor taps whether the item uses an absolute or comparative perspective. The results in Table 6 clearly favor the comparative approach. It may be that the provision of some "anchor points," as is required in the comparative approach, helps respondents give more precise answers.

Length of introduction and of question. Two item-design characteristics, the length of the introduction to a question and the length of the question itself, were combined into the single nine-category pattern variable that was used in the multiple classification analysis because preliminary exploration had shown these characteristics to have both curvilinear main effects and a first-order interaction.[20] Table 6 shows that validity tended to be highest and both types of error lowest when questions were preceded by a *medium*-length introduction (defined as an introduction of 16 to 64 words). Furthermore, given a medium length introduction, medium or long questions (16–24, or 25+ words, respectively) yielded higher data quality than shorter questions. The overall pattern of these results suggests that short introductions followed by short questions are not good (perhaps the respondent does not have an opportunity to get a clear understanding of what is being asked and/or does not have time to develop a precise answer) and neither are long introductions followed by long questions (respondents may lose track of what is being asked and/or get bored while waiting to answer).

Position of item in questionnaire. Table 6 shows a consistent, moderate-strength tendency for data quality to be lower when items were at the beginning of a questionnaire (within the first 25 items) or

---

[20] Andrews, et al. (1973) describe how interactions can be handled in a multiple classification analysis through the use of pattern variables.

far into a long questionnaire (beyond the 100th item). Better data quality comes from items that fell in the 26th to 100th positions.

It is not hard to imagine how this effect might come about. Items that come early in a questionnaire may be presented before the respondent is "warmed up" to the task and, in an interview, before rapport between interviewer and respondent has been developed. On the other hand, after the 100th item, respondents and/or interviewers may begin to suffer from fatigue or become careless.

Category labeling. The moderate-strength relationships associated with category labeling were a surprise and are not yet fully understood. The contrast is between items whose answer categories were fully labeled—i.e., an explicit meaning was indicated for every possible answer—and items where some of the answer categories were left unlabeled—as in a format where only the end points are labeled and some intermediate points take their meaning from their relative position on the page. Contrary to expectation, the results of the multivariate analysis suggest that data quality is below average when all categories are labeled.[21]

Predictors showing weak links to quality. All of the remaining predictors have average beta[2]s of .10 or less, and with just a single exception none of the individual beta[2]s associated with these predictors exceeds that level.[22] The fact that some of these relationships between survey design and data quality are weak is of great interest. It is helpful to know that the often debated issue of whether to allow respondents an "easy out" by including an explicit midpoint ("neutral," "pro-con," etc.) had only slight effects on data quality. It is also interesting to observe that it made little difference whether an item asked about things the respondent had already experienced or asked for predictions about the future. (The small effects that do appear here are in the expected direction—i.e., favoring things the respondent has experienced.) And the finding of only very small effects on validity and residual error attributable to whether data were collected by telephone interviews, face-to-face interviews, or group-administered questionnaires will also be encouraging to many survey

---

[21] It is possible that the surprisingly good quality associated with answer scales having 20+ categories (many of which consisted of reports of actual frequencies per month of doing various things, and hence which count as "fully labeled") has interacted with the category labeling predictor so as to produce an *over*estimate of the quality of data from 20+ answer categories and a corresponding *under*estimate of the data from fully labeled categories. Unfortunately, the data are not sufficient to clarify this matter and it merits further investigation.

[22] The exception is an indication that face-to-face interviews result in a slight enhancement of method effects, but this is *not* accompanied by any reduction in validity for measures obtained in face-to-face interviews.

researchers. That none of the characteristics of the substantive topic being asked about in a survey item had an important effect on data quality was in some respects a disappointment, for we had clear expectations about how these variables might relate. However, the fact that the relationships all proved very weak might be seen as a desirable outcome by many, for it suggests that—other things equal—data of at least average quality can be obtained about a wide range of topics.

RESPONDENT CHARACTERISTICS AND DATA QUALITY

The idea that characteristics of respondents may relate to data quality is an appealing one and can be readily investigated in a sophisticated way with these data. This analysis is possible because estimates of data quality were obtained for many different subgroups of respondents. For example, data quality estimates were obtained separately for young respondents, middle-aged respondents, and elderly respondents, and hence it is possible to see how validity, method effects, and residual error—each averaged across many survey items—varies with age.[23]

Analysis strategy. Because the respondent subgroups for which data quality estimates could be obtained varied from survey to survey, and because survey design characteristics (e.g., topics investigated, answer formats used, data collection procedures, etc.) also varied from survey to survey—and because survey design characteristics have a major impact on data quality, as discussed in the preceding section—it is necessary to remove the survey design effects before looking at the effects of respondent characteristics. This was accomplished through residualization.

The dependent variables in the analyses to be described are the deviations of the actual estimates of an item's validity, method effects, or residual error from *what would be predicted* to be that item's measurement quality given the design of the survey in which that item occurred. Each of these residualized scores were then related to a 53-category predictor variable that denoted the group of respondents on whom the estimates of measurement quality were calculated.[24] These respondent characteristics explained about 12 percent of the remaining variance in the validity estimates, 16 percent for the method effects, and 5 percent for residual error. Clearly, respondent characteristics were not a major predictor of variation in the quality of

---

[23] A separate paper (Andrews and Herzog, 1982) provides a detailed analysis of the relationship between survey data quality and respondent age.

[24] Space limitations permit only a summary of this analysis here. Full details appear in Andrews (1984).

measurement in these data, but there are some characteristics that showed interesting and potentially important links to measurement quality.

Specific effects of respondent characteristics. Validity was higher for more educated respondents, for younger respondents, and for whites. Residual error showed exactly the opposite trends. (Method effects had a clear trend only with respect to age, where it showed sharp increases with increasing age.) Of course these demographic characteristics are known to be substantially correlated among United States adults, and an immediate question is whether these trends would hold up under various controls. A series of subsidiary analyses (not shown) indicated that most of the race effects disappeared when education was controlled. Apparently they were attributable to the fact that blacks tend to have less education than whites. However, the age and education effects persisted even when the other variable was controlled.

There were virtually no relationships between the sex of the respondent and the indicators of data quality—a result that seems reasonable.

Interviewers' impressions about respondents' interest in the survey topics, general intelligence, sincerity with which questions were answered, suspiciousness, and reluctance to participate showed effects in the expected direction—i.e., high interest, intelligence, and/or sincerity tended to be associated with higher validity and lower errors—but none of the effects was very large. There was also evidence that respondents who had difficulty with the interview (e.g., received assistance provided by the interviewer, made requests for clarification and/or repetition of questions) tended to give answers with lower validity and higher residual error.

A persistent concern of survey organizations is whether it is "worth it" to try to contact hard-to-reach respondents. In this analysis no quality differences were observed between respondents contacted on the first attempt and those contacted only after five or more attempts. There also were no quality differences related to whether the respondent had participated in a previous survey conducted by the Survey Research Center.

In a few surveys we included five items selected from the Crowne-Marlowe (1964) scale of social desirability in order to obtain an indication of respondents' concern for presenting themselves in socially desirable ways. This scale produced results in the expected direction: Respondents who scored relatively high on this concern had a modest tendency to give data that were below average in validity and above average in residual error.

Further explorations. A legitimate concern is whether the effects on data quality of the various survey design characteristics explored in the previous section are the same for all types of respondents. In formal statistical terms, are there interactions involving respondent characteristics, survey design characteristics, and data quality? With 22 sets of contrasting respondent characteristics, 13 sets of survey design characteristics, and 3 data quality assessments, there were over 800 first-order interactions that might potentially occur. Eight of these that promised to be most interesting, and for which data were available in sufficient depth, were checked in detail. These included combinations of (1) age, education, or respondent concern for social desirability with (2) number of answer categories, data collection procedure, length of introduction and question, or item sensitivity to social desirability, as related to (3) mean levels of validity. The general result of this exploration was that no major interactions were found. While we cannot, of course, be sure that interactions do not exist where we have not checked for them, we have increased confidence that most of the survey design effects described in the preceding section will be generally applicable to a wide range of different types of respondents.

5. Implications of the Study

There are at least four ways in which the outcomes of this investigation may prove useful.

IMPLEMENTING THE TECHNIQUE

One of the most important outcomes of this research is the discovery that it was indeed feasible to generate measurement quality estimates using the new measurement modeling techniques in regular ongoing surveys. The marginal cost of obtaining measurement quality estimates for key concepts assessed in a survey can be quite low. Since the number of additional items is not large (rarely more than 10–20), this is not a major cost. The other component of cost arises from the staff time required for the initial design of the data collection and from the staff time and computing charges for the subsequent analysis of those data. For a professional with the requisite skills (or with access to skilled consultants), neither of these need be a major task.

RECOMMENDATIONS ABOUT SURVEY DESIGN

A second general implication of this investigation is the promise it holds for generating knowledge about how to design surveys that will yield higher quality measures. The multivariate analysis described in Part 4 of this report itself includes many suggestions for ways to enhance measurement quality, and it could be a prototype for similar analyses performed on other measurement quality estimates that may become available for other survey measures, for other national or cultural settings, and/or for specialized groups of respondents.

PREDICTING THE MEASUREMENT QUALITY OF OTHER ITEMS

One of the potential uses for the detailed set of coefficients presented in Table 6 is to generate predictions of measurement quality for survey items that were not actually included in this study. If it were not feasible for a survey team to develop its own multimethod-multitrait methodological supplement and generate its own estimates of measurement quality, estimates could be obtained by extrapolating the results from the present investigation. How accurate such estimates would be is, of course, open to question. However, almost certainly it would be better to use them than to totally disregard measurement error. The predictions derived by extrapolating from results in this study should be more accurate as (1) the items whose measurement qualities are being predicted are more similar in type of content and format to the items examined here, (2) the surveyed population is more similar to a general American or Canadian adult population, and (3) the surveying organization uses methods and procedures more similar to those of the University of Michigan's Survey Research Center.

To make a predicion of the measurement quality of a survey item, one would begin with the means shown in Table 4. These would be adjusted upward or downward according to the particular combination of survey design characteristics that pertain to the item for which one is making the prediction. The appropriate adjustment is determined by adding together relevant coefficients selected from Table 6. Of the 13 survey design characteristics presented in Table 6, all except the final four should be easy to determine for any item. (One would not go very far astray if the final four were simply neglected—because none of them correlates very strongly with other predicators and none has a strong effect on any of the measurement quality estimates.)

MEASUREMENT QUALITY AND OBSERVED RELATIONSHIPS

This report began by observing that measurement errors influence observed relationships. It is appropriate to conclude with a brief discussion of how one can use information about measurement error to make inferences about the true relationships.

Bivariate relationship between single-item measures. The basic assumptions of measurement modeling, which can be represented in the algebra of path analysis (Zeller and Carmines, 1980), predict that a simple observed relationship will be equal to the true relationship between the concepts being tapped times the product of the validities of the measures, plus the proportion of correlated error in the measures. Algebraically,

$$r_{AB} = r'_{AB} V_A V_B + E^c_{AB}, \tag{1}$$

where r_{AB} is the observed product-moment correlation between measures A and B,

r^1_{AB} is the true correlation between the concepts tapped by measures A and B,

V_A is the construct validity of measure A, i.e., the square root of the percentage of valid variance,

V_B is the construct validity of measure B, and

E^c_{AB} is the correlated error shared by measures A and B, i.e., the product of the *common* method effect coefficients for variables A and B.

This formula can be transformed to provide predictions of the true relationship based on information about the observed relationship and measurement quality:

$$r'_{AB} = (r_{AB} - E^c_{AB})/V_A V_B. \tag{2}$$

A couple of examples will illustrate how the kinds of measurement quality estimates obtained in this study can be combined with information about an observed relationship to predict the true relationship between the underlying concepts. (1) Assume a correlation of .40 is observed between two measures that have estimated validities of .6 and .7, respectively, and that use different methods (hence we assume correlated error is zero). In this case, Formula 2 predicts a true relationship of .95, which is obviously much higher than the observed .40 relationship, which reflects the effects of random measurement error. (2) Assume a similar relationship, .40, is observed between two measures that have validities estimated at .93 and .95, respectively, and that use the same response scale and include method effects estimated at .36 (on the basis of which we assume correlated error is .13—which is .36 squared). In this case, Formula 2 predicts a true relationship of .31, which is somewhat lower than the observed relationship.

Multi-item scales. The estimates of validity and error components obtained in this study are for measures based on *single* survey items. Many survey analyses, however, use scales derived by combining several items. An important rationale for using such scales is that they usually have higher construct validity than single-item measures. (Depending on how a scale is constructed, it may also reflect higher method effects.) If one has an observed relationship involving one or more multi-item scales and one wishes to predict the underlying true relationship, the measurement quality of the scale(s) must be determined before Formula 2 can be used.

In the simple and common situation where a set of items, all of which are assumed to tap the same underlying construct and have about equal validities and method effects, are added together to form a scale, a standard psychometric formula can be used to predict the validity of the scale. Guilford's (1954) Formula 14.37 can be adapted for this purpose as follows:

$$V_S = V_I/((1 - V_I^2 - M_I^2)/N + V_I^2 + M_I^2)^{1/2} \qquad (3)$$

where V_S is the estimated construct validity of the scale,
V_I is the estimated construct validity of a single item,
M_I is the estimated method effects in a single item, and
N is the number of items in the scale.

This same formula can be adapted to provide a prediction of the method effects reflected in a scale:

$$M_S = M_I/((1 - V_I^2 - M_I^2)/N + V_I^2 + M_I^2)^{1/2} \qquad (4)$$

where M_S is the estimated method effects in the scale, and all other terms are as above.

Once one has obtained estimates of the construct validity and method effects for a scale, the residual error effect can be obtained by the following formula:

$$E_S^R = (1 - V_S^2 - M_S^2)^{1/2} \qquad (5)$$

This is based on the definition that residual error is what is left after validity and method effects have been taken into account.

Predicting the validity and method effects for a scale is more complicated if the scale is not constructed by a simple addition of the items, if the items have different validities, and/or if the items reflect different method effects. There is some discussion of such situations in the literature (e.g., Green and Carmines, 1979), but the problem is complex and not fully solved. The new technology of structural modeling with latent variables, on which we comment below, offers a particularly useful way of handling some of these situations.

Multivariate relationships. Just as measurement errors affect bivariate relationships, so also do they have impacts on multivariate statistics—and here the effects are often harder to sort out. One approach for getting true multivariate relationships, uncontaminated by the effects of measurement error, is to use the procedures presented above for obtaining predictions of the true bivariate relationships, and then use these relationships as input to the calculation of the multivariate statistics. Another approach is to use structural modeling with latent variables, a powerful new approach for estimating the true relationships, either bivariate or multivariate, among underlying concepts (i.e., among latent variables). This is the structural modeling technology implemented in computer programs such as LISREL (Bentler, 1980; Joreskog, 1978; Joreskog and Sorbom, 1978).

If one had suitable data, one could use survey measures in such models and obtain useful estimates of underlying relationships without first making the corrections for measurement error just described. This requires, in effect, doing two things at once: estimating a set of measurement quality parameters and performing an analysis on the latent variables. However, sometimes one may not have data that permit simultaneous solution of both problems. In such circumstances, prior information about the validity and error components of the measures—information that might have been obtained using the approaches described in this report—can be incorporated into the structural equation model and allows one to proceed to an insightful analysis.

References

Alwin, D.
  1974 "Approaches to the interpretation of relationships in the multitrait-multimethod matrix." In H. L. Costner (ed.), Sociological Methodology 1973–74. San Francisco: Jossey-Bass.
Alwin, D. F., and D. J. Jackson
  1979 "Measurement models for response errors in surveys: issues and applications." In K. F. Schuessler (ed.), Sociological Methodology 1980. San Francisco: Jossey-Bass.
American Psychological Association
  1974 Standards for Educational and Psychological Tests. Washington, DC: American Psychological Association.
Andrews, F. M.
  1979 "Estimating the construct validity and correlated error components of the rated effectiveness measures." In F. M. Andrews (ed.), Scientific Productivity. Cambridge: Cambridge University Press/UNESCO.
  1984 "Construct validity and error components of survey measures." In C. F. Cannell and R. M. Groves (eds.). Health Survey Research Methods, 4th Conference. Rockville, Maryland: National Center for Health Services Research

Andrews, F. M., and R. Crandall
 1976 "The validity of measures of self-reported well-being." Social Indicators Research 3:1–19.
Andrews, F. M., and A. R. Herzog
 1982 "The quality of survey data as related to age of respondent." Ann Arbor, MI: Institute for Social Research, Working Paper #8032.
Andrews, F. M., J. N. Morgan, J. A. Sonquist, and L. Klem
 1973 Multiple Classification Analysis. Ann Arbor, MI: Institute for Social Research.
Asher, H. B.
 1974 "Some consequences of measurement error in survey design." American Journal of Political Science 18:469–85.
Bailar, B. A.
 1976 "Some sources of error and their effect on census statistics." Demography 13:273–86.
Bentler, P. M.
 1980 "Multivariate analysis with latent variables: causal modeling." Annual Review of Psychology 31:419–56.
Bentler, P. M., and D. G. Bonett
 1980 "Significance tests and goodness of fit in the analysis of covariance structures." Psychological Bulletin 88:588–606.
Bielby, W. T., and R. M. Hauser
 1977 "Response error in earnings functions for nonblack males." Sociological Methods and Research 6:241–80.
Bielby, W. T., R. M. Hauser, and D. L. Fetherman
 1977a "Response errors of black and nonblack males in models of the intergenerational transmission of socioeconomic status." American Journal of Sociology 82:242–88.
 1977b "Response errors of nonblack males in models of the stratification process." Journal of the American Statistical Association 72:723–75.
Bohrnstedt, G. W., and E. F. Borgatta
 1981 Social Measurement: Current Issues. Beverly Hills: Sage.
Bohrnstedt, G. W., and T. M. Carter
 1971 "Robustness in regression analysis." In H. L. Costner (ed.), Sociological Methodology. San Francisco: Jossey-Bass.
Bollen, K. A., and K. H. Barb
 1981 "Pearson's r and coarsely categorized measures." American Sociological Review 46:232–39.
Boruch, R. F., J. D. Larkin, L. Wolins, and A. C. MacKinney
 1970 "Alternative methods of analysis: multitrait-multimethod data." Educational and Psychological Measurement 30:833–53.
Campbell, D. T., and D. W. Fiske
 1959 "Convergent and discriminant validation by the multimethod-multitrait matrix." Psychological Bulletin 56:81–105.
Cochran, W. G.
 1968 "The effectiveness of adjustment by subclassifications in removing bias in observational studies." Biometrics 24:295–313.
 1970 "Some effects of errors of measurement on multiple correlation." Journal of the American Statistical Association 65:22–34.
Conner, R. J.
 1972 "Grouping for testing trends in categorical data." Journal of the American Statistical Association 67:601–04.
Corcoran, M.
 1980 "Sex differences in measurement error in status attainment models." Sociological Methods and Research 9:199–217.

Cox, E. P., III
1980 "The optimal number of response alternatives for a scale: a review." Journal of Marketing Research 17:407–22.
Cronbach, L. J., and P. E. Meehl
1955 "Construct validity in psychological tests." Psychological Bulletin 52:281–302.
Crowne, D. P., and D. Marlowe
1964 The Approval Motive: Studies in Evaluative Dependence. New York: Wiley.
Fellegi, I. P.
1974 "An improved method of estimating the correlated response variance." Journal of the American Statistical Association 69:496–501.
Green, V. L., and E. G. Carmines
1979 "Assessing the reliability of composites." In K. F. Schuessler (ed.), Sociological Methodology. San Francisco: Jossey-Bass.
Guilford, J. P.
1954 Psychometric Methods, 2nd ed. New York: McGraw-Hill.
Hansen, M. H., W. N. Hurwitz, and M. A. Bershad
1961 "Measurement errors in censuses and surveys." Bulletin of the International Statistical Institute 38:359–74.
Heise, D. R., and G. W. Bohrnstedt
1970 "Validity, invalidity, and reliability." In E. F. Borgatta and G. W. Bohrnstedt (eds.), Sociological Methodology. San Francisco: Jossey-Bass.
Hill, D. H.
1979 "A methodological note on obtaining MCA coefficients and standard errors." Working Paper #8008. Ann Arbor, MI: Institute for Social Research.
Joreskog, K. G.
1978 "Structural analysis of covariance and correlation matrices." Psychometrika 43:443–77.
Joreskog, K. G., and D. Sorbom
1978 LISREL IV Users Guide. Chicago: National Educational Resources.
Kluegel, J. R., R. Singleton, Jr., and C. E. Starnes
1977 "Subjective class identification: a multiple indicator approach." American Sociological Review 42:599–611.
Krotki, K. P.
1978 "Estimation of correlated response variance." Paper presented to the 1978 Annual Meeting of the American Statistical Association.
Krotki, K. P., and A. MacLeod
1979 "Two methods of measuring correlated response variance." Paper presented to the 1979 Annual Meeting of the American Statistical Association.
Linn, R. L., and C. E. Werts
1973 "Errors of inference due to errors of measurement." Educational and Psychological Measurement 33:531–44.
Lissitz, R. W., and S. B. Greene
1975 "Effect of the number of scale points on reliability: a Monte Carlo approach." Journal of Applied Psychology 60:10–13.
Mare, R. D., and W. M. Mason
1980 "A multiple group measurement model of children's reports of parental socioeconomic status." Sociological Methods and Research 9:178–98.
Martin, W. S.
1978 "Effects of scaling on the correlation coefficient." Journal of Marketing Research 15:304–8.
Mason, W. M., R. M. Hauser, A. C. Kerckhoff, S. S. Poss, and K. Manton
1976 "Models of response error in student reports of parental socioeconomic characteristics." In W. H. Sewell, et al. (eds.), Schooling and Achievement in American Society. New York: Academic Press.
Namboodiri, N. K., L. F. Carter, and H. M. Blalock, Jr.
1975 Applied Multivariate Analysis and Experimental Design. New York: McGraw-Hill.

Pearson, K.
   1913   "On the measurement of the influence of 'broad categories' on correlation."
           Biometrika 9:116–39.
Ramsey, J. O.
   1973   "The effect of number of categories in rating scales on precision of estimation
           of scale values." Psychometrika 38:513–32.
Robins, P. K., and R. W. West
   1977   "Measurement errors in the estimation of home value." Journal of the Ameri-
           can Statistical Association 72:290–94.
Schmitt, N., B. W. Coyle, and B. B. Saari
   1977   "A review and critique of analyses of multitrait-multimethod matrices." Mul-
           tivariate Behavioral Research 12:447–78.
Sonquist, J. A., E. L. Baker, and J. N. Morgan
   1974   Searching for Structure, rev. ed. Ann Arbor, MI: Institute for Social Re-
           search.
Sudman, S., and N. L. Bradburn
   1974   Response Effects in Surveys. Chicago: Aldine.
Sullivan, J. L., and S. Feldman
   1979   Multiple Indicators: An Introduction. Beverly Hills: Sage.
Survey Research Center Computer Support Group
   1981   OSIRIS IV: Statistical Analysis and Data Management Software System. Ann
           Arbor, MI: Institute for Social Research.
Wheaton, B., B. Muthen, D. F. Alwin, and G. F. Summers
   1977   "Assessing reliability and stability in panel models." In D. R. Heise (ed.),
           Sociological Methodology. San Francisco: Jossey-Bass.
Zeller, R. A., and E. G. Carmines
   1980   Measurement in the Social Sciences. New York: Cambridge University Press.

Pseudo-Opinions
on Public Affairs

GEORGE F. BISHOP, ROBERT W. OLDENDICK, ALFRED J. TUCHFARBER AND STEPHEN E. BENNETT

THE BELIEF that respondents often give opinions on issues, objects, or events they know nothing about has become one of the more ingrained superstitions in survey research. We say "superstition" because, aside from some scattered and not always well-documented accounts, such as the survey cited by Payne (1951), in which over two-thirds of a sample supposedly offered an opinion on a fictitious "Metallic Metals Act," we know very little about this potentially major source of nonsampling error.[1] There is even a hint in a recently published investigation by Schuman and Presser (1978) that researchers may have exaggerated the extent of "nonattitudes" in the

---

[1] Hartley's (1946) early studies of college students showed large majorities willing to offer opinions on such fictitious nationalities as the Wallonians. Kolson and Green (1970) discovered similar levels of opinionation in a sample of grade school children for a nonexistent political figure named Thomas Walker. Neither study, however, provides much theoretical guidance as to why this phenomenon occurs (cf. Bogart, 1967).

Abstract This article reports on the often suspected but rarely researched tendency of survey respondents to give opinions on topics to which they have given little or no thought. The findings, based on a question about a fictitious public affairs issue, do show that the magnitude of the problem is substantial. But the data also demonstrate that this phenomenon does not represent simple random error, reflecting instead basic social-psychological dispositions which can be elicited, unwittingly, in the context of the interview.

George F. Bishop is a Senior Research Associate, Robert W. Oldendick is a Research Associate, and Alfred J. Tuchfarber is Director, Behavioral Sciences Laboratory at the University of Cincinnati. Stephen E. Bennett is Associate Professor of Political Science at the University of Cincinnati. The research reported here was supported by a grant from the National Science Foundation (SOC78–07407). The authors want to thank Howard Schuman and Stanley Presser for their comments on a presentation of a previous version of this paper at the annual conference of the American Association for Public Opinion Research, Buck Hill Falls, Pennsylvania, June 1979.

American public (cf. Converse, 1970). For they found that a sizable majority (63 percent) of their respondents were quite willing to volunteer "don't know" when asked their opinion of the not-so-well-known military government in Portugal. But impressive as this figure might seem, it was based on a real subject that had been covered in varying degrees by the mass media.

A more direct approach would be simply to ask people whether they have an opinion about an issue or topic that theoretically does not exist. This, in fact, is what we did as part of a larger set of experiments on the effects of opinion filtering (Bishop et al., 1979). In this report we will look first at how extensive the nonattitude or "pseudo-opinion" problem may be in U.S. surveys. We will then try to identify the principal social and psychological sources of this disposition, including a partial assessment of the extent to which it reflects deliberate falsification. And finally, we will explore the probable consequences of excluding respondents who express such tendencies from analysis of other items within the same survey.

Research Design

The data for our analysis come from two separate field experiments. The first one was part of a broader RDD telephone survey of citizen alienation from local government carried out by the Behavioral Sciences Laboratory in July and August of 1978 ($N = 631$).[2] The second was part of an even larger omnibus vehicle known as the Greater Cincinnati Survey, the interviewing for which took place in November and December of 1978 ($N = 1,218$).[3] In each of these experiments respondents were randomly assigned to one of four conditions, and within one of these, to one of two subconditions:

Subgroup A. Respondents in this group were asked about their opinions on a number of policy issues (see Table 2)[4] using a version of

---

[2] Approximately 63 percent of the respondents in this study were members of a panel being interviewed for a second time, the rest being from a previously uninterviewed control group. The reinterview rate for the (14-month) panel was 62.7 percent. The response rate for the control group was 67.7 percent. There were no significant differences between these subsamples, however, in the proportions giving an opinion on our fictitious topic. Nor were there any on the major independent variables we analyzed—education, race, and trust.

[3] The response rate for this survey was 73.6 percent. For further documentation, see the technical report for *The Greater Cincinnati Survey: November—December, 1978.* The population used for this second survey consisted of residents (18 and over) of telephone households in the county, which includes the city, whereas the first survey was limited to telephone households in the city only.

[4] The exact wording of these other items can be obtained by writing to the authors.

a filter question that had originally appeared in the SRC 1956–1962 American National Election Studies: "Do you have an opinion on this or not?"

Subgroup B. Here the filter accompanying each issue was the one first introduced by SRC in the 1964 election study: "Have you been interested enough in this to favor one side over the other?"

Subgroup C1. Respondents received a variation of the filter currently used by the Michigan Center for Political Studies: "Have you thought much about this issue?"

Subgroup C2. Respondents were administered a slightly different version of the filter used in Subgroup C1: "Where do you stand on this issue, or haven't you thought much about it?"

Subgroup D. This group was *not* exposed to any filter question when asked about each of the policy issues.

Embedded within the series of domestic and foreign policy questions that we asked of each group was the following fictitious issue: "Some people say that the 1975 Public Affairs Act should be repealed."

If the respondent was in the nonfilter condition (D) he or she was immediately asked: "Do you agree or disagree with this idea?" Otherwise in the various filter conditions (A, B, C1, C2) they were initially screened for having an opinion. And if they did, they were asked: "Do you agree or disagree with the idea that the 1975 Public Affairs Act should be repealed?"[5]

In many of the tables which follow we have pooled the data from the two experiments, largely because of the need for adequate cell sizes. Generally speaking, the pattern of differences among experimental conditions in the two studies was highly similar. In some cases data were available from only one of the two experiments, however, and we note that accordingly. The reader should also know that the filter question accompanying the Public Affairs Act (PAA) item was identical in conditions C1 and C2. For this reason we collapse these subgroups in the tables below.

Findings

A substantial number of respondents claimed to have an opinion on the Public Affairs Act (Table 1). The estimate from our pooled sample of the Cincinnati area was about a third of the adult population, that

---

[5] An anonymous reviewer suggested that, since this item involves a possible acquiescence response set, it may maximize opinion giving. The results in Table 6 below, however, indicate that a more basic social-psychological disposition is implicated.

Table 1. Response to a Question about Repealing the 1975 Public Affairs Act by Filter-Nonfilter Condition (Pooled File)

Condition	Agree	Disagree	Filtered DK	Voluntary DK	Total	(N=)
A: "Do you have an opinion on this or not?"	3.9%	3.2	82.5	10.4	100%	(463)
B: "Have you been interested enough in this to favor one side over the other?"	3.8%	3.6	76.6	16.0	100%	(445)
C1/C2: "Have you thought much about this issue?"	2.9%	1.6	85.8	9.7	100%	(445)
D: (no filter)	15.6%	17.6	0.0	66.8	100%	(467)

Note: "Filtered" DK includes respondents who said they did not have an opinion, were not interested, or had not thought much about an issue when exposed to an explicit filter. "Voluntary" DK's indicate a nonsubstantive response given after the choices were read—i.e., the usual "don't know" response.

is, in the absence of an explicit filter.[6] Even in the face of such a hurdle, we found that roughly 5 to 10 percent of the respondents would persist in volunteering an opinion. Both of these figures are very similar to those found in a national sample by Schuman and Presser (1980) for a real but highly obscure federal statute called the "Agricultural Trade Act of 1978." Nor is the percentage with opinions on the PAA in our nonfilter condition (33 percent) that different from the percentage giving opinions in the same condition to their previously cited question about the Portuguese military government (37 percent).[7] Hence, the distinction between what is a real topic and what is not may be irrelevant for much of the mass public, for whom political content is of generally low salience.

Another striking feature of the marginals in Table 1 is the division of opinion among those who volunteered one. The agree/disagree split looks suspiciously close to 50:50 in most conditions; in fact, it is

[6] In Experiment I the figure was 41 percent in the nonfilter condition; in Experiment II, 32 percent. The difference is due largely to the greater proportion of blacks in the former survey who are generally more likely to offer opinions on this item (see Table 4 below). The reader may also be curious to know how these percentages compare to those found for real issues like the ones shown in Table 2 below. In the nonfilter condition we found a range from 85 percent with an opinion on the *arms to Turkey* item to approximately 97 percent on the *affirmative action* issue, whereas in the filter condition it ran from about 48 percent to 91 percent on the same two issues, respectively (see Bishop et al., 1979). On most other issues we have generally found about 85 to 95 percent of the population willing to volunteer an opinion in the absence of a filter, but which, when introduced, typically takes out about 20 to 25 percent of respondents, a figure that is quite similar to that reported by Schuman and Presser (1978).

[7] Schuman and Presser (1980) have pointed out, however, that these superficial similarities in the marginals of real and fictitious issues can conceal important differences in the relationship of opinions to other variables like education.

almost exactly that for the sample as a whole, suggesting perhaps that a random model of responding would provide an appropriate fit (cf. Converse, 1964; 1970). But, as we shall see shortly, this is not at all the case, at least not in terms of the way we normally conceptualize item-specific responses.

Furthermore, we have evidence which indicates that responding to a fictitious item like the Public Affairs Act is not simply a matter of deceit. In our second experiment we tested this proposition by also asking respondents whether they had heard of a nonexistent social service agency called ECTA.[8] About 10 percent said they had, but there was no significant association in either the filter or nonfilter conditions between responses to this item and giving an opinion on the PAA. This does not, of course, rule out deception in response to specific items, but it does suggest that it is not a general characteristic.

Of greater significance to many researchers is the question of whether respondents who offer opinions on the Public Affairs Act will do the same on topics that are real but not especially salient in their daily lives. The figures in Table 2 tell us that such people were indeed more likely to express an opinion on *all* other issues we investigated.[9] This was particularly true in the filter condition and for the more abstract matters of policy, such as resumption of arms shipments to Turkey and the SALT negotiations. The most plausible reason for the larger differences in the filter condition is that it acts as a "test" which more sharply differentiates those respondents who tend to volunteer opinions on topics they are unfamiliar with from those who are more willing to acknowledge their ignorance. And apparently the more remote the topic becomes from day-to-day concerns, the greater is the effect of this predisposition.

SOCIAL AND PSYCHOLOGICAL SOURCES

Probably our strongest expectation was that respondents with lower levels of education would be most likely to say they had an opinion on the Public Affairs Act. Even though we knew from a number of previous studies that such people were less likely to have opinions on matters of public policy (Faulkenberry and Mason, 1978; Francis and Busch, 1975; J. Converse. 1976–77; Schuman and Presser, 1978), we

---

[8] ECTA is an acronym for the computer program, Everyman's Contingency Table Analysis, developed by Leo Goodman and his associates at the University of Chicago.
[9] We collapsed across filter conditions because of the need, again, for adequate subgroup sizes.

Table 2. Percentage with Opinions on Other Policy Issues, in Filter and Nonfilter Conditions, by Opinion/No Opinion on the Public Affairs Act

	Filter		Nonfilter	
	Opinion	No Opinion	Opinion	No Opinion
Policy Issue	PAA	PAA	PAA	PAA
Government vs. private	88.4	68.0	98.1	93.6
solution of problems	(86)	(1,263)	(155)	(311)
Affirmation action	94.2	91.3	97.4	96.5
for blacks	(86)	(1,266)	(155)	(310)
Tax cut if loss of	80.2	71.7	97.4	89.1
jobs for public employees	(86)	(1,264)	(155)	(309)
Government vs. private	90.7	80.9	98.1	90.9
health insurance	(86)	(1,265)	(155)	(311)
Reestablishment of diplo-	71.8	57.2	92.2	84.0
matic relations with Cuba	(85)	(1,266)	(154)	(312)
Resumption of arms	68.2	47.2	94.2	80.4
shipments to Turkey	(85)	(1,264)	(155)	(312)
	Experiment II			
SALT negotiations and				
Soviet interference in	91.7	68.1	93.3	88.4
African affairs	(48)	(831)	(89)	(216)

NOTE: Entries are percentages of respondents giving an opinion on an issue (subgroup sizes shown in parentheses).

reasoned that they would also be less likely to realize that our questions on the PAA was a dummy. In addition, there was evidence from the classic study by Lenski and Leggett (1960) showing lower-status respondents to be more deferential or acquiescent toward middle-class interviewers. Thus we thought they would be more inclined to "go along" by offering an opinion on "another one of those questions," particularly in the absence of an explicit filter. The results for the nonfilter condition in Table 3 confirm the hypothesis without question, but in the filtered subgroup the relationship is not only much weaker, it tends in the opposite direction, with college-level respondents most likely to offer an opinion. One way to interpret this

Table 3. Percentages with Opinion on Public Affairs Act, in Filter and Nonfilter Conditions, by Education

Education	Filter[a]	Nonfilter[b]
0–11 yrs.	6.6 (333)	40.2 (122)
12	3.9 (431)	35.6 (149)
13+	8.2 (562)	26.2 (189)

NOTE: χ^2 for response by education by filter/nonfilter interaction = 12.06, $df = 2$, $p < .01$.

[a] $\chi^2 = 7.34$, $df = 2$, $p < .05$ (Gamma = $-.14$).

[b] $\chi^2 = 6.93$, $df = 2$, $p < .05$ (Gamma = $.21$).

interaction is in terms of a "floor effect." That is, in the filter condition, there are so few respondents who offer an opinion on the PAA (4 to 8 percent) that there is little opportunity for education (or any other variable) to produce substantial variation, whereas in the nonfilter condition this floor is removed.

Notice also in Table 3 that using a filter tends to be considerably more effective in reducing the magnitude of volunteered opinions in the less educated subgroups. This may help explain the somewhat higher level of opinion-giving among college-educated respondents; that is, they may be simply less willing to admit that they do not have an opinion on some issue of "public affairs," perhaps because of their need to appear well-informed (see, e.g., Ferber, 1956). Two quite different processes may then be operating to produce the same result: in one case because respondents don't know any better (i.e., the less educated); in the other, because they don't want anyone to know that they "don't know." Or perhaps they are both variations of a more generic process of "saving face."

A form of face-saving may likewise explain the association between race and opinions on the Public Affairs Act (Table 4). In both the filter and nonfilter conditions blacks volunteered an opinion far more frequently than whites. Our speculation is that it represents an attempt by many blacks not to fit stereotypes about being "uninformed" to our presumptively white middle-class interviewing staff . . . "calling from the University of Cincinnati."[10] If that is true, there are some disturbing implications for the ever-growing use of telephone interviewing, with which it is technically impossible to achieve any adequate matching of race of interviewer with race of respondent.

Table 4. Percentage with Opinion on Public Affairs Act, in Filter and Nonfilter Conditions, by Race

Race	Filter[a]	Nonfilter[b]
Black	11.4 (290)	48.5 (97)
White	4.9 (1028)	28.6 (357)

NOTE: χ^2 for response by race by filter/nonfilter interaction = .04, $df = 1$, n.s.
[a] $\chi^2 = 15.19$, $df = 1$, $p < .001$ ($Q = .43$).
[b] $\chi^2 = 12.79$, $df = 1$, $p < .001$ ($Q = .40$).

[10] While a respondent's color may not be "visible" over the phone, we have discovered an extremely high correlation ($Q = .99$) between the perceived race of the respondent in the first wave of the panel study we identified in footnote 2 and reported race in the second wave. We suspect that much of this is based on stereotypic, but accurate, inferences by our interviewers from vocal cues; if they were so aware of race, so too must our respondents have been.

The only practical alternative would be to increase, substantially, the number of black interviewers on our staffs, randomize properly the assignment of telephone numbers, and control for this extraneous source of variation statistically.

We also examined the influence of several other sociodemographic variables—age, sex, and income—but none of them was of any real consequence (data not shown here). There was a slight, statistically significant tendency for males in the filter condition to report more frequently having an opinion on the PAA, but this difference was not substantively important. Education and race thus appear to be the principal social sources of this phenomenon.

The only other variable that we expected to mediate responses to our fictitious issue was interest or involvement in politics, which, while correlated with education, will generally have an independent effect on the expression of opinions on public affairs (see, e.g., Francis and Busch, 1975). Our data (not shown here) supported this expectation, showing a pattern that was very similar to the one we found for education (Table 3).[11] In the filter condition it was respondents with higher levels of interest in politics who were more likely to offer an opinion on the PAA, whereas the reverse was true in the nonfilter condition. When we controlled education, however, the relationship between interest in politics and opinion on the PAA was significant only in the filter condition (data not shown here).

Our next finding was totally serendipitous. Along with a number of questions concerning political alienation in the first experiment we had included the three-item index used by the Michigan Survey Research Center to measure interpersonal trust (see Robinson and Shaver, 1973), or what Rosenberg (1957) had originally developed as the Faith-in-People Scale. When we correlated responses to this index with those on the public affairs question, a highly significant interaction emerged: in the filter condition there was virtually no association at all, but in the nonfilter condition mistrustful respondents were more than twice as likely to say they had an opinion on the PAA then those with more faith in other people (Table 5).[12]

[11] To measure political interest we used the standard Michigan CPS question: "Now . . . some people seem to follow what's going on in government and public affairs most of the time, whether there's an election going on or not. Others aren't that interested. Would you say that you follow what's going on in government and public affairs most of the time, some of the time, only now and then, hardly at all?" Respondents who said they followed these matters "most of the time" were defined as the *high* interest group, the rest were collapsed into a *low* interest category.

[12] We created the index by first summing responses to the three dichotomous items, yielding a range from 0 to 3. We then dichotomized this distribution into the *high* (2, 3) and *low* (0,1) trust subgroups shown in Table 5.

Table 5. Percentage with Opinion on Public Affairs Act, in Filter and Nonfilter Conditions, by Interpersonal Trust

Trust	Filter[a]	Nonfilter[b]
High	7.0 (230)	26.3 (76)
Low	9.4 (212)	57.3 (75)

NOTE: χ^2 for response by trust by filter/nonfilter interaction $= 4.03$, $df = 1$, $p < .05$.
[a] $\chi^2 = .60$, $df = 1$, n.s.
[b] $\chi^2 = 13.69$, $df = 1$, $p < .001$ (Q = .58).

Since we knew from previous investigations that blacks and less educated respondents were generally less trusting of others (Robinson and Shaver, 1973)[13] and since they were also more likely to express opinions on the PAA, we suspected that this finding might be spurious. However, controlling these variables, both separately and simultaneously (data not shown here), had virtually no effect on the original association. Race, education, and trust all appear, then, to produce relatively independent effects on the expression of opinions on a fictitious issue.

The interesting question, of course, is why people with little faith in others more often give opinions than those with greater faith. The answer perhaps lies in the documented connection between trust and self-esteem (see, e.g., Robinson and Shaver, 1973). Our question about a credible-sounding Public Affairs Act can be viewed as a threat to the sense of personal competence of a misanthropic individual, and so he or she volunteers an opinion as a form of self-protection against being thought "stupid" or "uninformed." This interpretation fits in with our earlier discussion of "saving face" as an explanation for racial and educational differences. Each of these variables may be tapping somewhat different aspects of an underlying factor of self-confidence. It does, after all, take a certain amount of confidence in oneself to acknowledge that one does not have an opinion on something that sounds important.

Opinions on the PAA, once expressed, may not be just a matter of randomly flipping mental coins (cf. Converse, 1964). Indeed, the data in Table 6 tell us that many respondents also fall back on their general disposition to trust or mistrust other people or institutions—in this case, the government or public sector—when deciding to agree or disagree with the proposition concerning our ambiguous PAA stimulus. Thus we find those low on trust more inclined to agree with the idea of repealing the act and those high on trust more likely to

[13] We found similar associations in our dataset between race and the trust index (Q = $-.67$, $p < .001$), and between education and trust (Q = $.54$, $p < .001$).

Table 6. Substantive Response to Repeal of Public Affairs Act, by Interpersonal Trust and Filter/Nonfilter Conditions (Experiment 1)

Response	Filter Condition		Nonfilter Condition	
	High Trust	Low Trust	High Trust	Low Trust
Agree	25.0%	70.0%	35.0%	41.9%
Disagree	75.0	30.0	65.0	58.1
Total	100.0%	100.0%	100.0%	100.0%
(N=)	(16)	(20)	(20)	(43)
	$\chi^2 = 5.51, df = 1,$			
	$p < .05 (Q = -.75)$		$\chi^2 = .06, df = 1,$ n.s.	

NOTE: χ^2 for response by trust by filter/nonfilter interaction = 3.19, $df = 1$, $p = .073$.

disagree, though the relationship reaches statistical significance in the filter condition only.

SUBSTANTIVE CONSEQUENCES

Because we already know that respondents who volunteered opinions on the Public Affairs Act tended to be black, less educated, less interested in politics, and less trusting of others, it should not surprise us to learn that they also differed in the kinds of substantive responses they gave to other policy items (Table 7). In general, they

Table 7. Relationships Between Opinion/No Opinion on the Public Affairs Act and Substantive Response to Other Policy Issues by Filter-Nonfilter Condition

Policy Issue	Filter	Nonfilter
Government vs. private solution of problems	−.29* (935)	−.52*** (443)
Affirmative action for blacks	.27 (1,237)	.33* (450)
Tax cut if loss of jobs for public employees	−.24 (975)	−.47*** (428)
Government vs. private health insurance	.26* (1,102)	.27** (433)
Reestablishment of diplomatic relations with Cuba	.01 (785)	.10 (404)
Resumption of arms shipments to Turkey	.01 (655)	−.06 (397)
Experiment II		
SALT negotiations and Soviet interference in African affairs	−.09 (610)	−.11 (274)

NOTE: Entries are Yule's Q-coefficients.
  * $p < .05$.
  ** $p < .01$.
  *** $p < .001$.

were more in favor of the "liberal" or progovernment position on domestic issues, an association which is considerably stronger (as we might expect) in the nonfilter condition. In contrast, there was little or no relationship between giving an opinion on the PAA item and responses to the three foreign affairs questions. Moreover, when we controlled education and race (data not shown here), many of the original relations shown in Table 7 remained about the same in magnitude, though there were several noticeable specifications. In other words, volunteering an opinion on the PAA appears to be independently related to expressing a progovernment position on domestic issues.

These findings led us to speculate whether respondents who answered the PAA item might not have derived a good deal of its meaning from the immediately preceding context of the interview schedule, which consisted of the four domestic issues which which it was correlated. Inferring that it had to do with "the government," albeit vaguely, they would thus rely on their general disposition to trust or mistrust this institution in deciding how to answer. So far from being a random or thoughtless reaction, it tells us something about how readily respondents will engender meaning where public opinion analysts think there is none, or where such researchers think there is one, and they substitute another.

At the same time, we should not lose sight of the unintended consequences of our general failure in public opinion surveys to remove such respondents with a filter question or a dummy item of the kind we have used here. If they are indeed more likely to give a "liberal" response to domestic policy issues, based on some vague sense of trust or mistrust toward the government sector, then we risk distorting, perhaps considerably in the case of more abstract matters, the level of public support for various social and economic programs. To express it still another way, for a significant segment of the population (a third?), we may be measuring not much more than their general positive or negative affect toward the government, rather than specific beliefs about the policy alternatives contained in our questions.

And yet, how are we to say that such responses, once elicited, are any less "real" than any others? Insofar as they represent more enduring (personality) dispositions, one might even argue that they are more genuine or "substantial" than the opinions elicited by the specific content of public policy items. Ultimately, it comes down to the old question of validity: What is it that we are trying to measure?

References

Bishop, George F., Robert W. Oldendick, Alfred J. Tuchfarber, and Stephen
E. Bennett
  1979 "Opinion filtering and political attitude structure." Paper presented
        at the annual conference of the Midwest Political Science Associa-
        tion, Chicago, Illinois, April 1979.
Bogart, Leo
  1967 "No opinion, don't know, and maybe no answer." Public Opinion
        Quarterly 31:331–45.
Converse, Jean M.
  1976– "Predicting no opinion in the polls." Public Opinion Quarterly
  77   40:515–30.
Converse, Philip E.
  1970 "Attitudes and non-attitudes: continuation of a dialogue." Pp.
        168–89 in E. R. Tufte (ed.) The Quantitative Analysis of Social
        Problems. Reading, Mass.: Addison-Wesley.
Faulkenberry, G. David, and Robert Mason
  1978 "Characteristics of nonopinion and no opinion response groups."
        Public Opinion Quarterly 42:533–43.
Ferber, Robert
  1956 "The effect of respondent ignorance on survey results." Journal of
        the American Statistical Association 51:576–86.
Francis, Joe D., and Lawrence Busch
  1975 "What we now know about 'I don't know.'" Public Opinion Quar-
        terly 39:207–18.
Hartley, Eugene L.
  1946 Problems in Prejudice. New York: Octagon Books.
Kolson, Kenneth L., and Justin J. Green
  1970 "Response set bias and political socialization research." Social Sci-
        ence Quarterly 51:527–38.
Lenski, Gerhard E., and John C. Leggett
  1960 "Caste, class, and deference in the research interview." American
        Journal of Sociology 65:463–67.
Payne, Stanley L.
  1951 The Art of Asking Questions. Princeton: Princeton University Press.
Robinson, John P., and Phillip R. Shaver
  1973 Measures of Social Psychological Attitudes. (rev. ed.) Ann Arbor:
        Institute for Social Research, University of Michigan.
Rosenberg, Morris
  1957 Occupations and Values. Glencoe, Illinois: The Free Press.
Schuman, Howard, and Stanley Presser
  1978 "The assessment of 'no opinion' in attitude surveys." Pp. 241–75 in
        K. R. Schuessler (ed.), Sociological Methodology 1979. San Fran-
        cisco: Jossey-Bass.
  1980 "Public opinion and public ignorance: the fine line between attitudes
        and non-attitudes." American Journal of Sociology (in press).